Märchen Prince

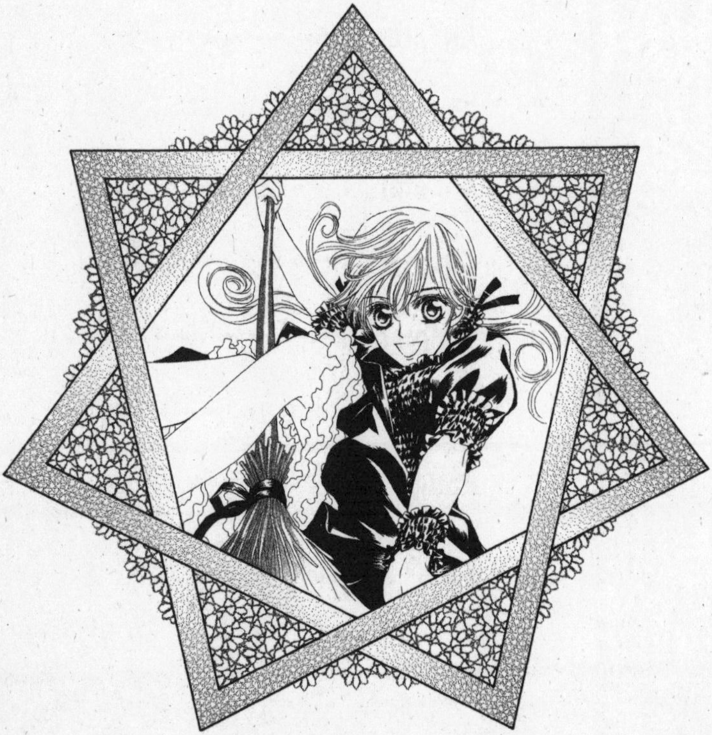

Volume 3

Story & Art by Matsuri Hino

Contents

MeruPuri: Märchen Prince

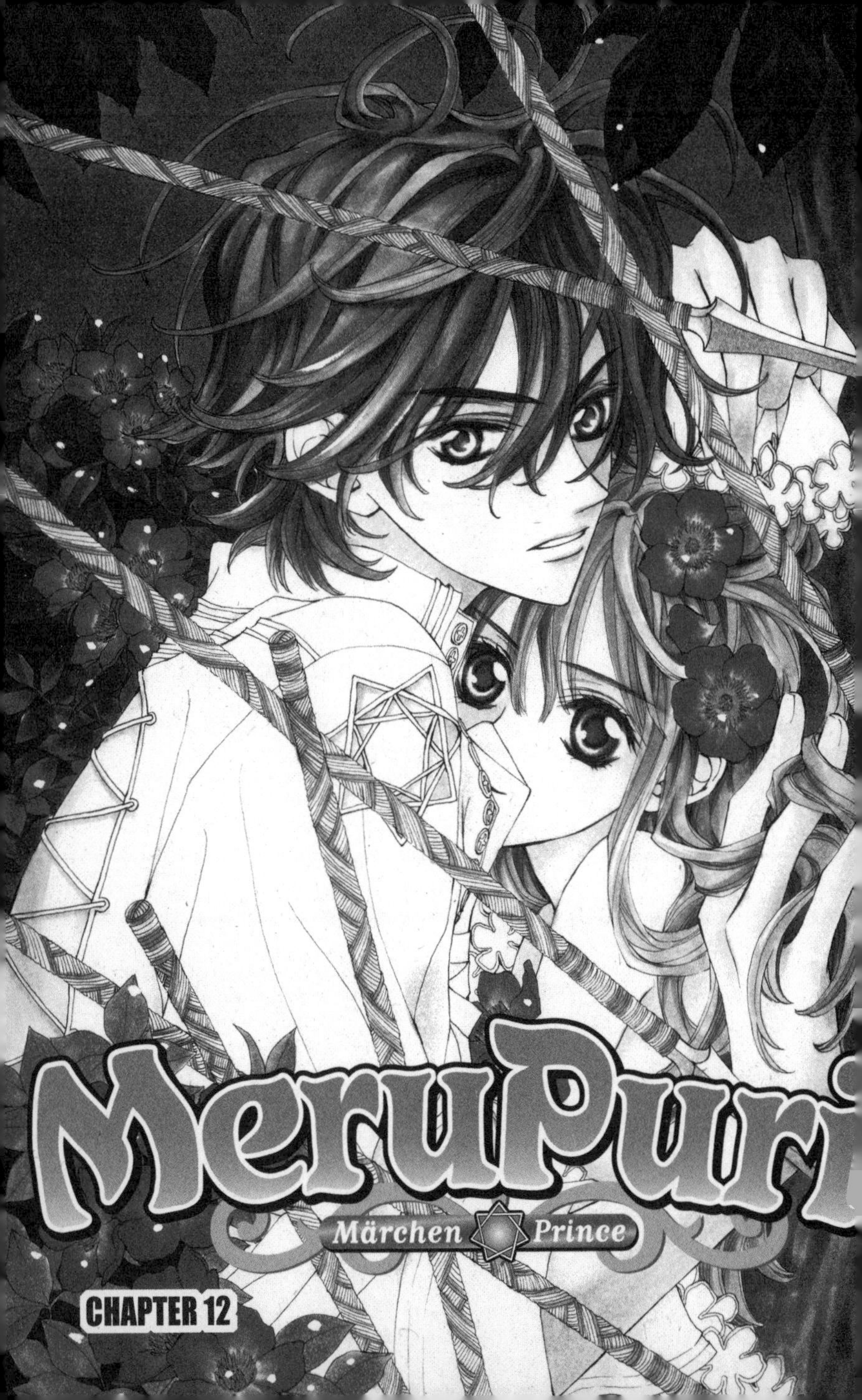
MeruPuri
Märchen Prince
CHAPTER 12

MERUPURI CHARACTERS

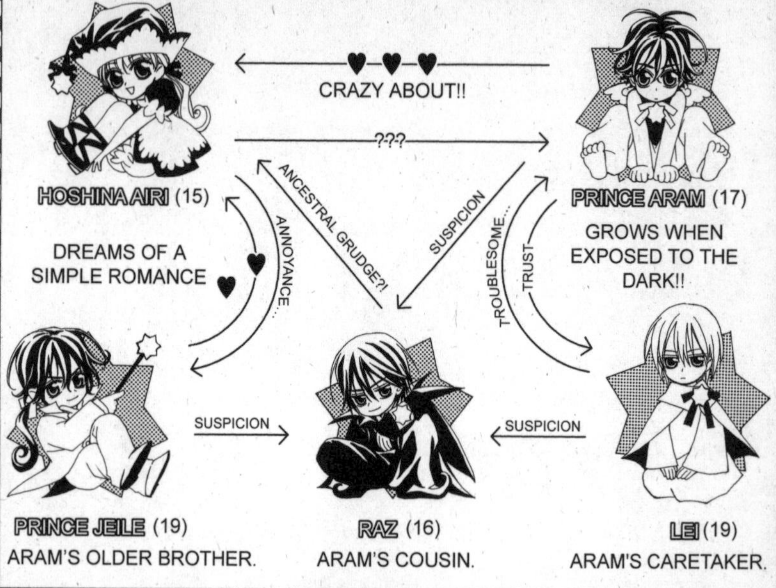
CRAZY ABOUT!!
???
ANCESTRAL GRUDGE?!
SUSPICION
TROUBLESOME...
TRUST
ANNOYANCE...
HOSHINA AIRI (15)
DREAMS OF A SIMPLE ROMANCE
PRINCE ARAM (17)
GROWS WHEN EXPOSED TO THE DARK!!
SUSPICION
SUSPICION
PRINCE JEILE (19)
ARAM'S OLDER BROTHER.
RAZ (16)
ARAM'S COUSIN.
LEI (19)
ARAM'S CARETAKER.

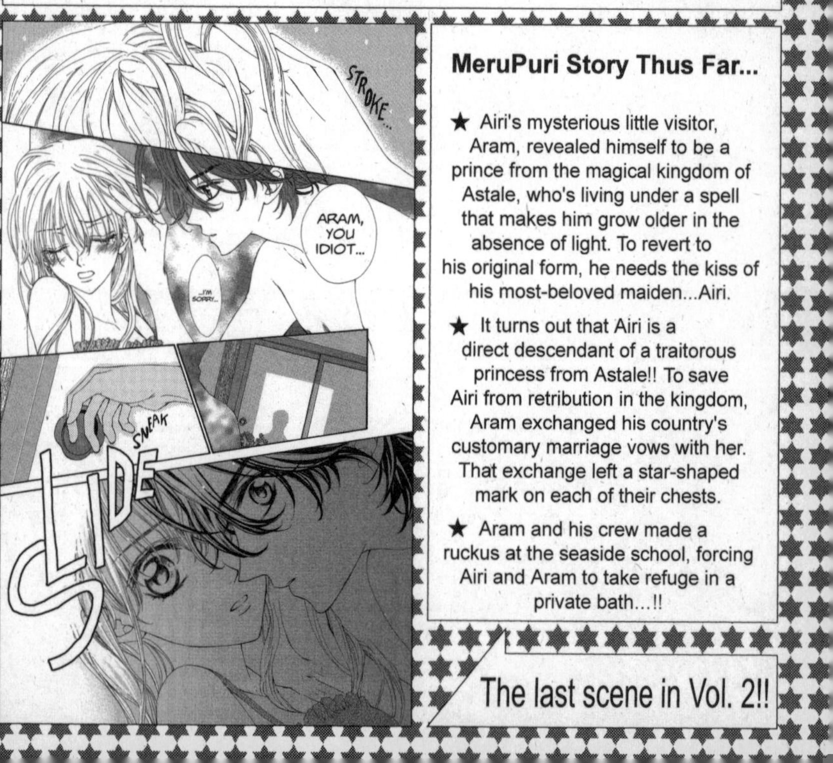
STROKE...
ARAM, YOU IDIOT...
I'M SORRY...
SNEAK
SLIDE

MeruPuri Story Thus Far...

★ Airi's mysterious little visitor, Aram, revealed himself to be a prince from the magical kingdom of Astale, who's living under a spell that makes him grow older in the absence of light. To revert to his original form, he needs the kiss of his most-beloved maiden...Airi.

★ It turns out that Airi is a direct descendant of a traitorous princess from Astale!! To save Airi from retribution in the kingdom, Aram exchanged his country's customary marriage vows with her. That exchange left a star-shaped mark on each of their chests.

★ Aram and his crew made a ruckus at the seaside school, forcing Airi and Aram to take refuge in a private bath...!!

The last scene in Vol. 2!!

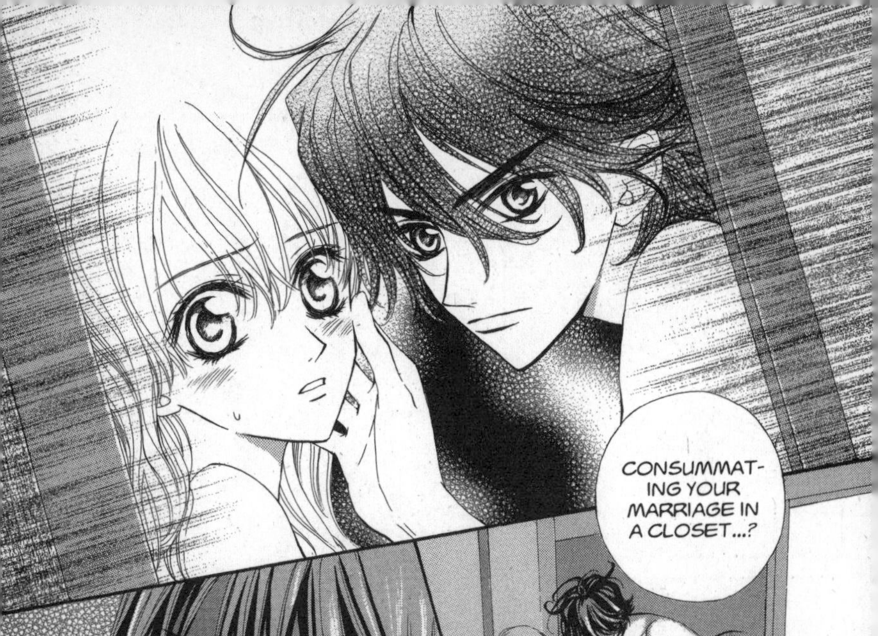
CONSUMMATING YOUR MARRIAGE IN A CLOSET...?
WELL...
YOU'RE LEGIT IN ASTALE. I GUESS YOU CAN DO IT HOWEVER YOU WANT...

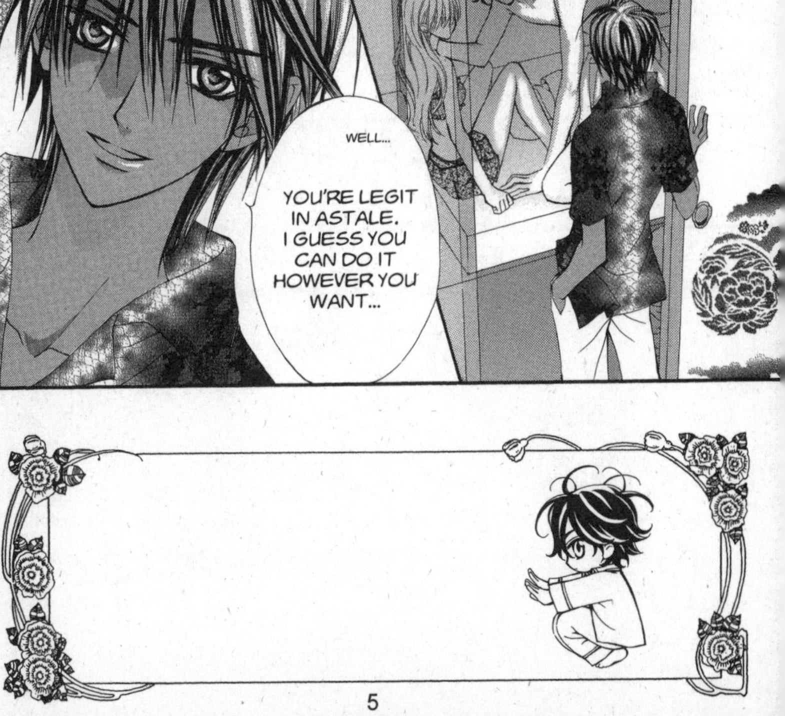

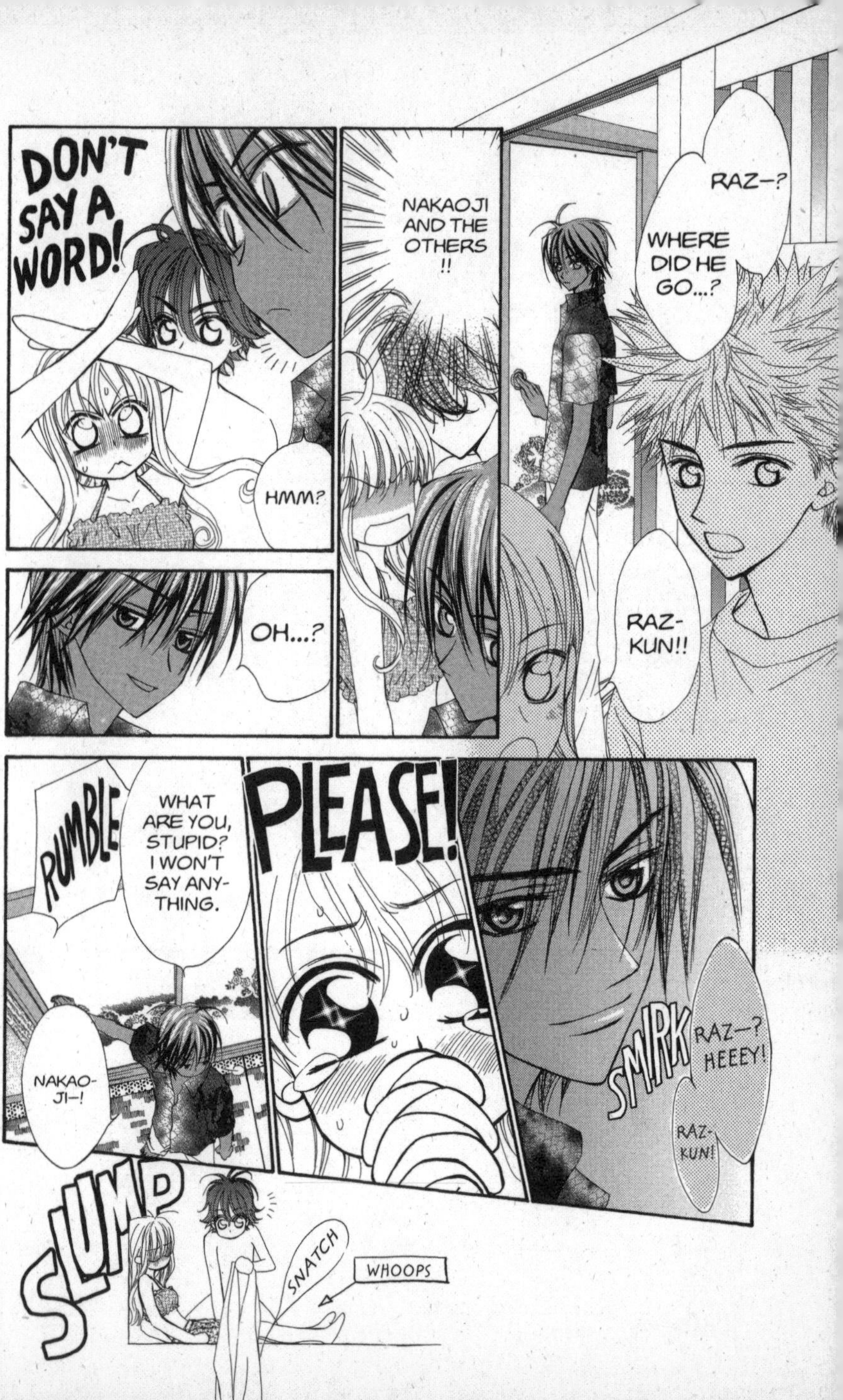
RAZ—?
WHERE DID HE GO...?
RAZ-KUN!!
NAKAOJI AND THE OTHERS !!
DON'T SAY A WORD!
HMM?
OH...?
SMIRK
RAZ—? HEEEY!
RAZ-KUN!
PLEASE!
RUMBLE
WHAT ARE YOU, STUPID? I WON'T SAY ANY-THING.
NAKAOJI-!
SLUMP
SNATCH
WHOOPS

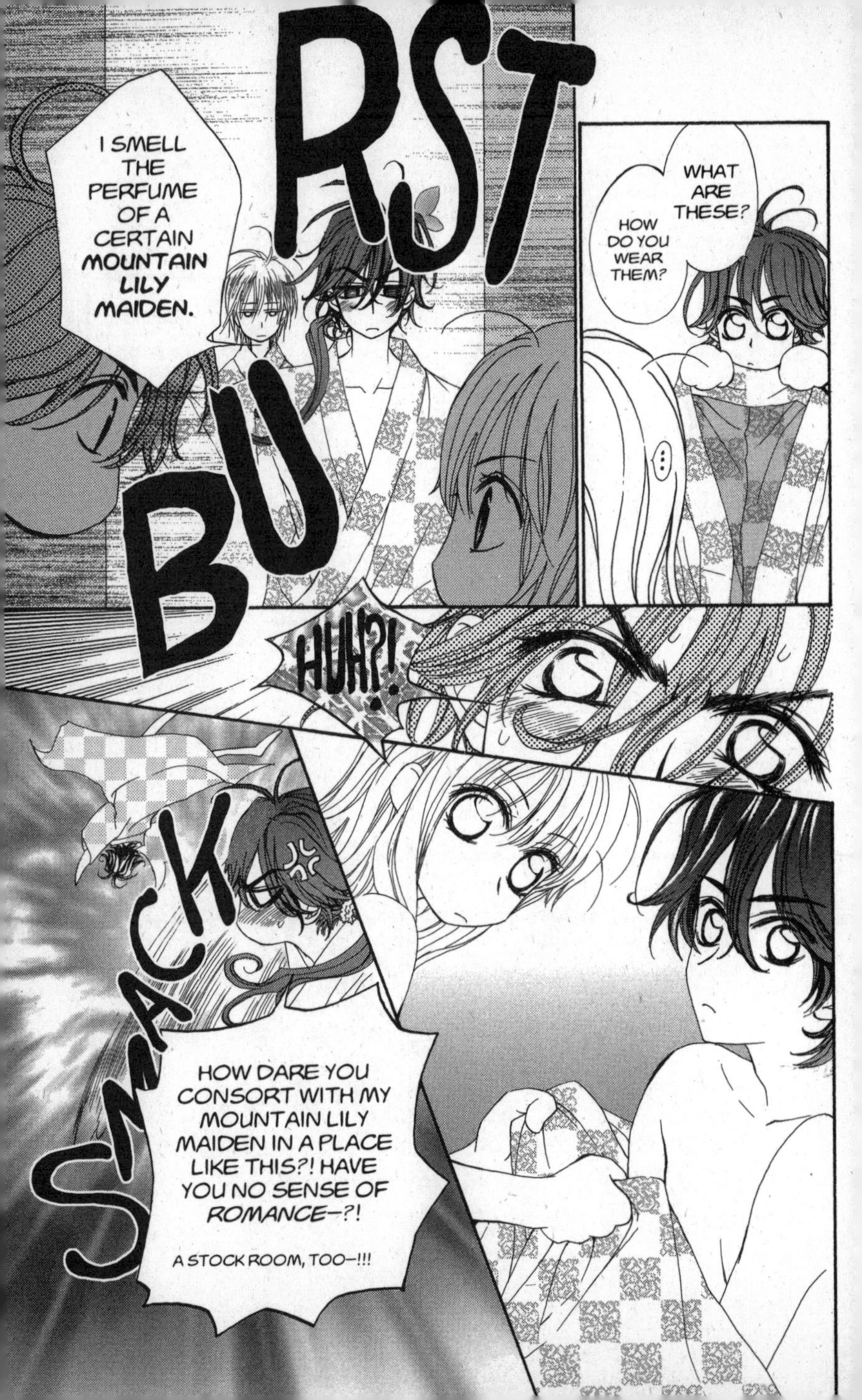
WHAT ARE THESE?
HOW DO YOU WEAR THEM?
...
BURST
I SMELL THE PERFUME OF A CERTAIN MOUNTAIN LILY MAIDEN.
HUH?!
SMACK
HOW DARE YOU CONSORT WITH MY MOUNTAIN LILY MAIDEN IN A PLACE LIKE THIS?! HAVE YOU NO SENSE OF ROMANCE–?!
A STOCK ROOM, TOO–!!!

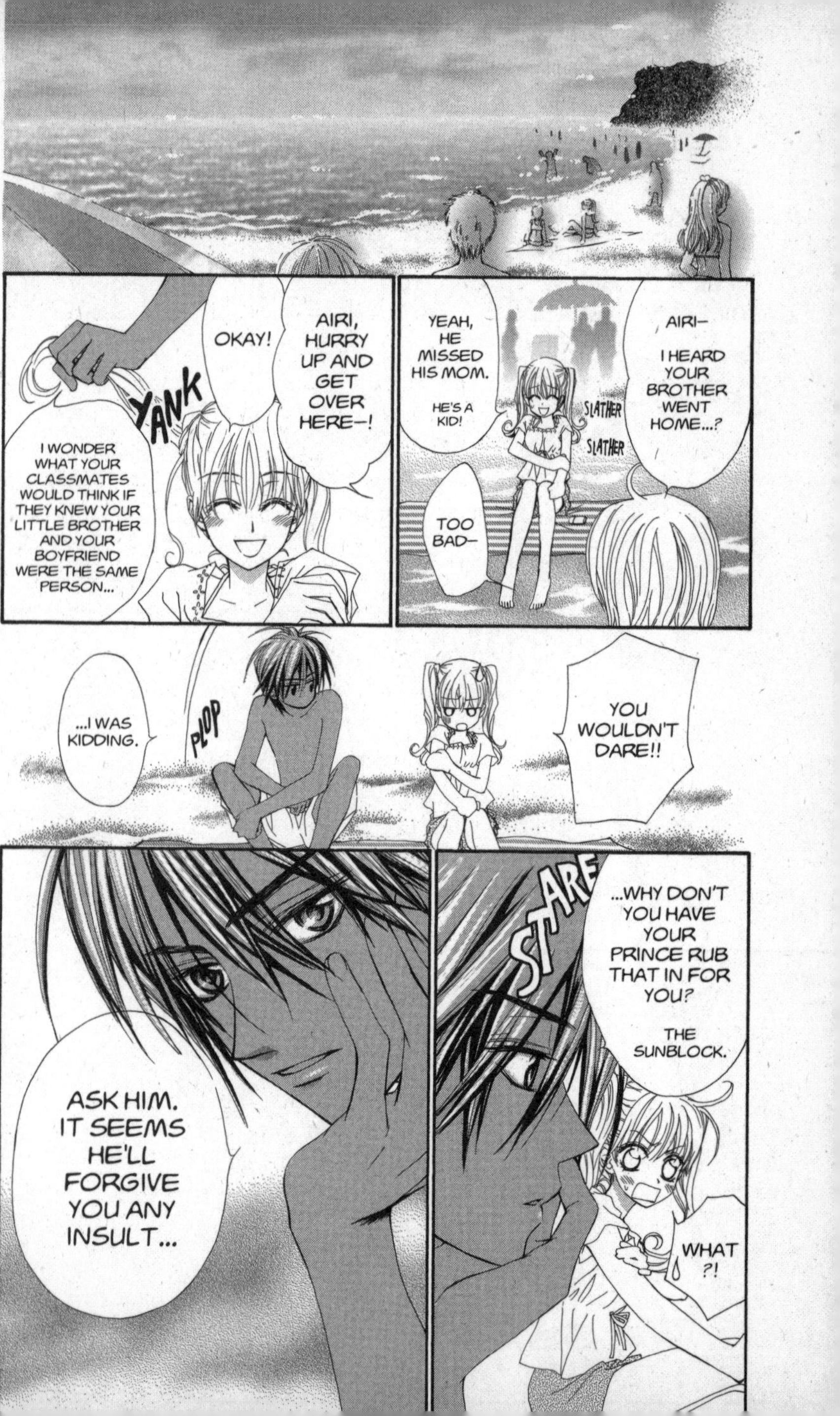
AIRI— I HEARD YOUR BROTHER WENT HOME...?
SLATHER
SLATHER
YEAH, HE MISSED HIS MOM.
HE'S A KID!
TOO BAD—
AIRI, HURRY UP AND GET OVER HERE—!
OKAY!
YANK
I WONDER WHAT YOUR CLASSMATES WOULD THINK IF THEY KNEW YOUR LITTLE BROTHER AND YOUR BOYFRIEND WERE THE SAME PERSON...
YOU WOULDN'T DARE!!
PLOP
...I WAS KIDDING.
STARE
...WHY DON'T YOU HAVE YOUR PRINCE RUB THAT IN FOR YOU?
THE SUNBLOCK.
WHAT?!
ASK HIM. IT SEEMS HE'LL FORGIVE YOU ANY INSULT...

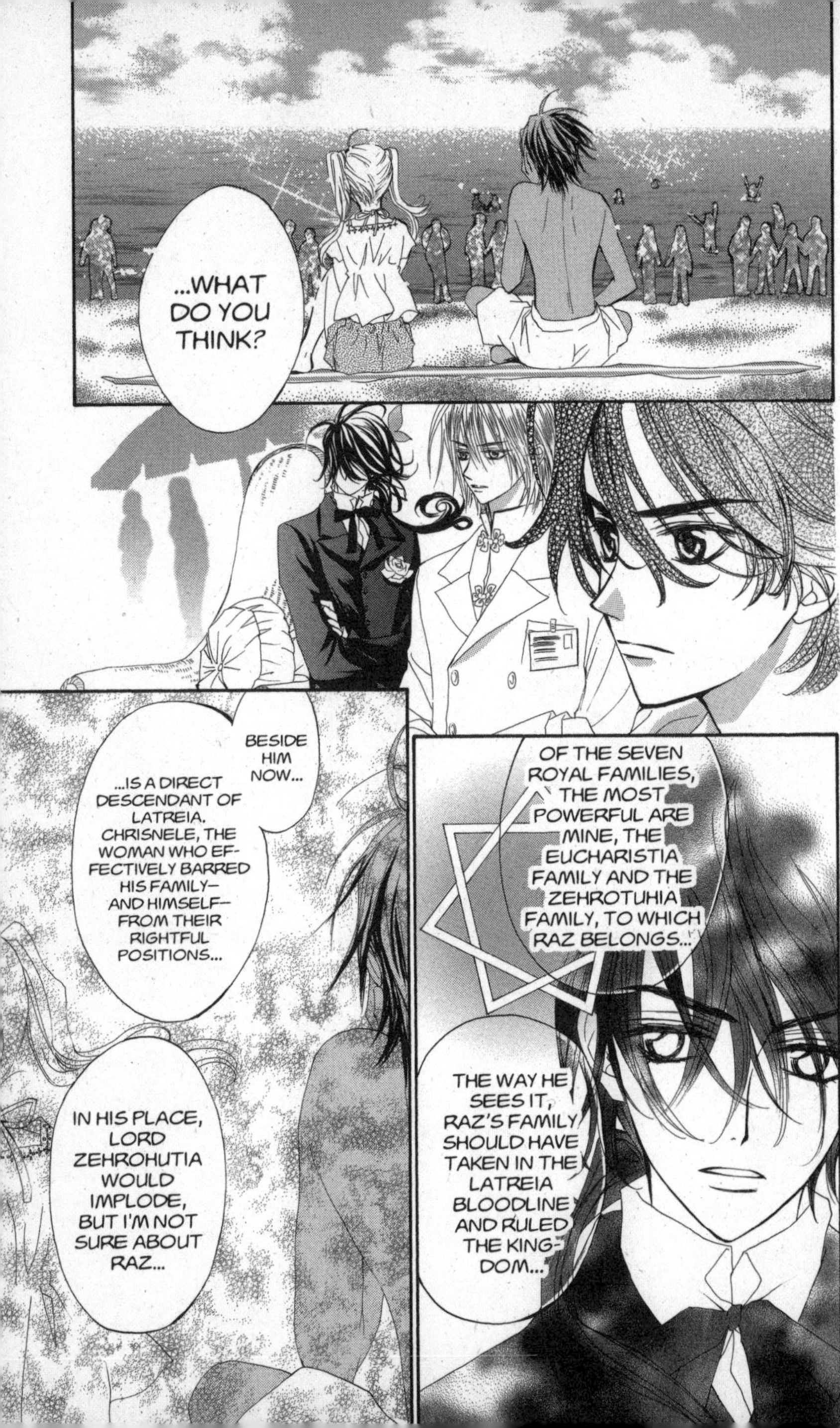
...WHAT DO YOU THINK?
OF THE SEVEN ROYAL FAMILIES, THE MOST POWERFUL ARE MINE, THE EUCHARISTIA FAMILY AND THE ZEHROTUHIA FAMILY, TO WHICH RAZ BELONGS...
THE WAY HE SEES IT, RAZ'S FAMILY SHOULD HAVE TAKEN IN THE LATREIA BLOODLINE AND RULED THE KING-DOM...
BESIDE HIM NOW...
...IS A DIRECT DESCENDANT OF LATREIA. CHRISNELE, THE WOMAN WHO EF-FECTIVELY BARRED HIS FAMILY—AND HIMSELF—FROM THEIR RIGHTFUL POSITIONS...
IN HIS PLACE, LORD ZEHROHUTIA WOULD IMPLODE, BUT I'M NOT SURE ABOUT RAZ...

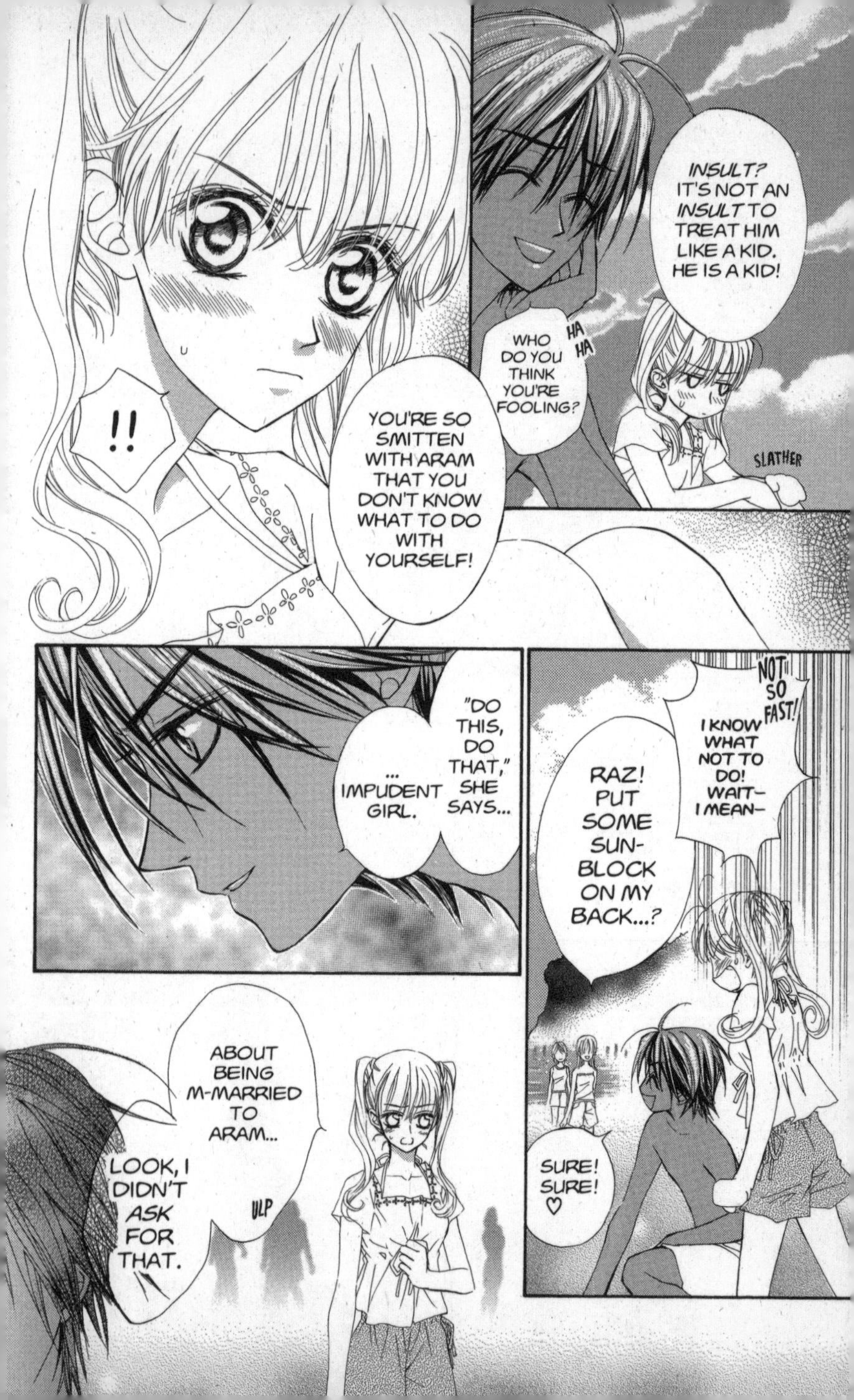
INSULT? IT'S NOT AN INSULT TO TREAT HIM LIKE A KID. HE IS A KID!
HA HA
WHO DO YOU THINK YOU'RE FOOLING?
SLATHER
YOU'RE SO SMITTEN WITH ARAM THAT YOU DON'T KNOW WHAT TO DO WITH YOURSELF!
!!
RAZ! PUT SOME SUN-BLOCK ON MY BACK...?
SURE! SURE! ♡
NOT SO FAST!
I KNOW WHAT NOT TO DO! WAIT- I MEAN-
"DO THIS, DO THAT," SHE SAYS...
... IMPUDENT GIRL.
ABOUT BEING M-MARRIED TO ARAM...
LOOK, I DIDN'T ASK FOR THAT.
ULP

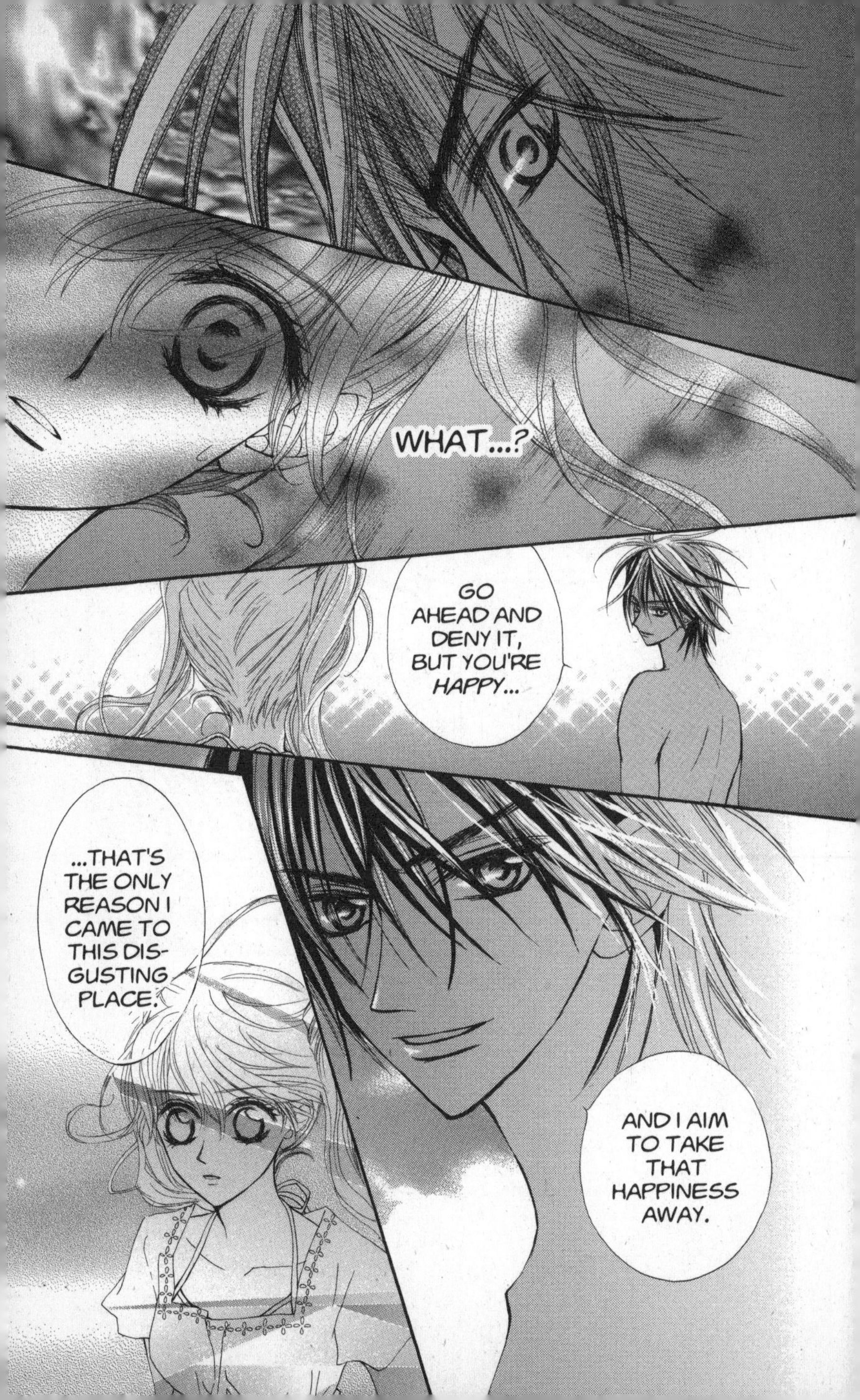
WHAT...?
GO AHEAD AND DENY IT, BUT YOU'RE HAPPY...
...THAT'S THE ONLY REASON I CAME TO THIS DIS-GUSTING PLACE.
AND I AIM TO TAKE THAT HAPPINESS AWAY.

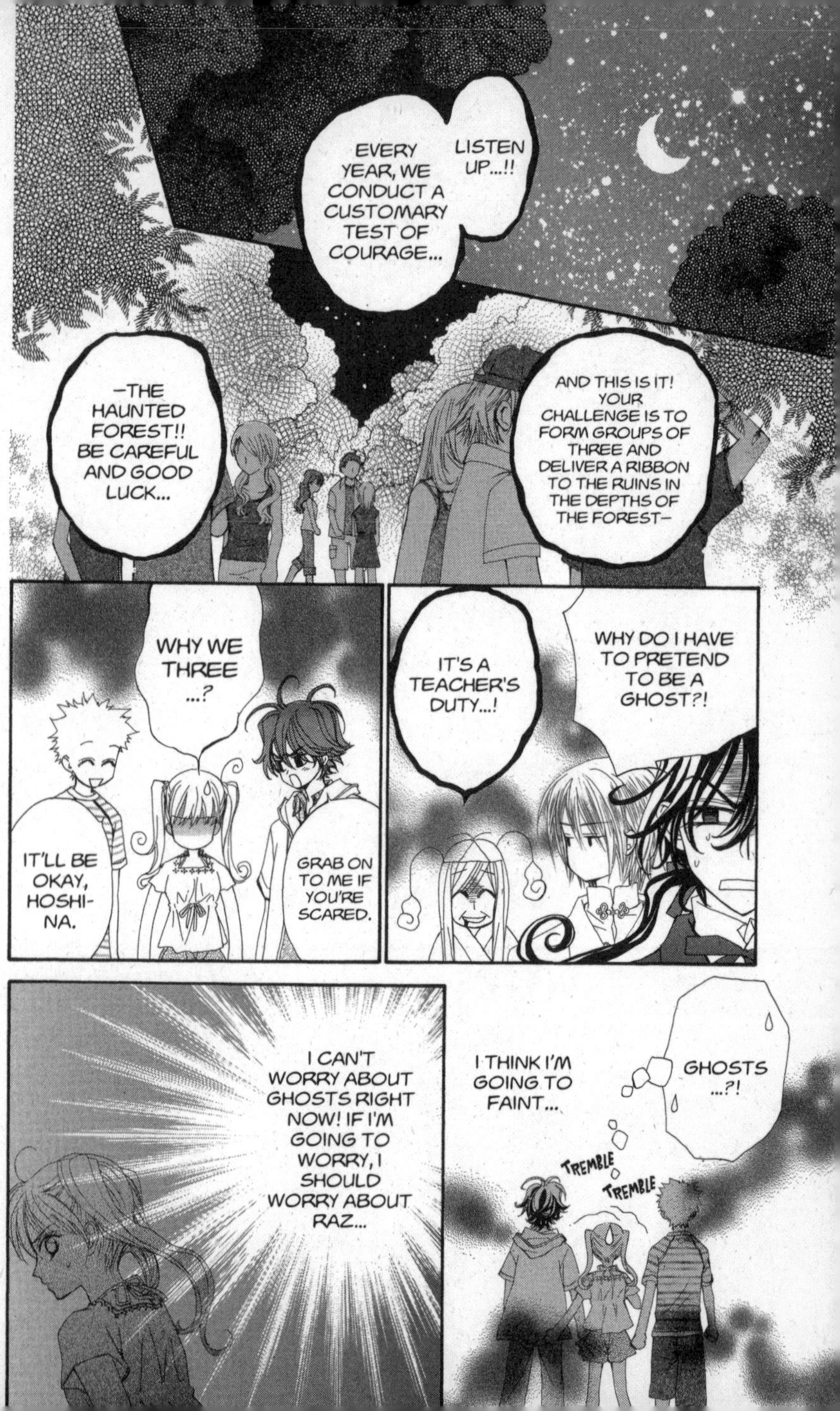

LISTEN UP...!!
EVERY YEAR, WE CONDUCT A CUSTOMARY TEST OF COURAGE...
AND THIS IS IT! YOUR CHALLENGE IS TO FORM GROUPS OF THREE AND DELIVER A RIBBON TO THE RUINS IN THE DEPTHS OF THE FOREST—
—THE HAUNTED FOREST!! BE CAREFUL AND GOOD LUCK...
WHY DO I HAVE TO PRETEND TO BE A GHOST?!
IT'S A TEACHER'S DUTY...!
WHY WE THREE ...?
GRAB ON TO ME IF YOU'RE SCARED.
IT'LL BE OKAY, HOSHI-NA.
GHOSTS ...?!
I THINK I'M GOING TO FAINT...
TREMBLE
TREMBLE
I CAN'T WORRY ABOUT GHOSTS RIGHT NOW! IF I'M GOING TO WORRY, I SHOULD WORRY ABOUT RAZ...

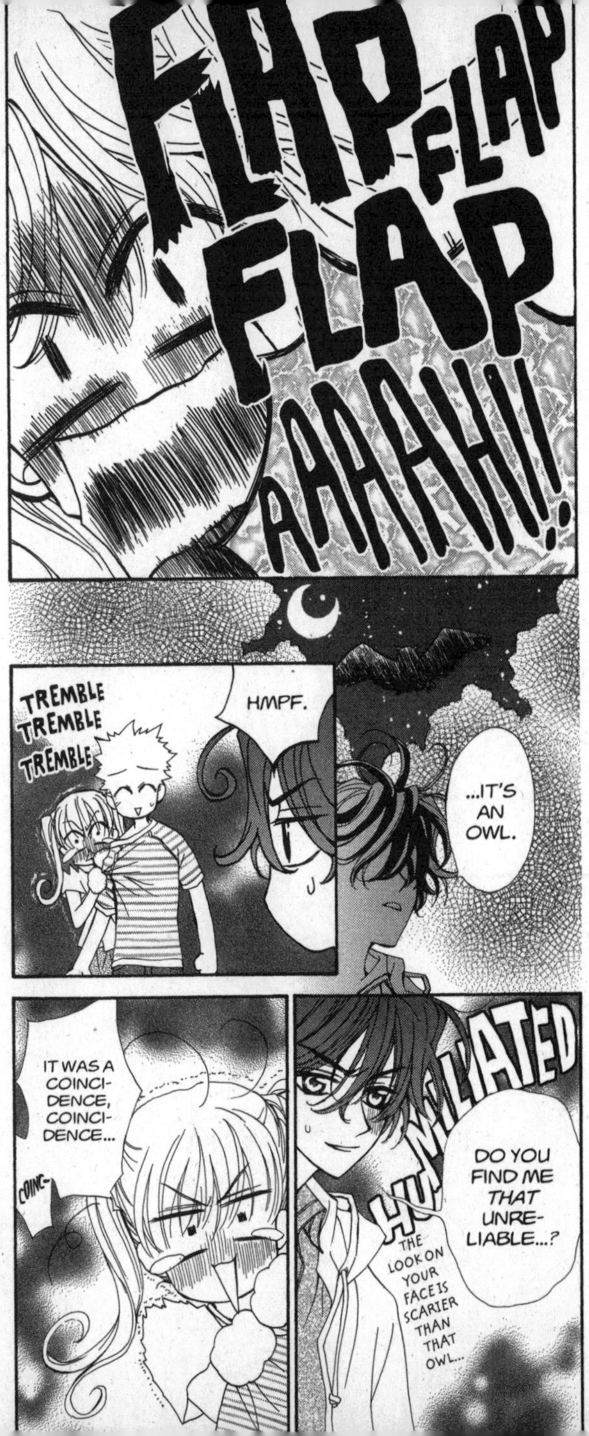
FLAP
FLAP
FLAP
AAAAH!!
...IT'S AN OWL.
HMPF.
TREMBLE
TREMBLE
TREMBLE
HUMILIATED
DO YOU FIND ME THAT UNRELIABLE...?
THE LOOK ON YOUR FACE IS SCARIER THAN THAT OWL...
IT WAS A COINCIDENCE, COINCIDENCE...
COINC-

I

Hello. This is Hino Matsuri! Thank you for reading MeruPuri Vol. 3! This is the first time I've drawn a love triangle on the cover of one of my own comics! You don't think there's an extra guy there, do you? (bitter grin).

One thing, though...it feels like...I mean, what kind of cosplay bar do they hang out at?!

The theme is meant to be something like "Poor, lovable Airi is being pulled every-which-way by the rich kids!" Heh.

The concept for the Chapter 12 cover was "The two of them wed on a southern island and disappear afterward, escaping into the jungle where they encounter the natives!" (Did you get that...?)

Oh, by the way...

Continued in II.

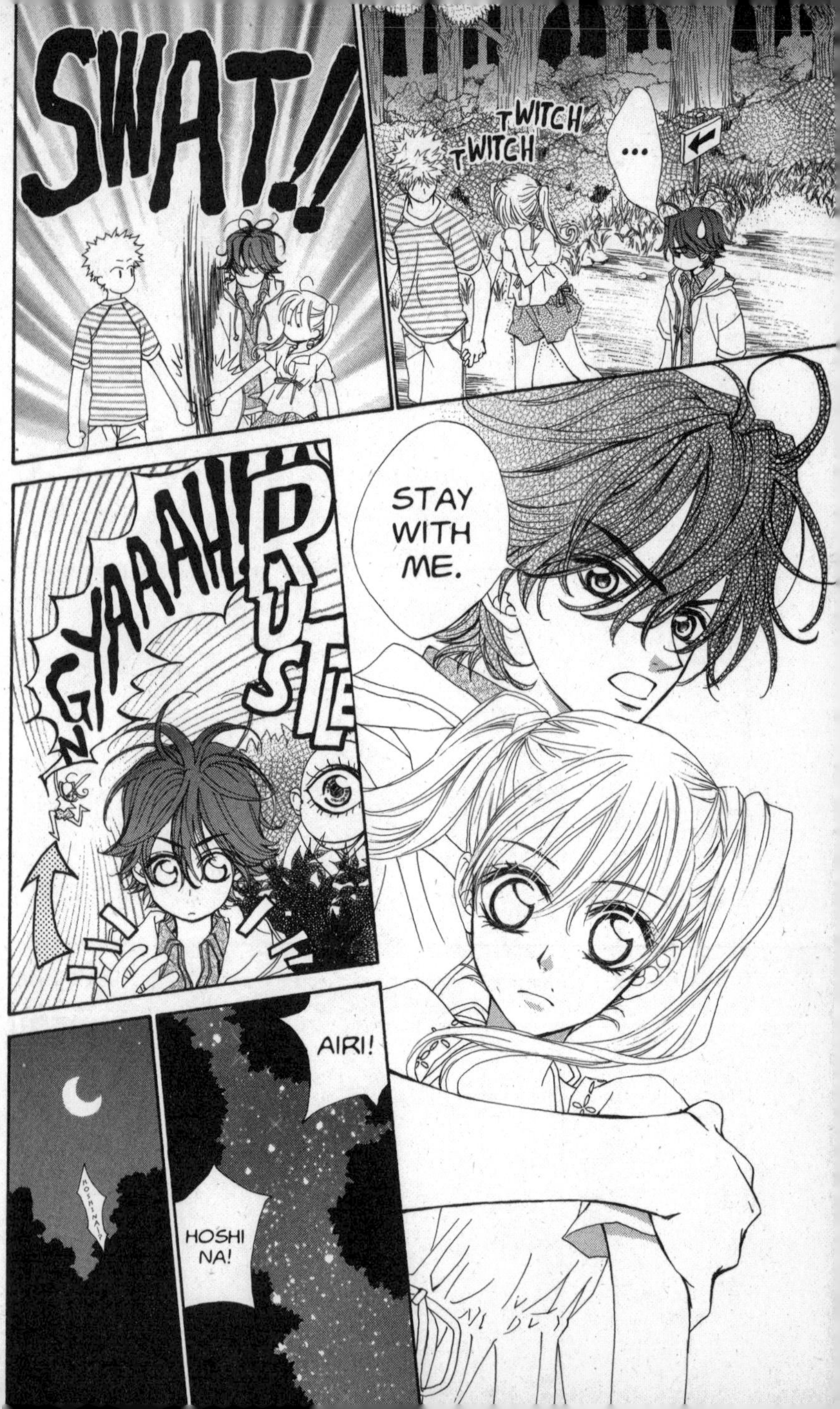
TWITCH
TWITCH
...
SWAT!!
STAY WITH ME.
GYAAAH
RUSTLE
AIRI!
HOSHI NA!
HOSHINA!?

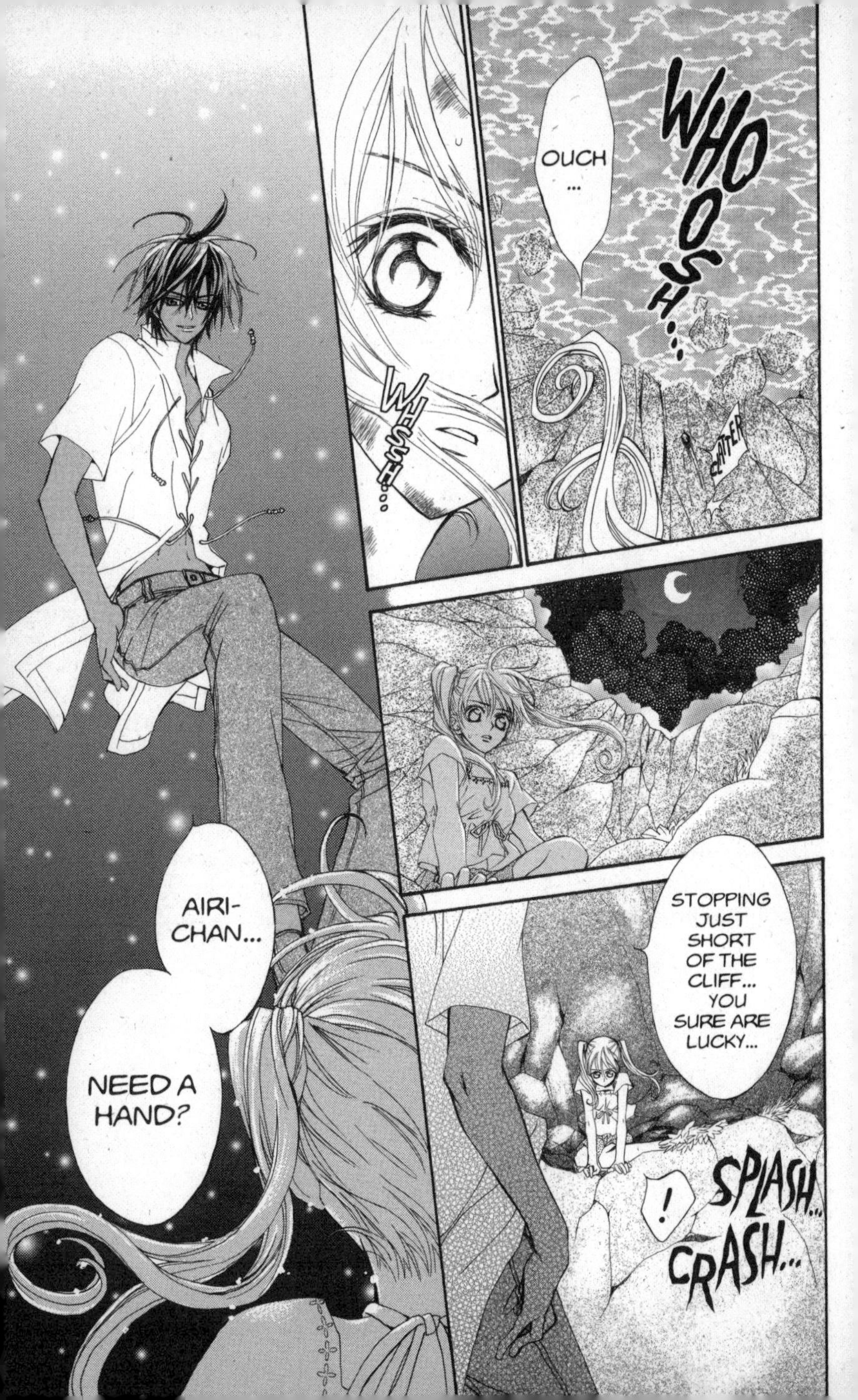
WHOOSH...
OUCH...
CLATTER
WHSSH...
STOPPING JUST SHORT OF THE CLIFF... YOU SURE ARE LUCKY...
!
SPLASH... CRASH...
AIRI-CHAN...
NEED A HAND?

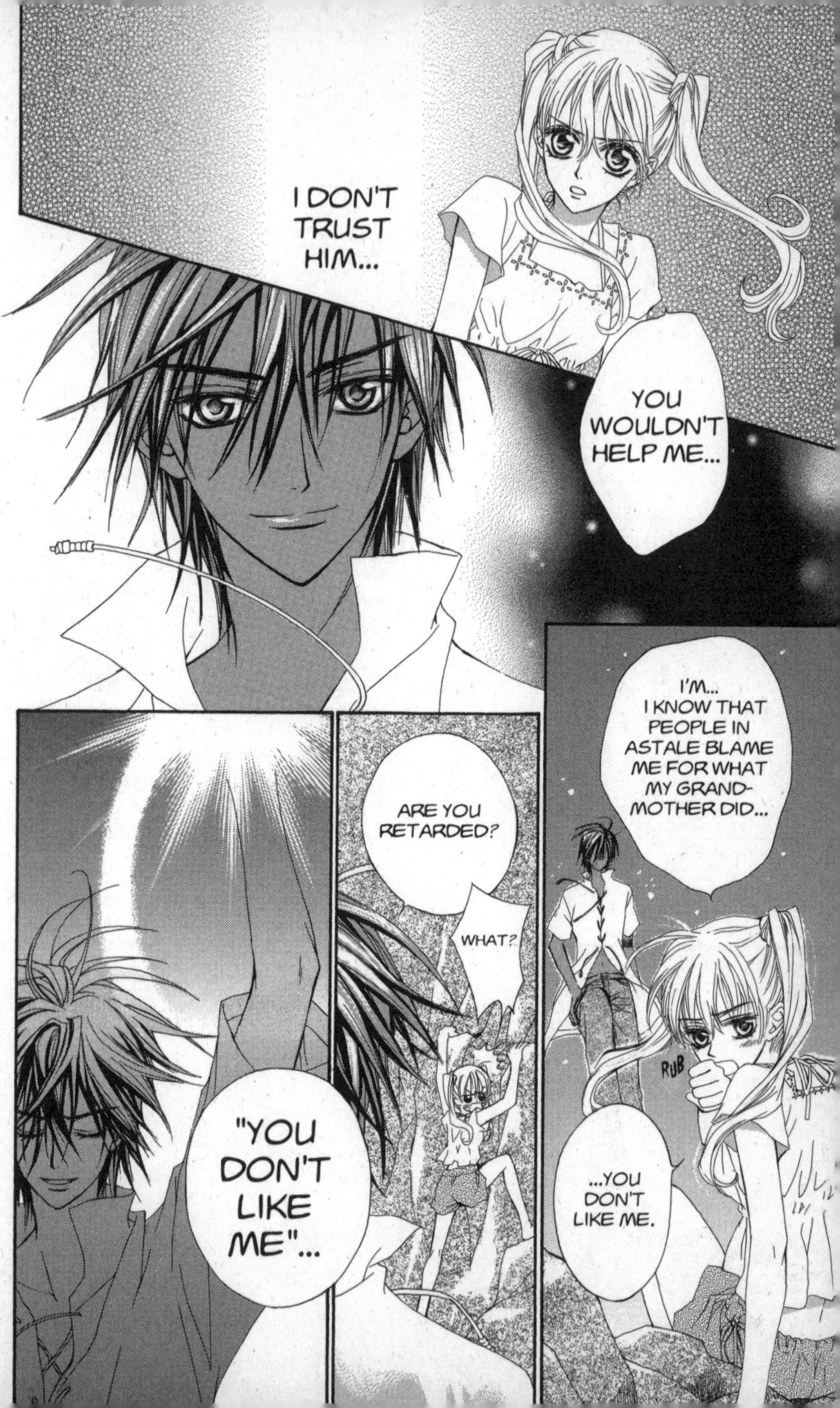
I DON'T TRUST HIM...
YOU WOULDN'T HELP ME...
I'M... I KNOW THAT PEOPLE IN ASTALE BLAME ME FOR WHAT MY GRAND-MOTHER DID...
RUB
...YOU DON'T LIKE ME.
ARE YOU RETARDED?
WHAT?
"YOU DON'T LIKE ME"...

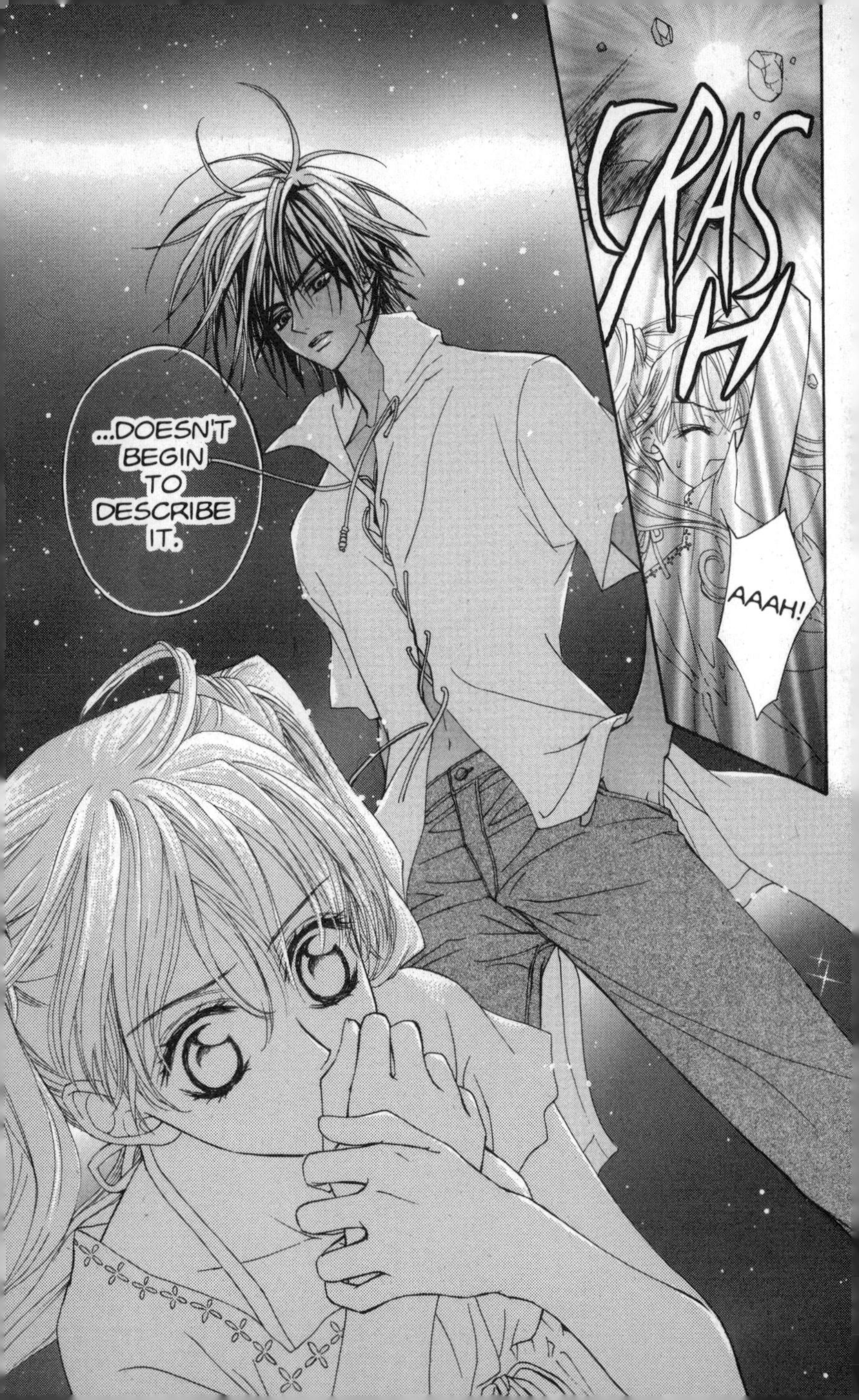
CRASH
AAAH!
...DOESN'T BEGIN TO DESCRIBE IT.

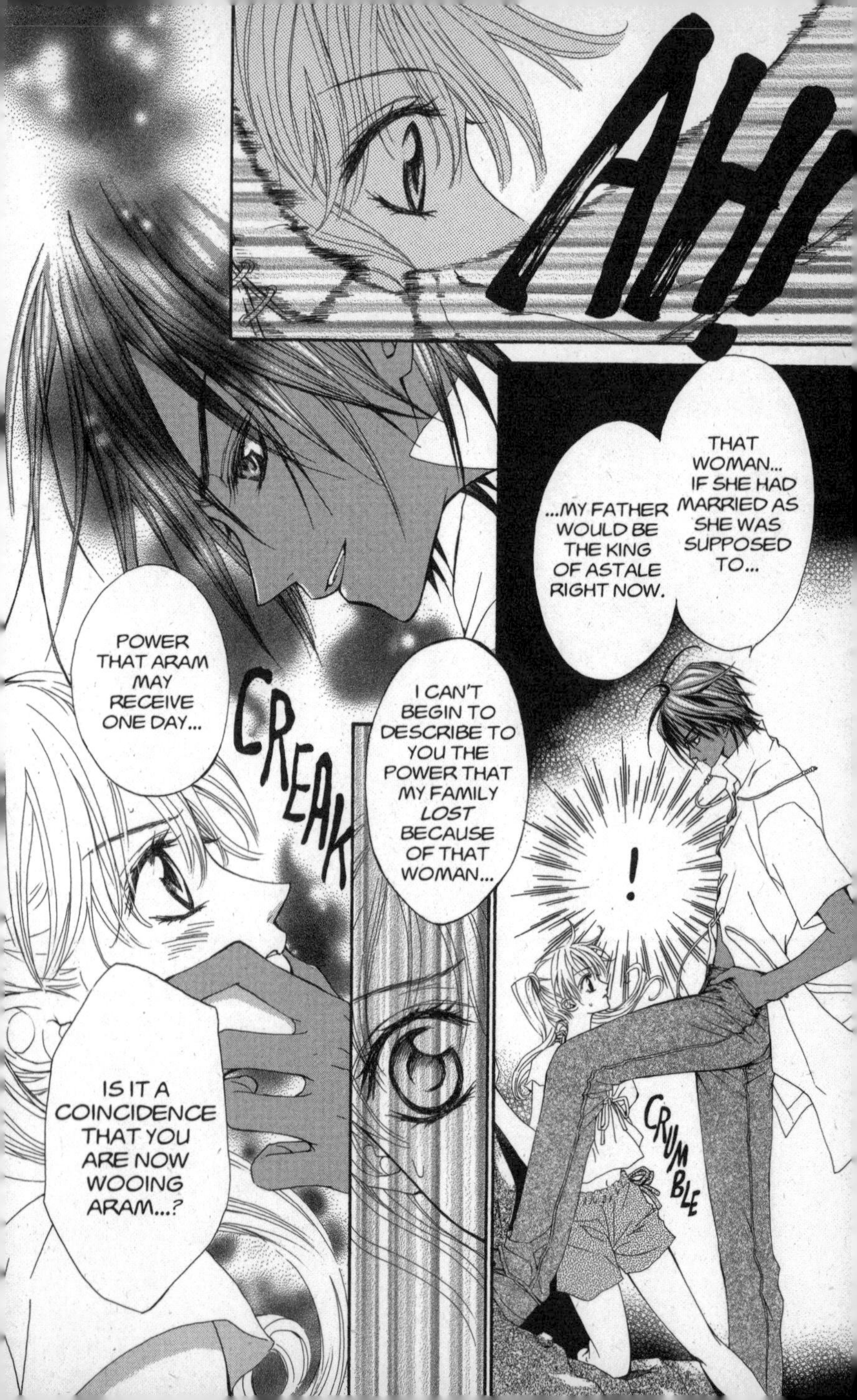
AH!
THAT WOMAN... IF SHE HAD MARRIED AS SHE WAS SUPPOSED TO...
...MY FATHER WOULD BE THE KING OF ASTALE RIGHT NOW.
!
CRUMBLE
I CAN'T BEGIN TO DESCRIBE TO YOU THE POWER THAT MY FAMILY *LOST* BECAUSE OF THAT WOMAN...
CREAK
POWER THAT ARAM MAY RECEIVE ONE DAY...
IS IT A COINCIDENCE THAT YOU ARE NOW WOOING ARAM...?

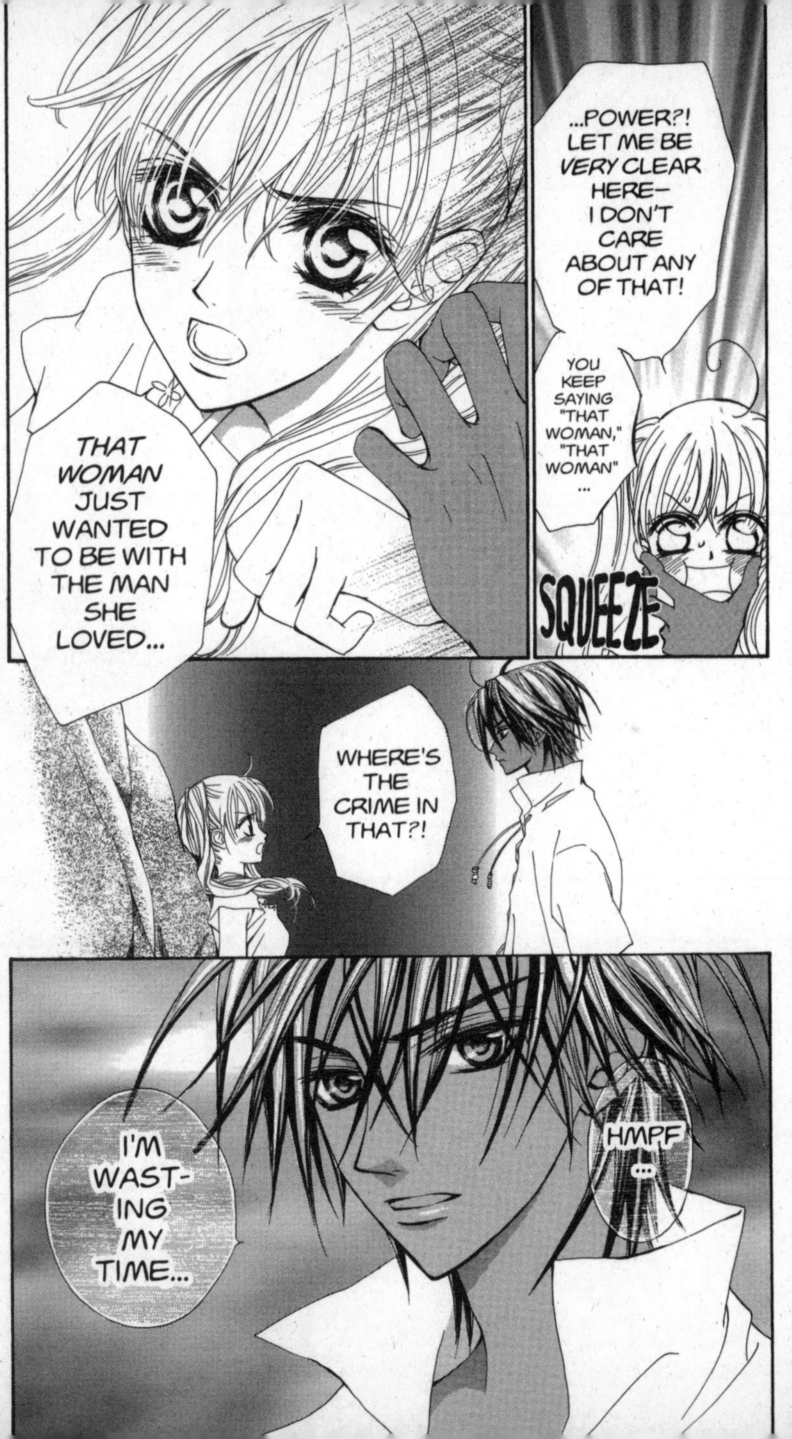
...POWER?! LET ME BE VERY CLEAR HERE— I DON'T CARE ABOUT ANY OF THAT!
YOU KEEP SAYING "THAT WOMAN," "THAT WOMAN" ...
SQUEEZE
THAT WOMAN JUST WANTED TO BE WITH THE MAN SHE LOVED...
WHERE'S THE CRIME IN THAT?!
HMPF ...
I'M WASTING MY TIME...

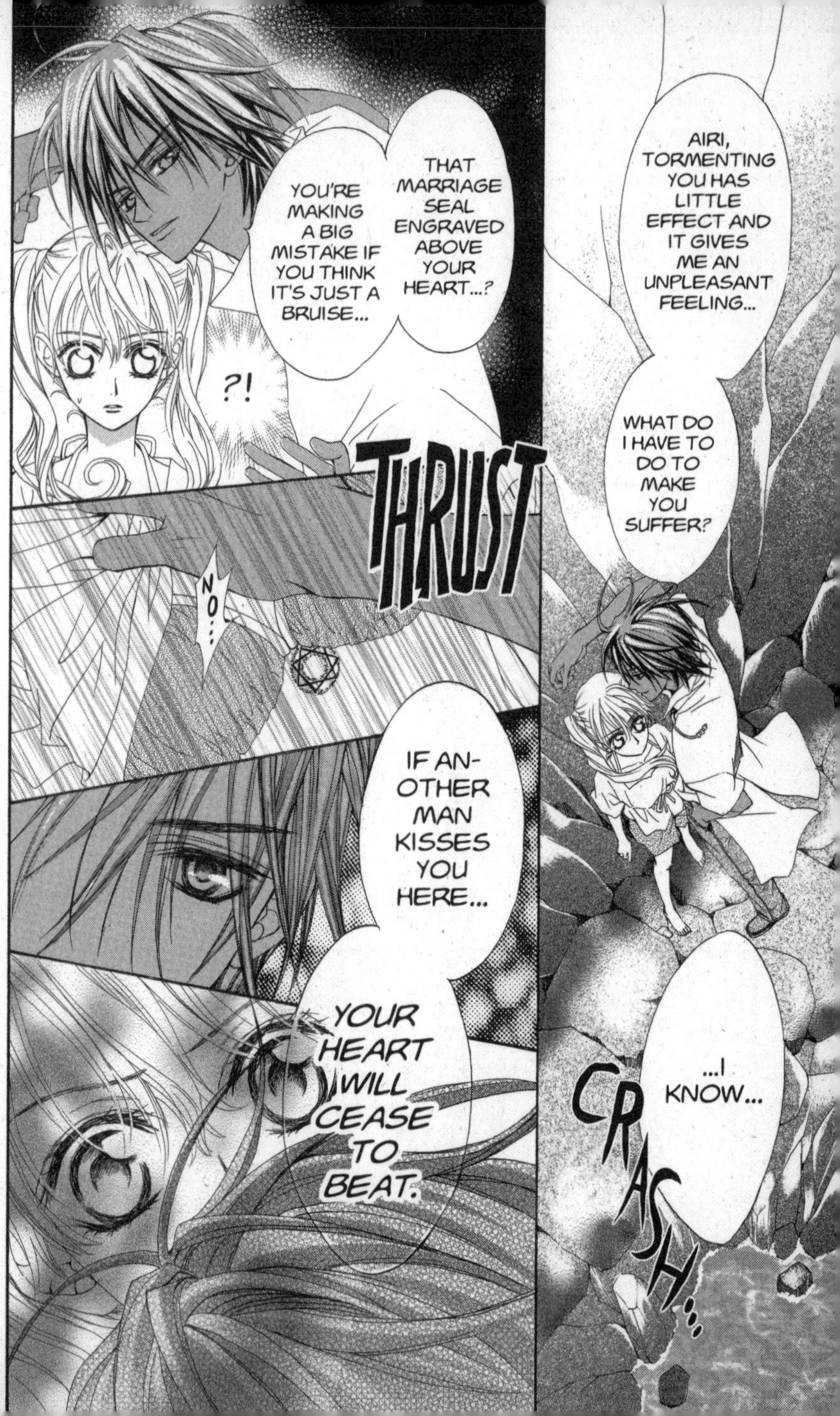
AIRI, TORMENTING YOU HAS LITTLE EFFECT AND IT GIVES ME AN UNPLEASANT FEELING...
WHAT DO I HAVE TO DO TO MAKE YOU SUFFER?
...I KNOW...
CRASH...
THAT MARRIAGE SEAL ENGRAVED ABOVE YOUR HEART...?
YOU'RE MAKING A BIG MISTAKE IF YOU THINK IT'S JUST A BRUISE...
?!
THRUST
NO...
IF AN-OTHER MAN KISSES YOU HERE...
YOUR HEART WILL CEASE TO BEAT.

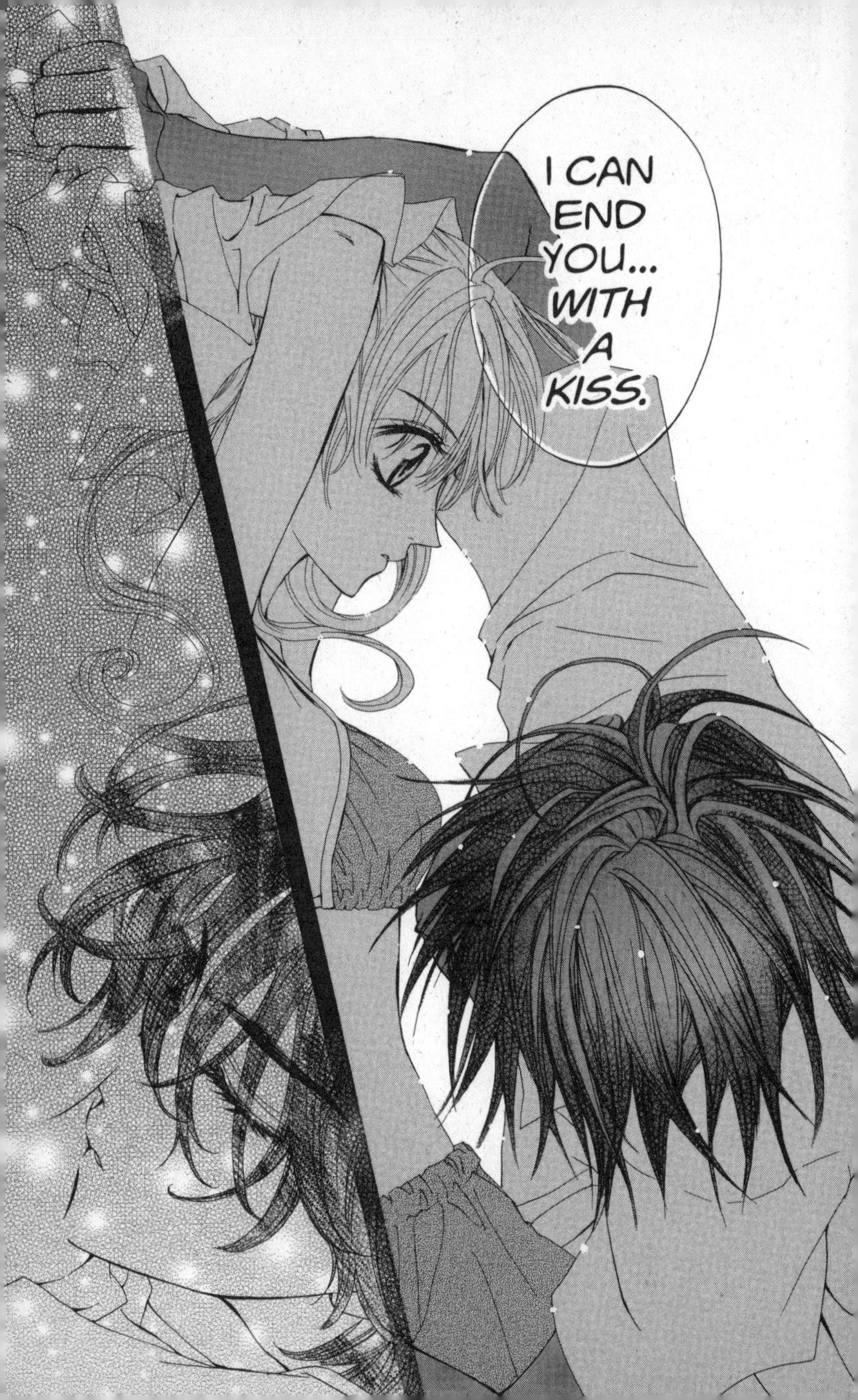
I CAN END YOU... WITH A KISS.

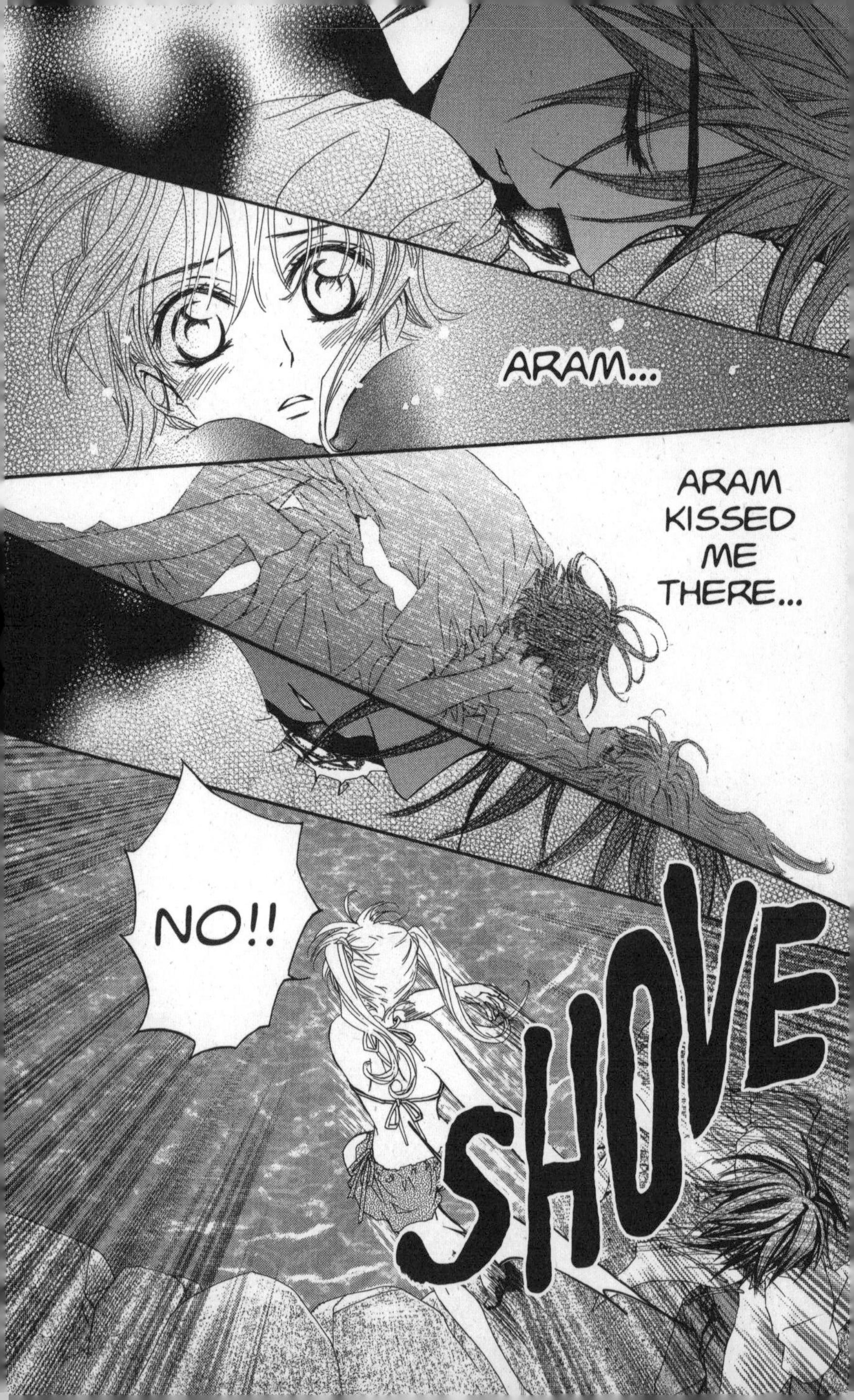
ARAM...
ARAM KISSED ME THERE...
NO!!
SHOVE

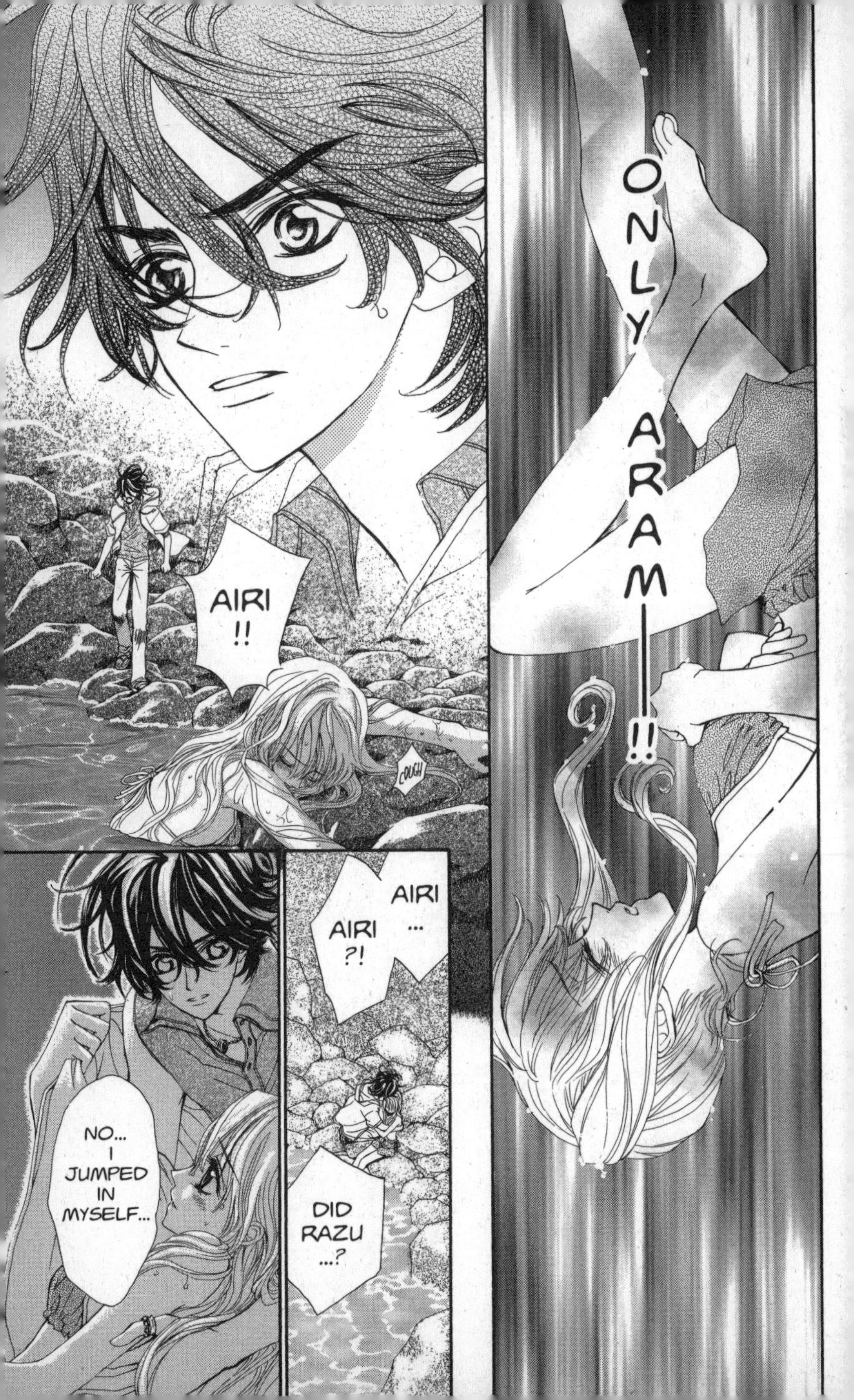

ONLY ARAM—!!
AIRI !!
COUGH
AIRI ...
AIRI ?!
DID RAZU ...?
NO... I JUMPED IN MYSELF...

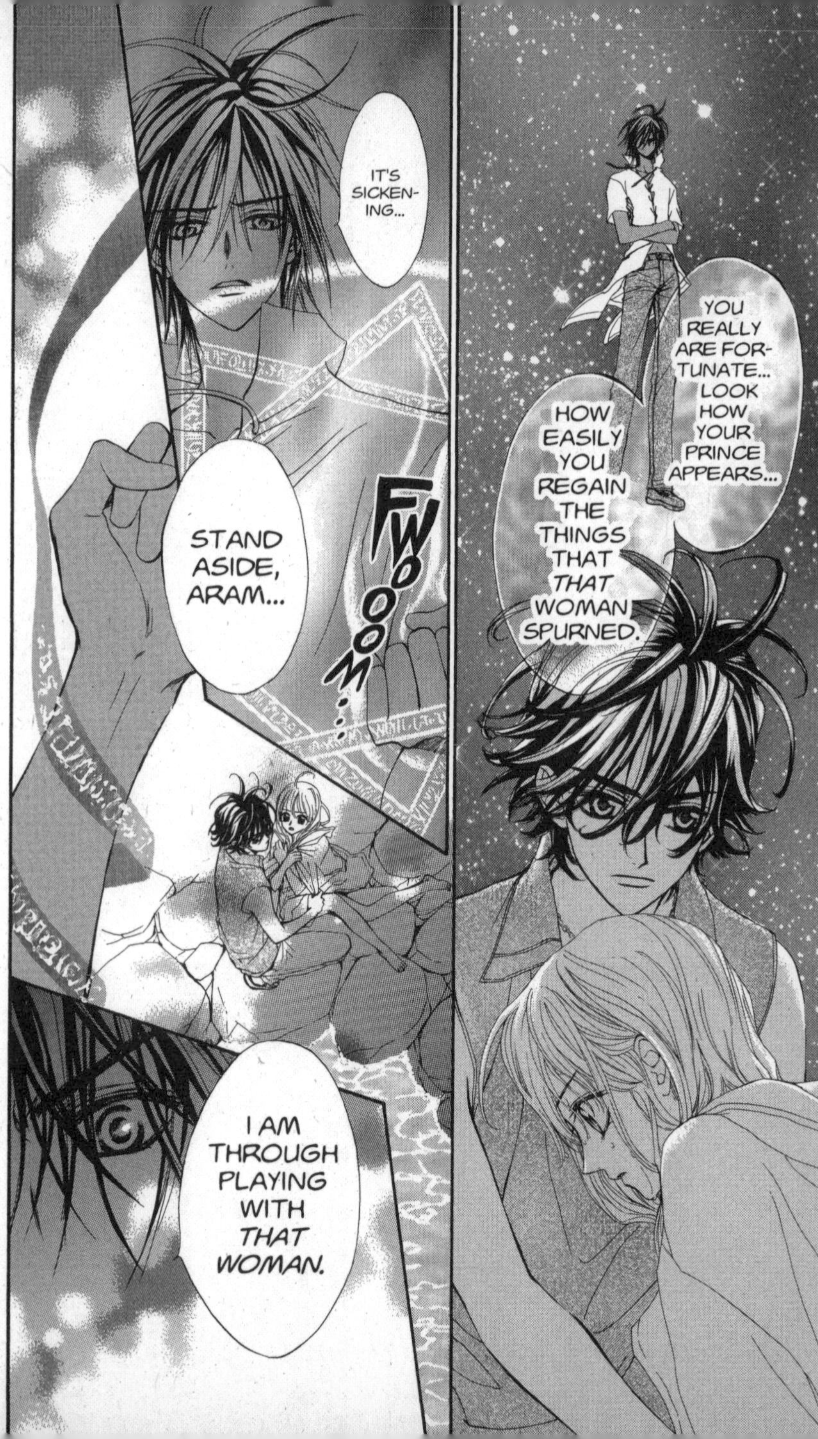
YOU REALLY ARE FOR-TUNATE... LOOK HOW YOUR PRINCE APPEARS...
HOW EASILY YOU REGAIN THE THINGS THAT *THAT* WOMAN SPURNED.
IT'S SICKEN-ING...
STAND ASIDE, ARAM...
FWOOOOM...
I AM THROUGH PLAYING WITH *THAT* WOMAN.

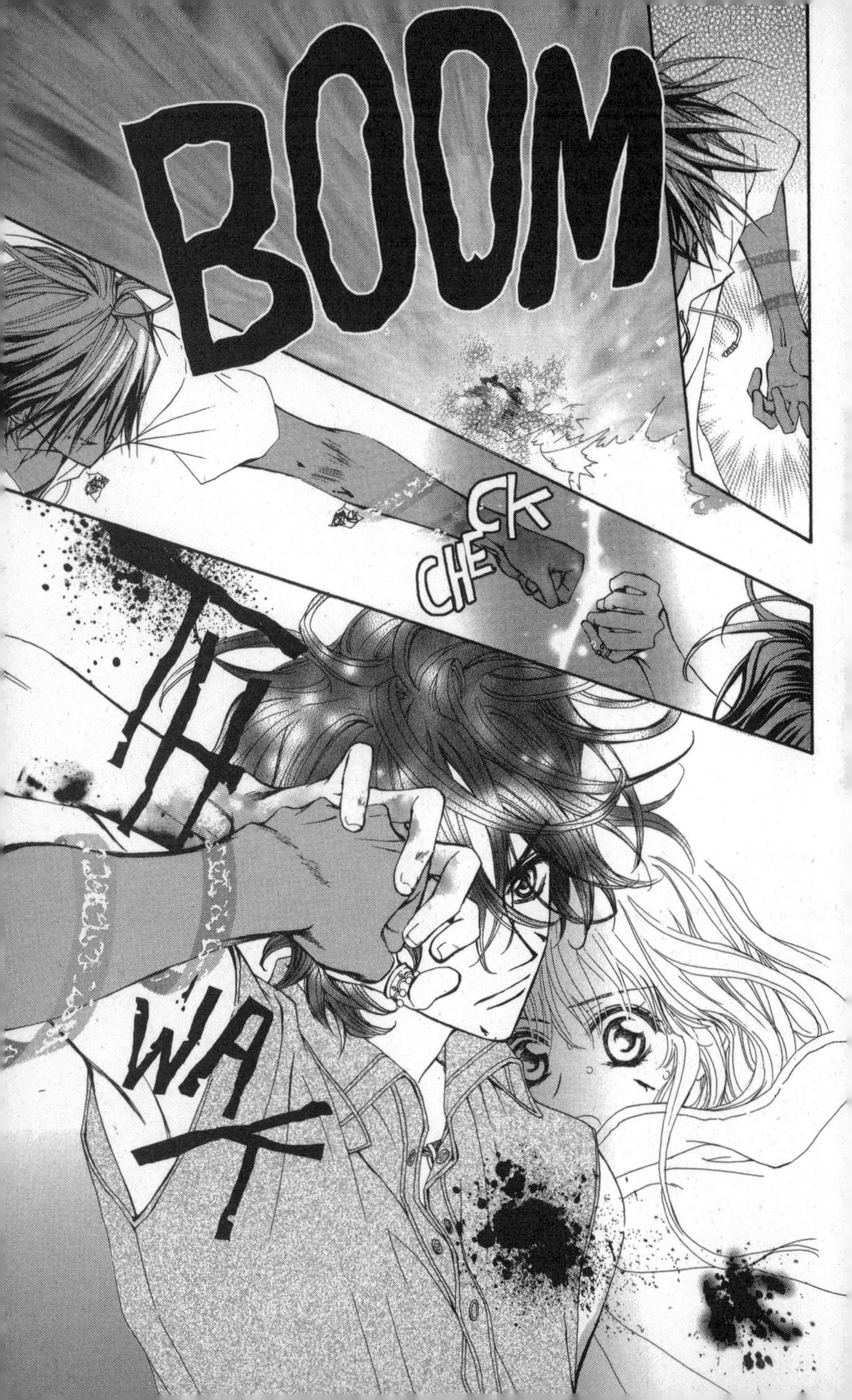
BOOM
CRACK
CRACK
CHECK
THWAT

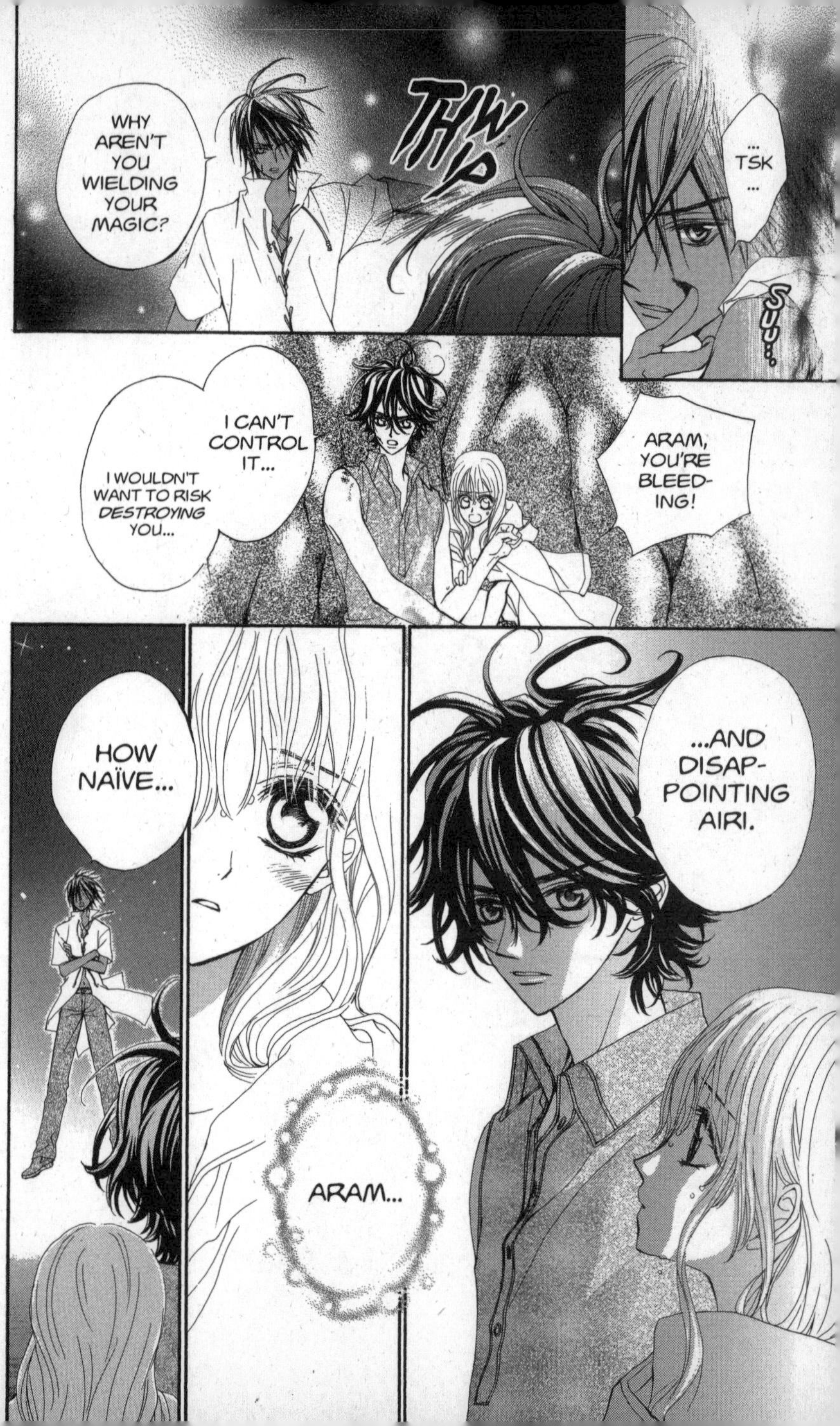
... TSK ...
SUU...
THWIP
WHY AREN'T YOU WIELDING YOUR MAGIC?
ARAM, YOU'RE BLEED-ING!
I CAN'T CONTROL IT...
I WOULDN'T WANT TO RISK DESTROYING YOU...
...AND DISAP-POINTING AIRI.
ARAM...
HOW NAÏVE...

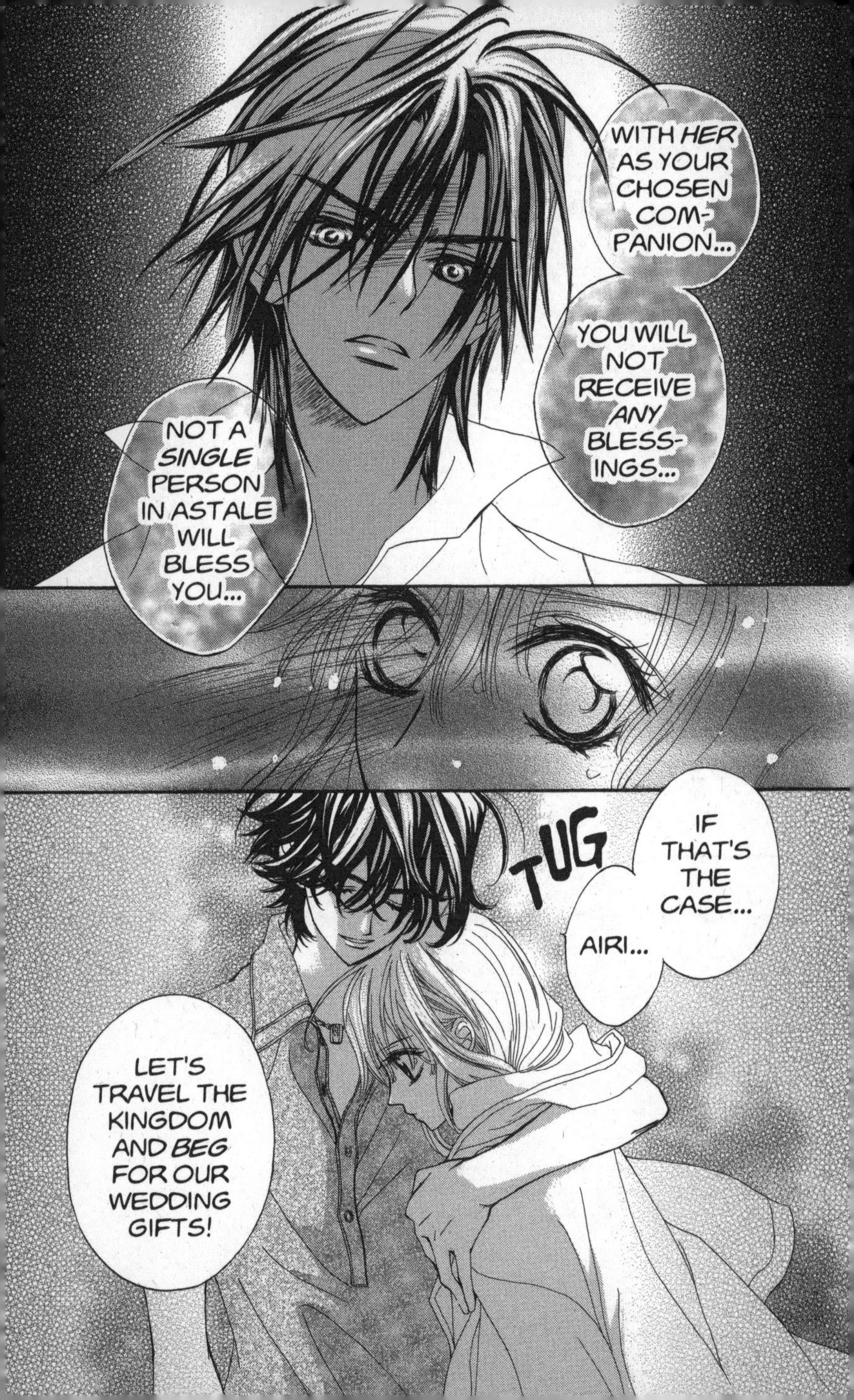
WITH *HER* AS YOUR CHOSEN COM-PANION...
YOU WILL NOT RECEIVE *ANY* BLESS-INGS...
NOT A *SINGLE* PERSON IN ASTALE WILL BLESS YOU...
IF THAT'S THE CASE...
TUG
AIRI...
LET'S TRAVEL THE KINGDOM AND *BEG* FOR OUR WEDDING GIFTS!

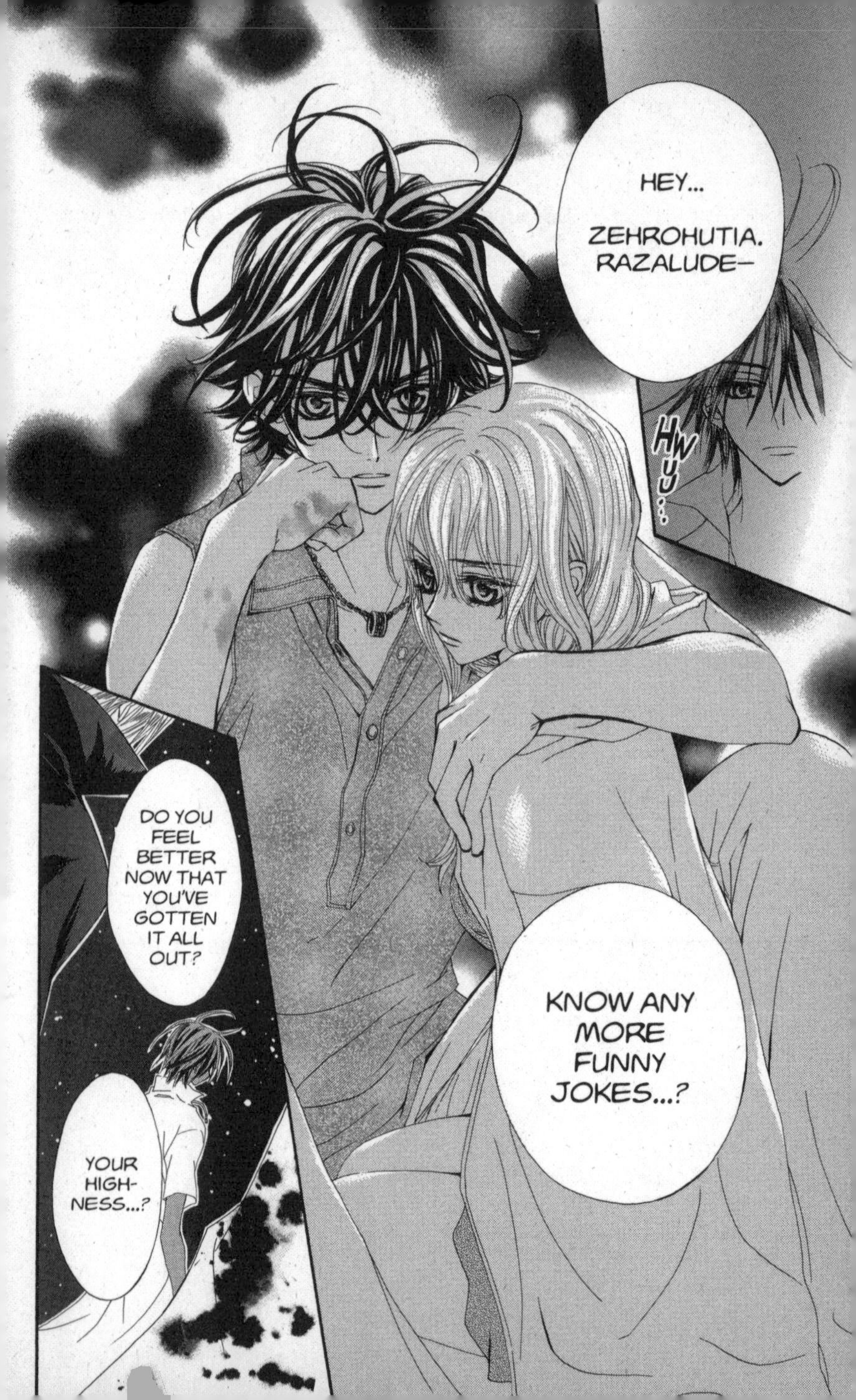
HEY... ZEHROHUTIA. RAZALUDE–
HWUU..
KNOW ANY MORE FUNNY JOKES...?
DO YOU FEEL BETTER NOW THAT YOU'VE GOTTEN IT ALL OUT?
YOUR HIGHNESS...?

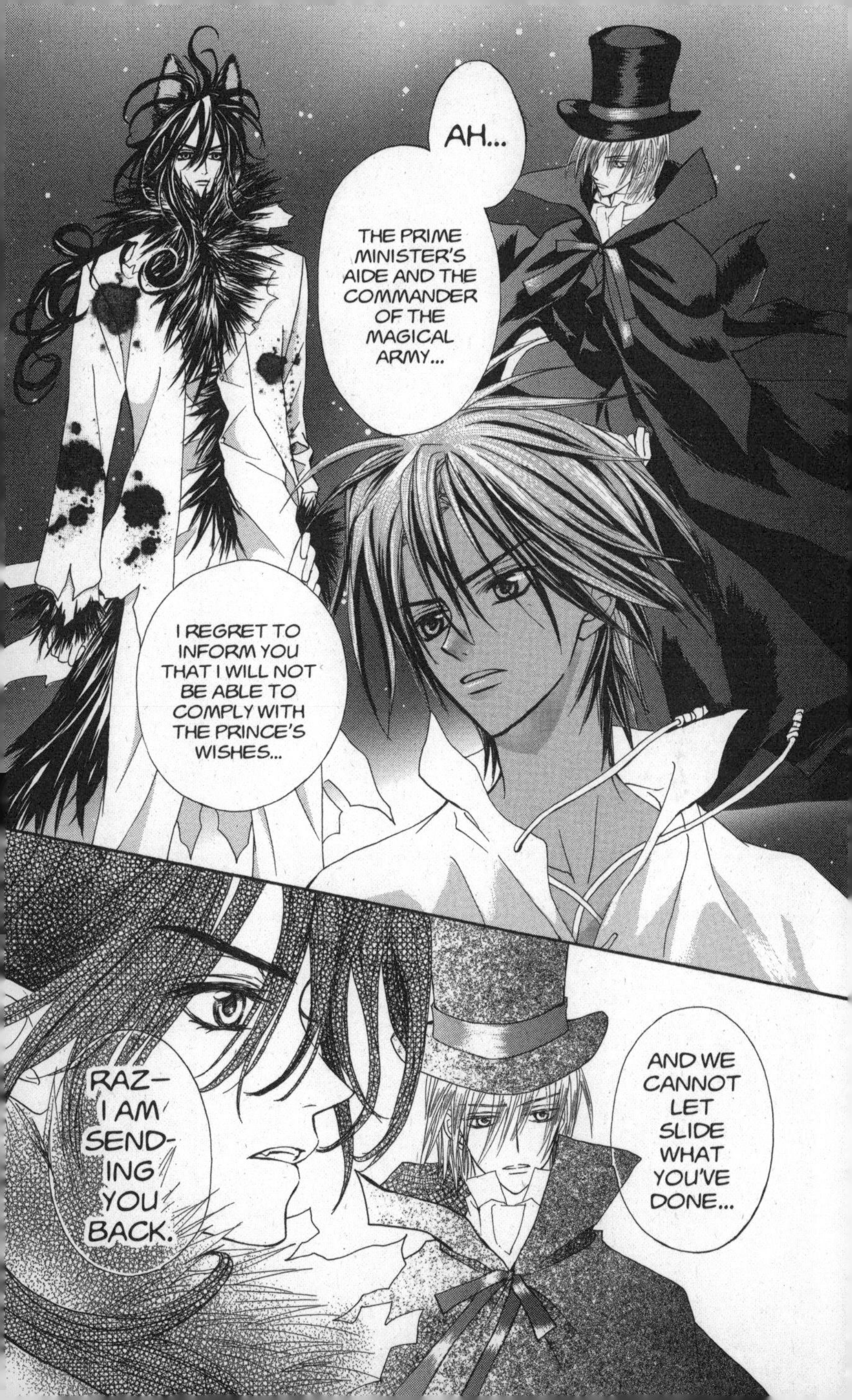
AH...
THE PRIME MINISTER'S AIDE AND THE COMMANDER OF THE MAGICAL ARMY...
I REGRET TO INFORM YOU THAT I WILL NOT BE ABLE TO COMPLY WITH THE PRINCE'S WISHES...
AND WE CANNOT LET SLIDE WHAT YOU'VE DONE...
RAZ—I AM SEND-ING YOU BACK.

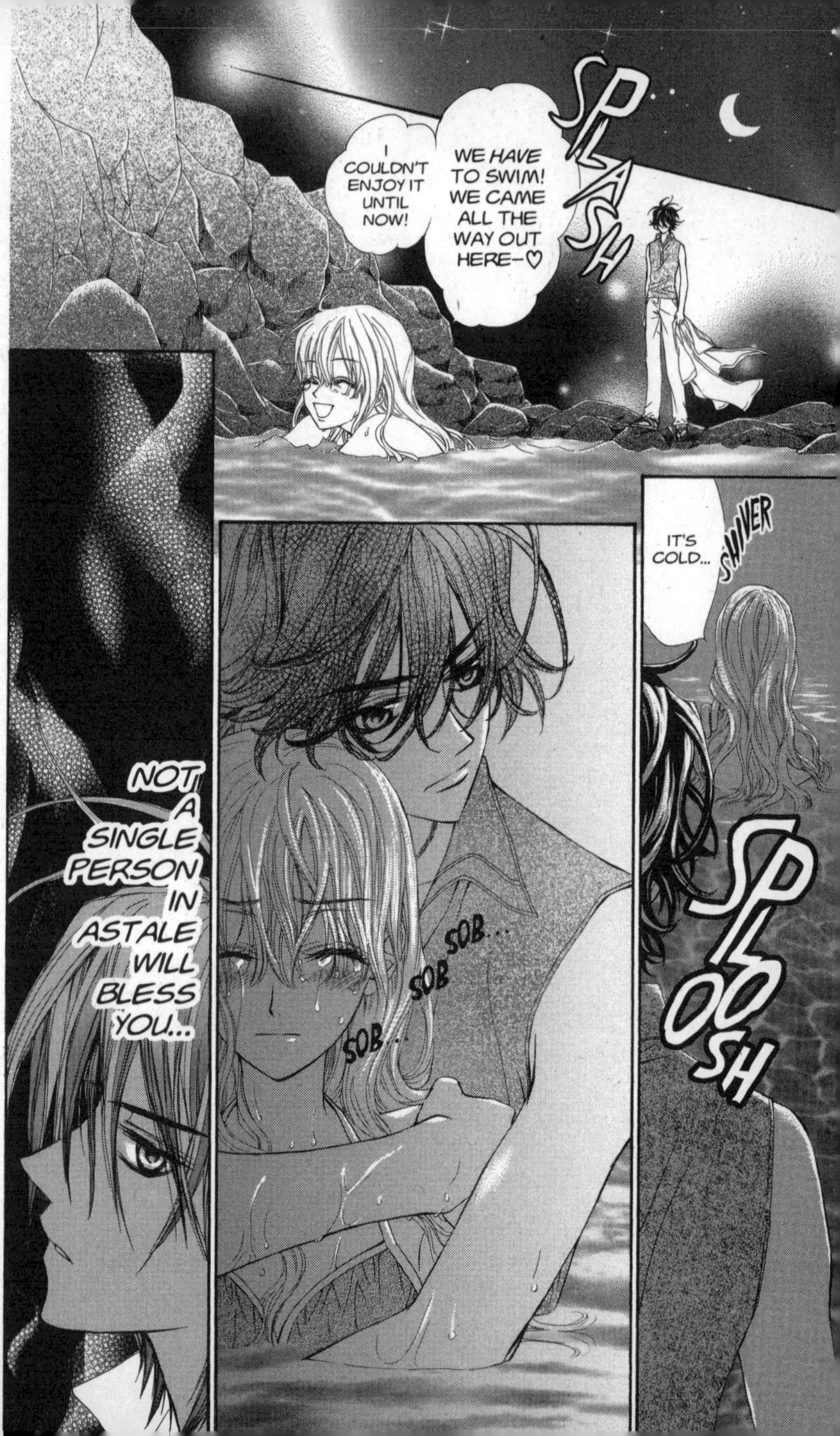
SPLASH
WE HAVE TO SWIM! WE CAME ALL THE WAY OUT HERE—♡
I COULDN'T ENJOY IT UNTIL NOW!
IT'S COLD...
SHIVER
SPLOOSH
SOB... SOB SOB...
NOT A SINGLE PERSON IN ASTALE WILL BLESS YOU...

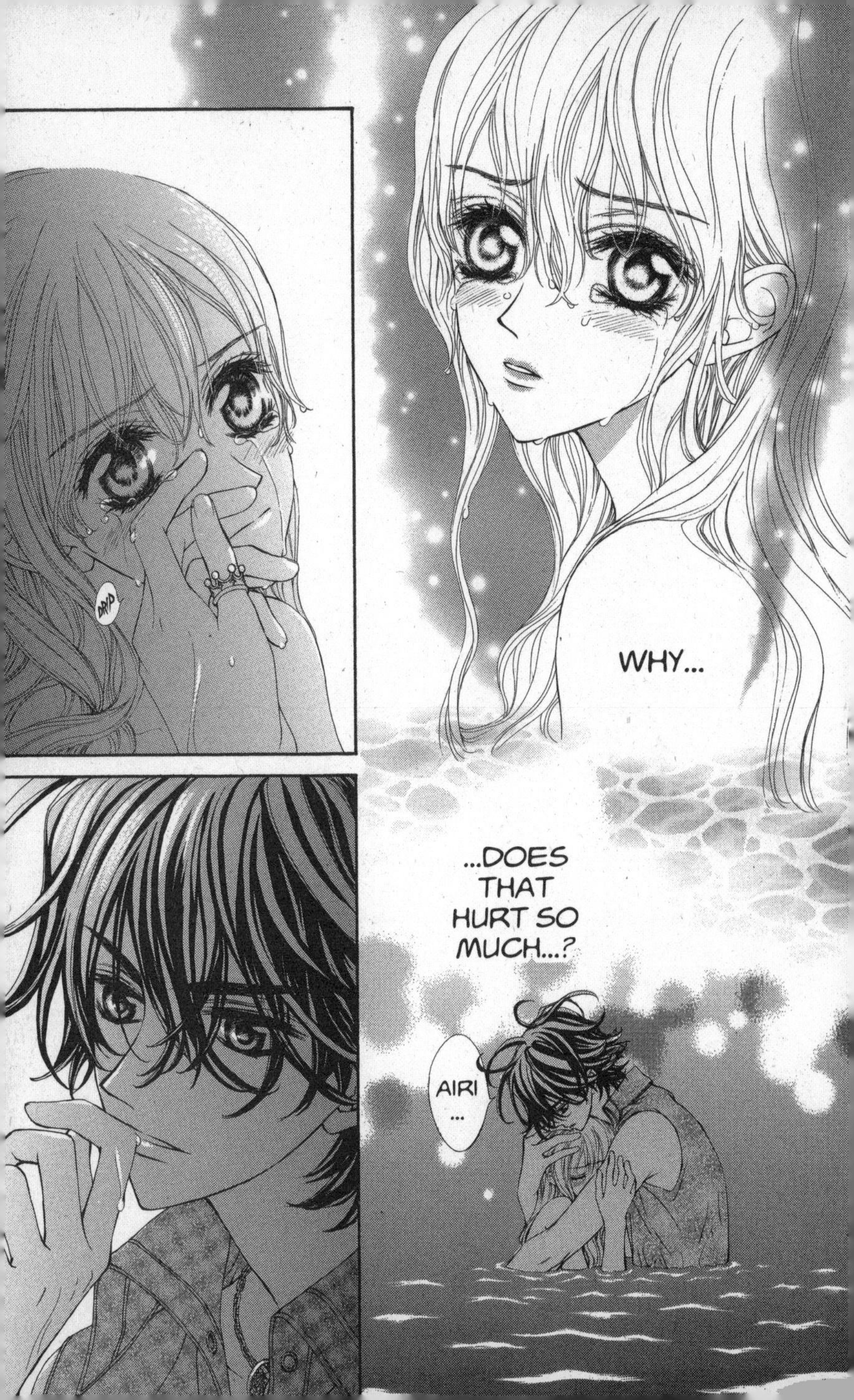
WHY...
...DOES THAT HURT SO MUCH...?
AIRI...
DRIP

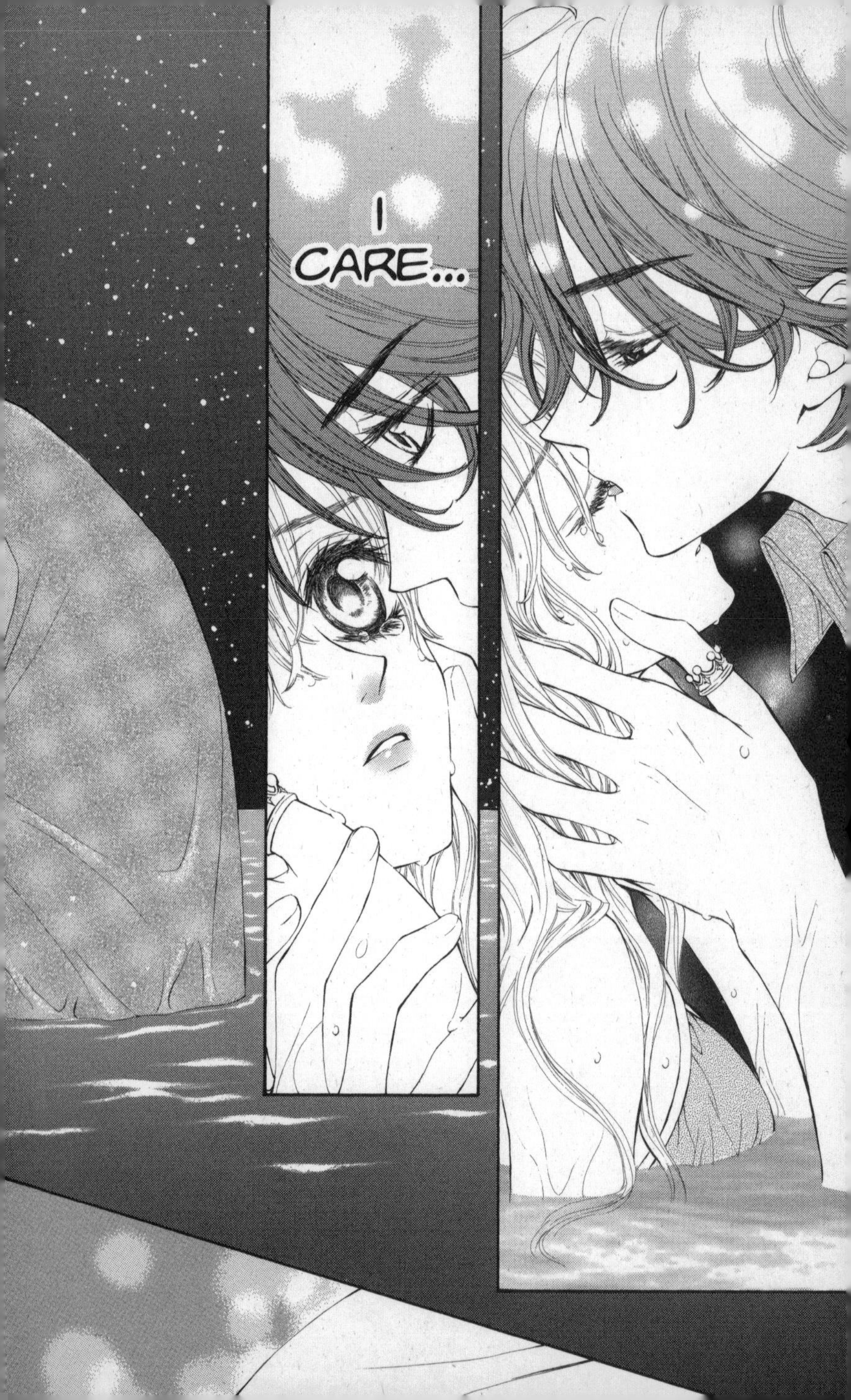
I CARE...

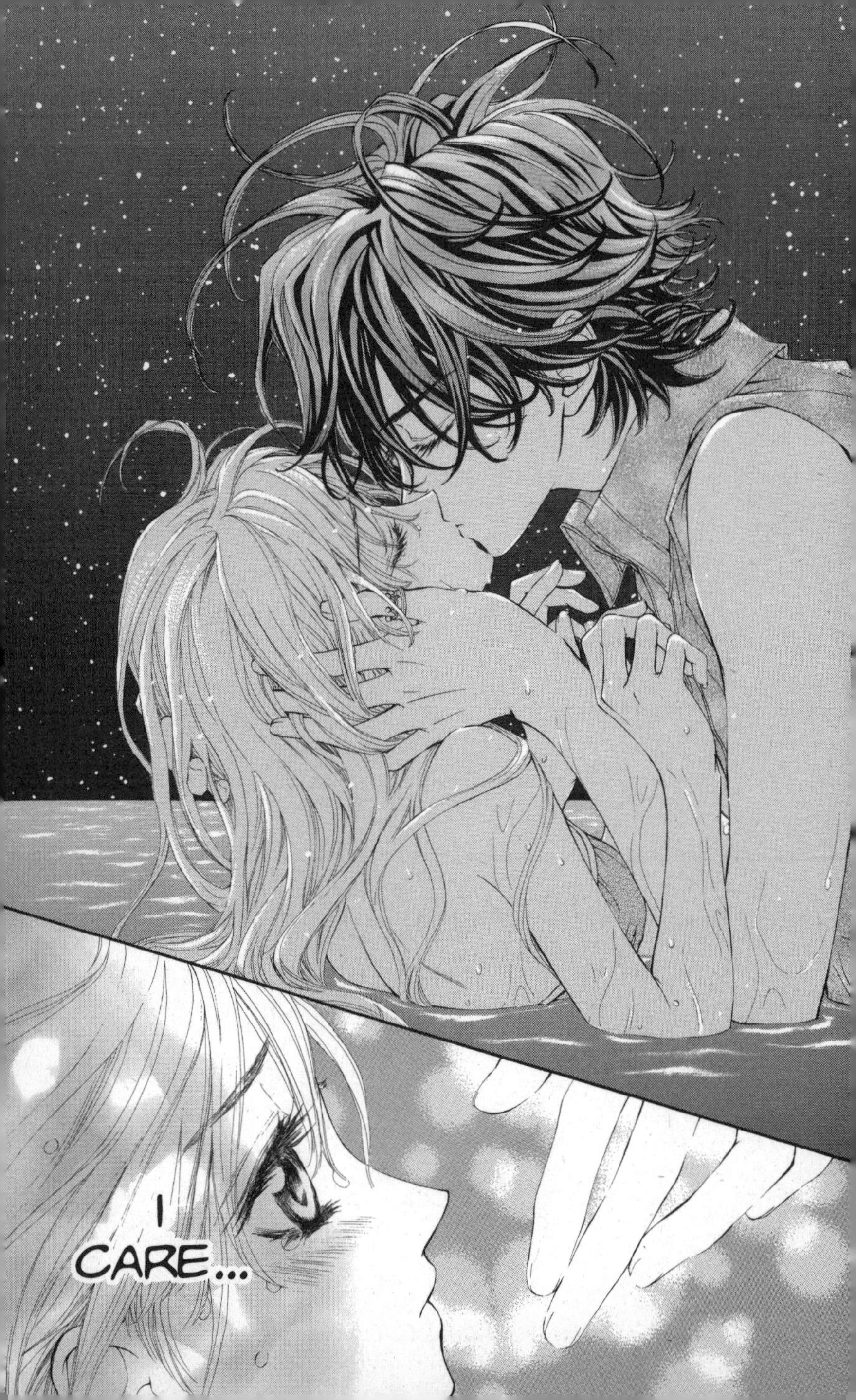
I CARE...

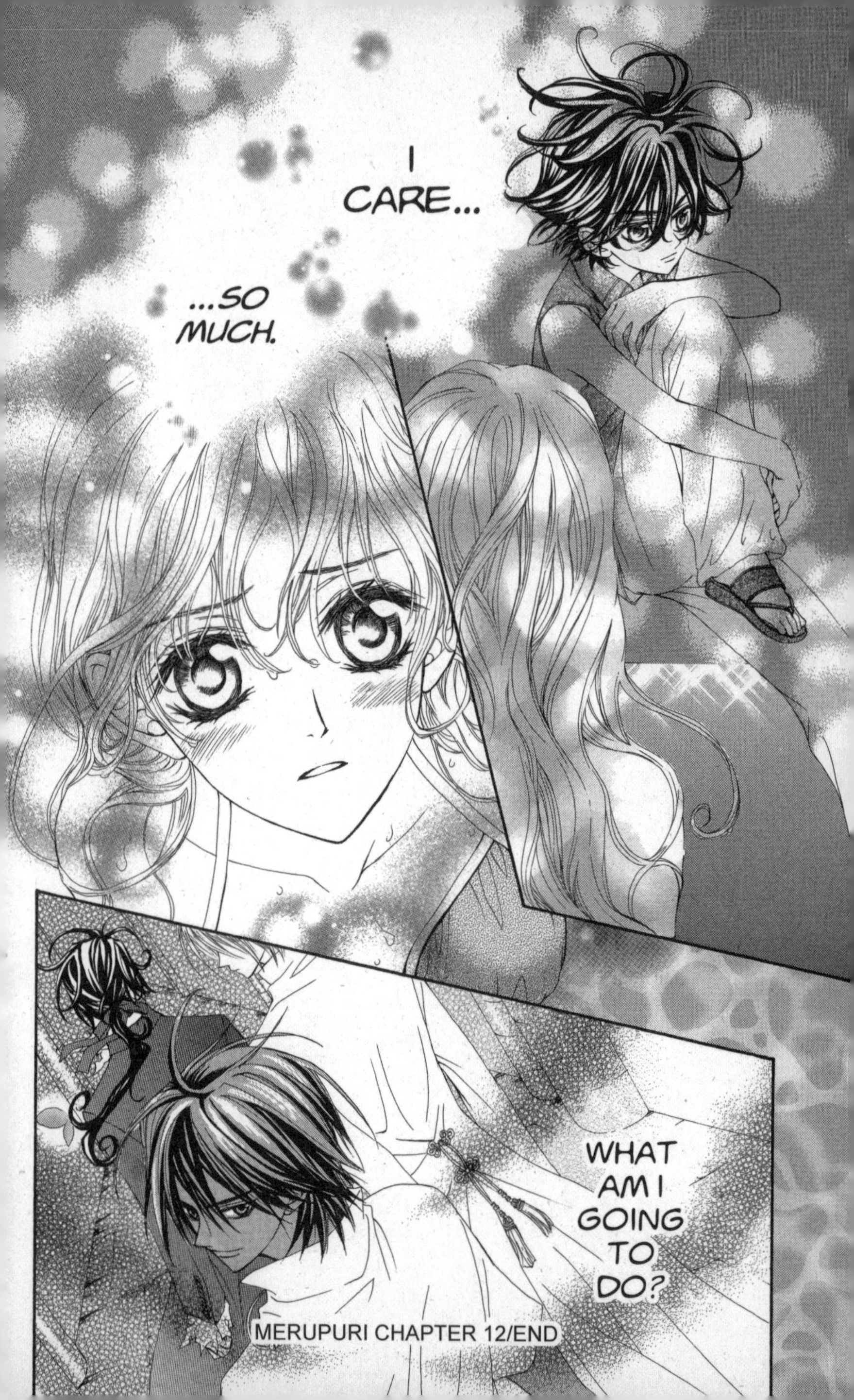
I CARE...
...SO MUCH.
WHAT AM I GOING TO DO?
MERUPURI CHAPTER 12/END

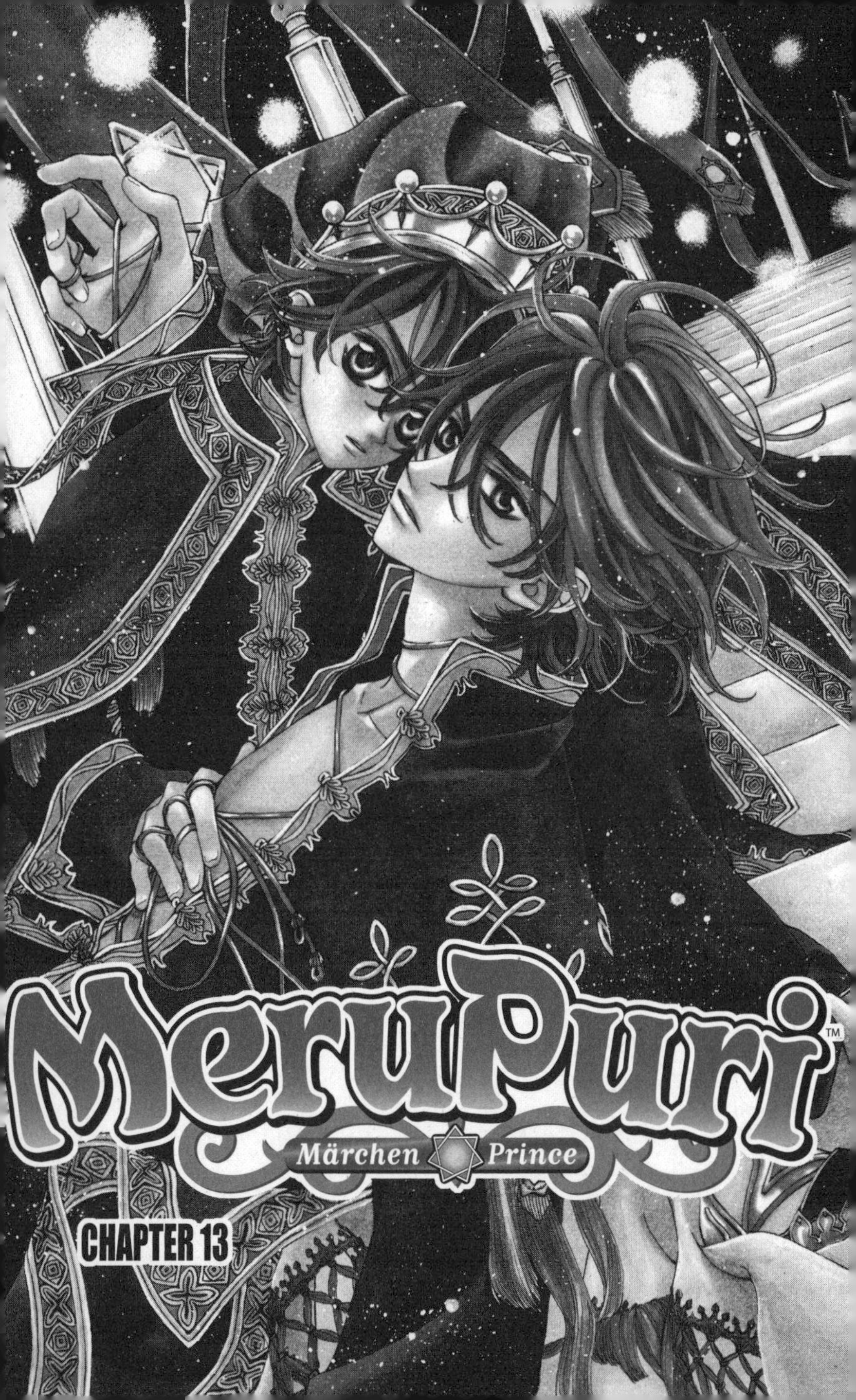
MeruPuri™
Märchen Prince
CHAPTER 13

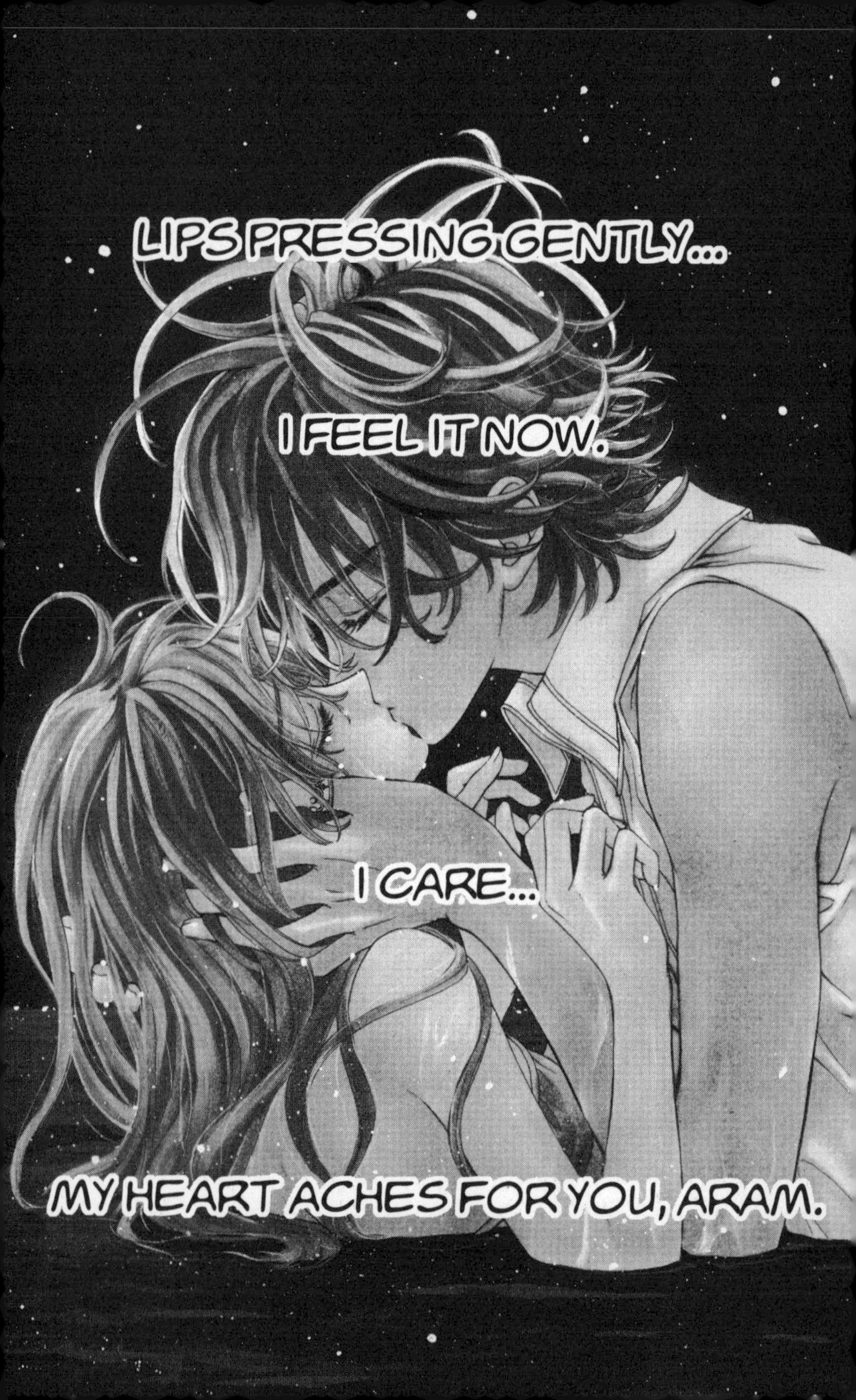
LIPS PRESSING GENTLY...
I FEEL IT NOW.
I CARE...
MY HEART ACHES FOR YOU, ARAM.

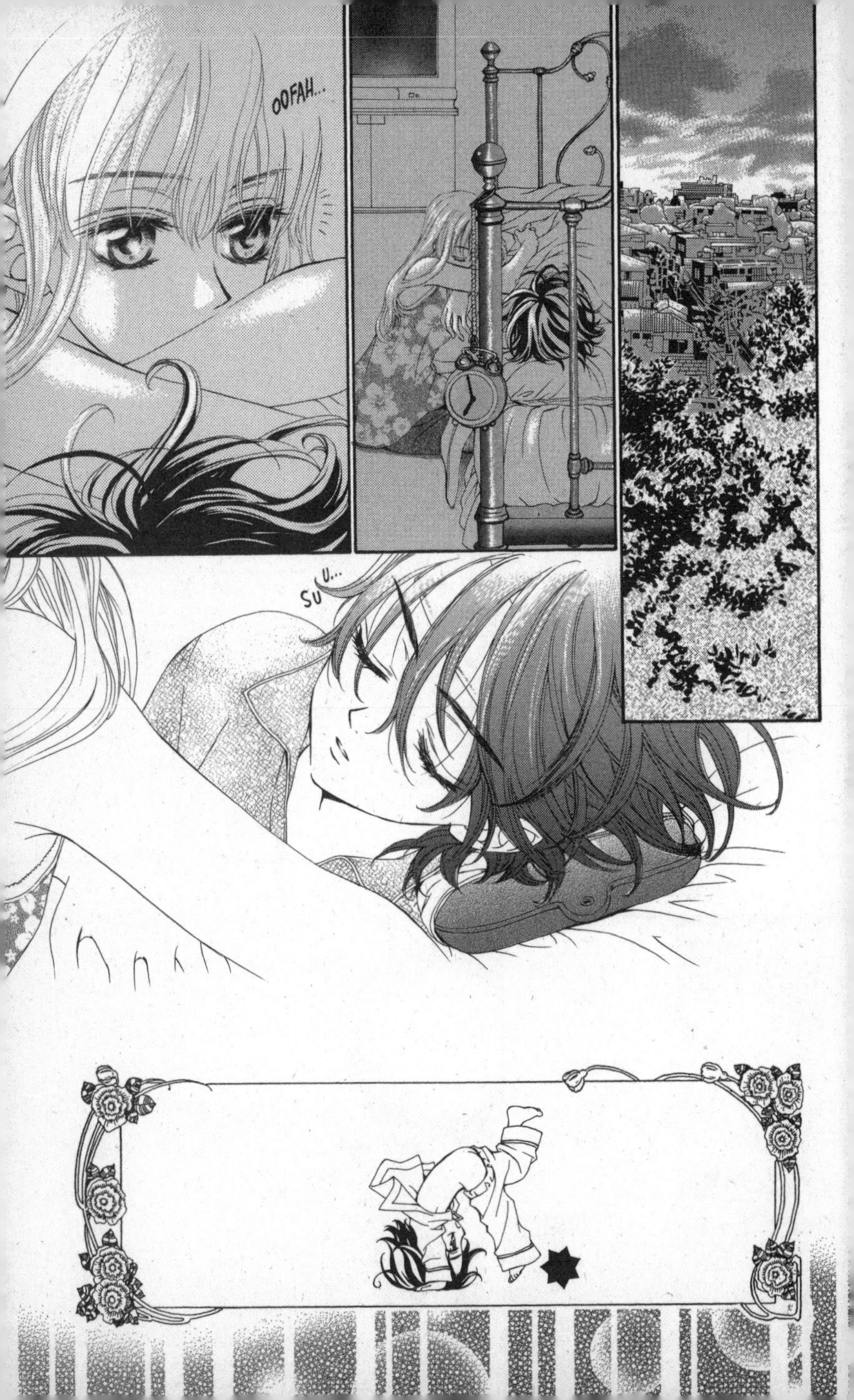
OOFAH...
SUU...

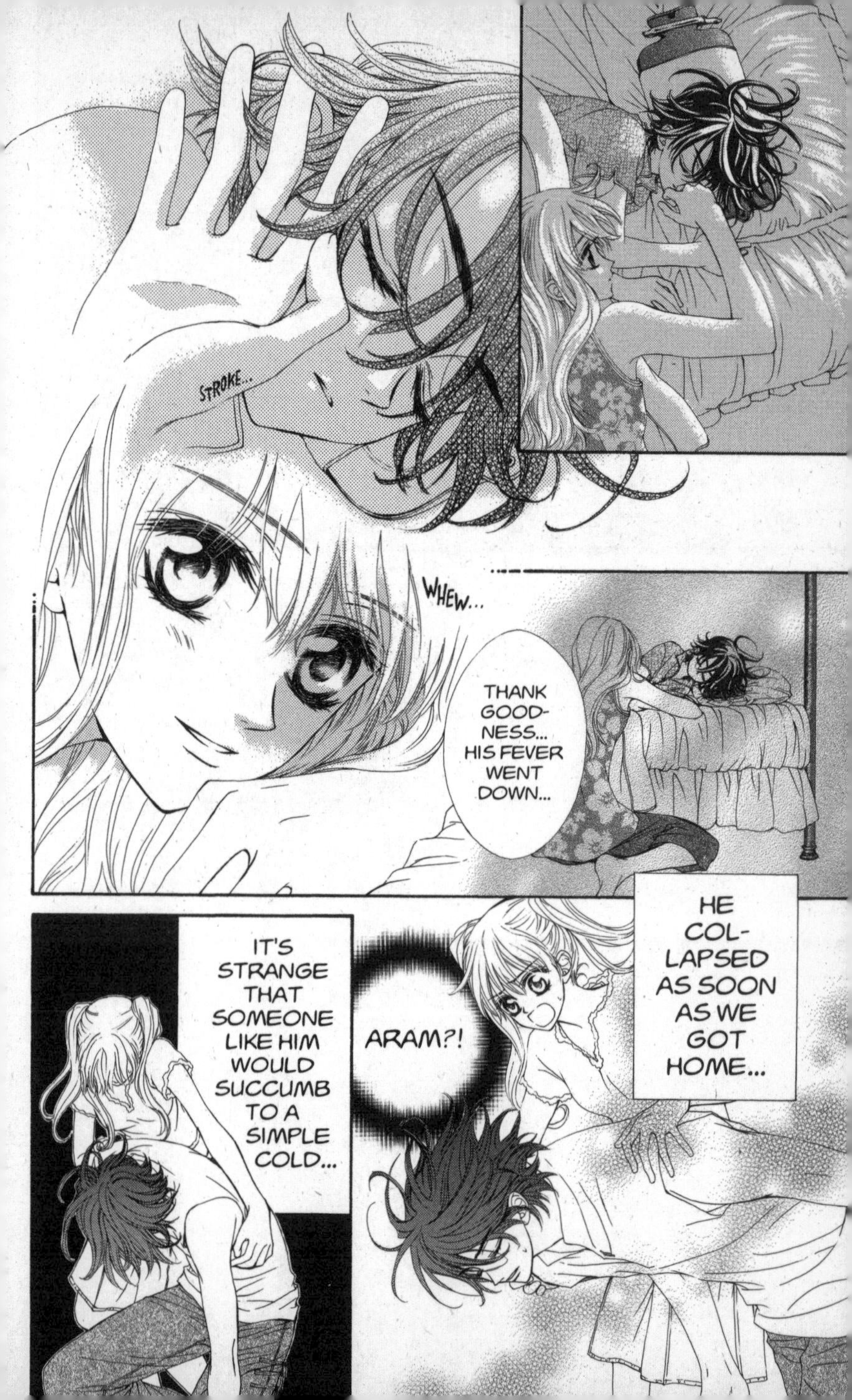
THANK GOODNESS... HIS FEVER WENT DOWN...
STROKE...
WHEW...
HE COLLAPSED AS SOON AS WE GOT HOME...
ARAM?!
IT'S STRANGE THAT SOMEONE LIKE HIM WOULD SUCCUMB TO A SIMPLE COLD...

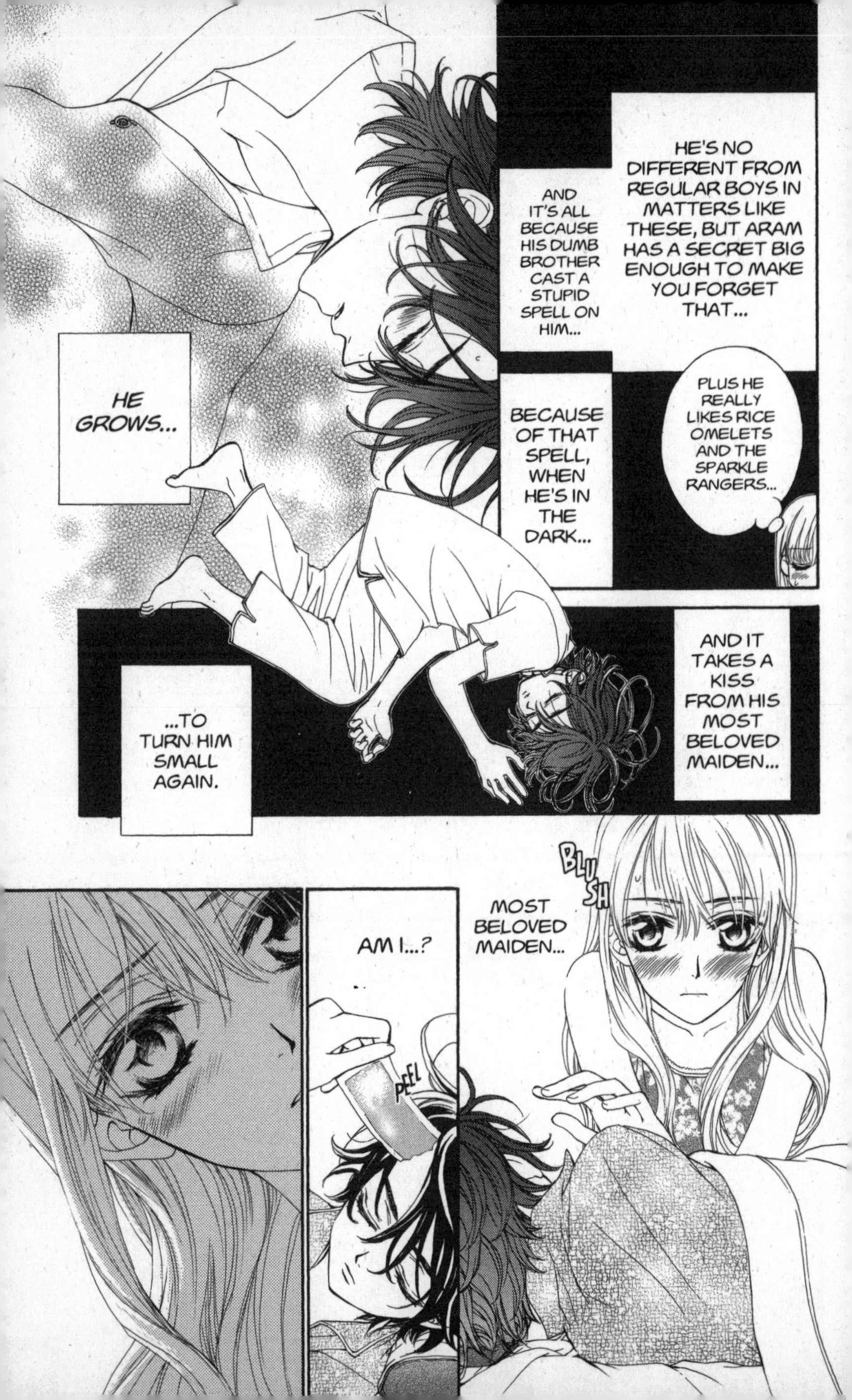
HE'S NO DIFFERENT FROM REGULAR BOYS IN MATTERS LIKE THESE, BUT ARAM HAS A SECRET BIG ENOUGH TO MAKE YOU FORGET THAT...
AND IT'S ALL BECAUSE HIS DUMB BROTHER CAST A STUPID SPELL ON HIM...
PLUS HE REALLY LIKES RICE OMELETS AND THE SPARKLE RANGERS...
BECAUSE OF THAT SPELL, WHEN HE'S IN THE DARK...
HE GROWS...
AND IT TAKES A KISS FROM HIS MOST BELOVED MAIDEN...
...TO TURN HIM SMALL AGAIN.
BLUSH
MOST BELOVED MAIDEN...
AM I...?
PEEL

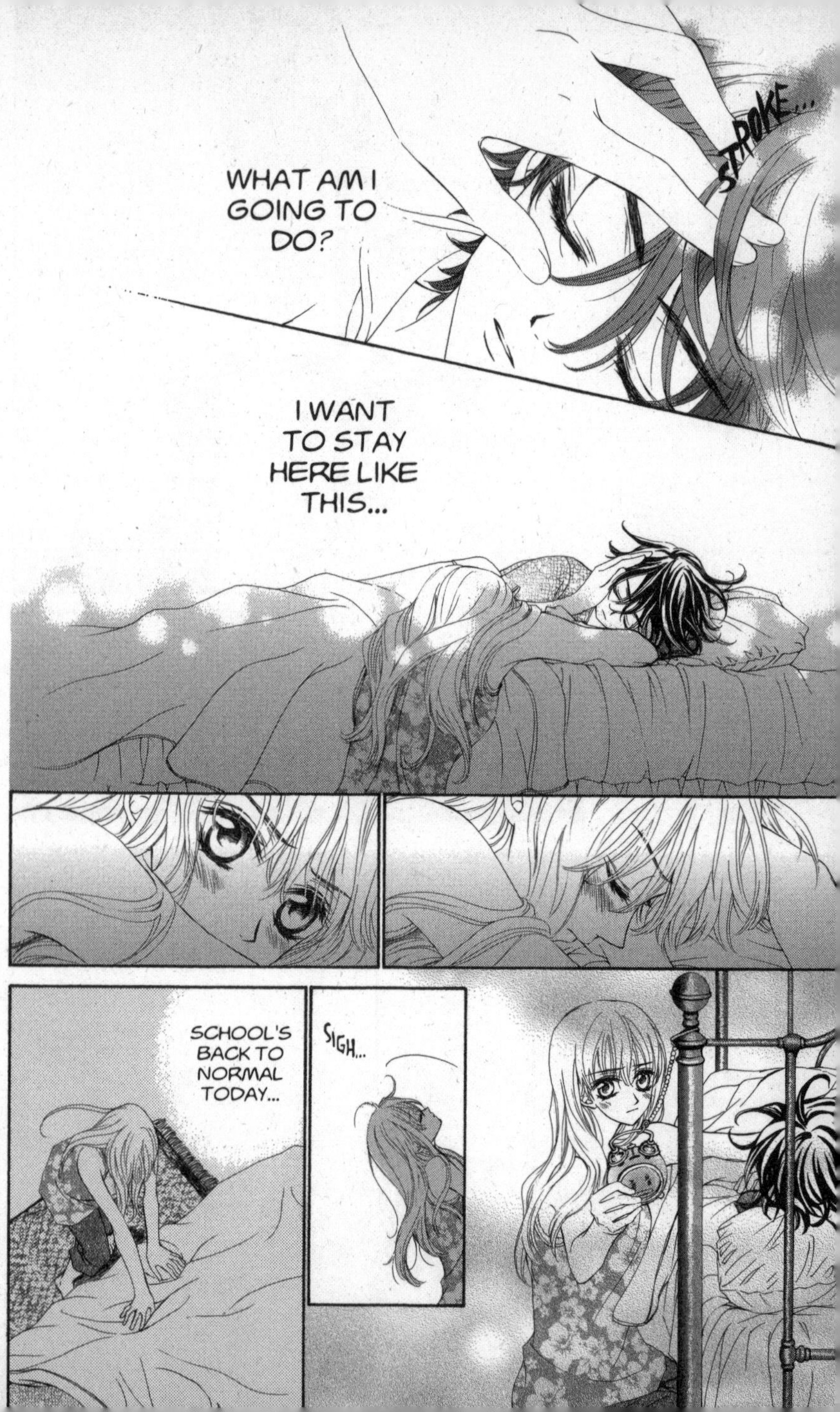
STROKE...
WHAT AM I GOING TO DO?
I WANT TO STAY HERE LIKE THIS...
SIGH...
SCHOOL'S BACK TO NORMAL TODAY...

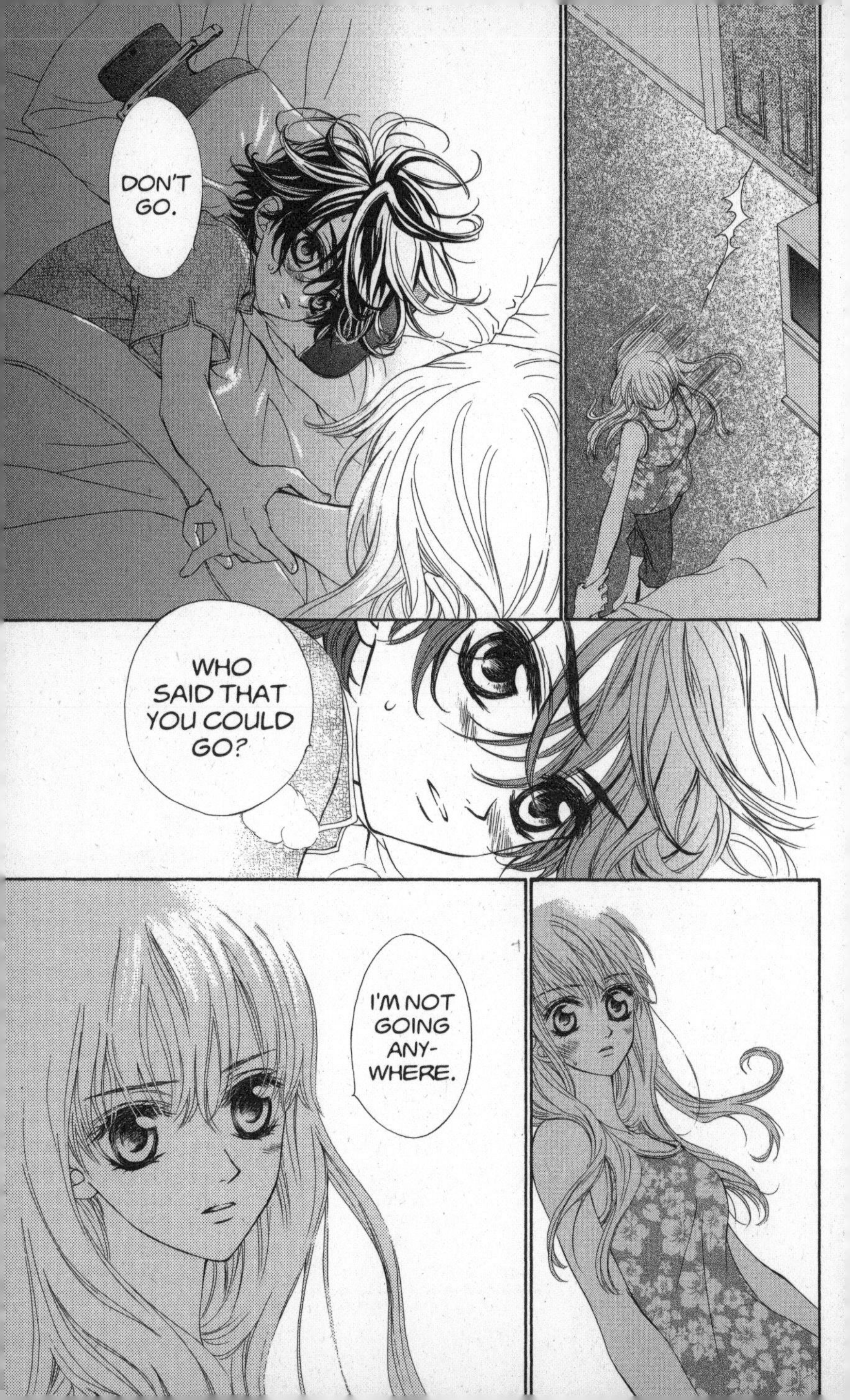
DON'T GO.
WHO SAID THAT YOU COULD GO?
I'M NOT GOING ANY-WHERE.

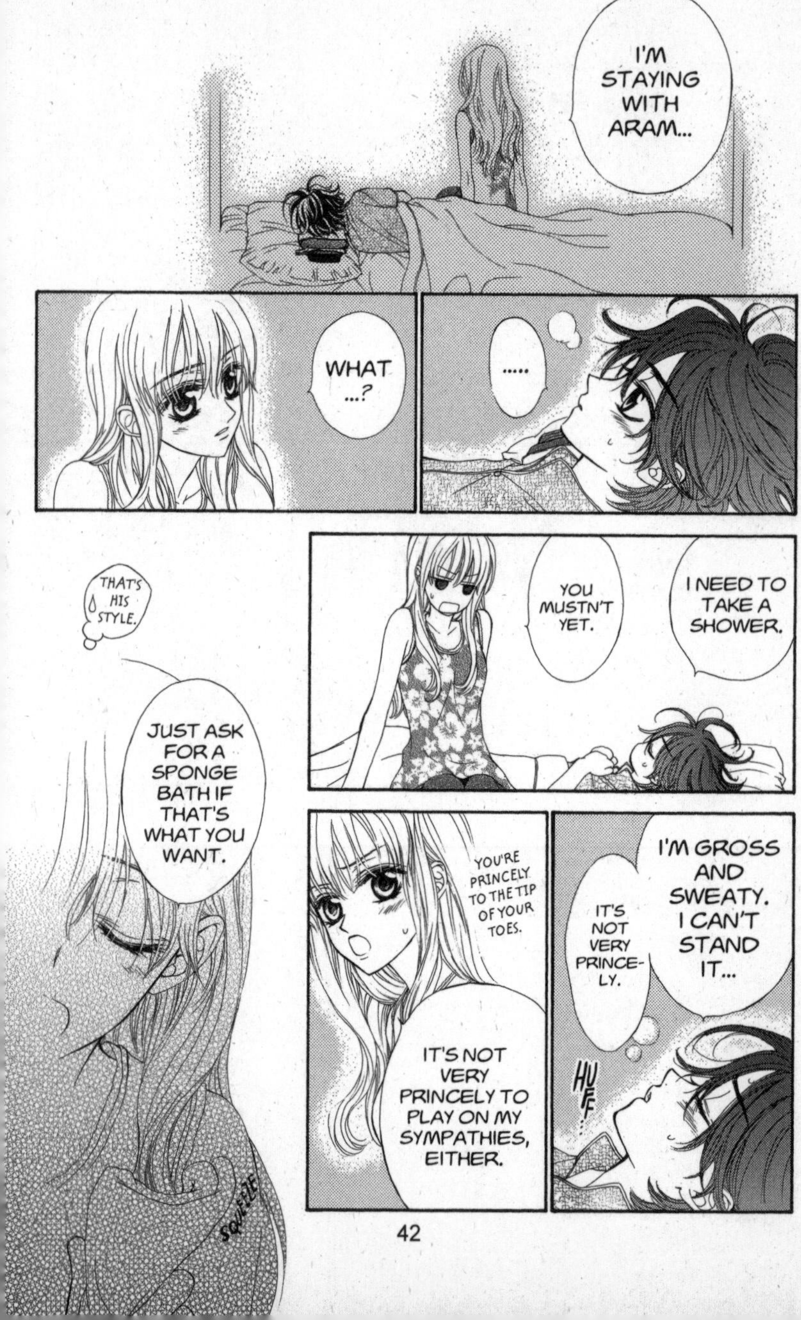
I'M STAYING WITH ARAM...
.....
WHAT ...?
I NEED TO TAKE A SHOWER.
YOU MUSTN'T YET.
I'M GROSS AND SWEATY. I CAN'T STAND IT...
IT'S NOT VERY PRINCE-LY.
HUFF...
YOU'RE PRINCELY TO THE TIP OF YOUR TOES.
IT'S NOT VERY PRINCELY TO PLAY ON MY SYMPATHIES, EITHER.
THAT'S HIS STYLE.
JUST ASK FOR A SPONGE BATH IF THAT'S WHAT YOU WANT.
SQUEEZE

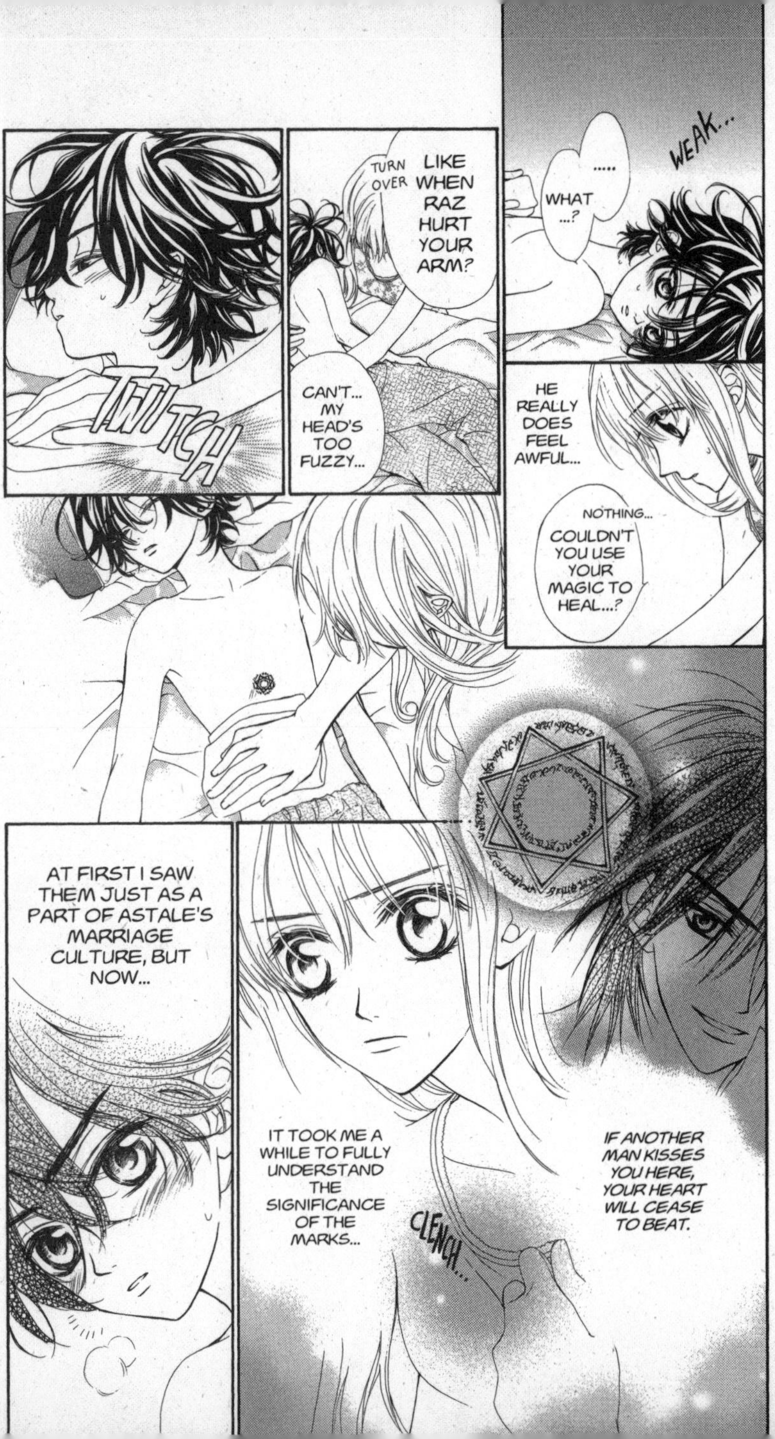
WEAK...
......
WHAT ...?
TURN OVER
LIKE WHEN RAZ HURT YOUR ARM?
CAN'T... MY HEAD'S TOO FUZZY...
TWITCH
HE REALLY DOES FEEL AWFUL...
NOTHING...
COULDN'T YOU USE YOUR MAGIC TO HEAL...?
IF ANOTHER MAN KISSES YOU HERE, YOUR HEART WILL CEASE TO BEAT.
IT TOOK ME A WHILE TO FULLY UNDERSTAND THE SIGNIFICANCE OF THE MARKS...
CLENCH...
AT FIRST I SAW THEM JUST AS A PART OF ASTALE'S MARRIAGE CULTURE, BUT NOW...

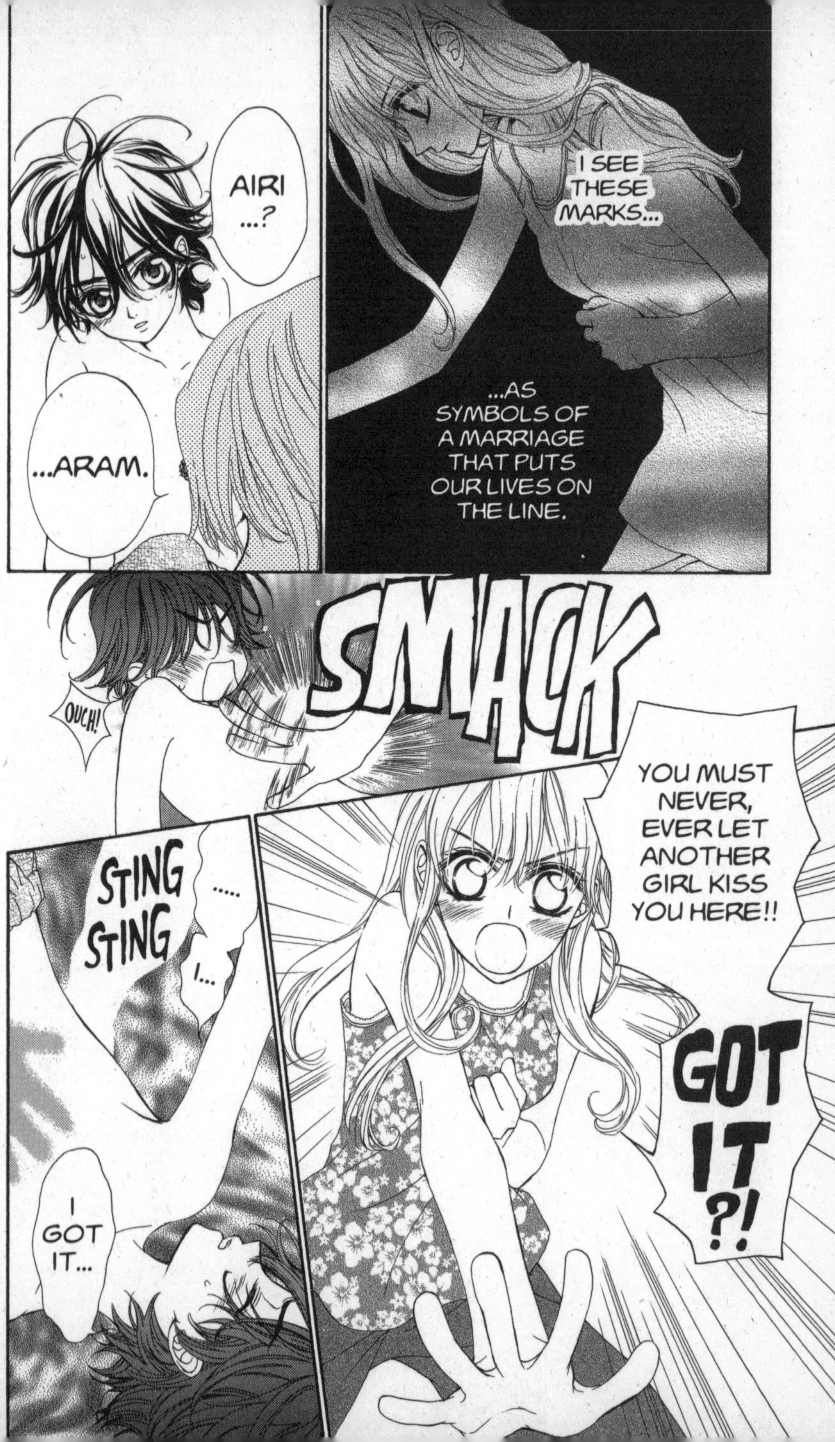
I SEE THESE MARKS...
...AS SYMBOLS OF A MARRIAGE THAT PUTS OUR LIVES ON THE LINE.
AIRI ...?
...ARAM.
SMACK
OUCH!
YOU MUST NEVER, EVER LET ANOTHER GIRL KISS YOU HERE!!
GOT IT?!
STING STING
.....
I...
I GOT IT...

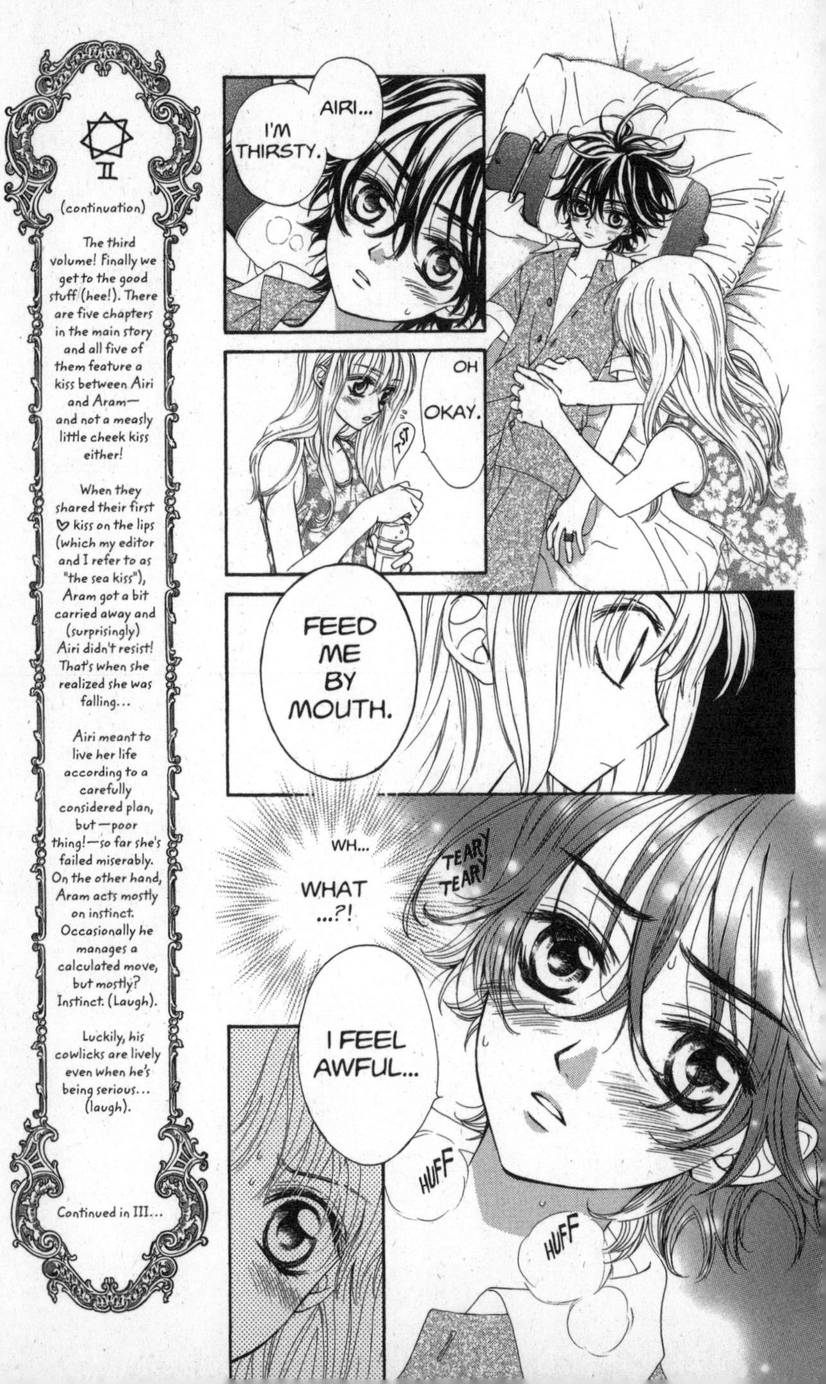
AIRI... I'M THIRSTY.
OH OKAY.
T-ST
FEED ME BY MOUTH.
TEARY TEARY
WH... WHAT ...?!
I FEEL AWFUL...
HUFF
HUFF

II

(continuation)

The third volume! Finally we get to the good stuff (hee!). There are five chapters in the main story and all five of them feature a kiss between Airi and Aram—and not a measly little cheek kiss either!

When they shared their first ♡ kiss on the lips (which my editor and I refer to as "the sea kiss"), Aram got a bit carried away and (surprisingly) Airi didn't resist! That's when she realized she was falling...

Airi meant to live her life according to a carefully considered plan, but—poor thing!—so far she's failed miserably. On the other hand, Aram acts mostly on instinct. Occasionally he manages a calculated move, but mostly? Instinct. (Laugh).

Luckily, his cowlicks are lively even when he's being serious... (laugh).

Continued in III...

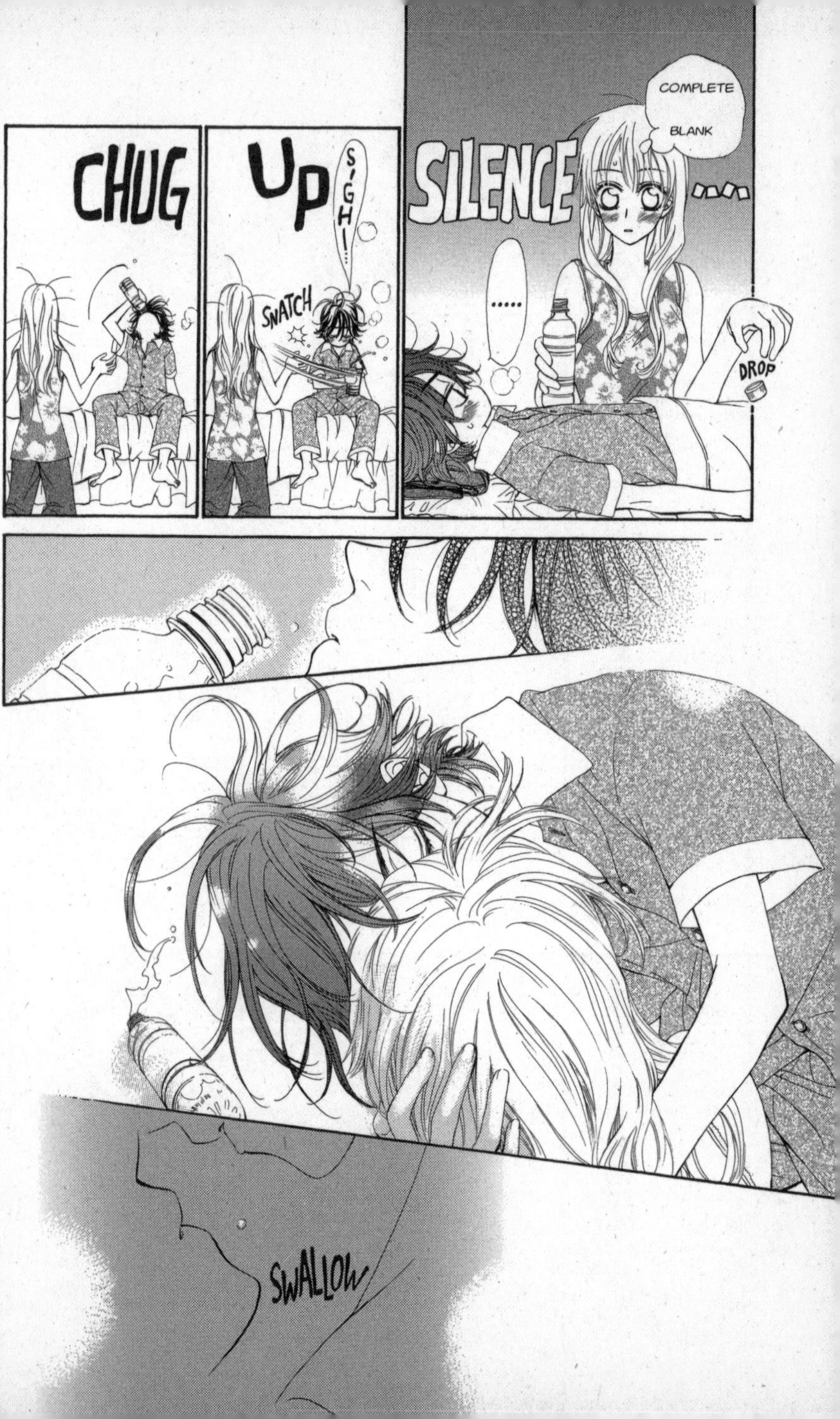

COMPLETE BLANK
SILENCE
.....
......
DROP
UP
SIGH!!
SNATCH
CHUG
SWALLOW

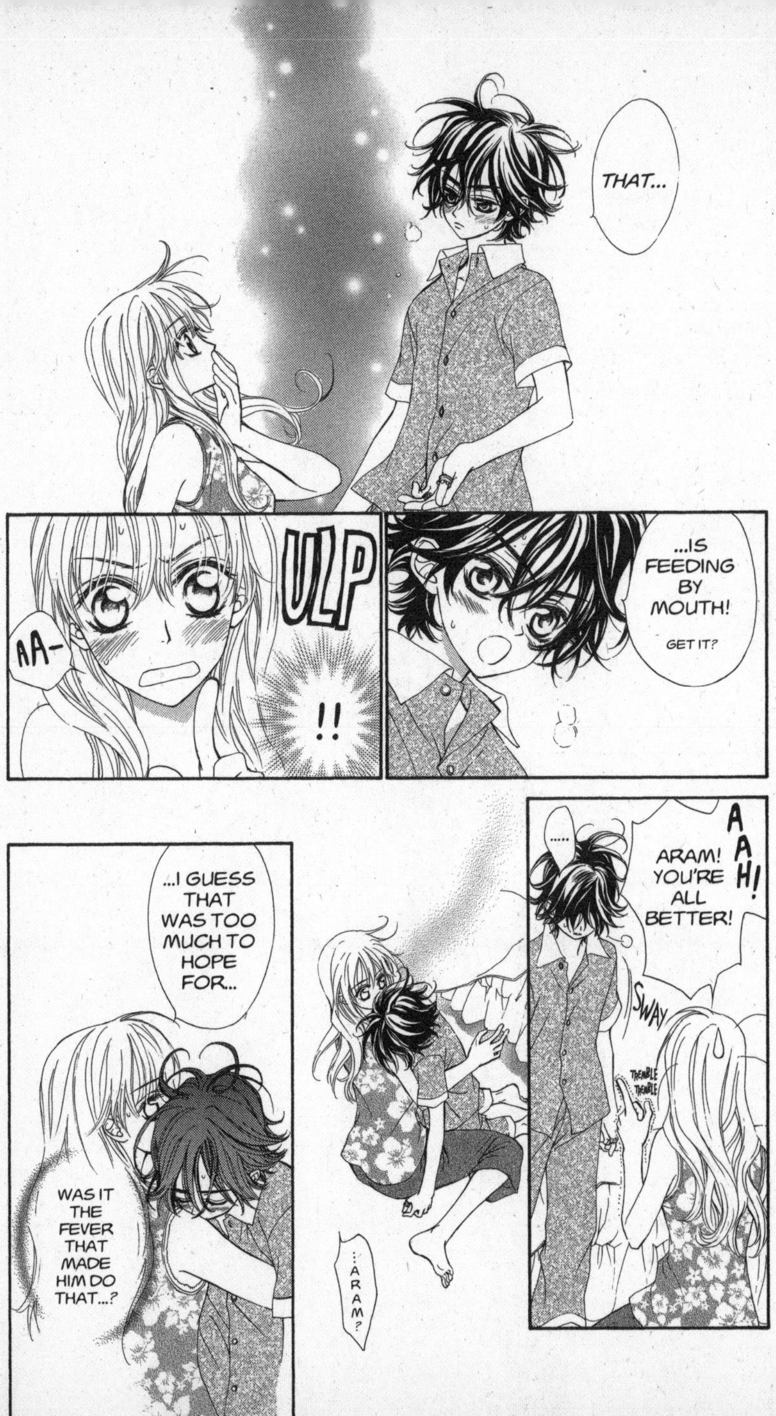
THAT...
...IS FEEDING BY MOUTH!
GET IT?
AA-
ULP
!!
.....
AAH!
ARAM! YOU'RE ALL BETTER!
SWAY
TREMBLE TREMBLE
...I GUESS THAT WAS TOO MUCH TO HOPE FOR...
...ARAM?
WAS IT THE FEVER THAT MADE HIM DO THAT...?

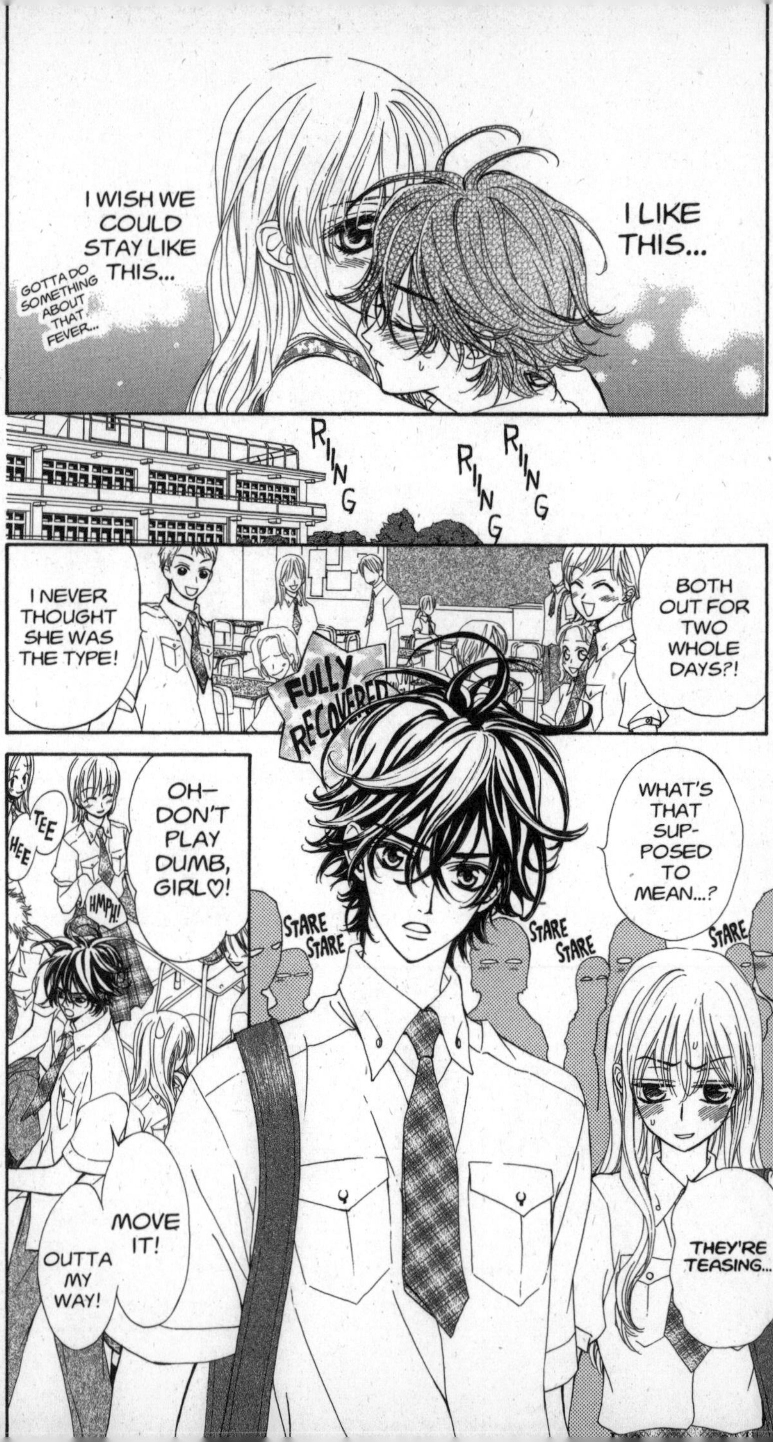
I LIKE THIS...
I WISH WE COULD STAY LIKE THIS...
GOTTA DO SOMETHING ABOUT THAT FEVER...
RIIING
RIIING
RIIING
BOTH OUT FOR TWO WHOLE DAYS?!
FULLY RECOVERED
I NEVER THOUGHT SHE WAS THE TYPE!
WHAT'S THAT SUP-POSED TO MEAN...?
STARE
STARE STARE
STARE STARE
THEY'RE TEASING...
OH— DON'T PLAY DUMB, GIRL♡!
TEE HEE
HMPH!
MOVE IT!
OUTTA MY WAY!

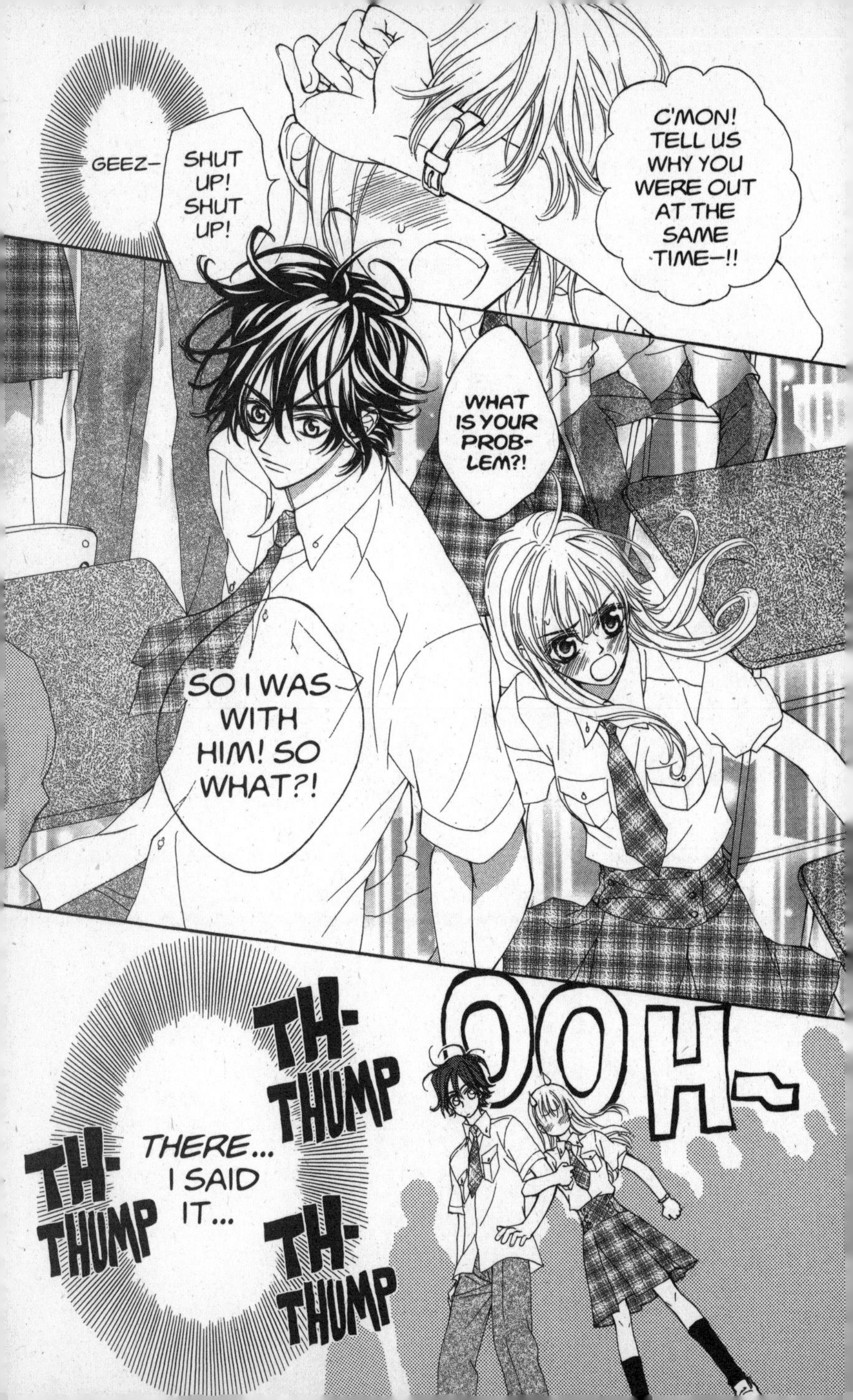
C'MON! TELL US WHY YOU WERE OUT AT THE SAME TIME—!!
SHUT UP! SHUT UP!
GEEZ—
WHAT IS YOUR PROBLEM?!
SO I WAS WITH HIM! SO WHAT?!
OOH~
TH-THUMP
TH-THUMP
THERE... I SAID IT...
TH-THUMP

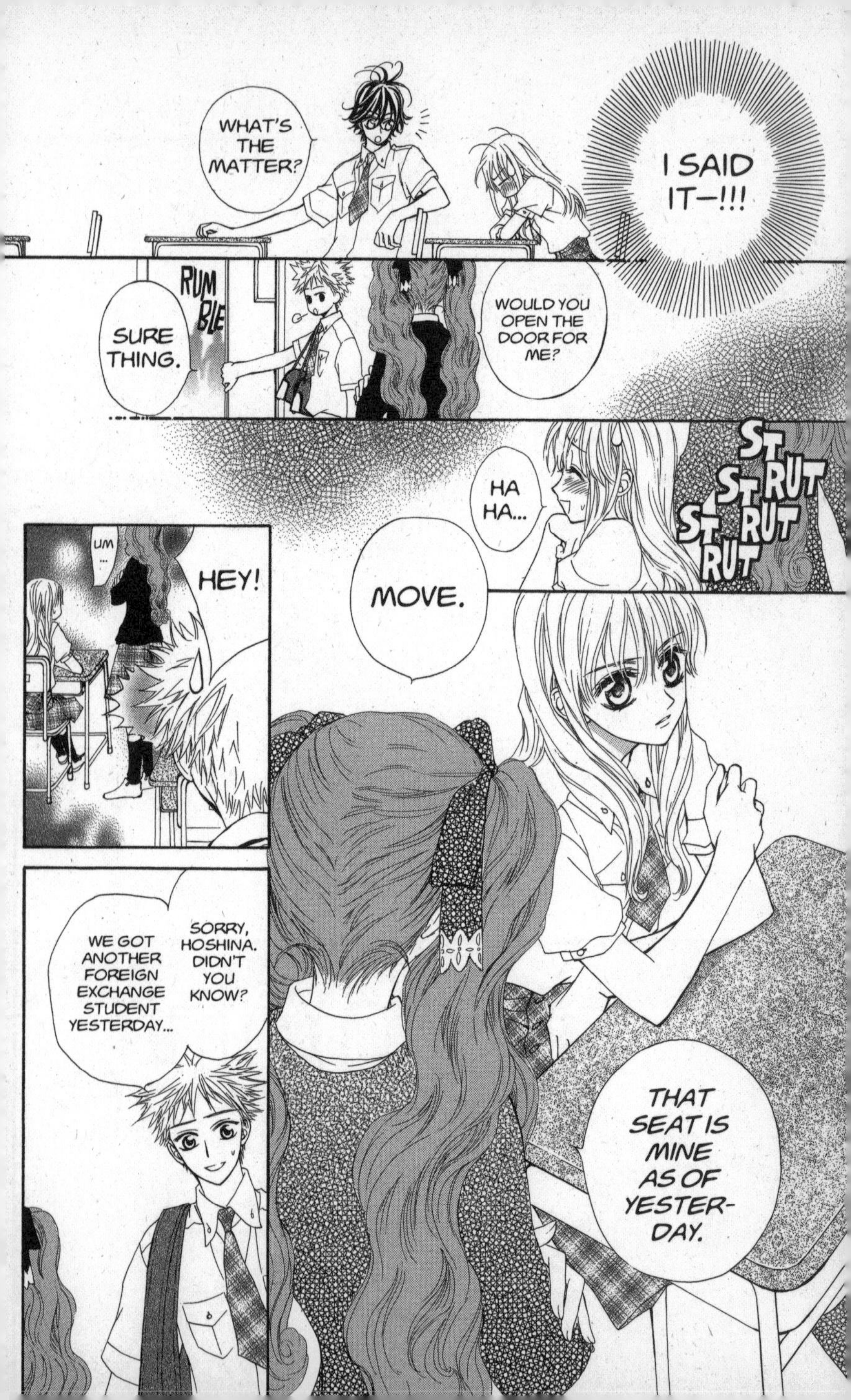
I SAID IT—!!!
WHAT'S THE MATTER?
WOULD YOU OPEN THE DOOR FOR ME?
RUMBLE
SURE THING.
STRUT STRUT STRUT
HA HA...
MOVE.
THAT SEAT IS MINE AS OF YESTERDAY.
UM ...
HEY!
SORRY, HOSHINA. DIDN'T YOU KNOW?
WE GOT ANOTHER FOREIGN EXCHANGE STUDENT YESTERDAY...

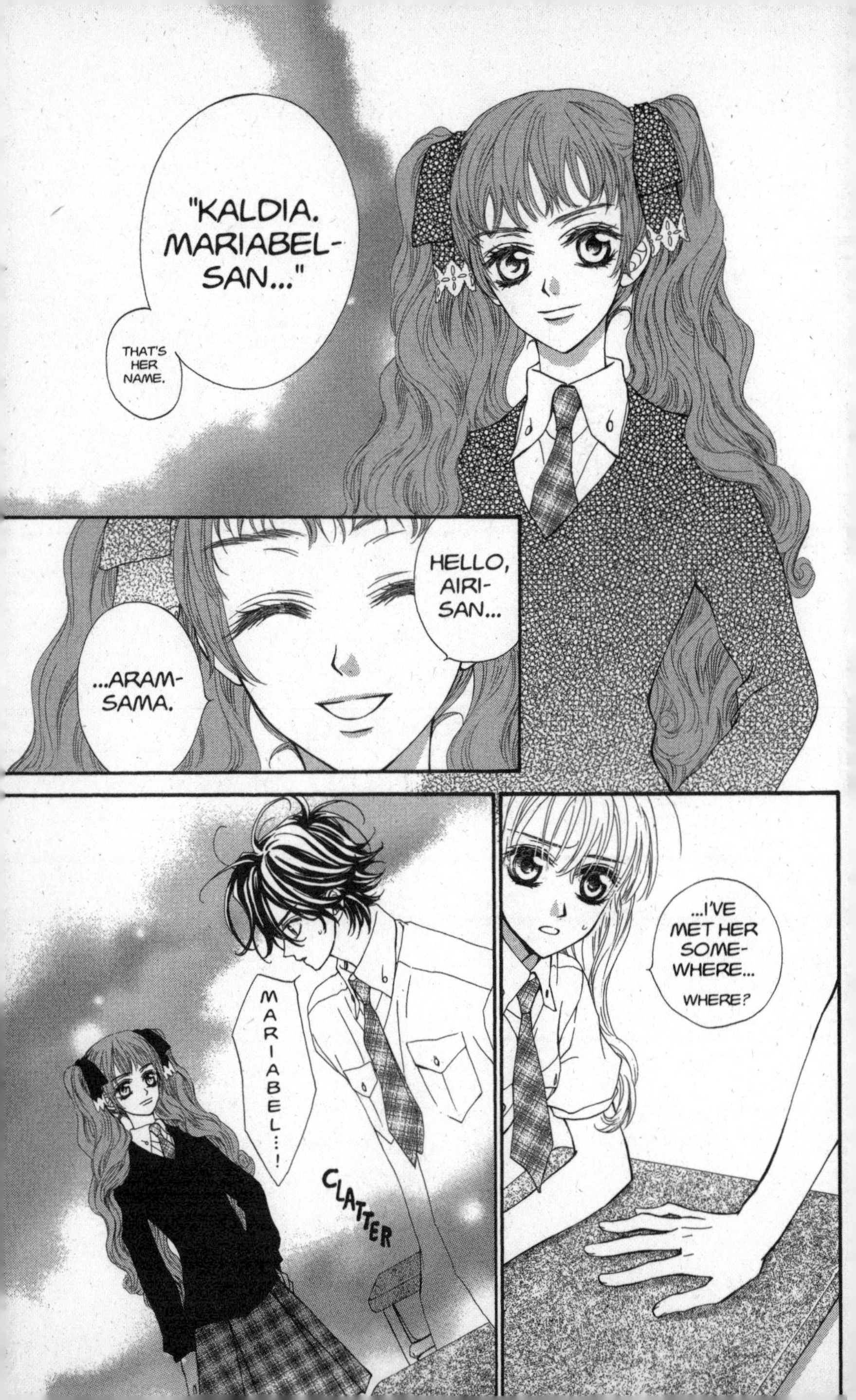
"KALDIA. MARIABEL-SAN..."
THAT'S HER NAME.
HELLO, AIRI-SAN...
...ARAM-SAMA.
...I'VE MET HER SOME-WHERE...
WHERE?
MARIABEL...!
CLATTER

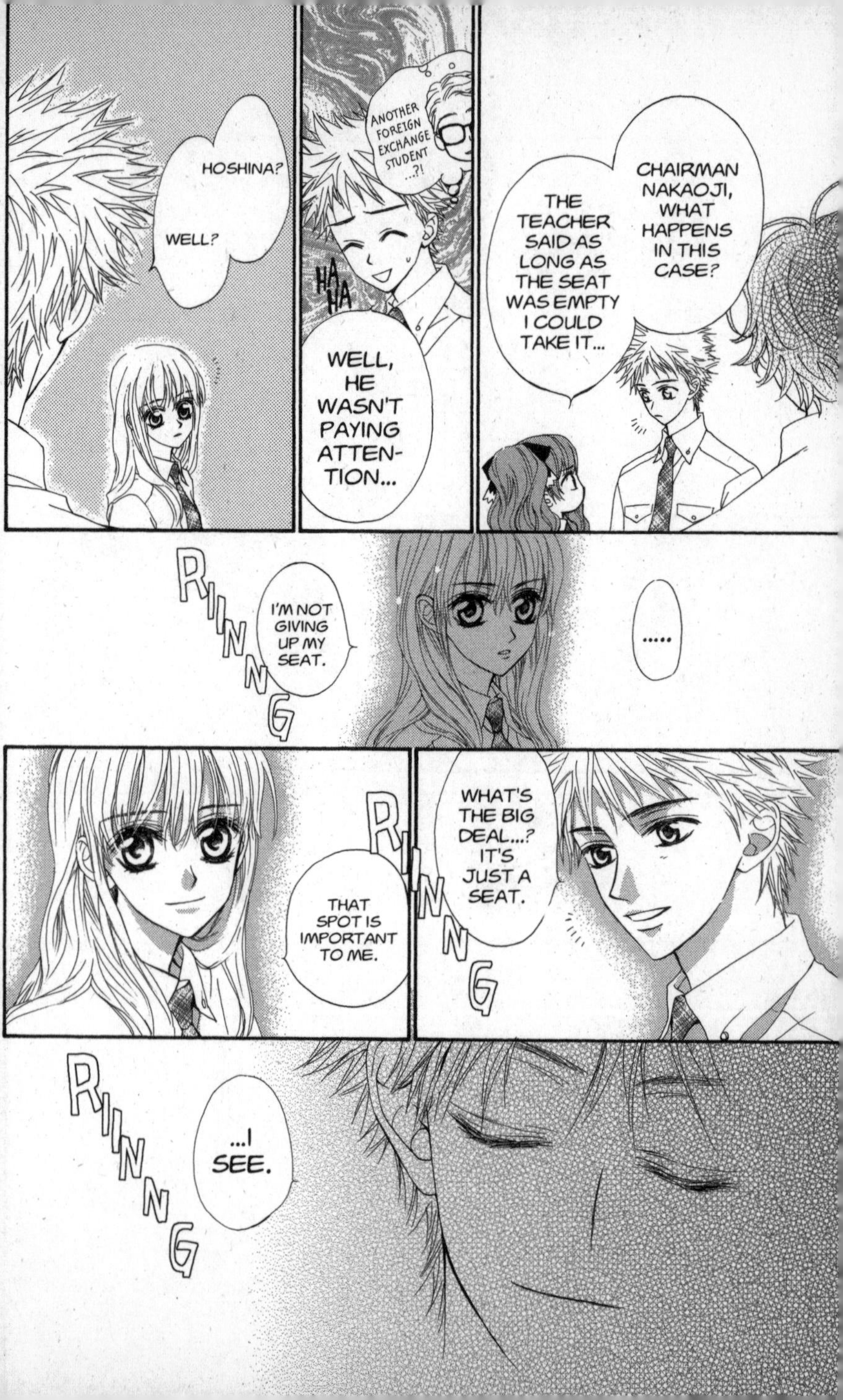
CHAIRMAN NAKAOJI, WHAT HAPPENS IN THIS CASE?
THE TEACHER SAID AS LONG AS THE SEAT WAS EMPTY I COULD TAKE IT...
ANOTHER FOREIGN EXCHANGE STUDENT ...?!
HA HA
WELL, HE WASN'T PAYING ATTEN-TION...
HOSHINA?
WELL?
.....
RIIINNG
I'M NOT GIVING UP MY SEAT.
WHAT'S THE BIG DEAL...? IT'S JUST A SEAT.
RIINNG
THAT SPOT IS IMPORTANT TO ME.
RIINNG
...I SEE.

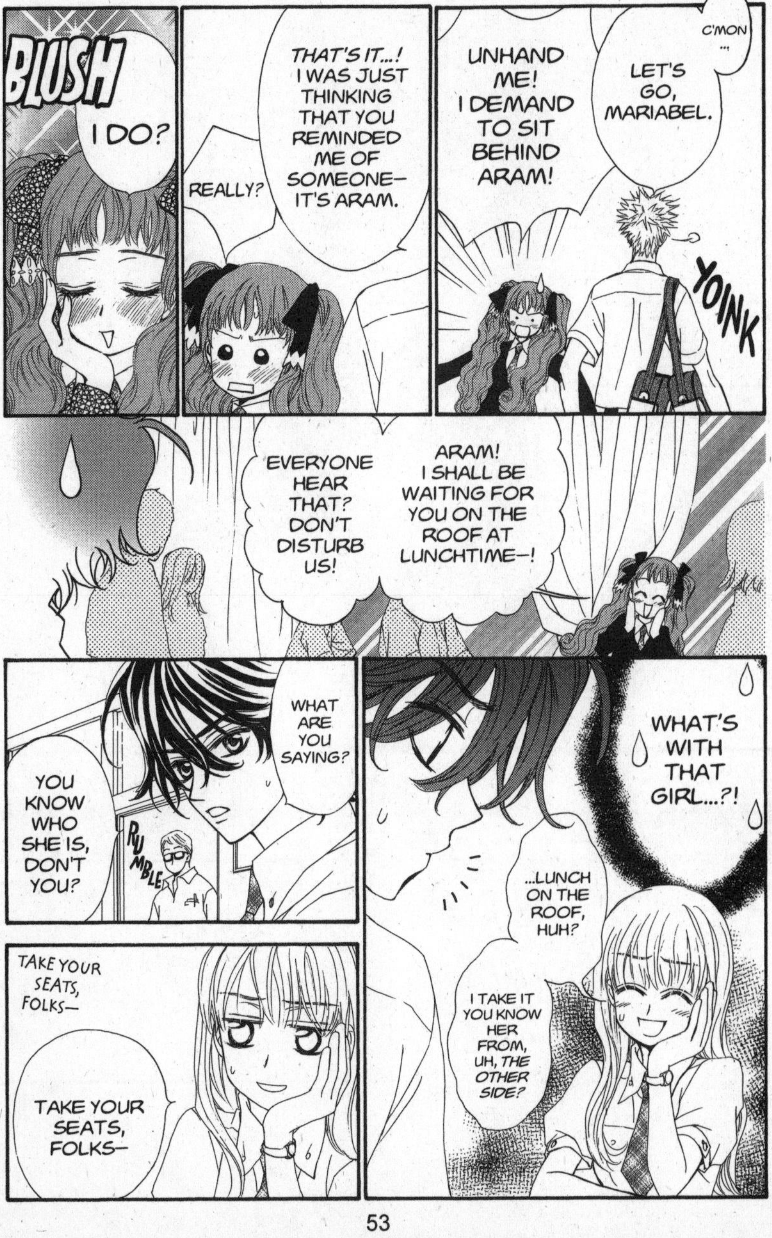
C'MON ...
LET'S GO, MARIABEL.
UNHAND ME! I DEMAND TO SIT BEHIND ARAM!
YOINK
THAT'S IT...! I WAS JUST THINKING THAT YOU REMINDED ME OF SOMEONE— IT'S ARAM.
REALLY?
BLUSH
I DO?
ARAM! I SHALL BE WAITING FOR YOU ON THE ROOF AT LUNCHTIME—!
EVERYONE HEAR THAT? DON'T DISTURB US!
WHAT'S WITH THAT GIRL...?!
...LUNCH ON THE ROOF, HUH?
I TAKE IT YOU KNOW HER FROM, UH, THE OTHER SIDE?
WHAT ARE YOU SAYING?
YOU KNOW WHO SHE IS, DON'T YOU?
RUMBLE
TAKE YOUR SEATS, FOLKS—
TAKE YOUR SEATS, FOLKS—

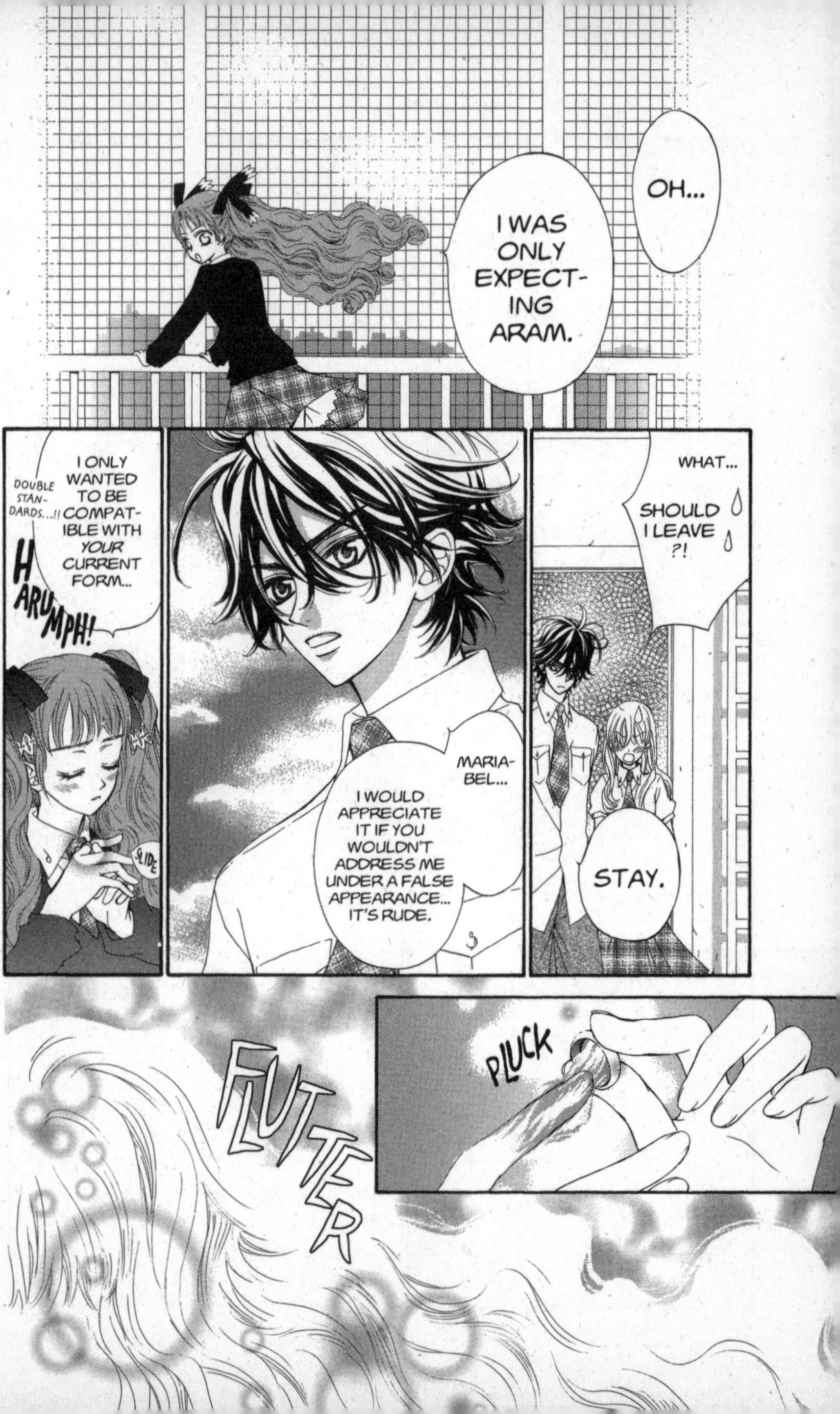
OH...
I WAS ONLY EXPECTING ARAM.
WHAT...
SHOULD I LEAVE ?!
STAY.
MARIA-BEL...
I WOULD APPRECIATE IT IF YOU WOULDN'T ADDRESS ME UNDER A FALSE APPEARANCE... IT'S RUDE.
I ONLY WANTED TO BE COMPATIBLE WITH *YOUR* CURRENT FORM...
DOUBLE STANDARDS...!!
HARUMPH!
SLIDE
PLUCK
FLUTTER

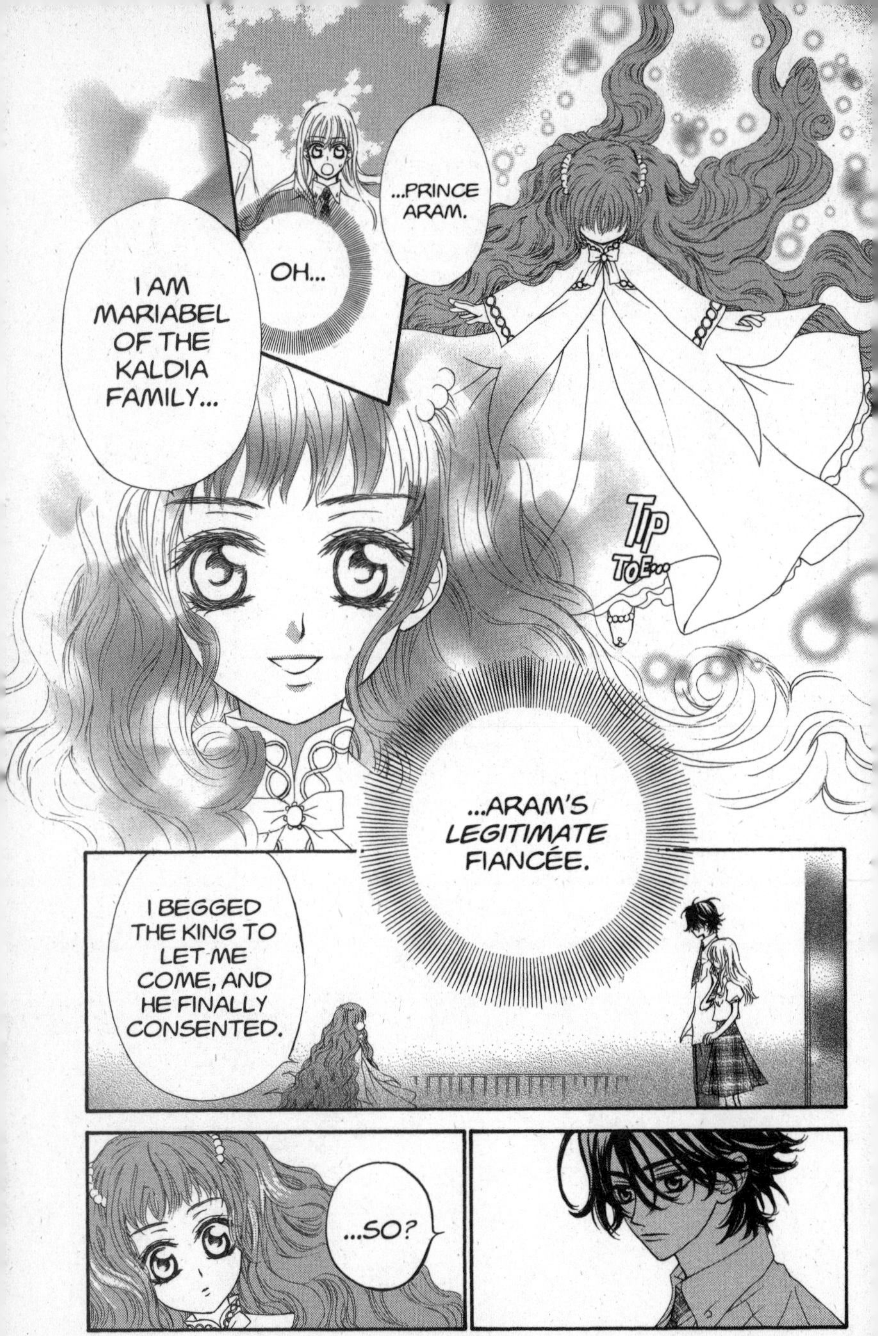
...PRINCE ARAM.
OH...
TIP TOE...
I AM MARIABEL OF THE KALDIA FAMILY...
...ARAM'S LEGITIMATE FIANCÉE.
I BEGGED THE KING TO LET ME COME, AND HE FINALLY CONSENTED.
...SO?

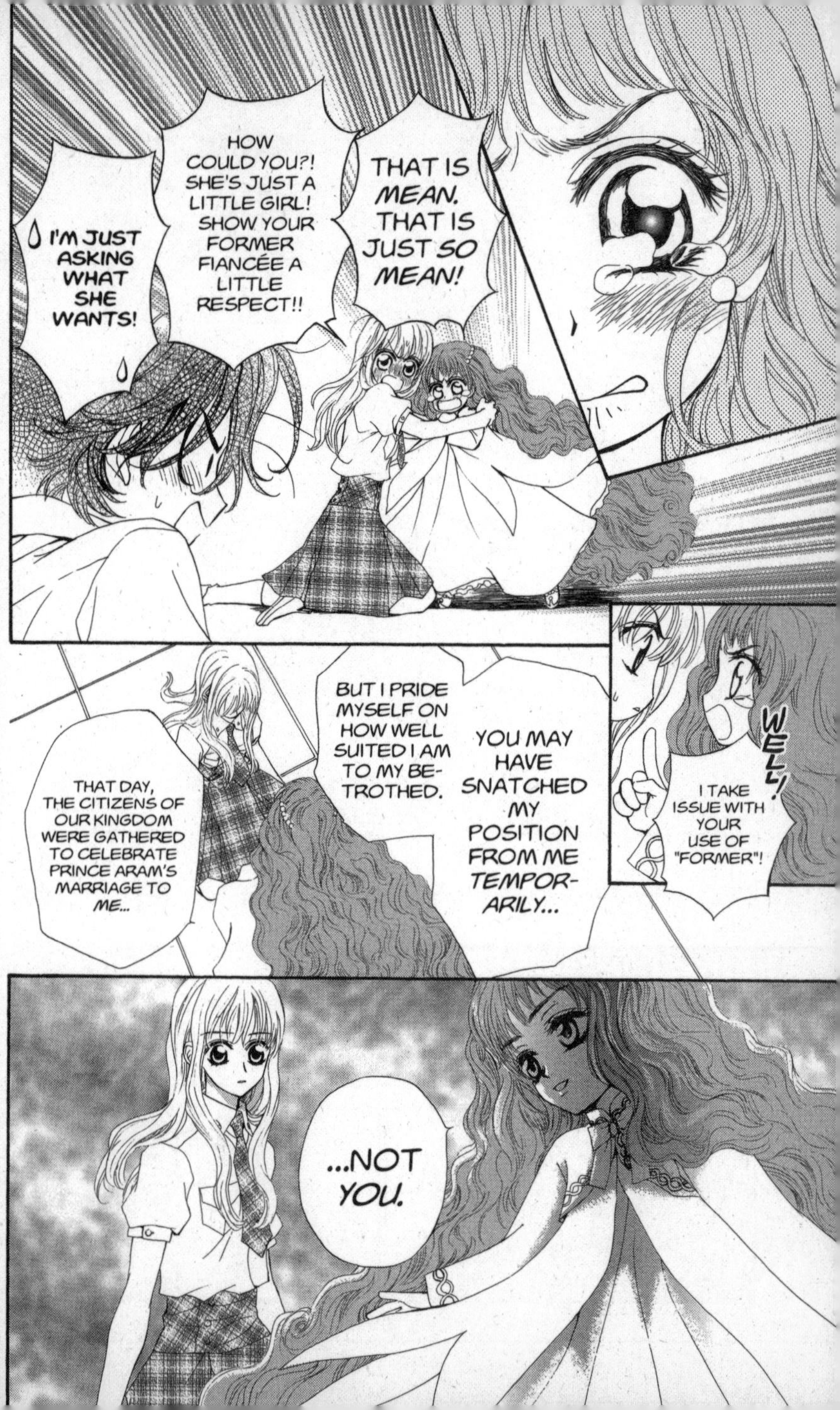
THAT IS MEAN. THAT IS JUST SO MEAN!
HOW COULD YOU?! SHE'S JUST A LITTLE GIRL! SHOW YOUR FORMER FIANCÉE A LITTLE RESPECT!!
I'M JUST ASKING WHAT SHE WANTS!
WELL!
I TAKE ISSUE WITH YOUR USE OF "FORMER"!
YOU MAY HAVE SNATCHED MY POSITION FROM ME TEMPOR-ARILY...
BUT I PRIDE MYSELF ON HOW WELL SUITED I AM TO MY BE-TROTHED.
THAT DAY, THE CITIZENS OF OUR KINGDOM WERE GATHERED TO CELEBRATE PRINCE ARAM'S MARRIAGE TO ME...
...NOT YOU.

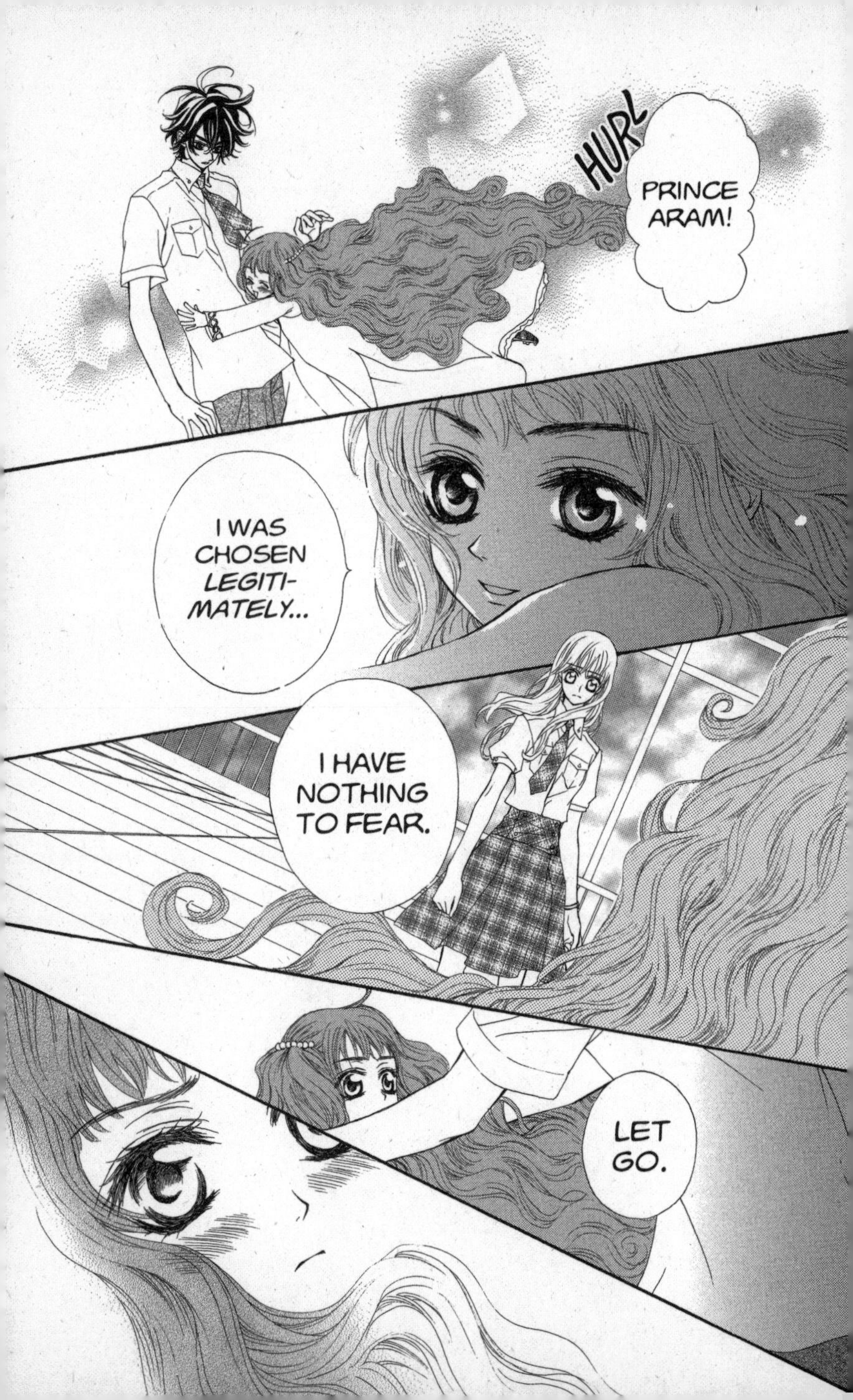
PRINCE ARAM!
HURL
I WAS CHOSEN LEGITI-MATELY...
I HAVE NOTHING TO FEAR.
LET GO.

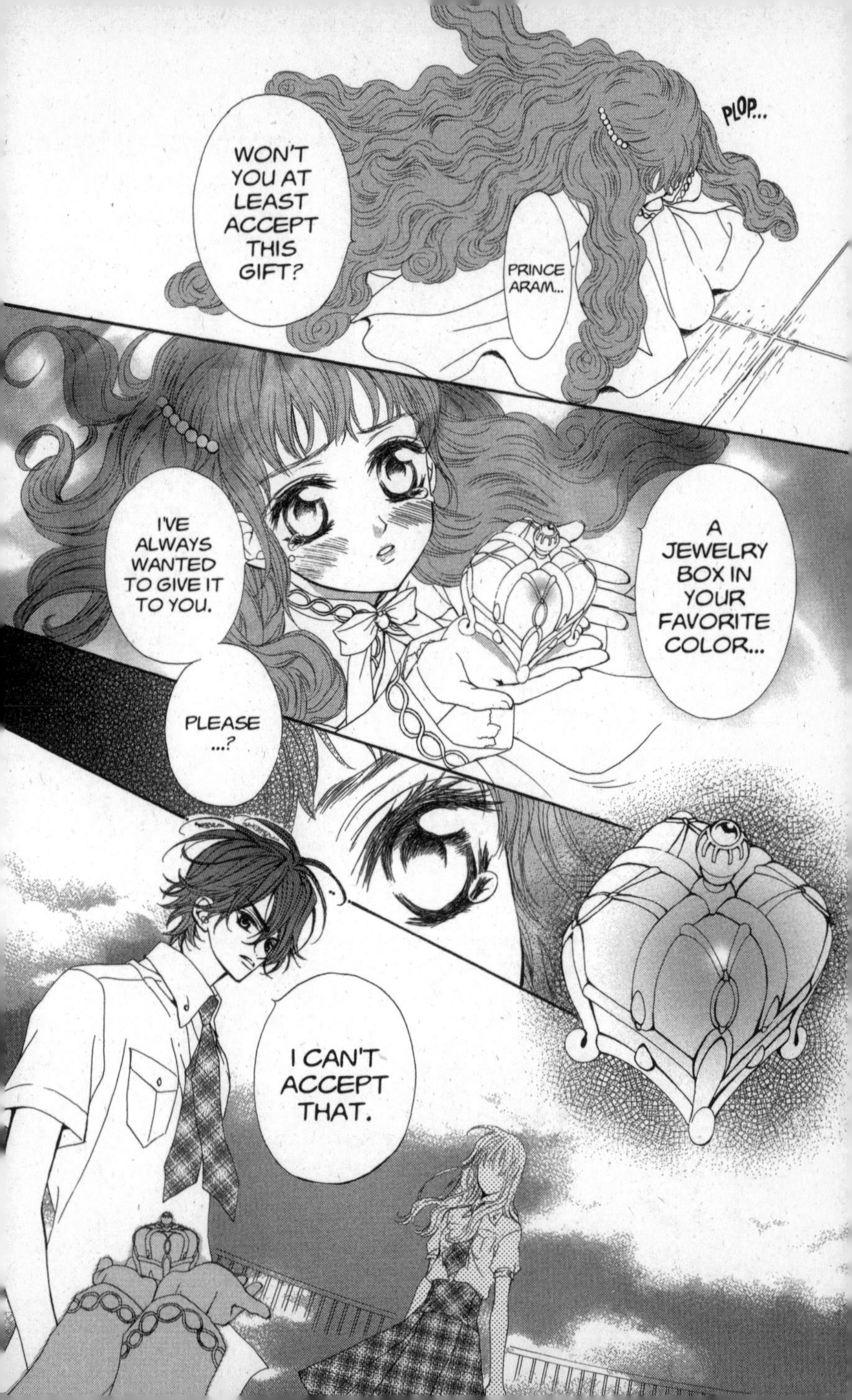
PLOP...
PRINCE ARAM...
WON'T YOU AT LEAST ACCEPT THIS GIFT?
A JEWELRY BOX IN YOUR FAVORITE COLOR...
I'VE ALWAYS WANTED TO GIVE IT TO YOU.
PLEASE ...?
I CAN'T ACCEPT THAT.

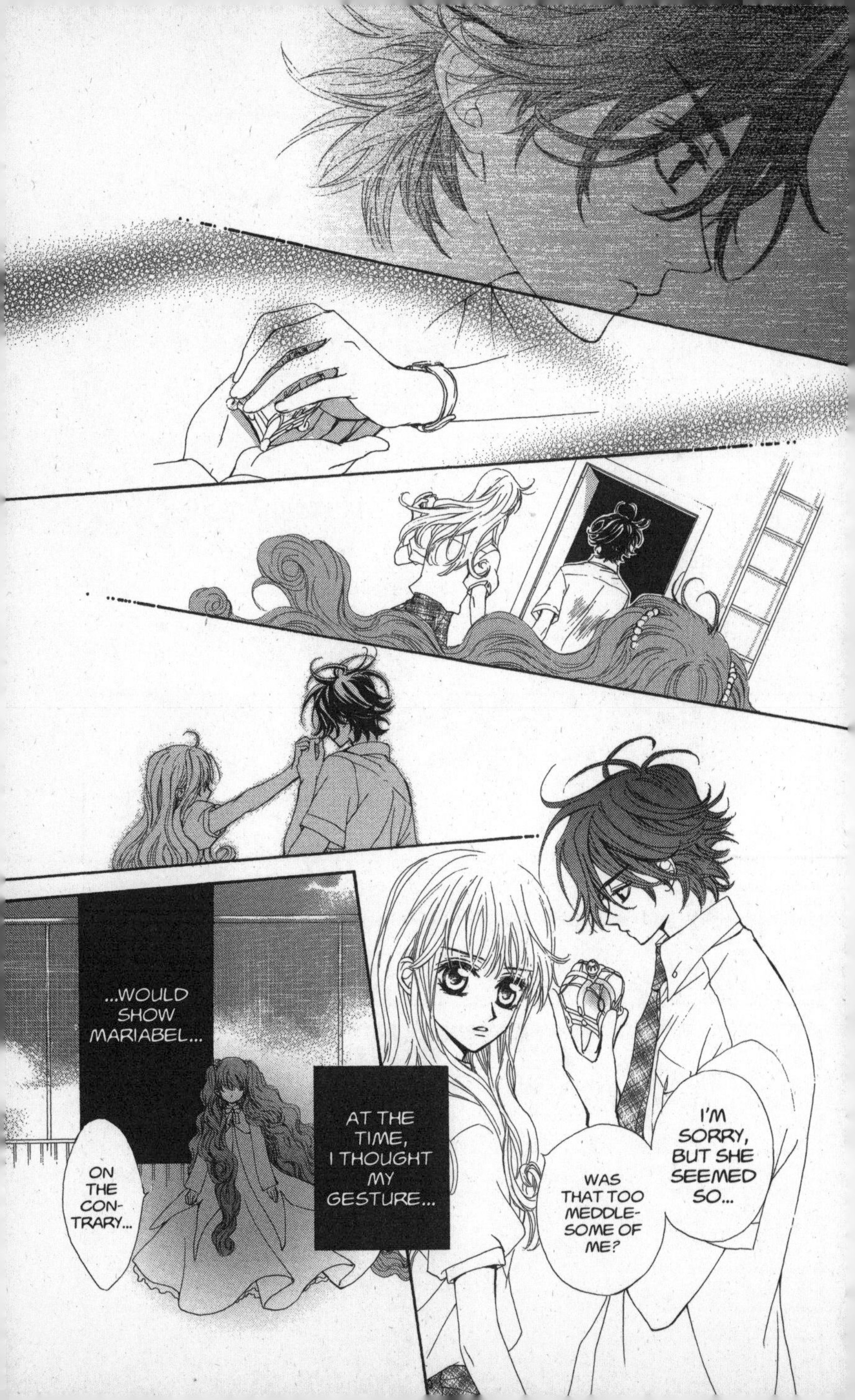
I'M SORRY, BUT SHE SEEMED SO...
WAS THAT TOO MEDDLE-SOME OF ME?
AT THE TIME, I THOUGHT MY GESTURE...
...WOULD SHOW MARIABEL...
ON THE CON-TRARY...

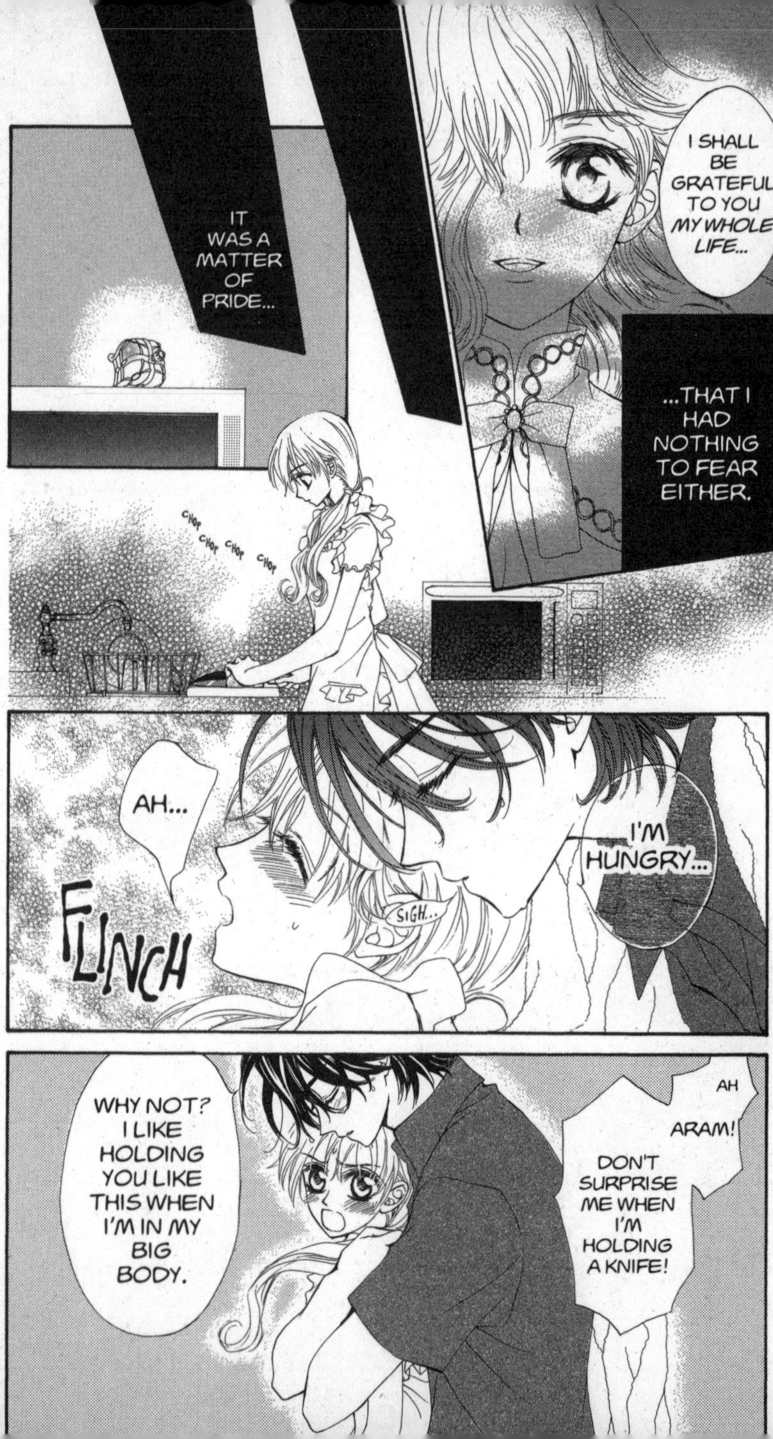
I SHALL BE GRATEFUL TO YOU *MY WHOLE LIFE...*
IT WAS A MATTER OF PRIDE...
...THAT I HAD NOTHING TO FEAR EITHER.
CHOP CHOP CHOP CHOP
I'M HUNGRY...
SIGH...
AH...
FLINCH
AH ARAM!
DON'T SURPRISE ME WHEN I'M HOLDING A KNIFE!
WHY NOT? I LIKE HOLDING YOU LIKE THIS WHEN I'M IN MY BIG BODY.

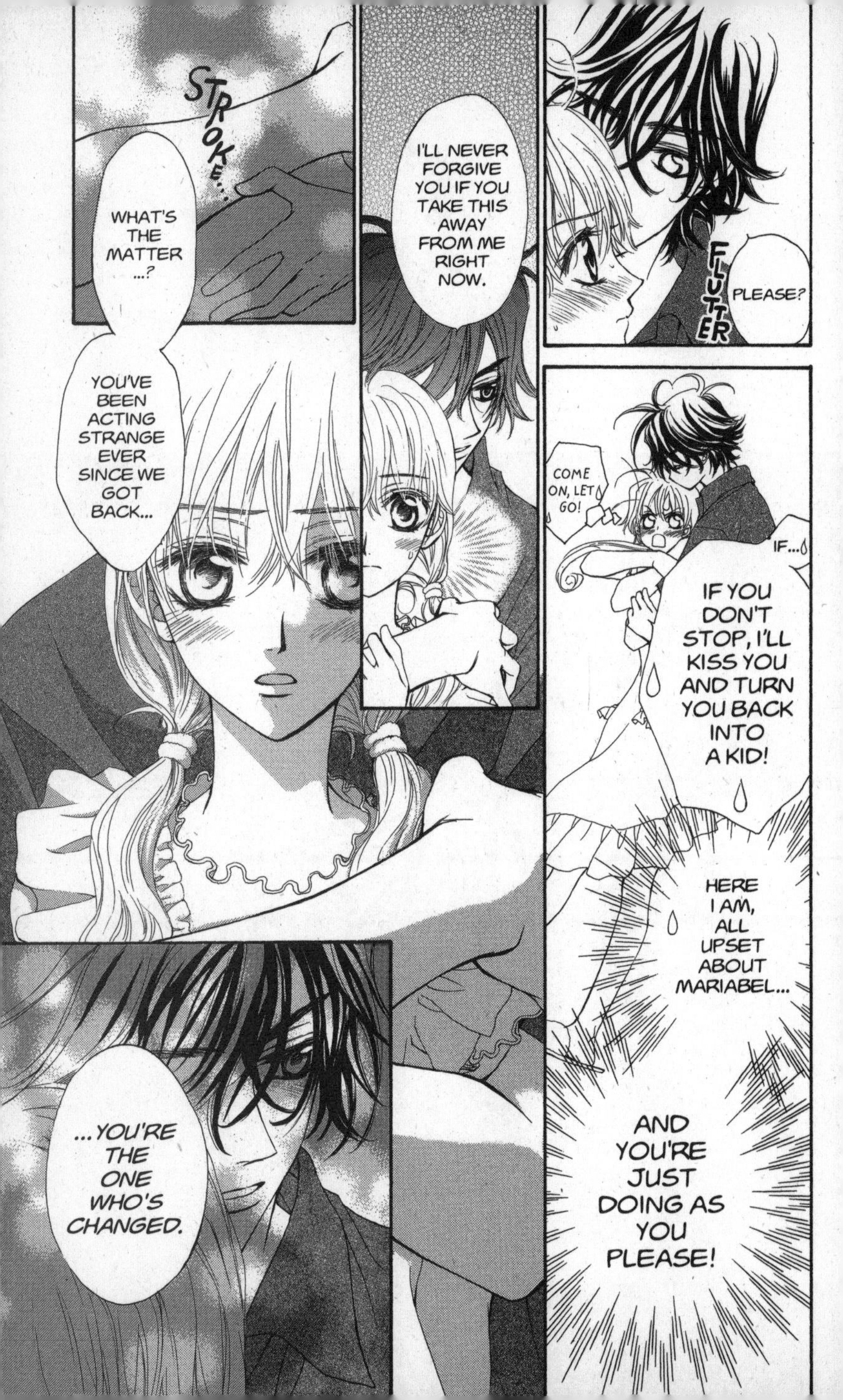
FLUTTER
PLEASE?
I'LL NEVER FORGIVE YOU IF YOU TAKE THIS AWAY FROM ME RIGHT NOW.
STROKE...
WHAT'S THE MATTER ...?
COME ON, LET GO!
IF...
IF YOU DON'T STOP, I'LL KISS YOU AND TURN YOU BACK INTO A KID!
HERE I AM, ALL UPSET ABOUT MARIABEL...
AND YOU'RE JUST DOING AS YOU PLEASE!
YOU'VE BEEN ACTING STRANGE EVER SINCE WE GOT BACK...
...YOU'RE THE ONE WHO'S CHANGED.

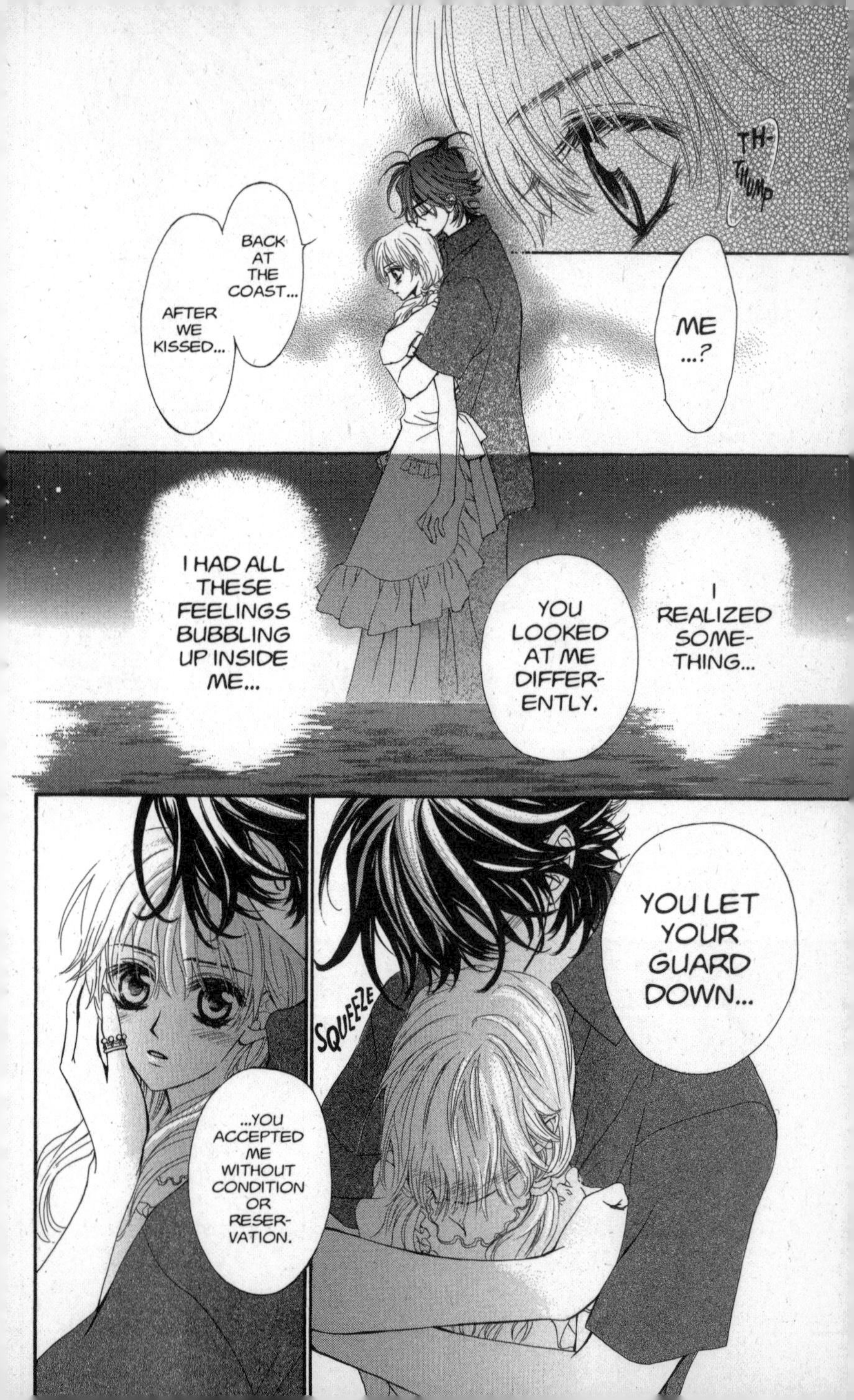
TH-THUMP
ME ...?
BACK AT THE COAST...
AFTER WE KISSED...
I REALIZED SOME-THING...
YOU LOOKED AT ME DIFFER-ENTLY.
I HAD ALL THESE FEELINGS BUBBLING UP INSIDE ME...
YOU LET YOUR GUARD DOWN...
SQUEEZE
...YOU ACCEPTED ME WITHOUT CONDITION OR RESER-VATION.

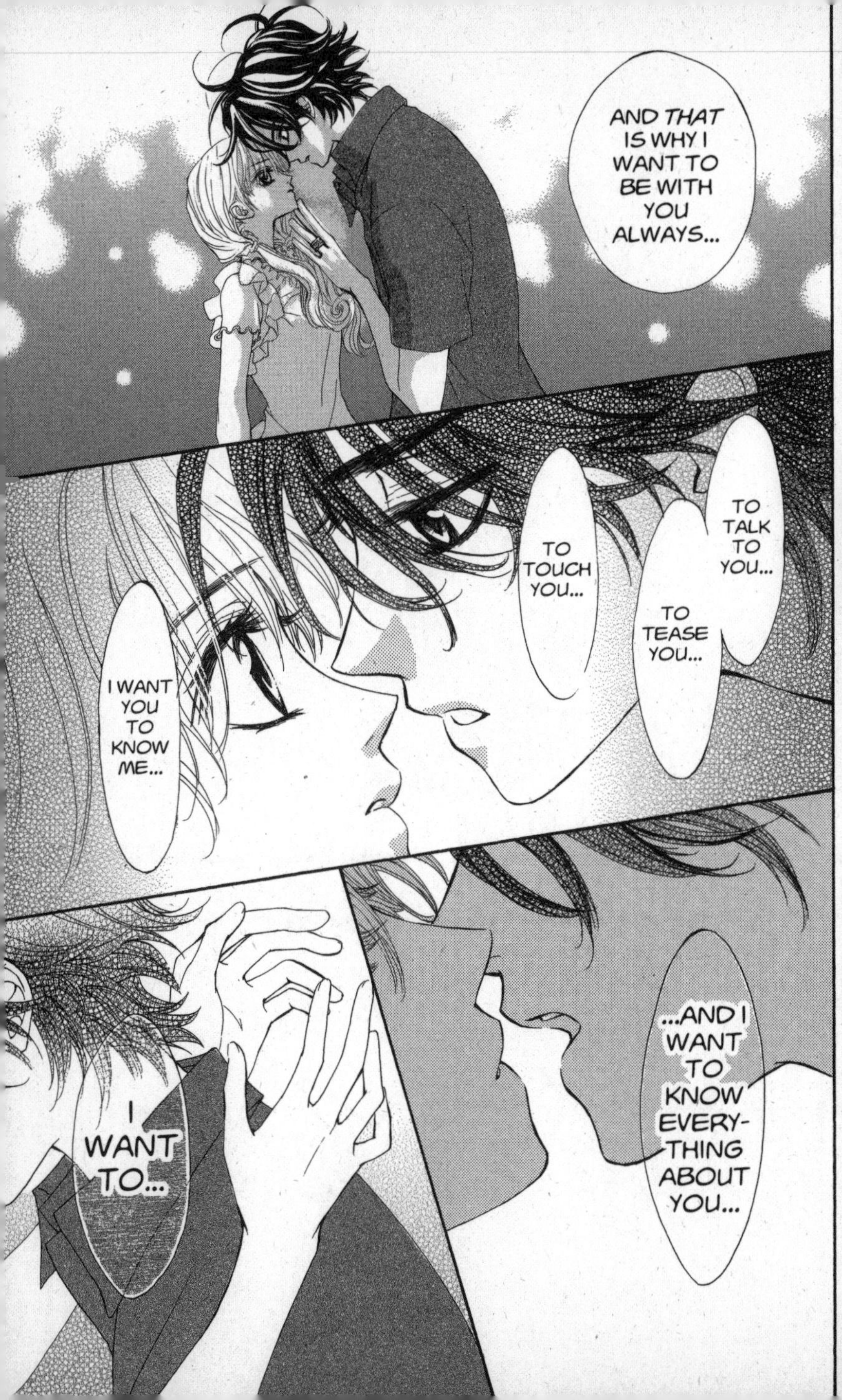
AND *THAT* IS WHY I WANT TO BE WITH YOU ALWAYS...
TO TALK TO YOU...
TO TEASE YOU...
TO TOUCH YOU...
I WANT YOU TO KNOW ME...
...AND I WANT TO KNOW EVERY-THING ABOUT YOU...
I WANT TO...

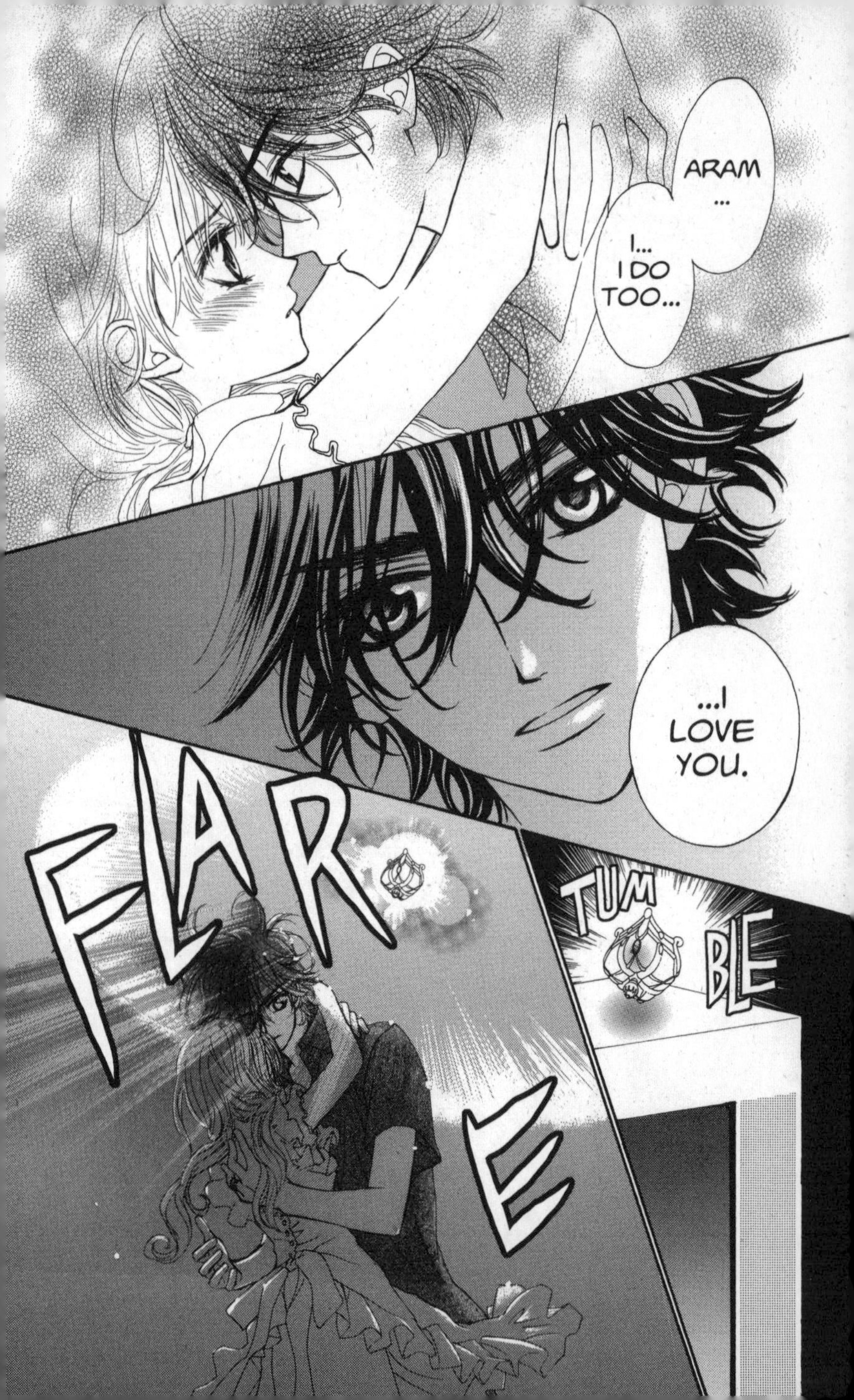
ARAM ...
I... I DO TOO...
...I LOVE YOU.
TUM BLE
FLARE

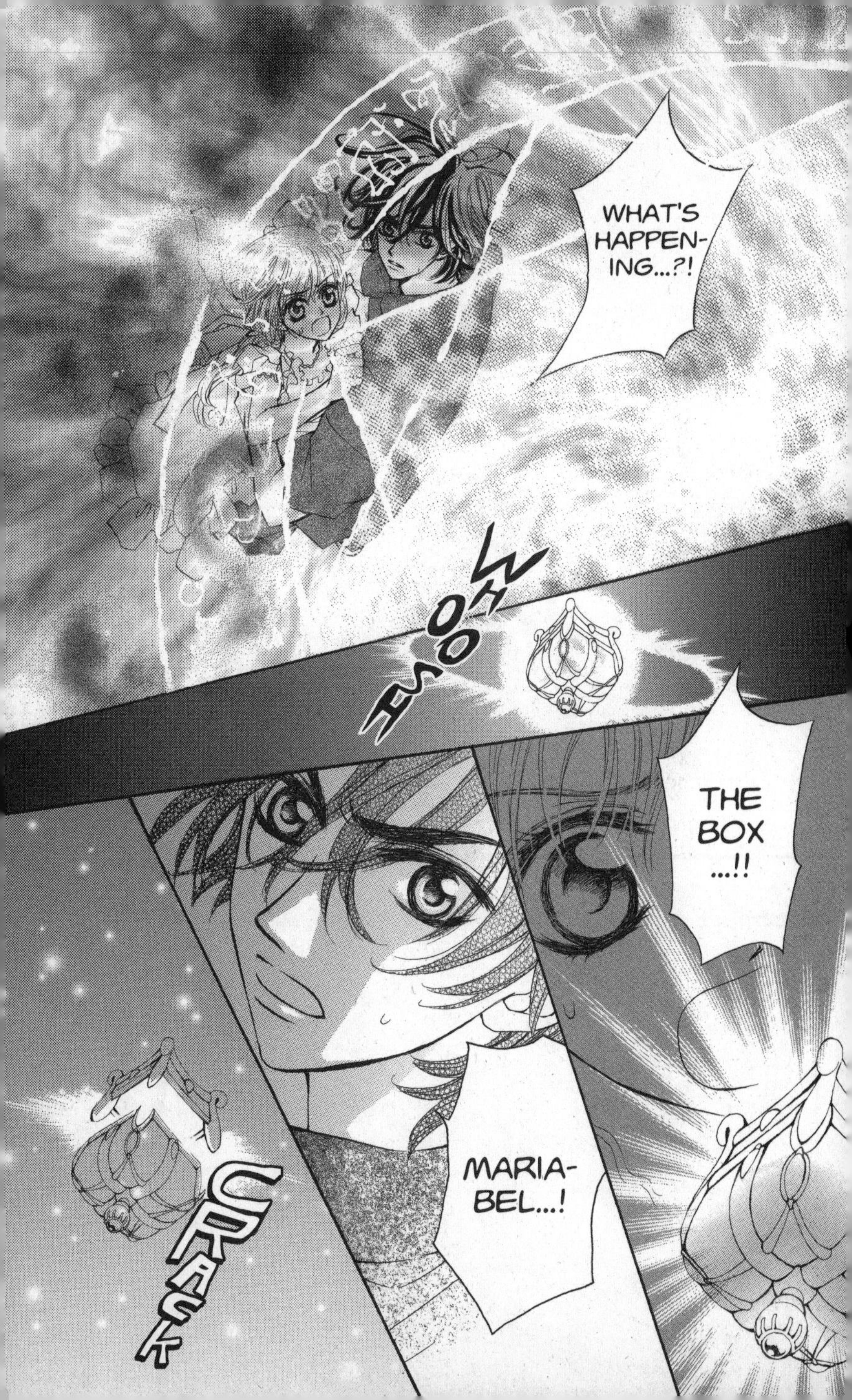
WHAT'S HAPPEN-ING...?!
WHOOSH
THE BOX ...!!
MARIA-BEL...!
CRACK

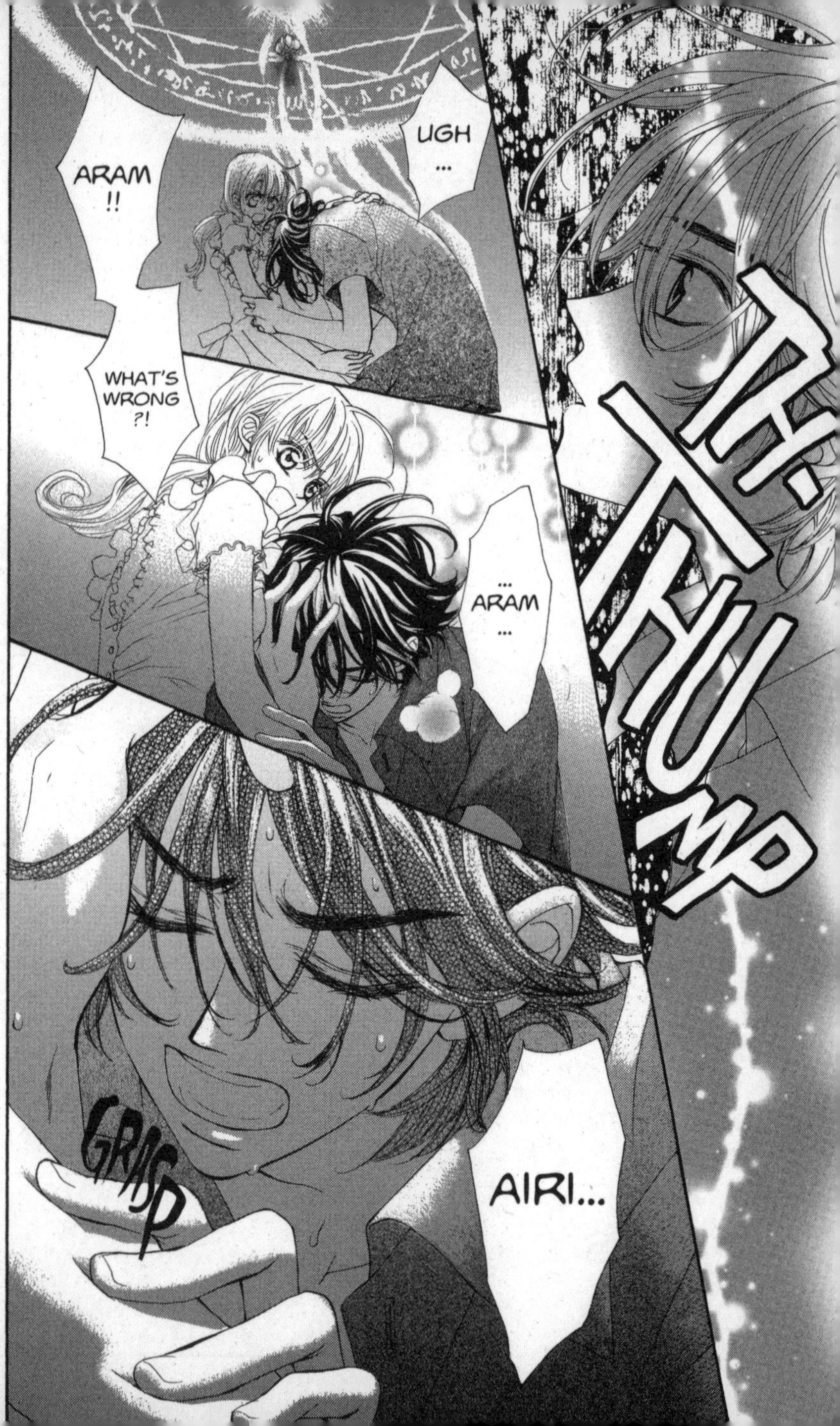
THA-THUMP
UGH ...
ARAM !!
... ARAM ...
WHAT'S WRONG ?!
AIRI...
GRASP

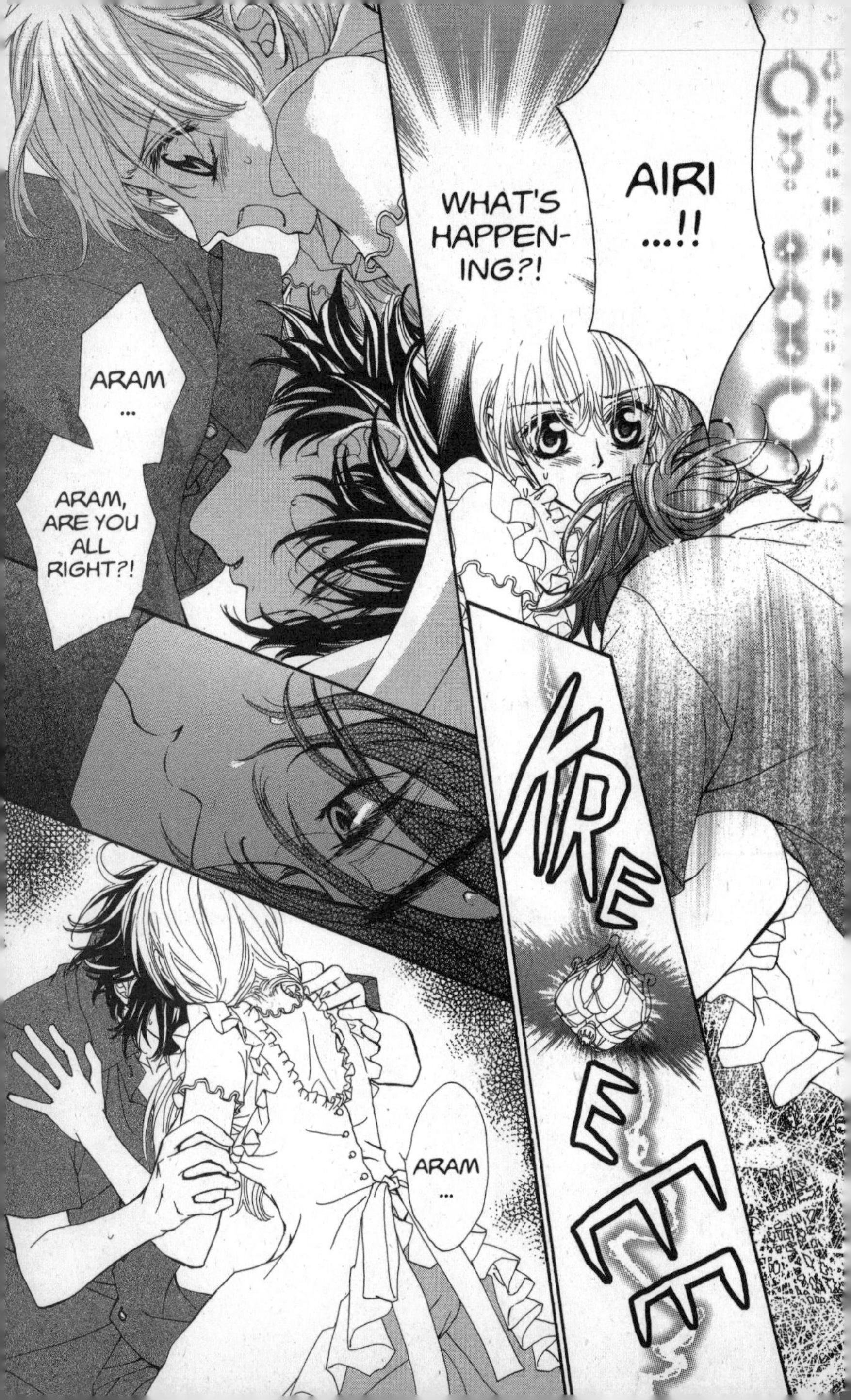
AIRI ...!!
WHAT'S HAPPEN-ING?!
ARAM ...
ARAM, ARE YOU ALL RIGHT?!
KREEEE
ARAM ...

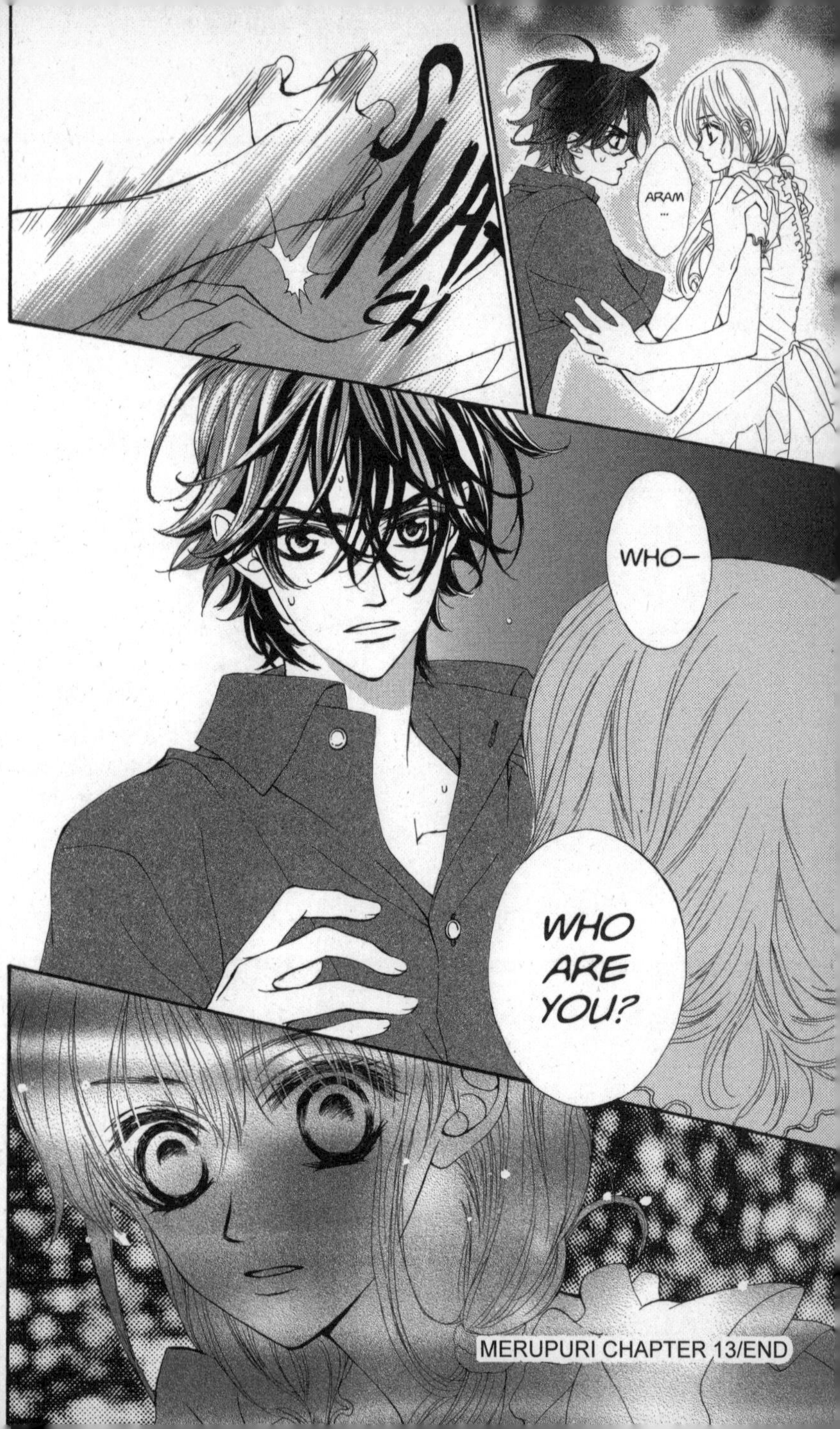
ARAM ...
SNATCH
WHO—
WHO ARE YOU?
MERUPURI CHAPTER 13/END

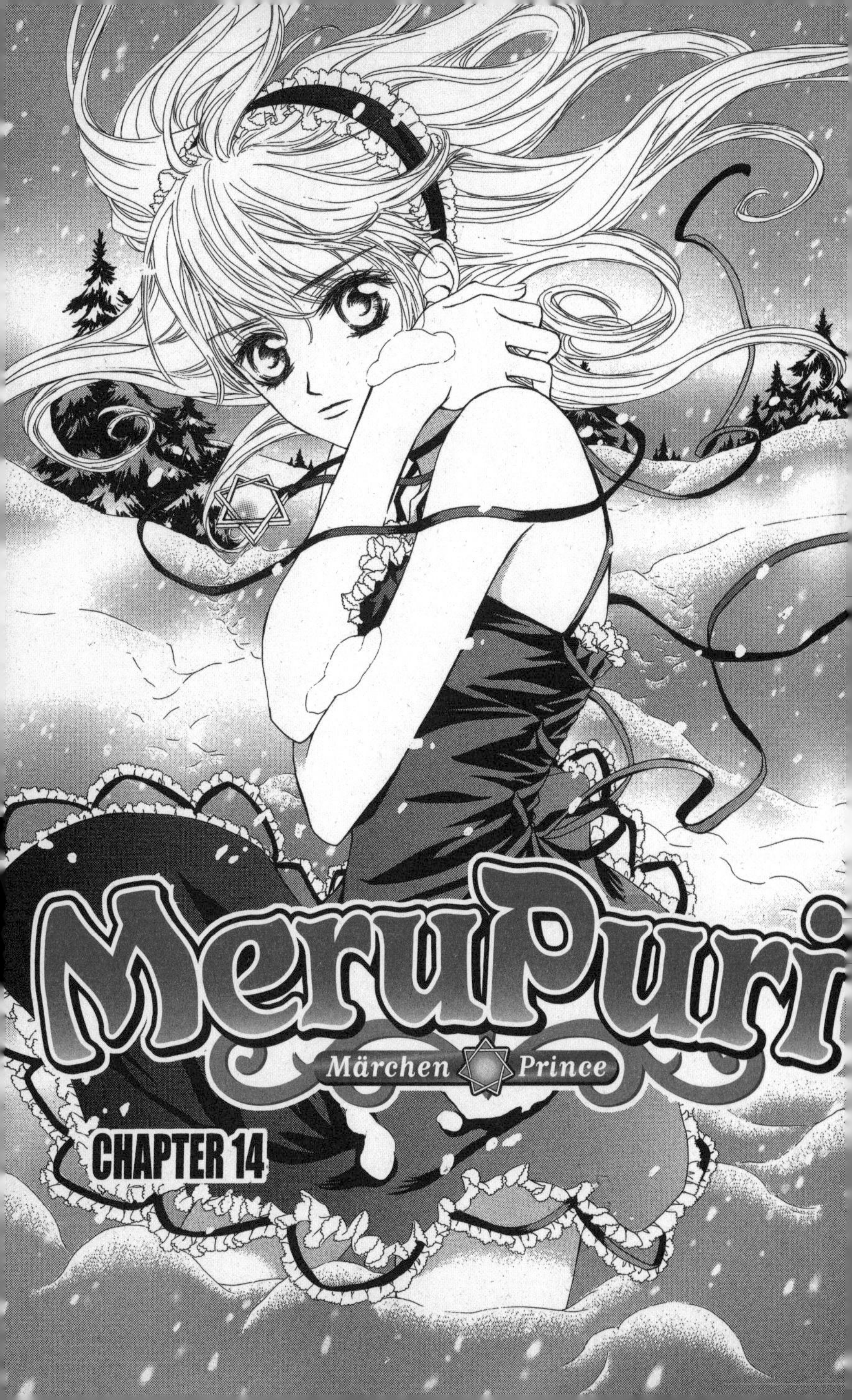
MeruPuri
Märchen Prince
CHAPTER 14

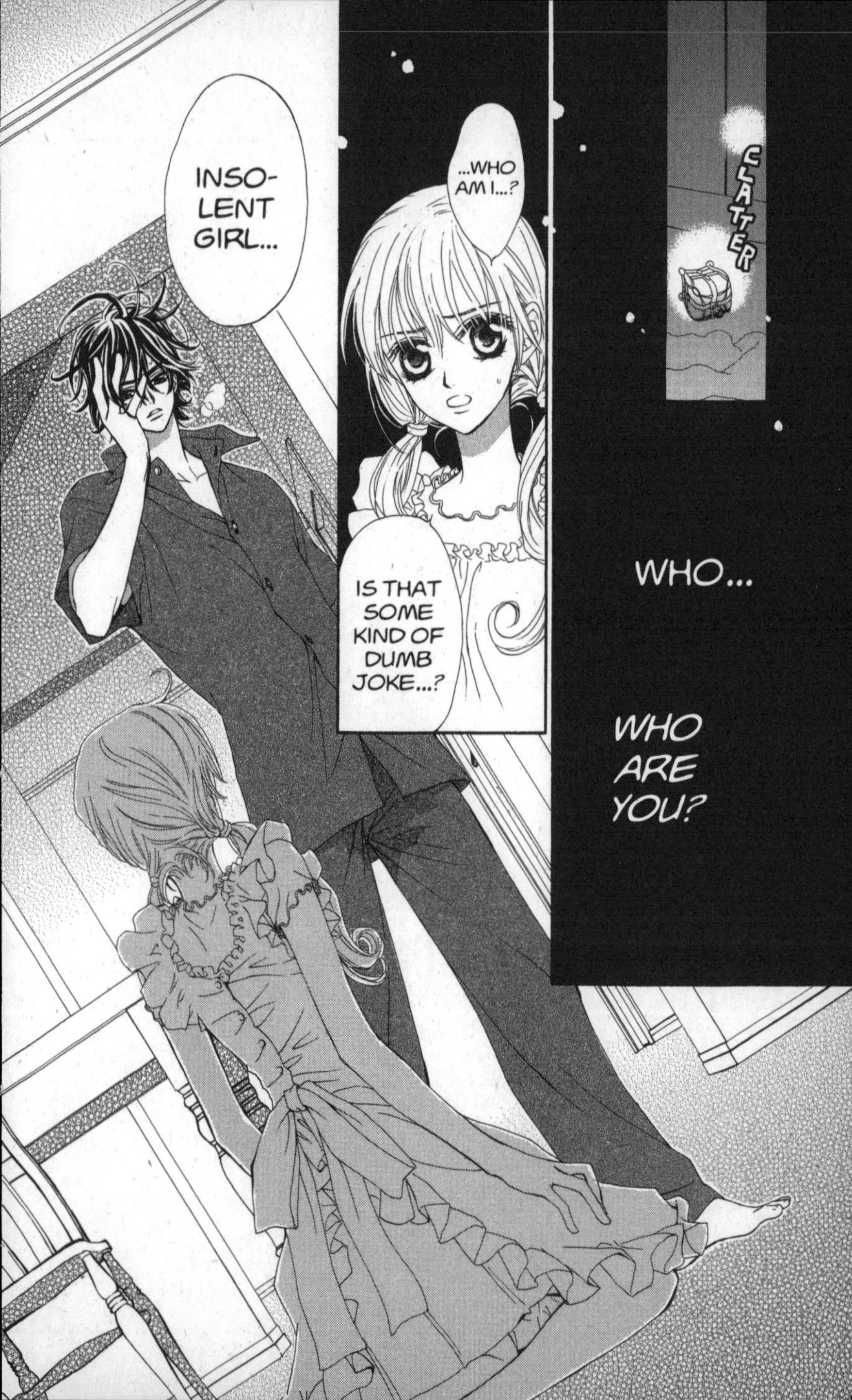
CLATTER
WHO...
WHO ARE YOU?
...WHO AM I...?
IS THAT SOME KIND OF DUMB JOKE...?
INSO-LENT GIRL...

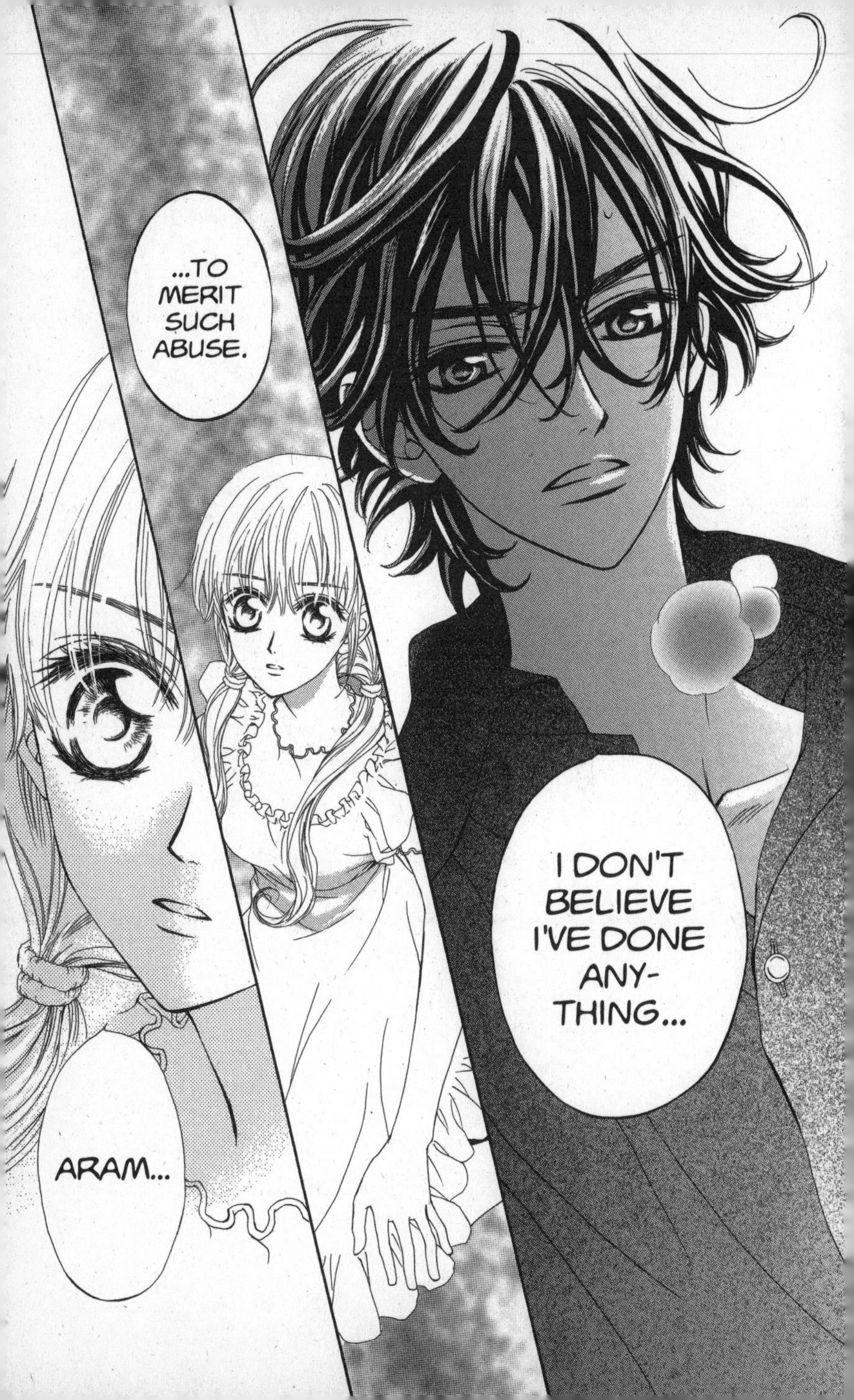
I DON'T BELIEVE I'VE DONE ANY-THING...
...TO MERIT SUCH ABUSE.
ARAM...

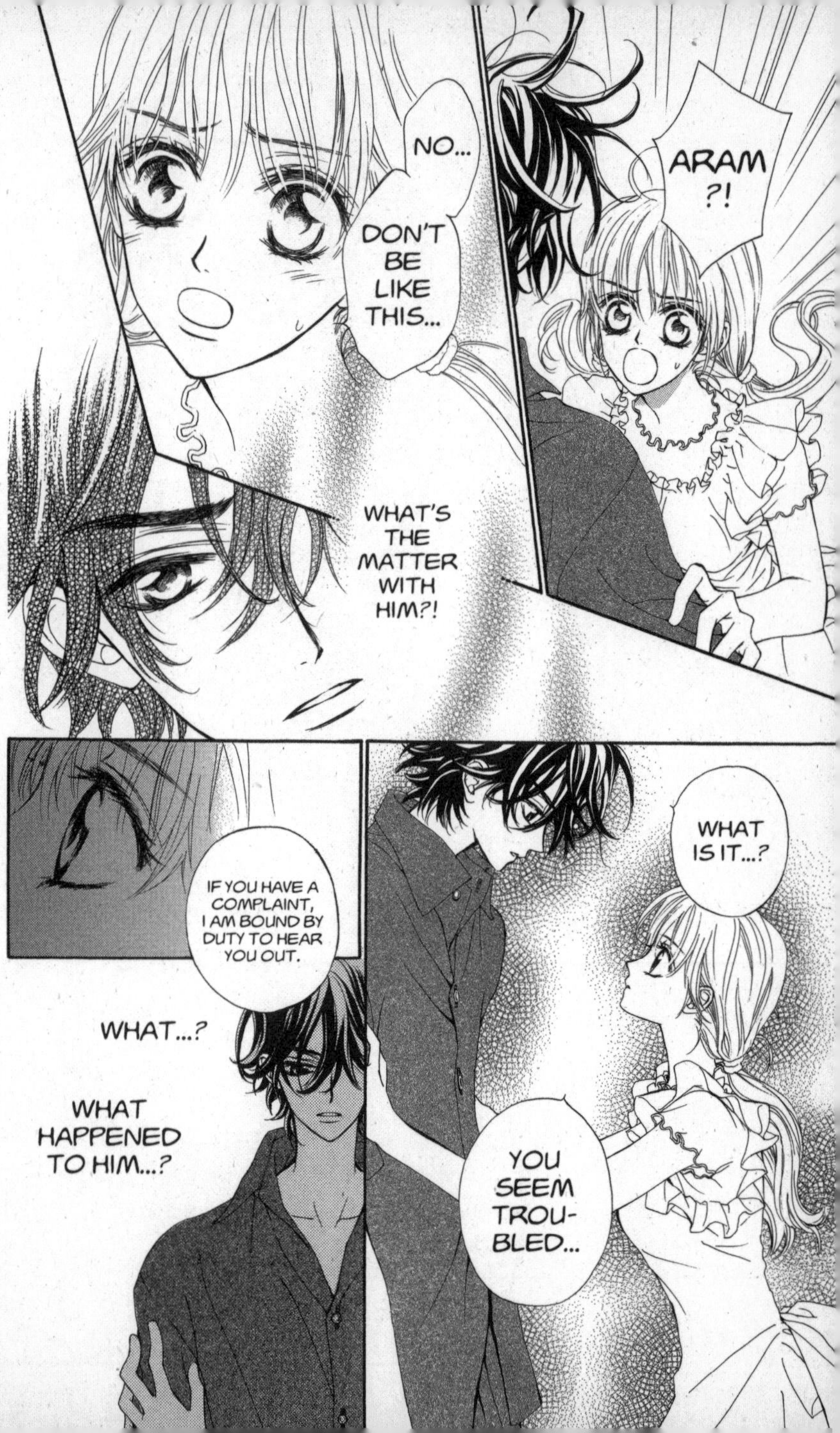
ARAM ?!
NO...
DON'T BE LIKE THIS...
WHAT'S THE MATTER WITH HIM?!
WHAT IS IT...?
YOU SEEM TROU-BLED...
IF YOU HAVE A COMPLAINT, I AM BOUND BY DUTY TO HEAR YOU OUT.
WHAT...?
WHAT HAPPENED TO HIM...?

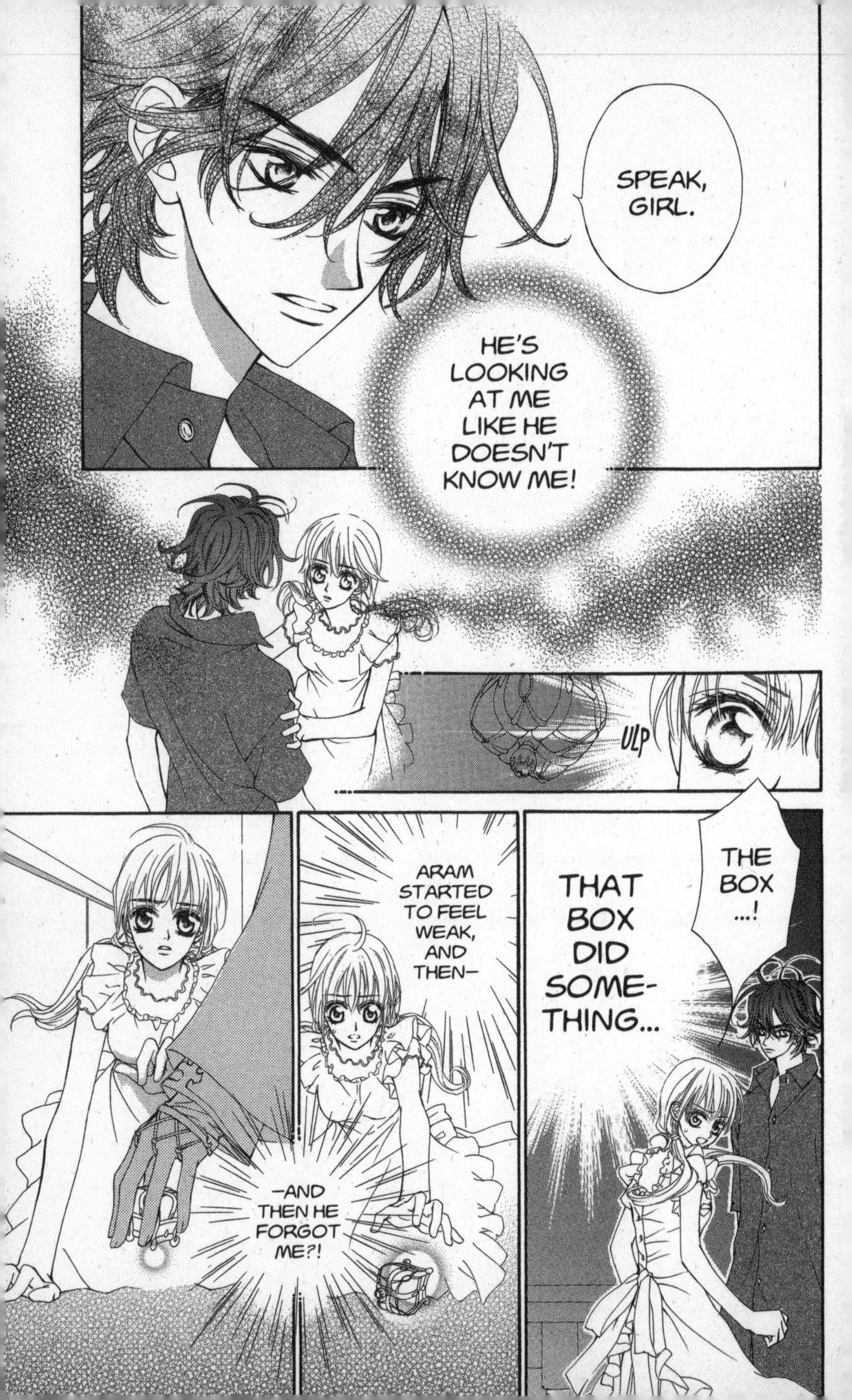
SPEAK, GIRL.
HE'S LOOKING AT ME LIKE HE DOESN'T KNOW ME!
ULP
THE BOX ...!
THAT BOX DID SOME-THING...
ARAM STARTED TO FEEL WEAK, AND THEN—
—AND THEN HE FORGOT ME?!

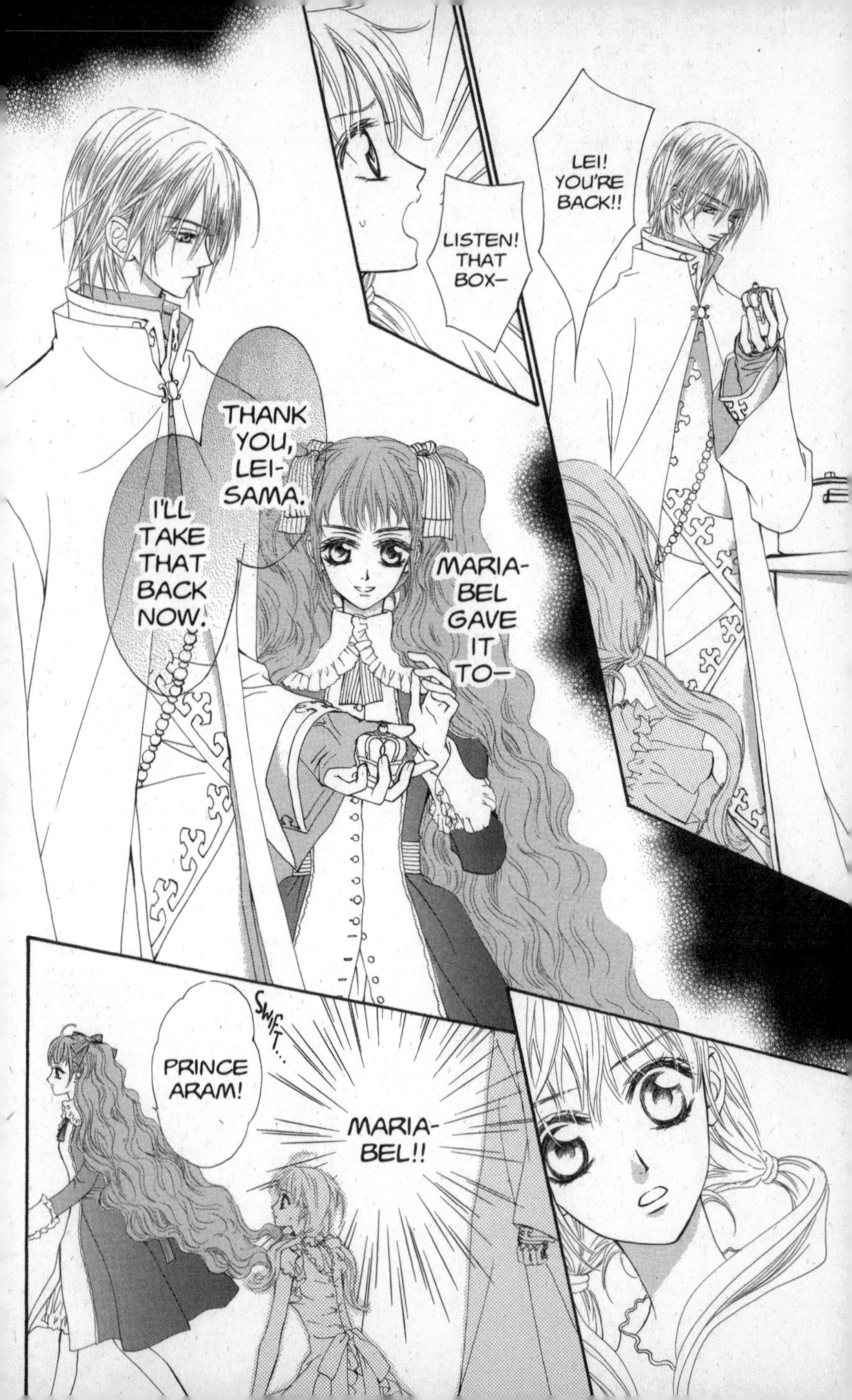
LEI! YOU'RE BACK!!
LISTEN! THAT BOX—
MARIA-BEL GAVE IT TO—
THANK YOU, LEI-SAMA.
I'LL TAKE THAT BACK NOW.
SWIFT...
MARIA-BEL!!
PRINCE ARAM!

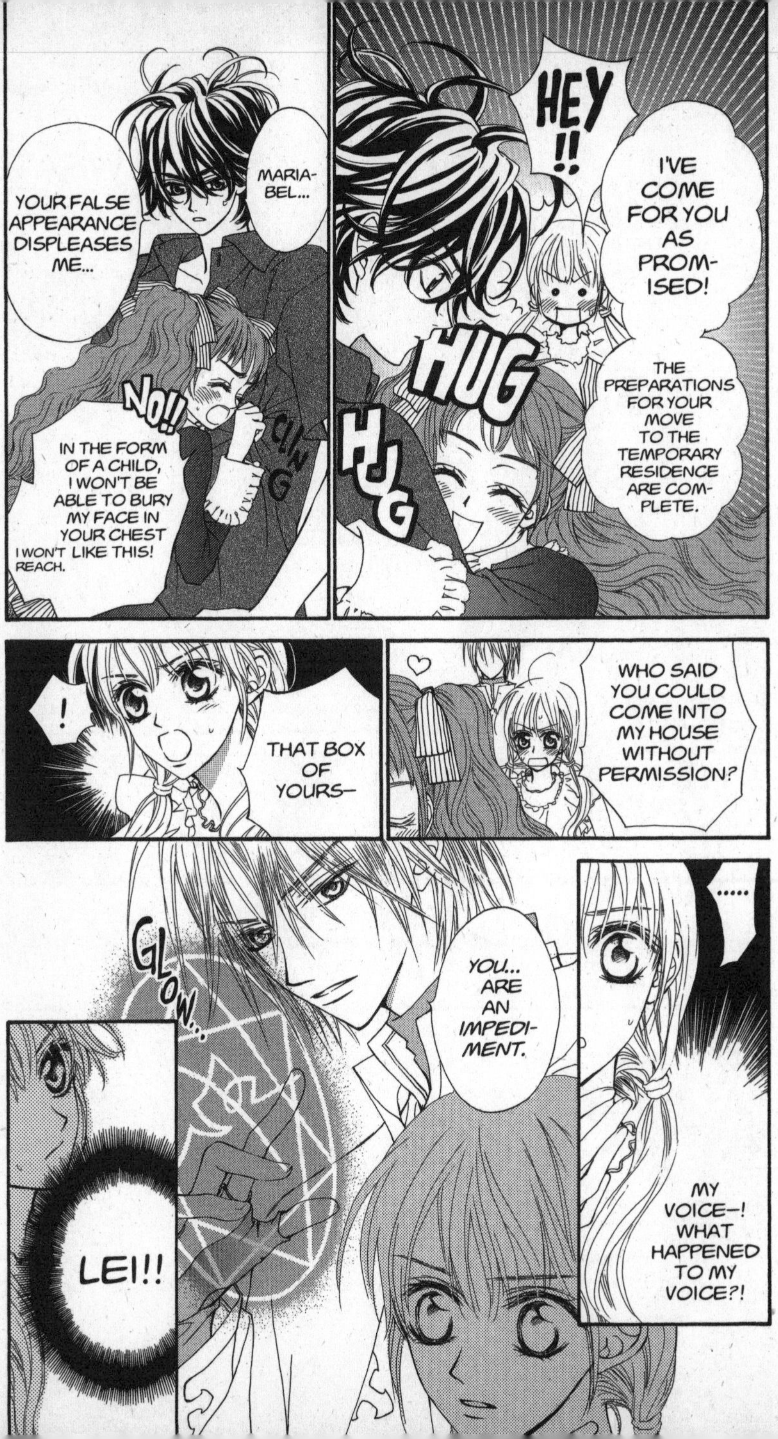
HEY!!
I'VE COME FOR YOU AS PROMISED!
HUG
HUG
THE PREPARATIONS FOR YOUR MOVE TO THE TEMPORARY RESIDENCE ARE COMPLETE.
MARIA-BEL...
YOUR FALSE APPEARANCE DISPLEASES ME...
NO!!
CLING
IN THE FORM OF A CHILD, I WON'T BE ABLE TO BURY MY FACE IN YOUR CHEST LIKE THIS!
I WON'T REACH.
WHO SAID YOU COULD COME INTO MY HOUSE WITHOUT PERMISSION?
!
THAT BOX OF YOURS–
.....
MY VOICE–! WHAT HAPPENED TO MY VOICE?!
YOU... ARE AN IMPEDIMENT.
GLOW...
LEI!!

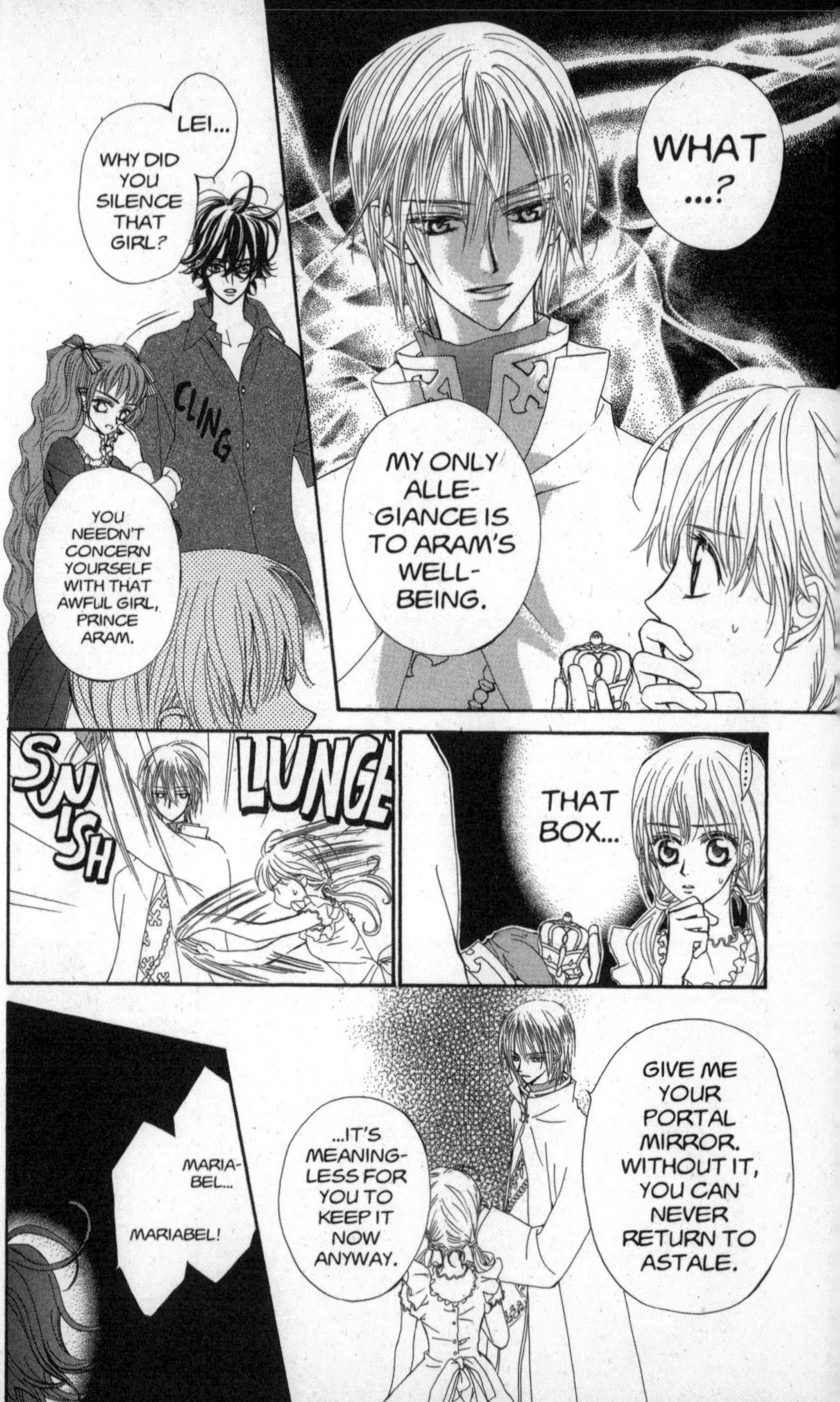
WHAT ...?
MY ONLY ALLE-GIANCE IS TO ARAM'S WELL-BEING.
LEI...
WHY DID YOU SILENCE THAT GIRL?
CLING
YOU NEEDN'T CONCERN YOURSELF WITH THAT AWFUL GIRL, PRINCE ARAM.
THAT BOX...
LUNGE
SWISH
GIVE ME YOUR PORTAL MIRROR. WITHOUT IT, YOU CAN NEVER RETURN TO ASTALE.
...IT'S MEANING-LESS FOR YOU TO KEEP IT NOW ANYWAY.
MARIA-BEL...
MARIABEL!

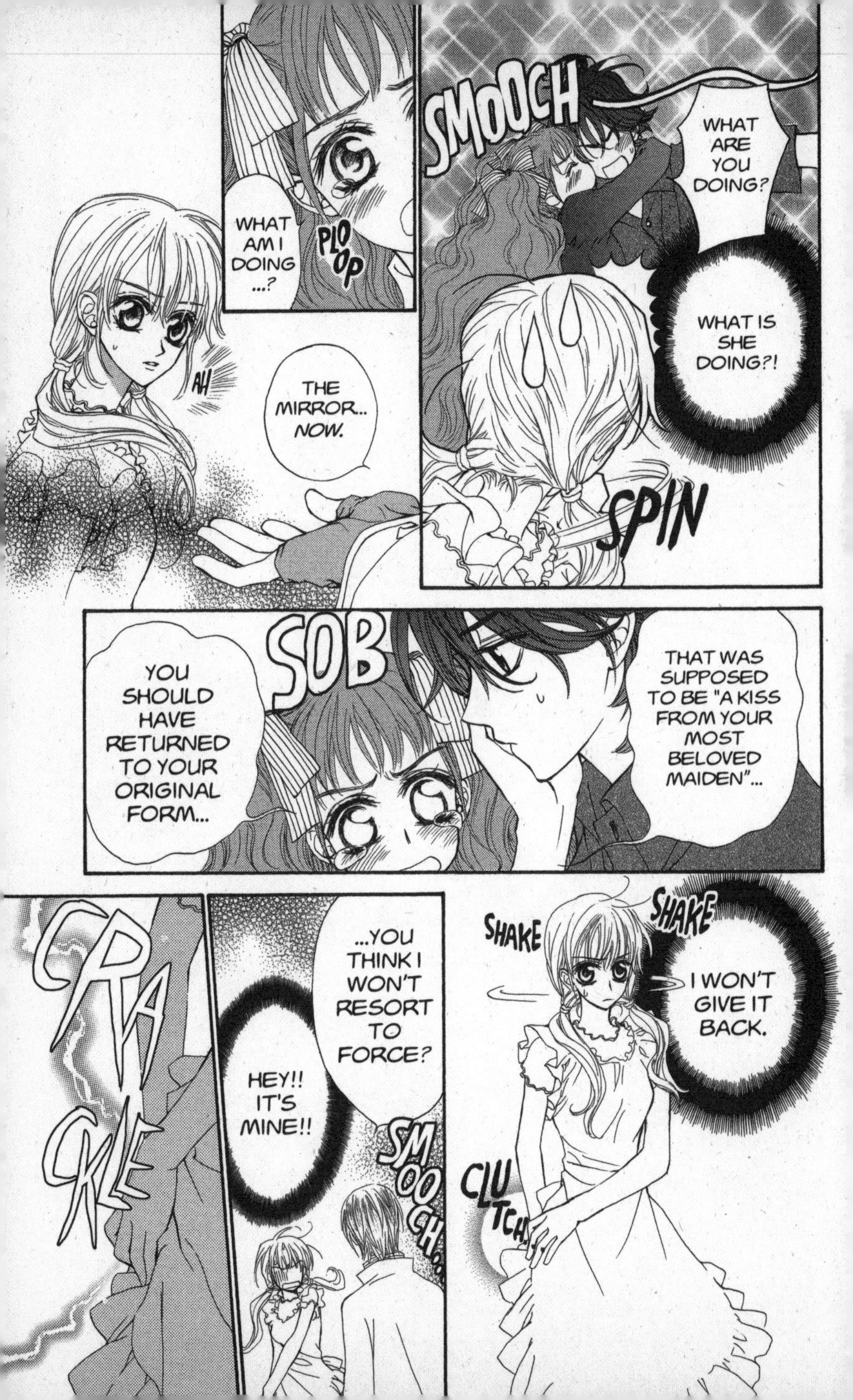
SMOOCH
WHAT ARE YOU DOING?
WHAT IS SHE DOING?!
SPIN
WHAT AM I DOING ...?
PLOOP
AH
THE MIRROR... NOW.
THAT WAS SUPPOSED TO BE "A KISS FROM YOUR MOST BELOVED MAIDEN"...
SOB
YOU SHOULD HAVE RETURNED TO YOUR ORIGINAL FORM...
SHAKE
SHAKE
I WON'T GIVE IT BACK.
CLUTCH
...YOU THINK I WON'T RESORT TO FORCE?
HEY!! IT'S MINE!!
SMOOCH...
CRACKLE

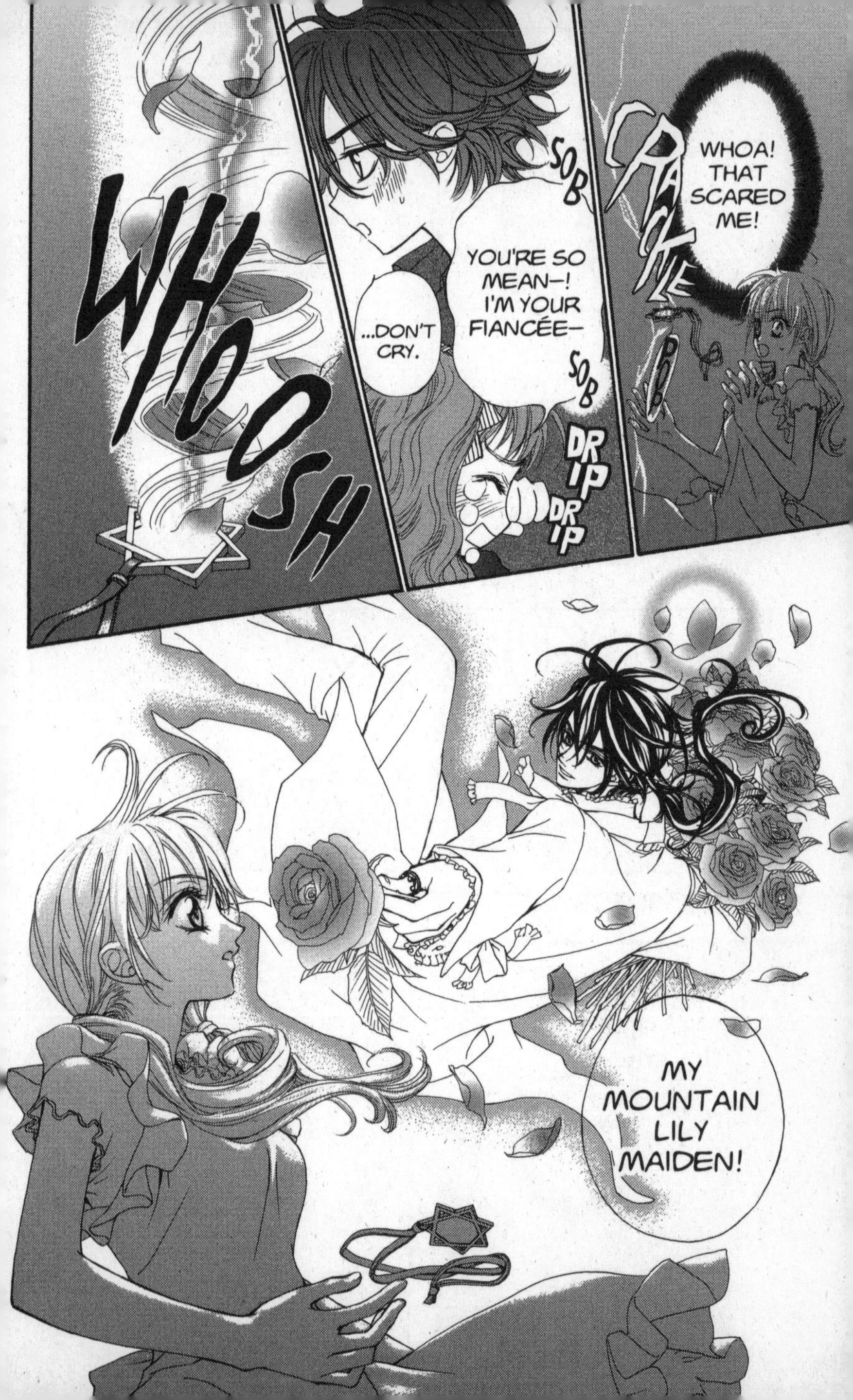
WHOA! THAT SCARED ME!
CRACKLE
POP
SOB
YOU'RE SO MEAN—! I'M YOUR FIANCÉE—
...DON'T CRY.
SOB
DRIP DRIP
DRIP DRIP
WHOOSH
MY MOUNTAIN LILY MAIDEN!

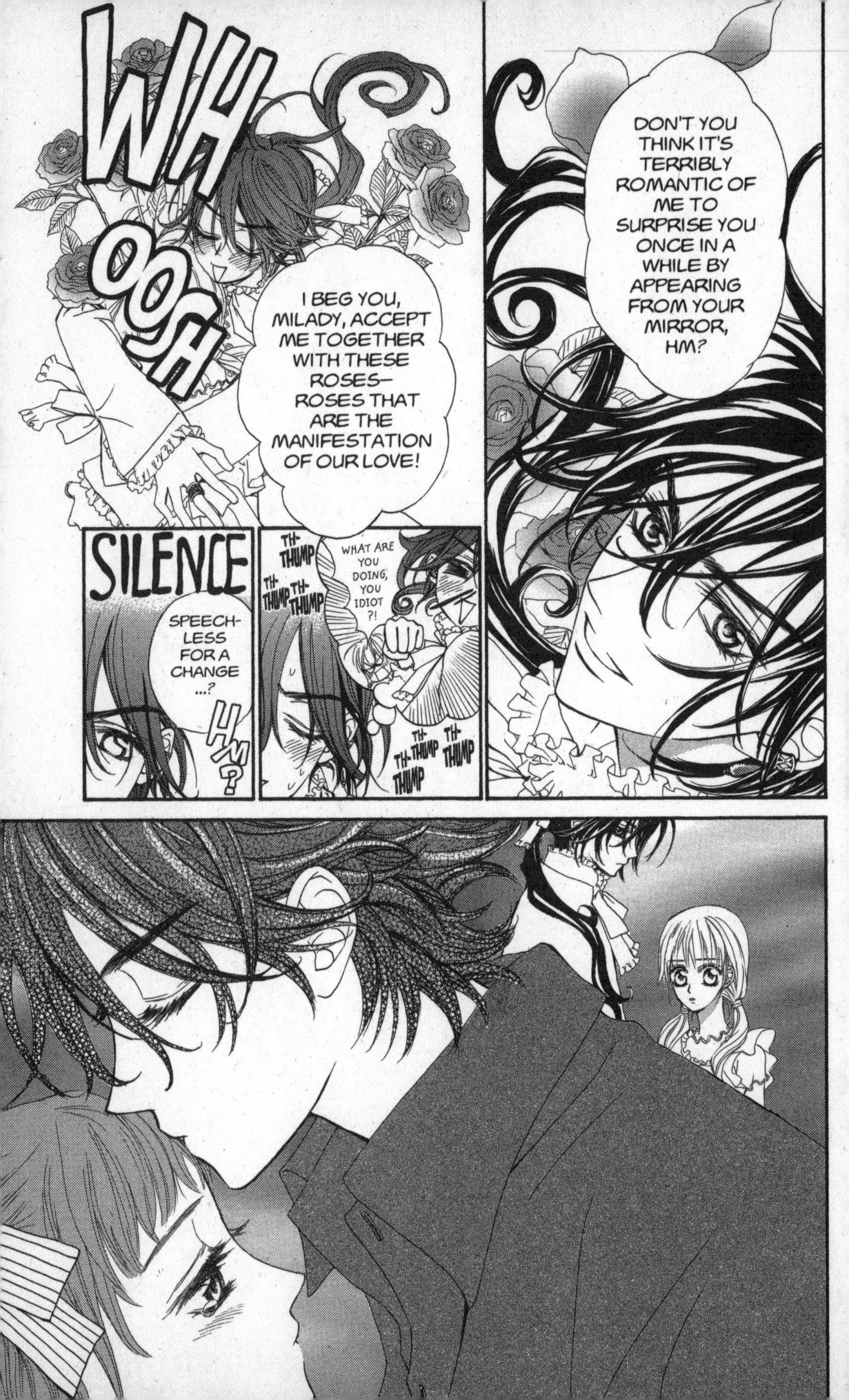
DON'T YOU THINK IT'S TERRIBLY ROMANTIC OF ME TO SURPRISE YOU ONCE IN A WHILE BY APPEARING FROM YOUR MIRROR, HM?
WHHOOSH
I BEG YOU, MILADY, ACCEPT ME TOGETHER WITH THESE ROSES—ROSES THAT ARE THE MANIFESTATION OF OUR LOVE!
TH-THUMP
TH-THUMP TH-THUMP
WHAT ARE YOU DOING, YOU IDIOT?!
TH-THUMP TH-THUMP
TH-THUMP TH-THUMP
SILENCE
SPEECHLESS FOR A CHANGE...?
HM?

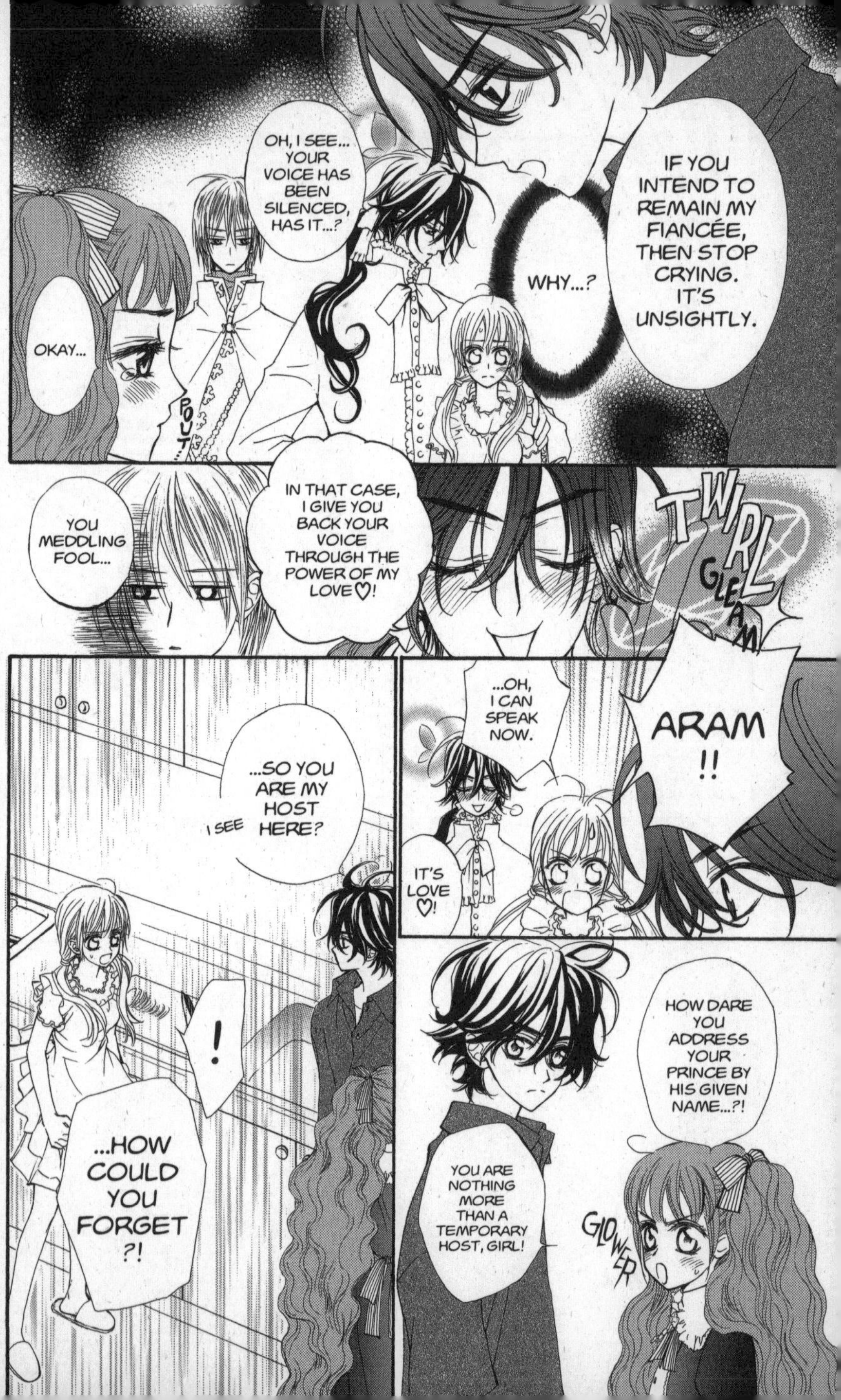
IF YOU INTEND TO REMAIN MY FIANCÉE, THEN STOP CRYING. IT'S UNSIGHTLY.
WHY...?
OH, I SEE... YOUR VOICE HAS BEEN SILENCED, HAS IT...?
OKAY...
POUT...
TWIRL
GLEAM
IN THAT CASE, I GIVE YOU BACK YOUR VOICE THROUGH THE POWER OF MY LOVE♡!
YOU MEDDLING FOOL...
ARAM !!
...OH, I CAN SPEAK NOW.
IT'S LOVE♡!
HOW DARE YOU ADDRESS YOUR PRINCE BY HIS GIVEN NAME...?!
YOU ARE NOTHING MORE THAN A TEMPORARY HOST, GIRL!
GLOWER
...SO YOU ARE MY HOST HERE?
I SEE
!
...HOW COULD YOU FORGET ?!

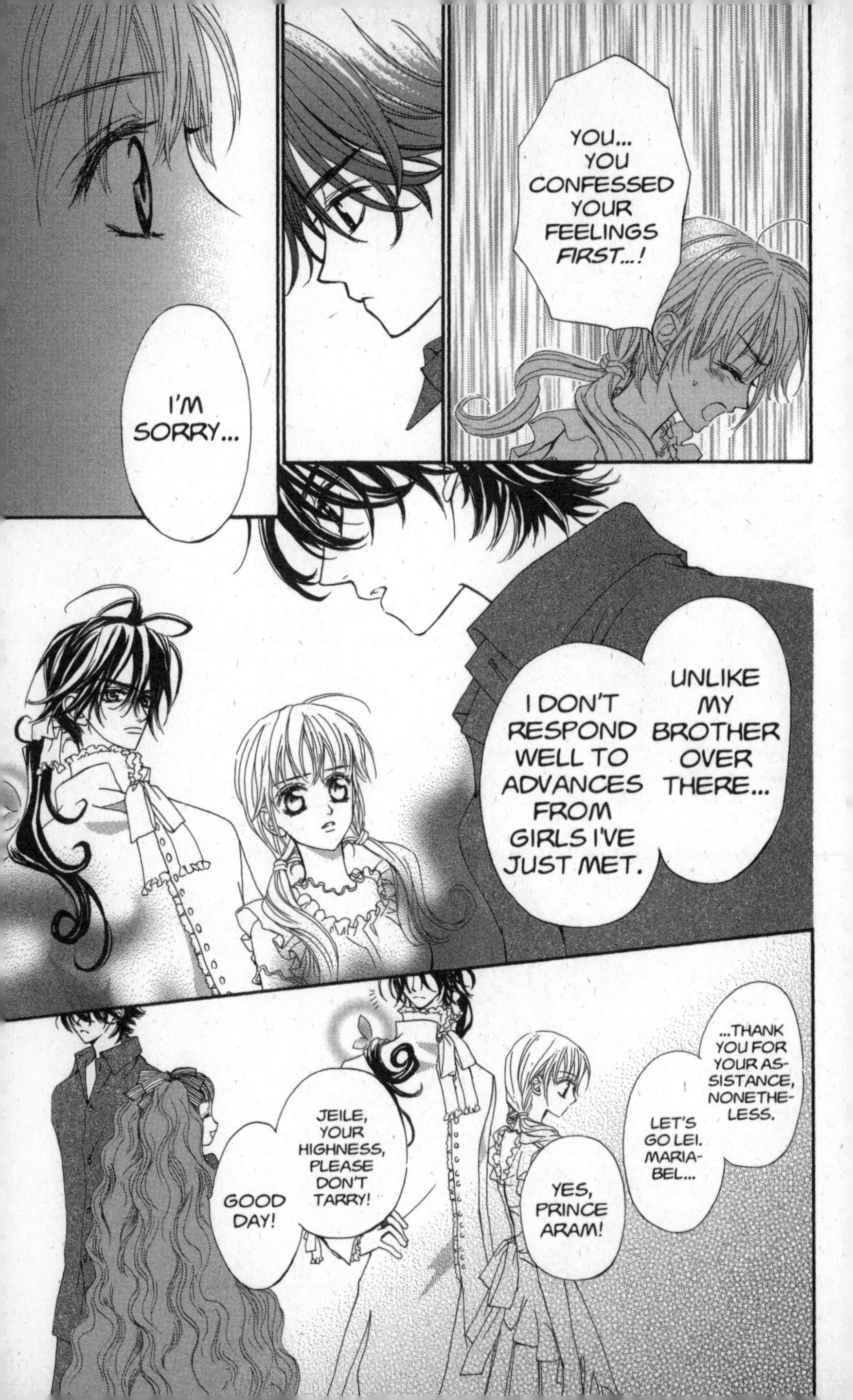
YOU... YOU CONFESSED YOUR FEELINGS FIRST...!
I'M SORRY...
UNLIKE MY BROTHER OVER THERE...
I DON'T RESPOND WELL TO ADVANCES FROM GIRLS I'VE JUST MET.
...THANK YOU FOR YOUR AS-SISTANCE, NONETHE-LESS.
LET'S GO LEI. MARIA-BEL...
YES, PRINCE ARAM!
JEILE, YOUR HIGHNESS, PLEASE DON'T TARRY!
GOOD DAY!

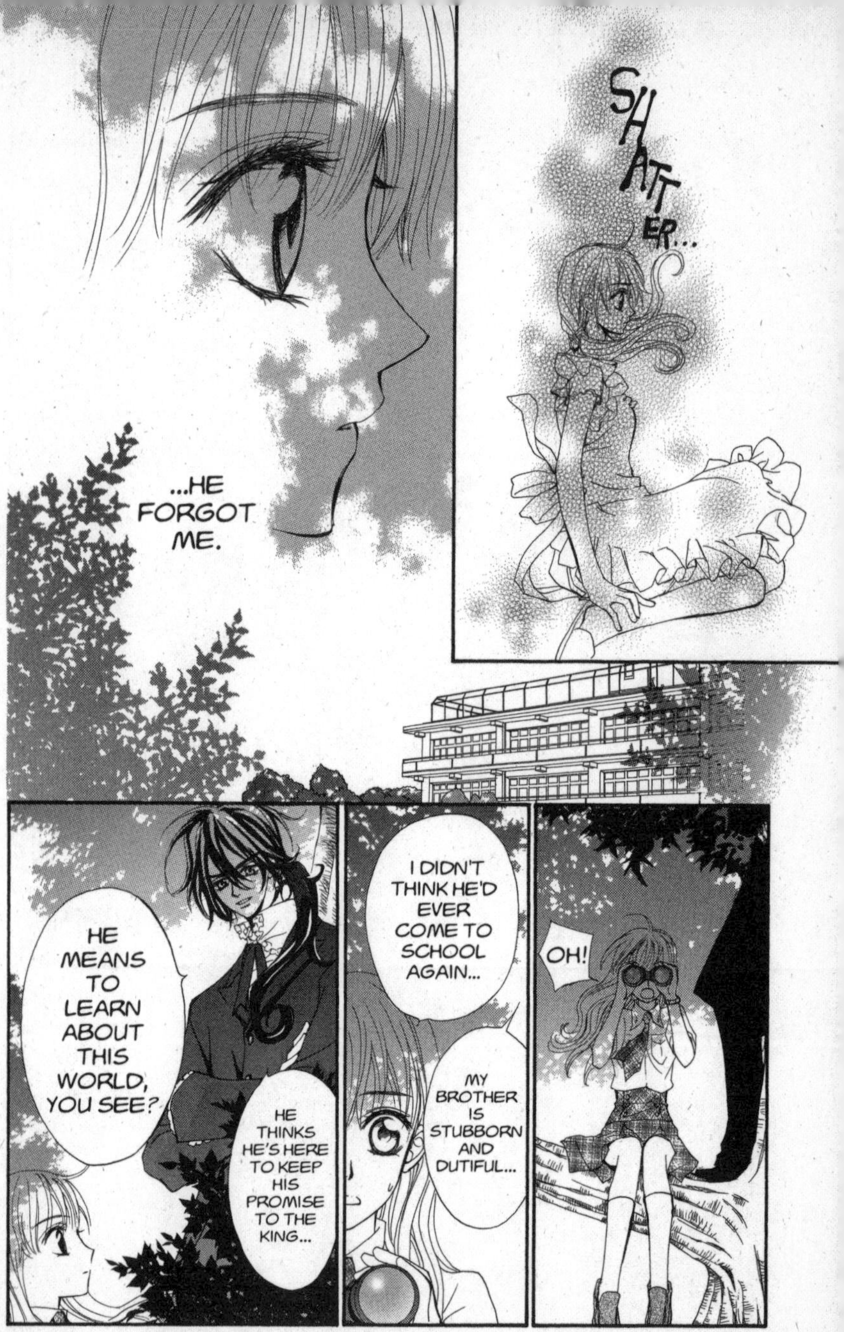
SHATTER...
...HE FORGOT ME.
OH!
I DIDN'T THINK HE'D EVER COME TO SCHOOL AGAIN...
MY BROTHER IS STUBBORN AND DUTIFUL...
HE MEANS TO LEARN ABOUT THIS WORLD, YOU SEE?
HE THINKS HE'S HERE TO KEEP HIS PROMISE TO THE KING...

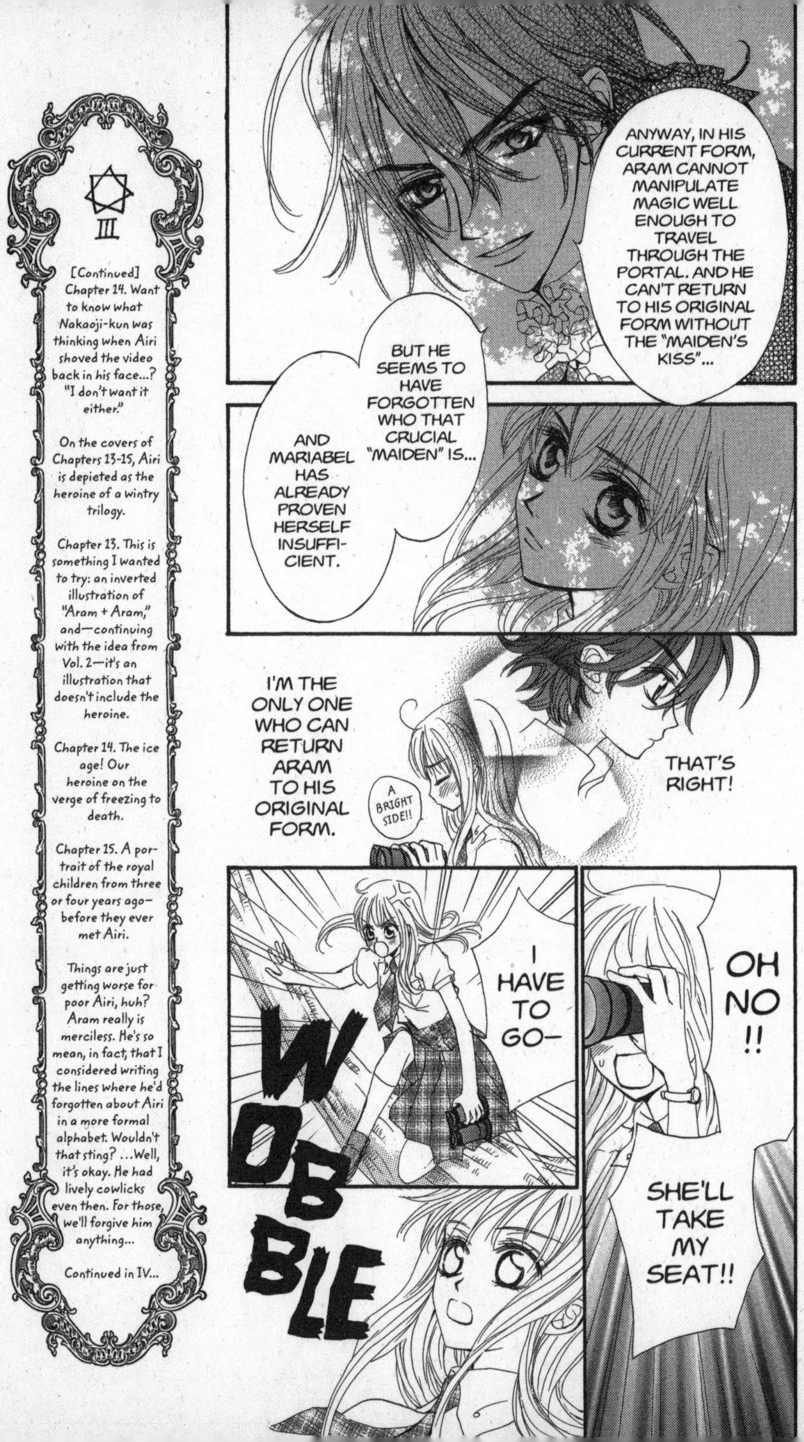
ANYWAY, IN HIS CURRENT FORM, ARAM CANNOT MANIPULATE MAGIC WELL ENOUGH TO TRAVEL THROUGH THE PORTAL. AND HE CAN'T RETURN TO HIS ORIGINAL FORM WITHOUT THE "MAIDEN'S KISS"...
BUT HE SEEMS TO HAVE FORGOTTEN WHO THAT CRUCIAL "MAIDEN" IS...
AND MARIABEL HAS ALREADY PROVEN HERSELF INSUFFI-CIENT.
THAT'S RIGHT!
I'M THE ONLY ONE WHO CAN RETURN ARAM TO HIS ORIGINAL FORM.
A BRIGHT SIDE!!
OH NO!!
SHE'LL TAKE MY SEAT!!
I HAVE TO GO—
WOBBLE

III

[Continued] Chapter 14. Want to know what Nakaoji-kun was thinking when Airi shoved the video back in his face...? "I don't want it either."

On the covers of Chapters 13-15, Airi is depicted as the heroine of a wintry trilogy.

Chapter 13. This is something I wanted to try: an inverted illustration of "Aram + Aram," and—continuing with the idea from Vol. 2—it's an illustration that doesn't include the heroine.

Chapter 14. The ice age! Our heroine on the verge of freezing to death.

Chapter 15. A portrait of the royal children from three or four years ago—before they ever met Airi.

Things are just getting worse for poor Airi, huh? Aram really is merciless. He's so mean, in fact, that I considered writing the lines where he'd forgotten about Airi in a more formal alphabet. Wouldn't that sting? ...Well, it's okay. He had lively cowlicks even then. For those, we'll forgive him anything...

Continued in IV...

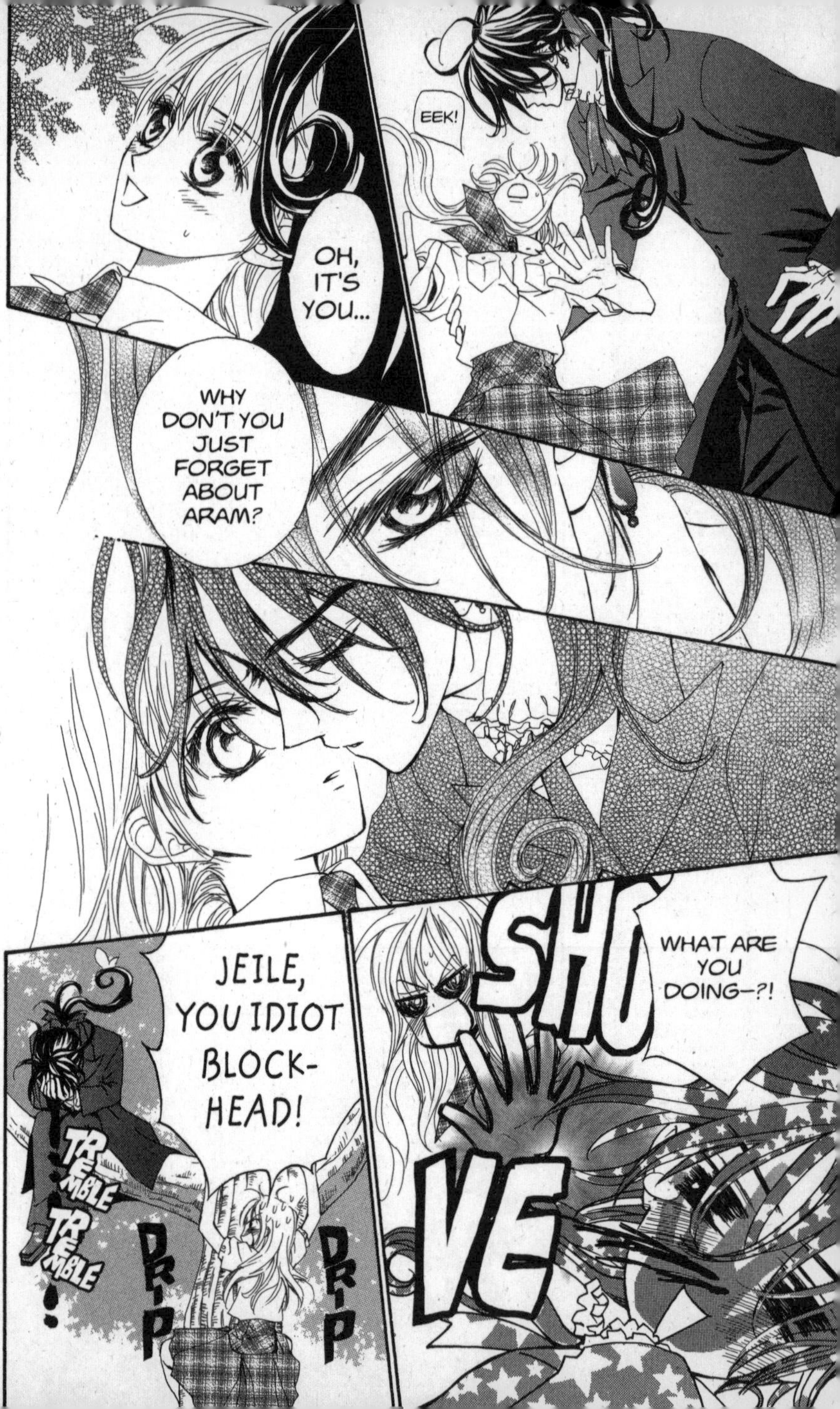
EEK!
OH, IT'S YOU...
WHY DON'T YOU JUST FORGET ABOUT ARAM?
SHOVE
WHAT ARE YOU DOING—?!
JEILE, YOU IDIOT BLOCK-HEAD!
TREMBLE TREMBLE
DRIP DRIP

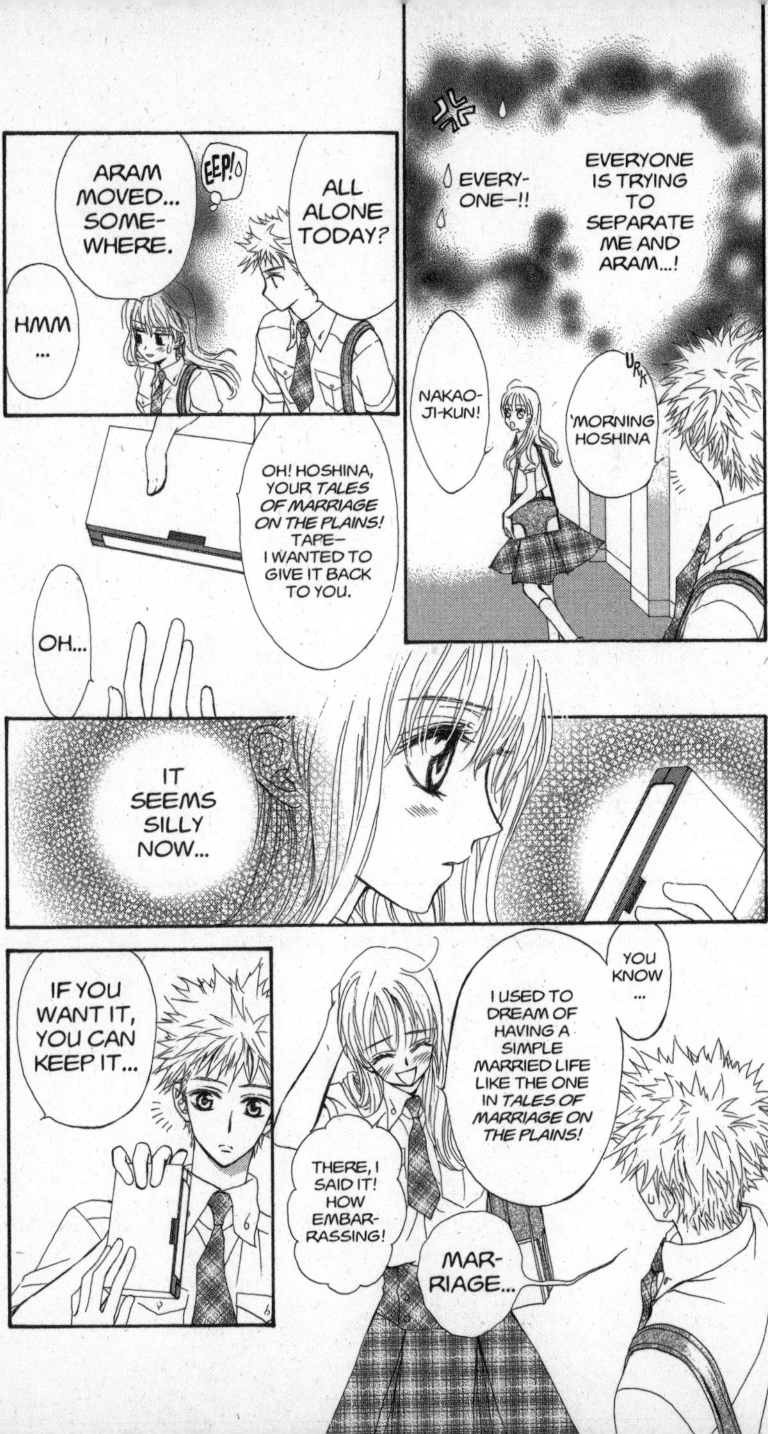
EVERYONE IS TRYING TO SEPARATE ME AND ARAM...!
EVERY-ONE--!!
URK
'MORNING HOSHINA
NAKAOJI-KUN!
ALL ALONE TODAY?
EEP!
ARAM MOVED... SOME-WHERE.
HMM ...
OH! HOSHINA, YOUR *TALES OF MARRIAGE ON THE PLAINS!* TAPE-- I WANTED TO GIVE IT BACK TO YOU.
OH...
IT SEEMS SILLY NOW...
YOU KNOW ...
I USED TO DREAM OF HAVING A SIMPLE MARRIED LIFE LIKE THE ONE IN *TALES OF MARRIAGE ON THE PLAINS!*
THERE, I SAID IT! HOW EMBAR-RASSING!
MAR-RIAGE...
IF YOU WANT IT, YOU CAN KEEP IT...

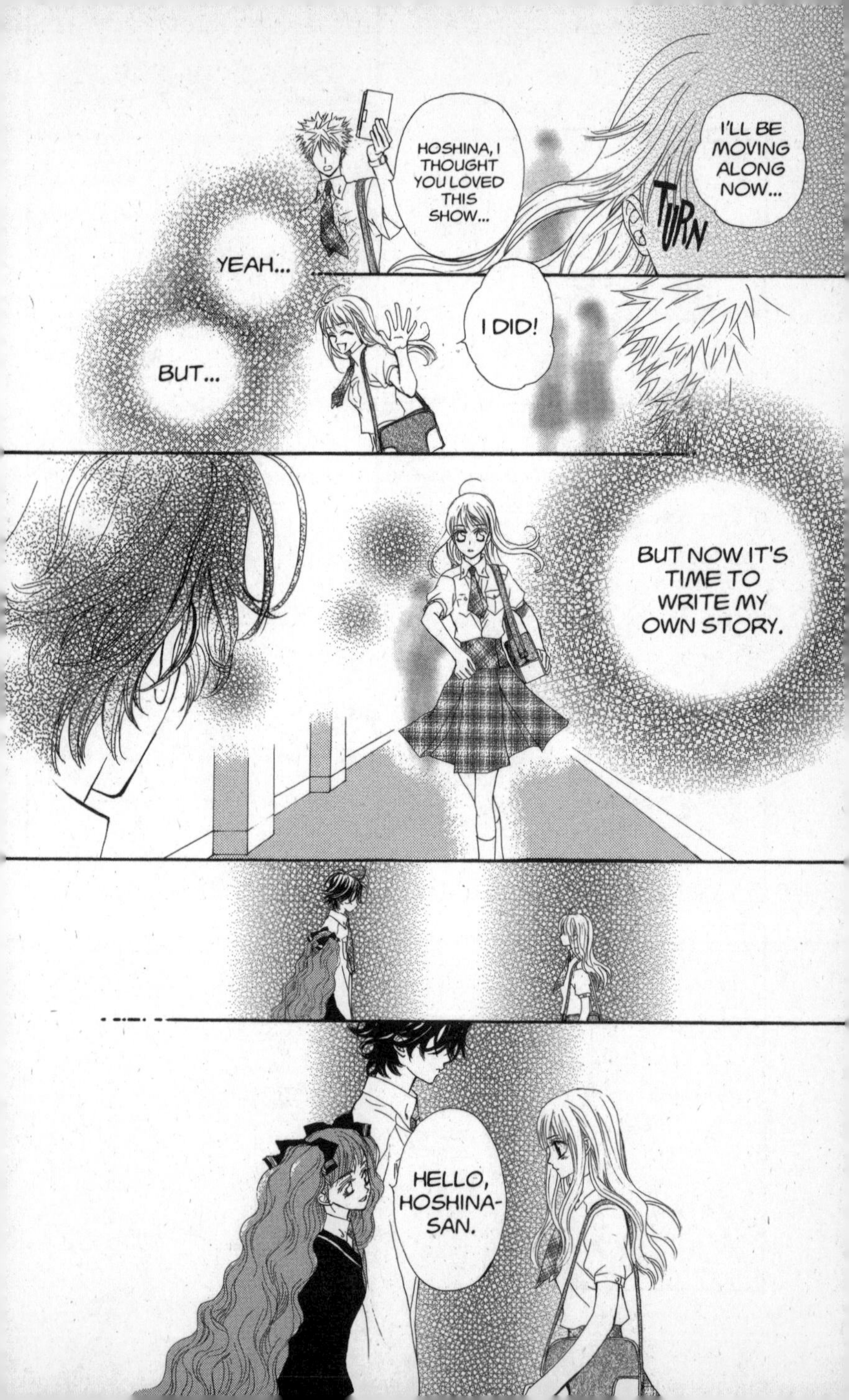
I'LL BE MOVING ALONG NOW...
TURN
HOSHINA, I THOUGHT YOU LOVED THIS SHOW...
YEAH...
I DID!
BUT...
BUT NOW IT'S TIME TO WRITE MY OWN STORY.
HELLO, HOSHINA-SAN.

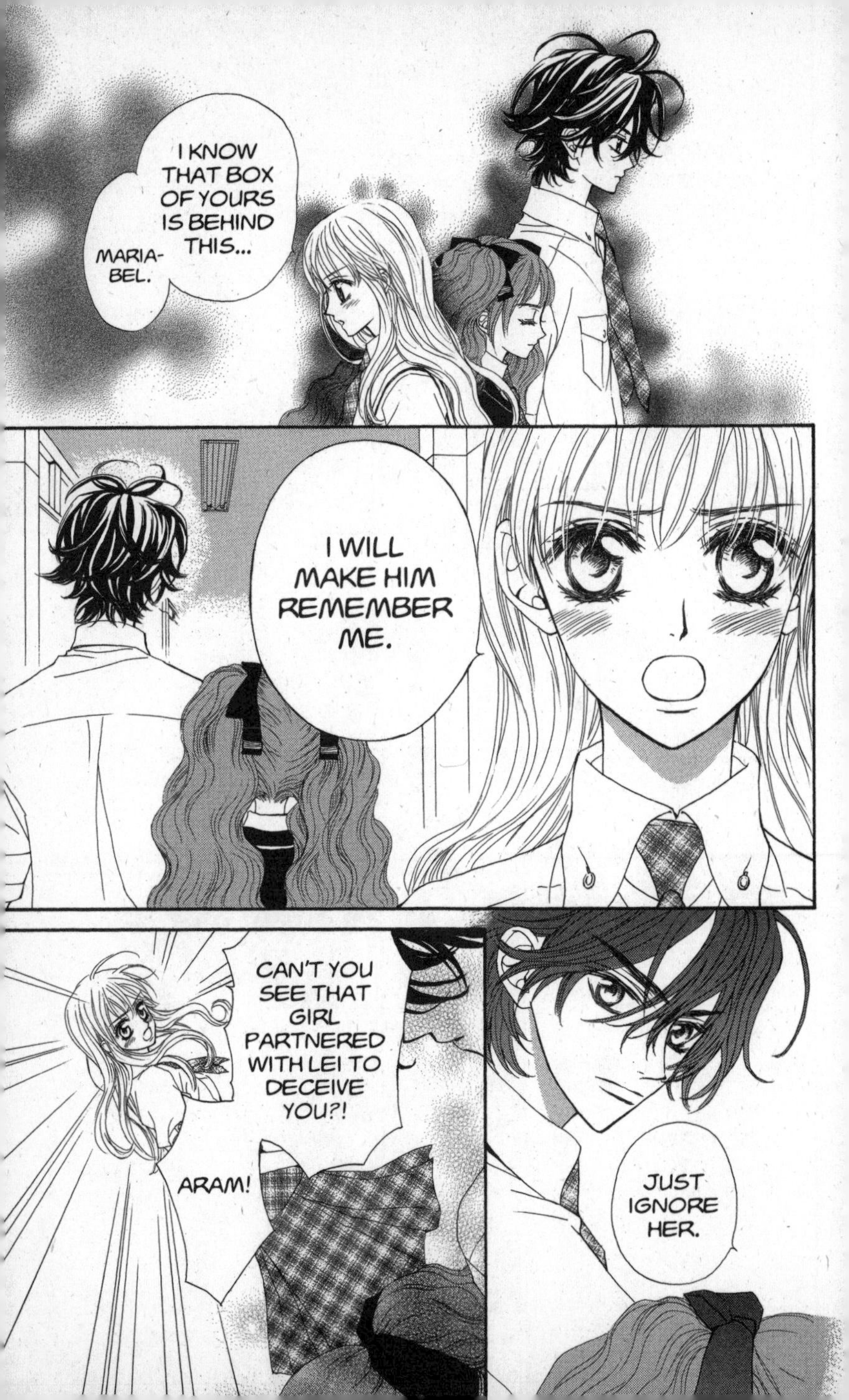
I KNOW THAT BOX OF YOURS IS BEHIND THIS...
MARIA-BEL.
I WILL MAKE HIM REMEMBER ME.
JUST IGNORE HER.
CAN'T YOU SEE THAT GIRL PARTNERED WITH LEI TO DECEIVE YOU?!
ARAM!

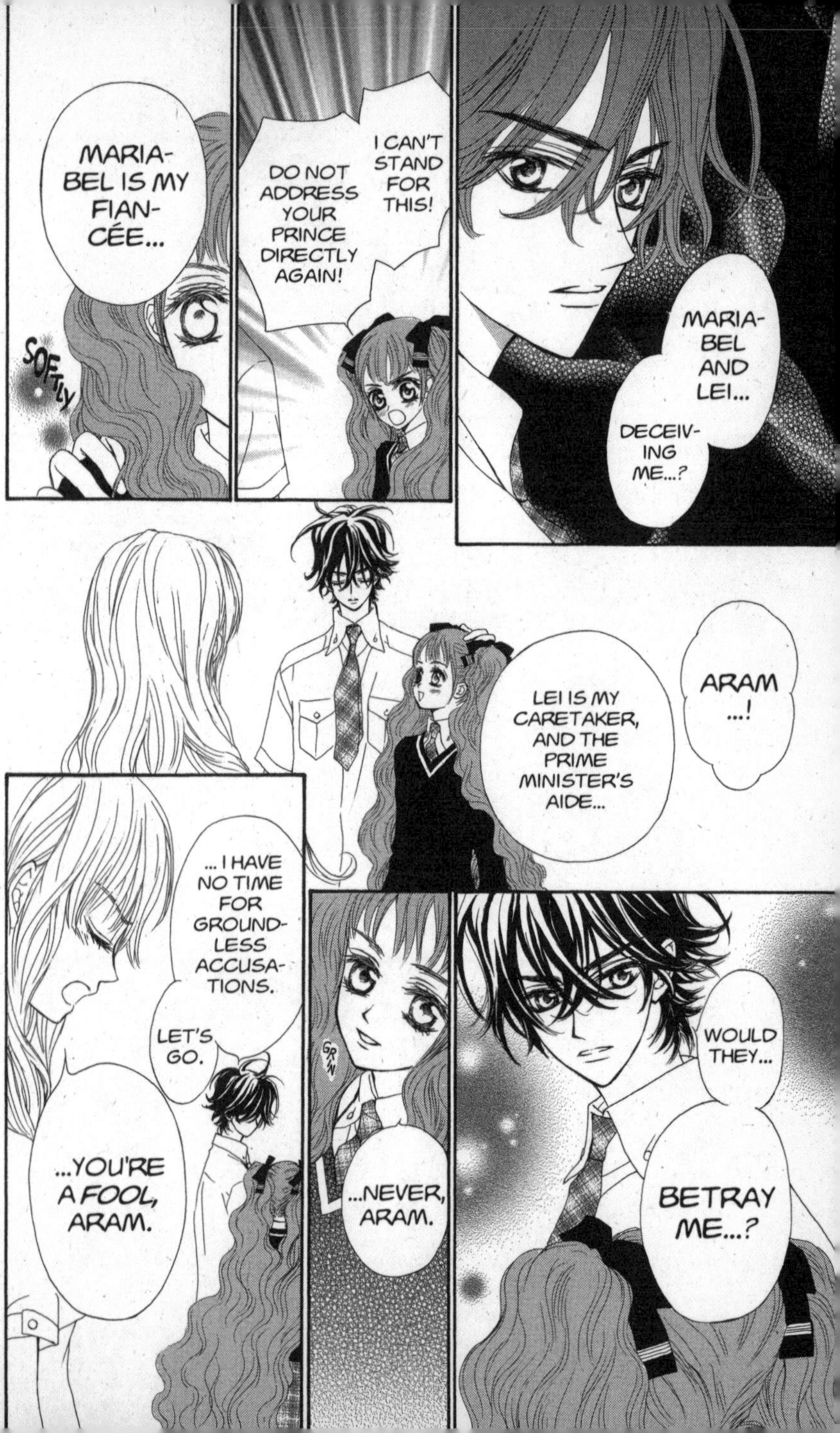
MARIABEL AND LEI...
DECEIVING ME...?
I CAN'T STAND FOR THIS!
DO NOT ADDRESS YOUR PRINCE DIRECTLY AGAIN!
MARIABEL IS MY FIANCÉE...
SOFTLY
ARAM ...!
LEI IS MY CARETAKER, AND THE PRIME MINISTER'S AIDE...
WOULD THEY...
BETRAY ME...?
GRIN
...NEVER, ARAM.
...I HAVE NO TIME FOR GROUNDLESS ACCUSATIONS.
LET'S GO.
...YOU'RE A FOOL, ARAM.

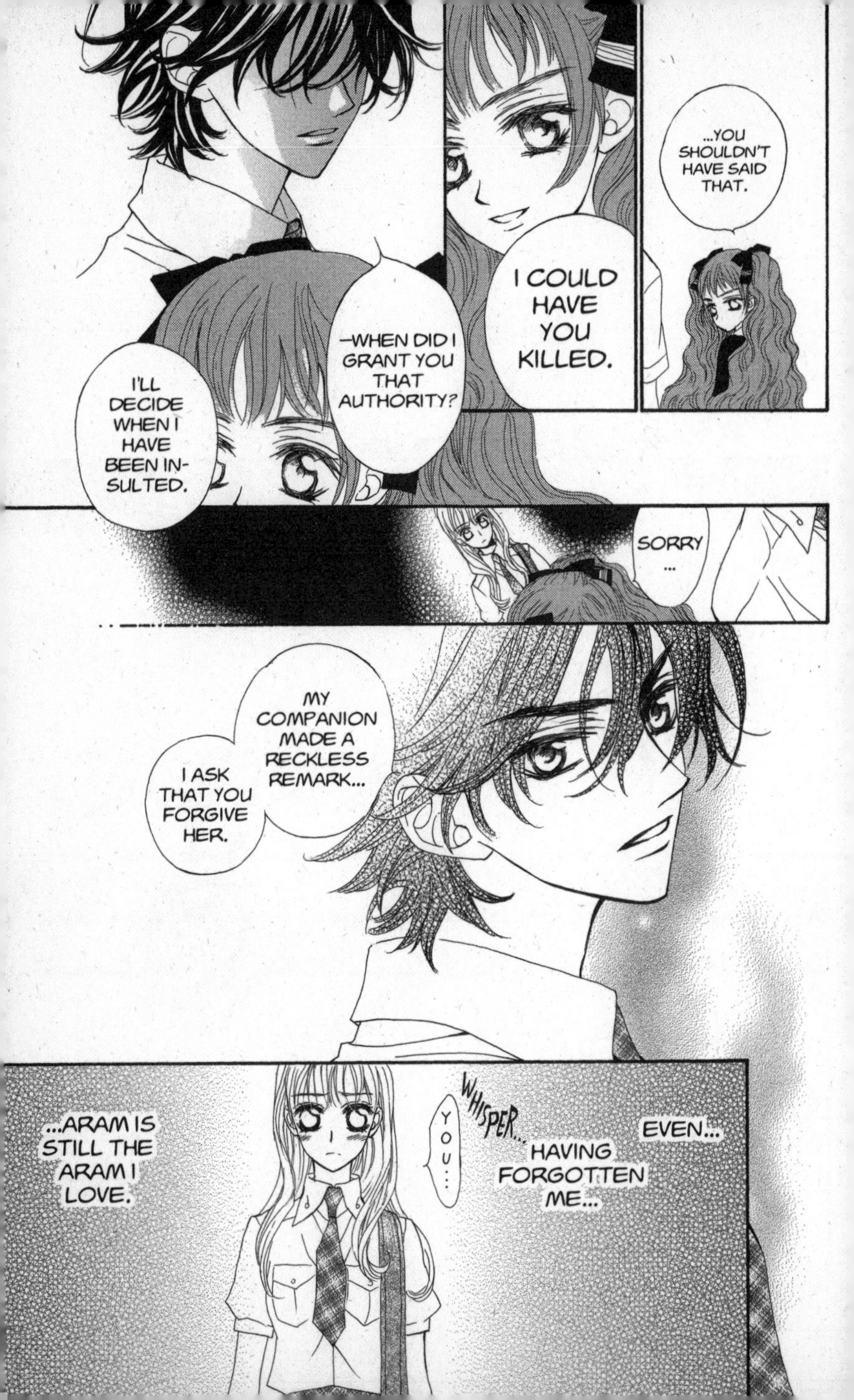
...YOU SHOULDN'T HAVE SAID THAT.
I COULD HAVE YOU KILLED.
—WHEN DID I GRANT YOU THAT AUTHORITY?
I'LL DECIDE WHEN I HAVE BEEN IN-SULTED.
SORRY...
MY COMPANION MADE A RECKLESS REMARK...
I ASK THAT YOU FORGIVE HER.
WHISPER...
YOU...
EVEN...
HAVING FORGOTTEN ME...
...ARAM IS STILL THE ARAM I LOVE.

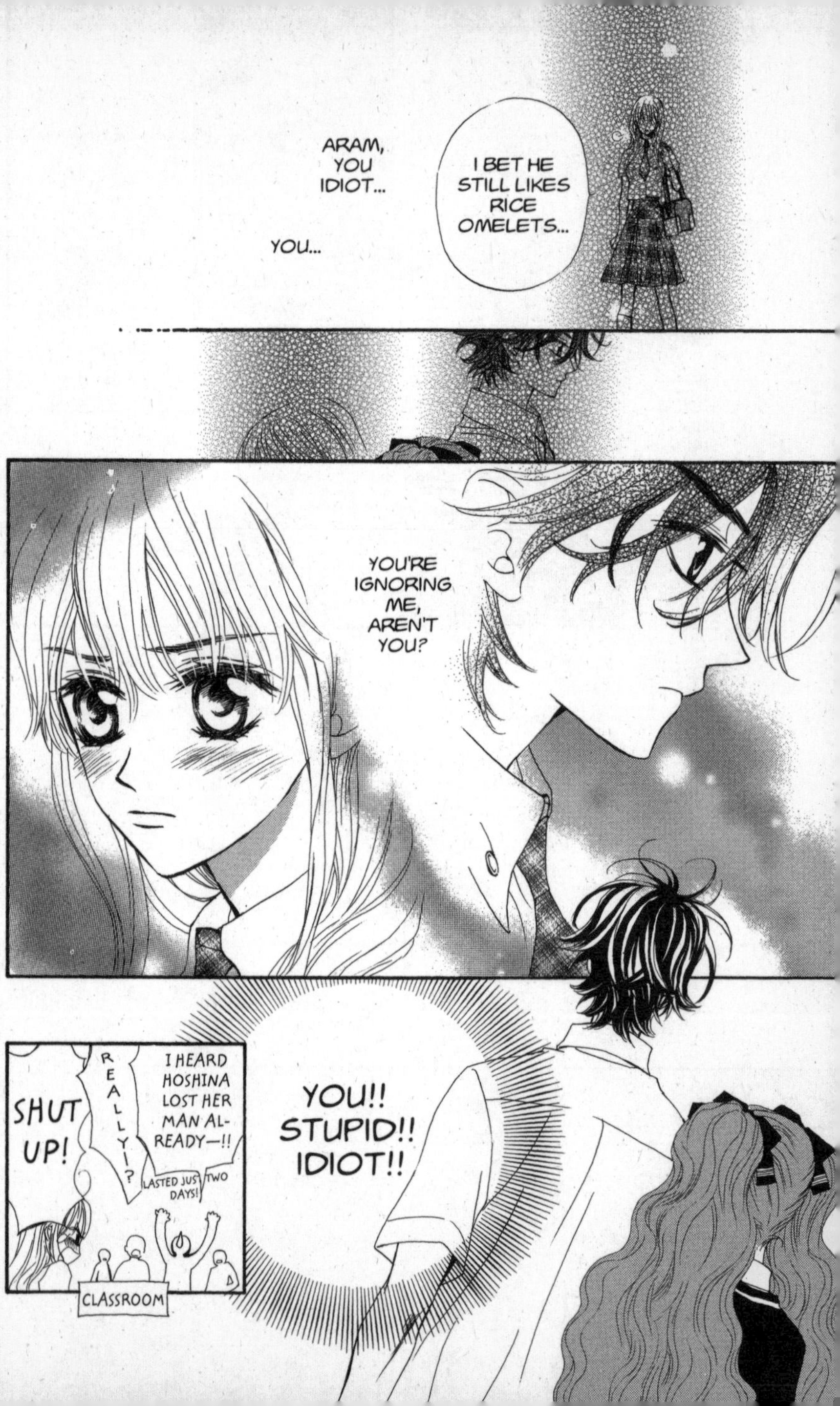
I BET HE STILL LIKES RICE OMELETS...
ARAM, YOU IDIOT...
YOU...
YOU'RE IGNORING ME, AREN'T YOU?
YOU!! STUPID!! IDIOT!!
I HEARD HOSHINA LOST HER MAN AL-READY—!!
REALLY!?
LASTED JUST TWO DAYS!
SHUT UP!
CLASSROOM

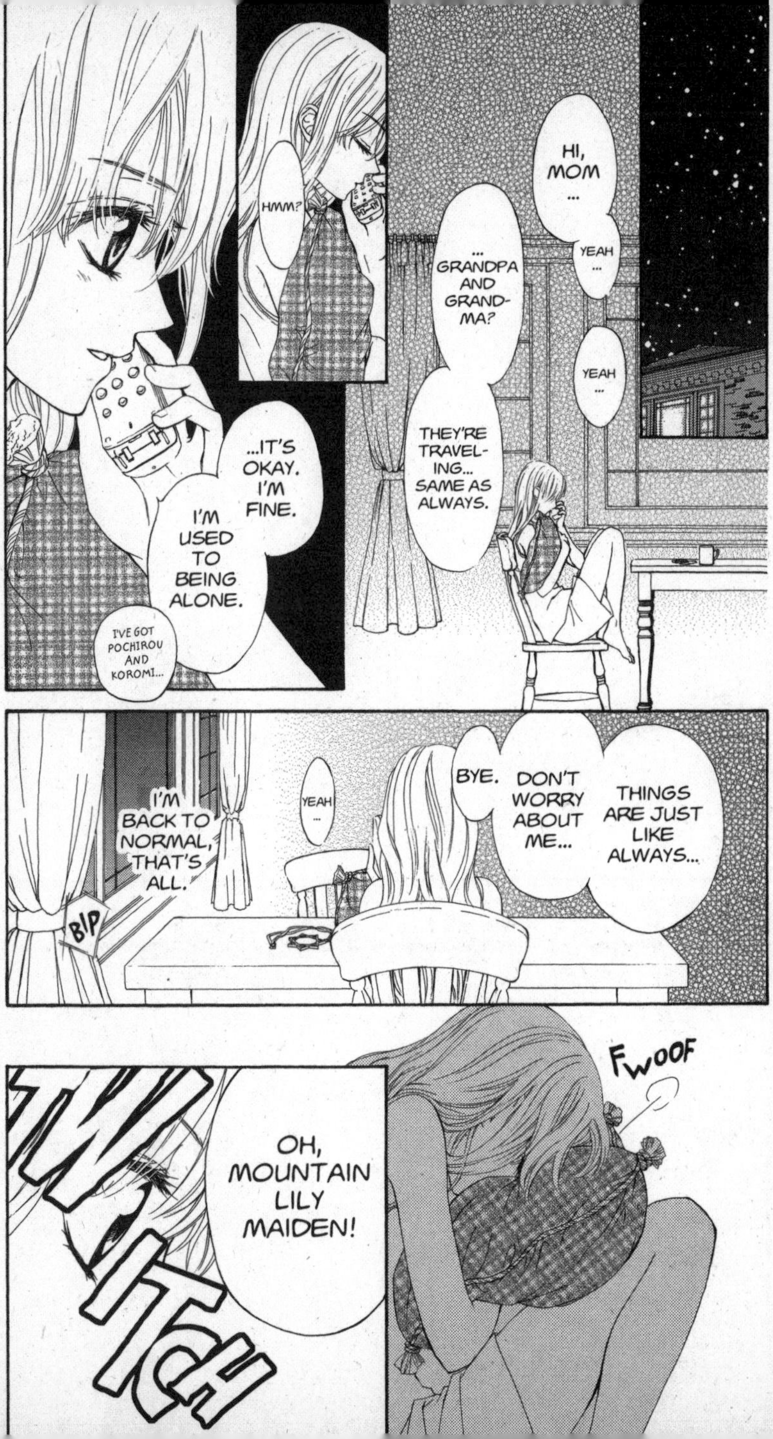
HI, MOM ...
YEAH ...
... GRANDPA AND GRAND-MA?
YEAH ...
THEY'RE TRAVEL-ING... SAME AS ALWAYS.
HMM?
...IT'S OKAY. I'M FINE.
I'M USED TO BEING ALONE.
I'VE GOT POCHIROU AND KOROMI...
THINGS ARE JUST LIKE ALWAYS...
DON'T WORRY ABOUT ME...
BYE.
YEAH ...
I'M BACK TO NORMAL, THAT'S ALL.
BIP
FWOOF
OH, MOUNTAIN LILY MAIDEN!
TWITCH

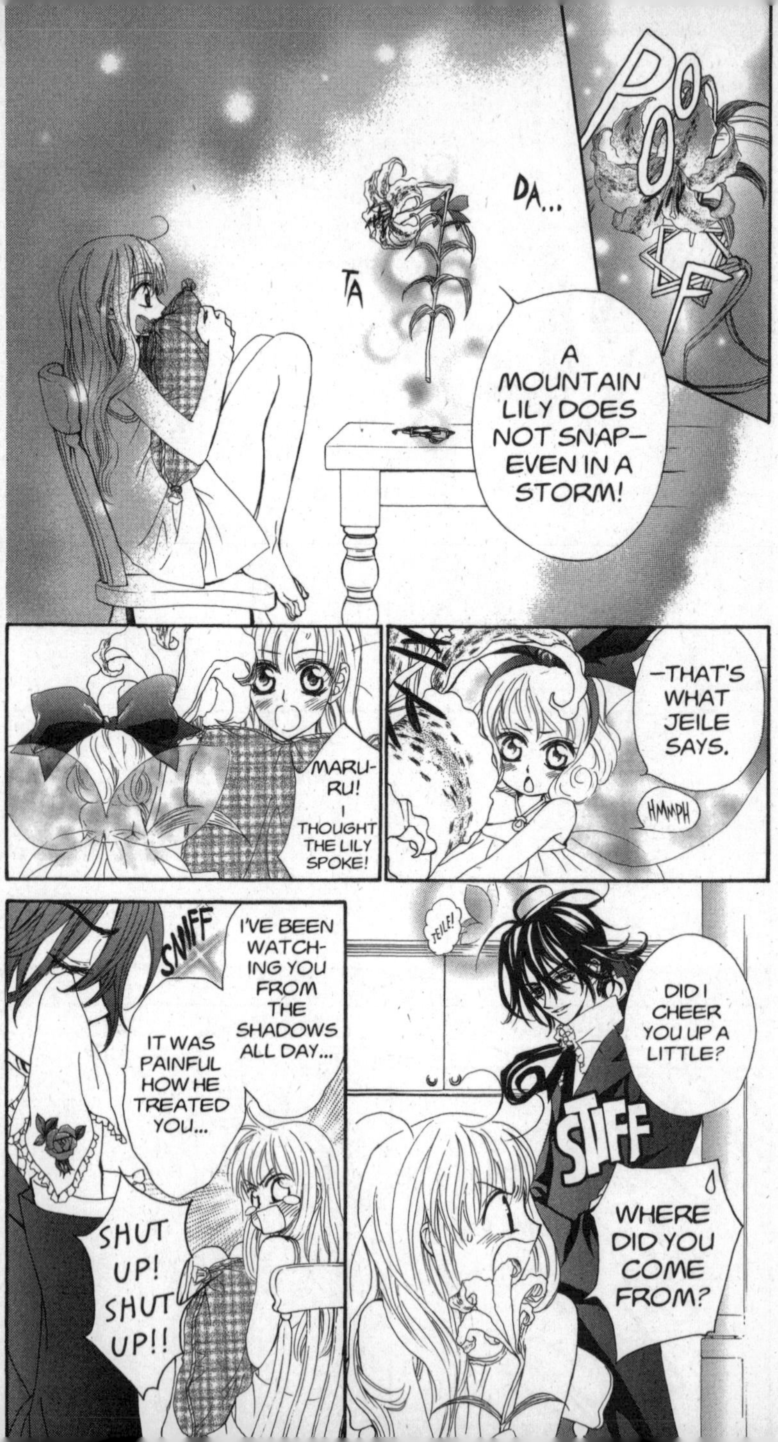
POOF
DA...
TA
A MOUNTAIN LILY DOES NOT SNAP—EVEN IN A STORM!
—THAT'S WHAT JEILE SAYS.
HMMPH
MARU-RU! I THOUGHT THE LILY SPOKE!
JEILE!
DID I CHEER YOU UP A LITTLE?
STIFF
WHERE DID YOU COME FROM?
SNIFF
I'VE BEEN WATCHING YOU FROM THE SHADOWS ALL DAY...
IT WAS PAINFUL HOW HE TREATED YOU...
SHUT UP! SHUT UP!!

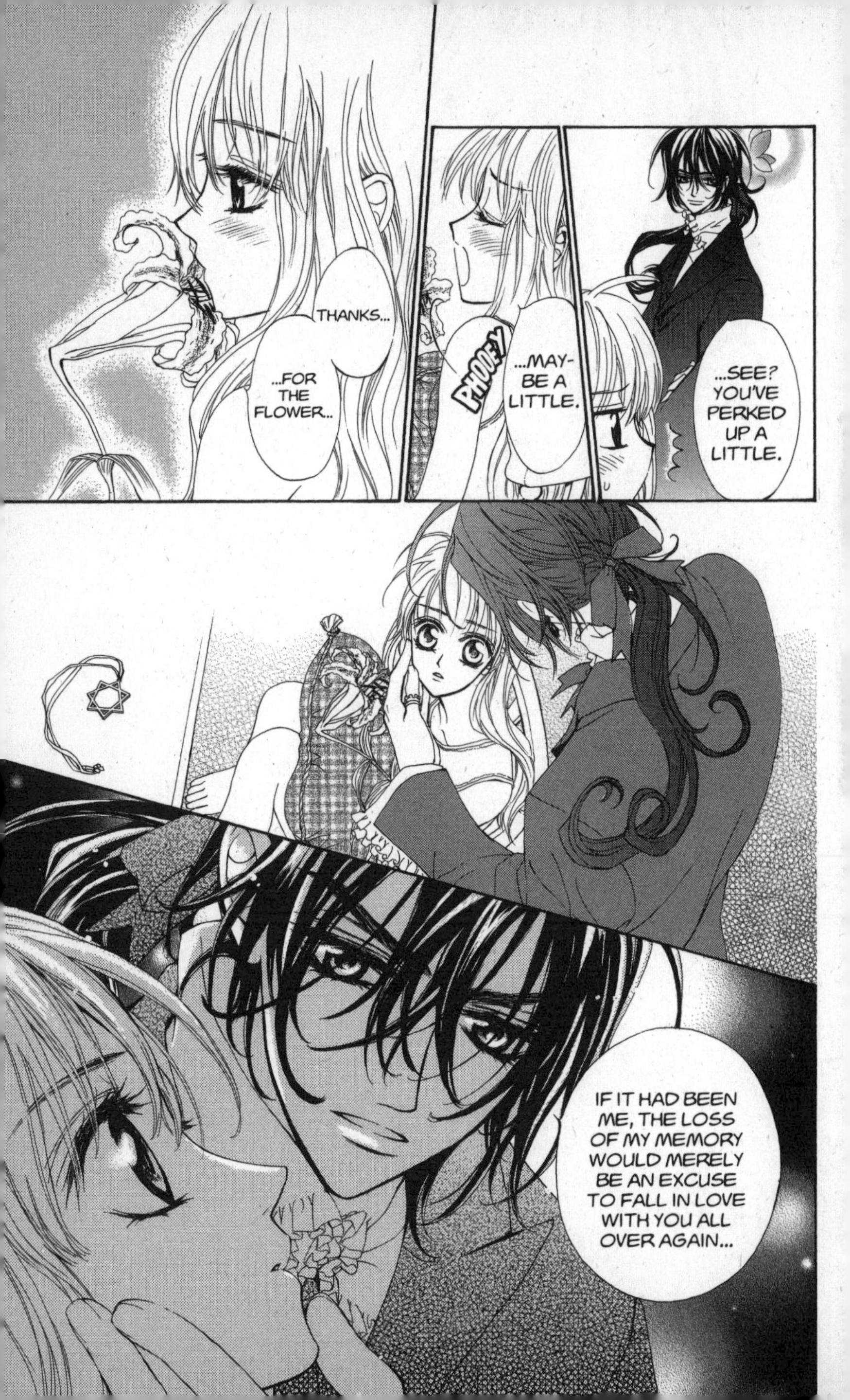
...SEE? YOU'VE PERKED UP A LITTLE.
PHOOEY
...MAY-BE A LITTLE.
THANKS...
...FOR THE FLOWER..
IF IT HAD BEEN ME, THE LOSS OF MY MEMORY WOULD MERELY BE AN EXCUSE TO FALL IN LOVE WITH YOU ALL OVER AGAIN...

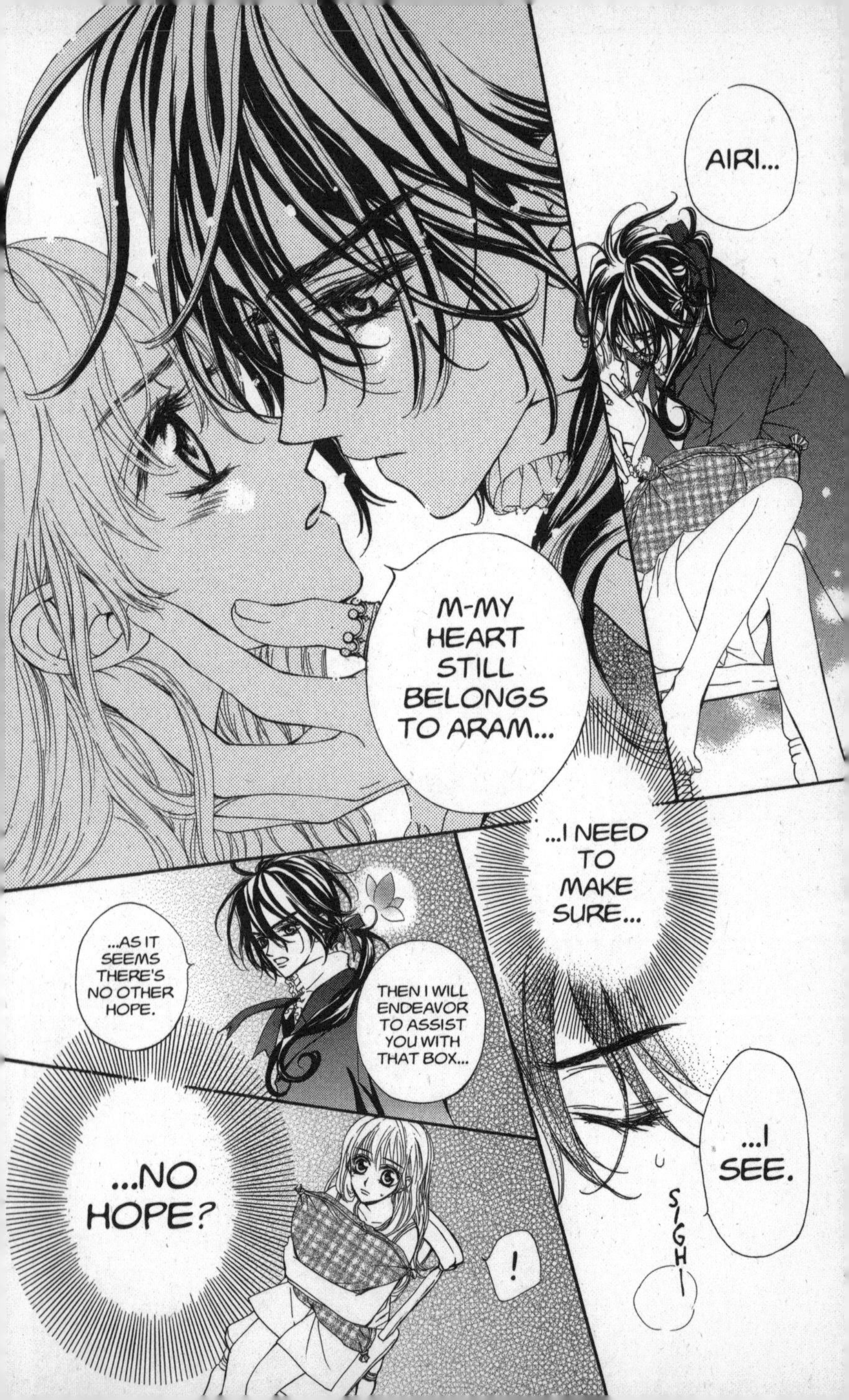
AIRI...
M-MY HEART STILL BELONGS TO ARAM...
...I NEED TO MAKE SURE...
...I SEE.
SIGH
THEN I WILL ENDEAVOR TO ASSIST YOU WITH THAT BOX...
...AS IT SEEMS THERE'S NO OTHER HOPE.
...NO HOPE?
!

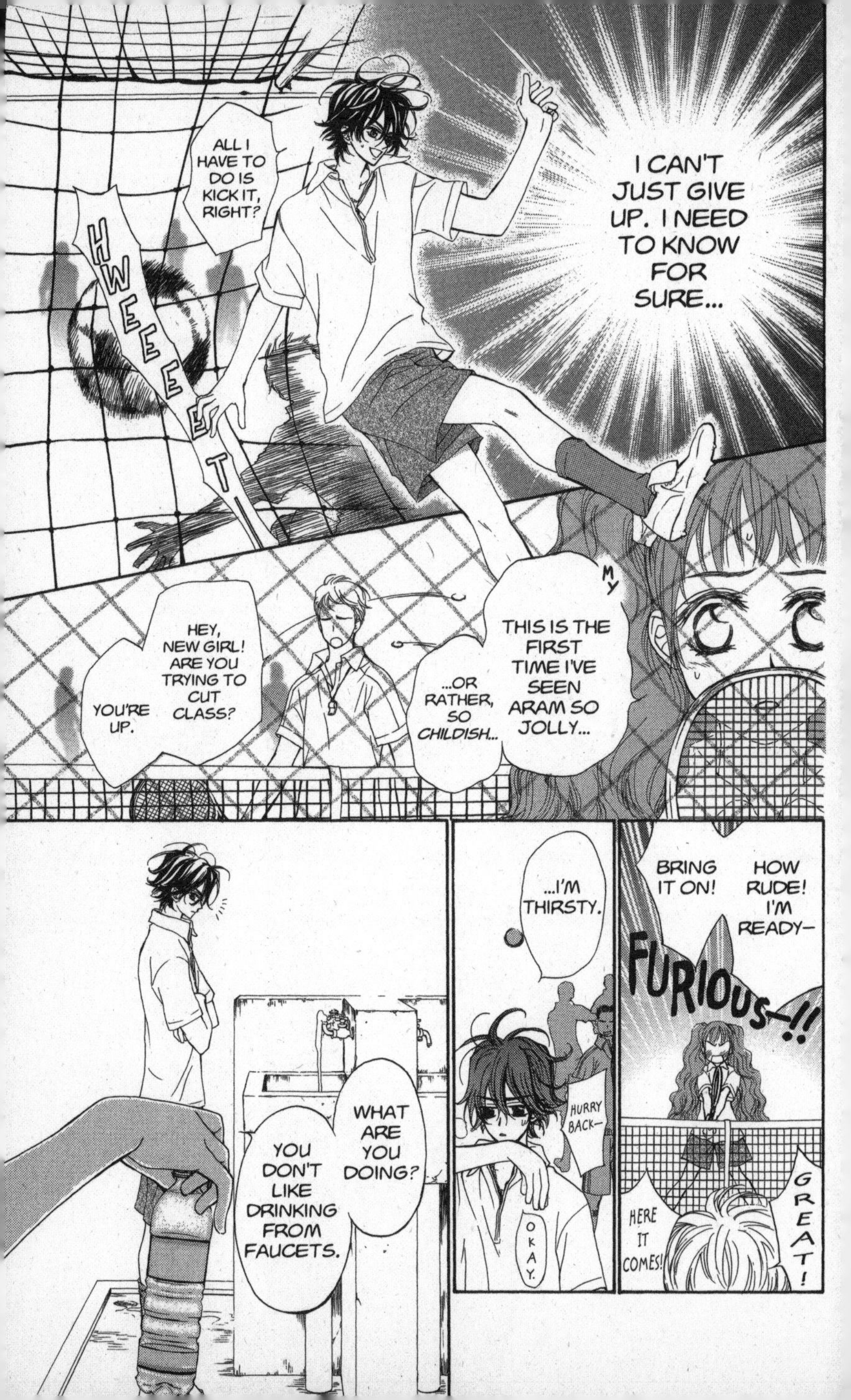
I CAN'T JUST GIVE UP. I NEED TO KNOW FOR SURE...
ALL I HAVE TO DO IS KICK IT, RIGHT?
HWEEEEET
MY
THIS IS THE FIRST TIME I'VE SEEN ARAM SO JOLLY...
...OR RATHER, SO CHILDISH...
HEY, NEW GIRL! ARE YOU TRYING TO CUT CLASS?
YOU'RE UP.
HOW RUDE! I'M READY—
BRING IT ON!
FURIOUS—!!
GREAT!
HERE IT COMES!
...I'M THIRSTY.
HURRY BACK—
OKAY.
WHAT ARE YOU DOING?
YOU DON'T LIKE DRINKING FROM FAUCETS.

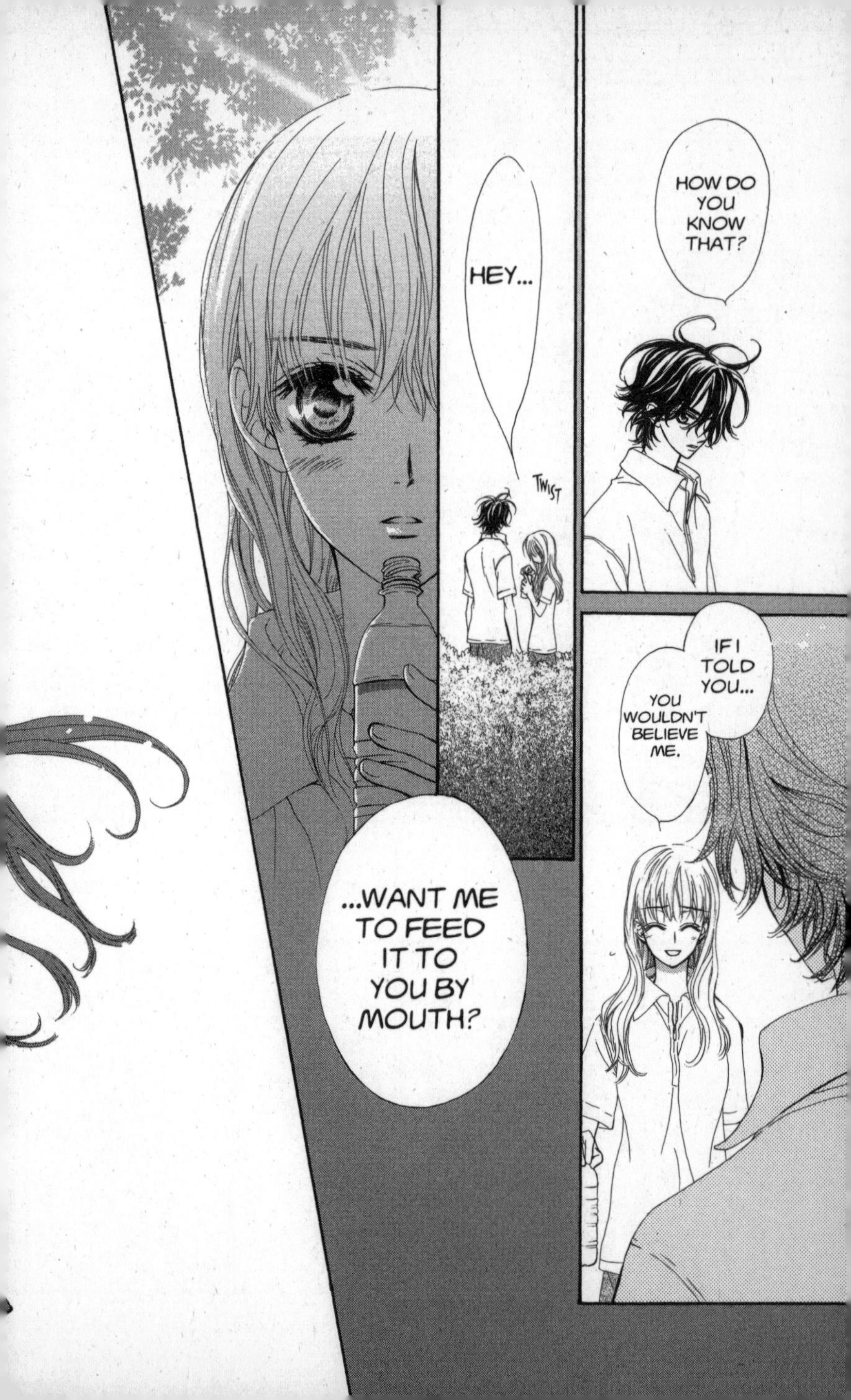
HOW DO YOU KNOW THAT?
IF I TOLD YOU...
YOU WOULDN'T BELIEVE ME.
HEY...
TWIST
...WANT ME TO FEED IT TO YOU BY MOUTH?

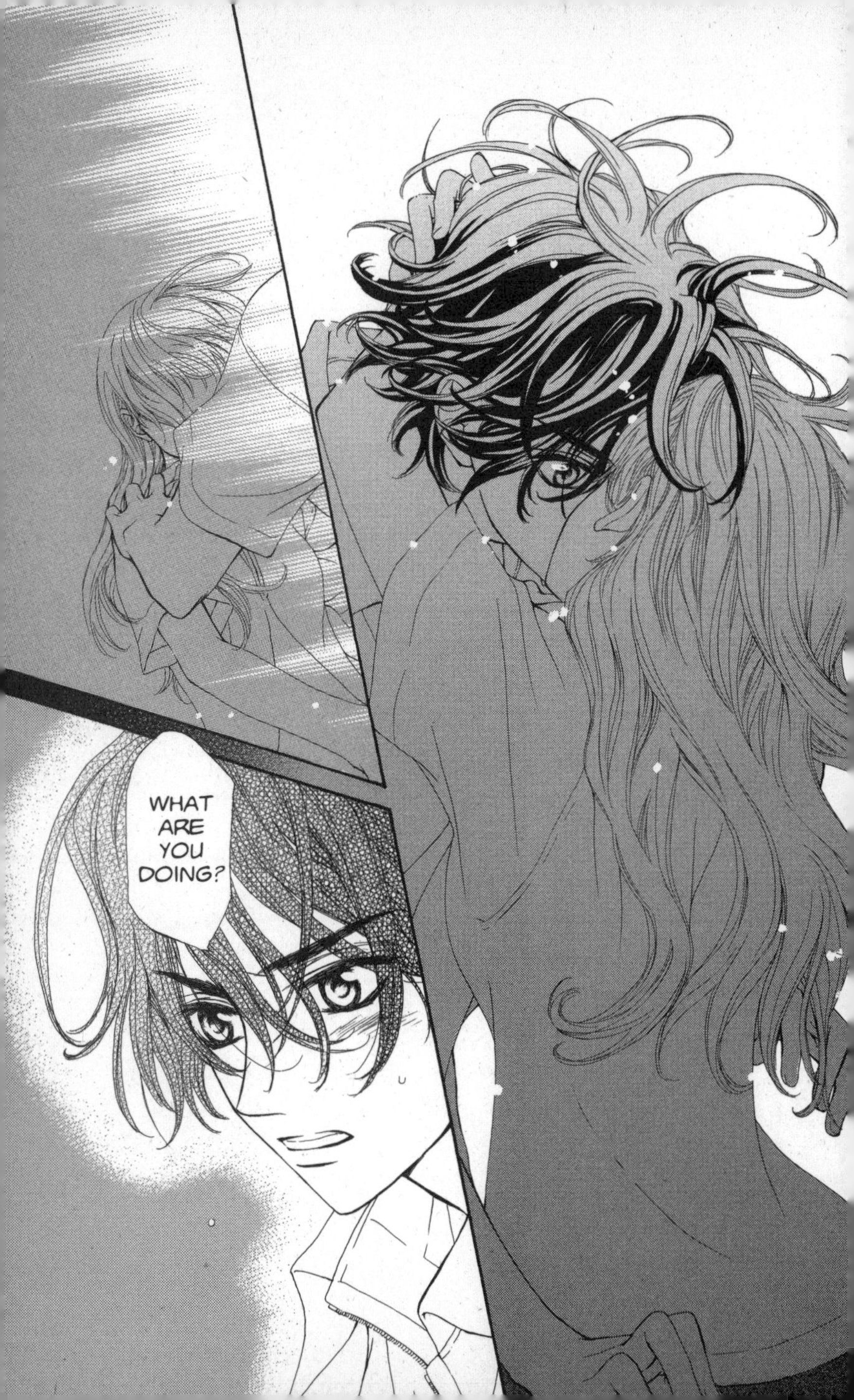
WHAT ARE YOU DOING?

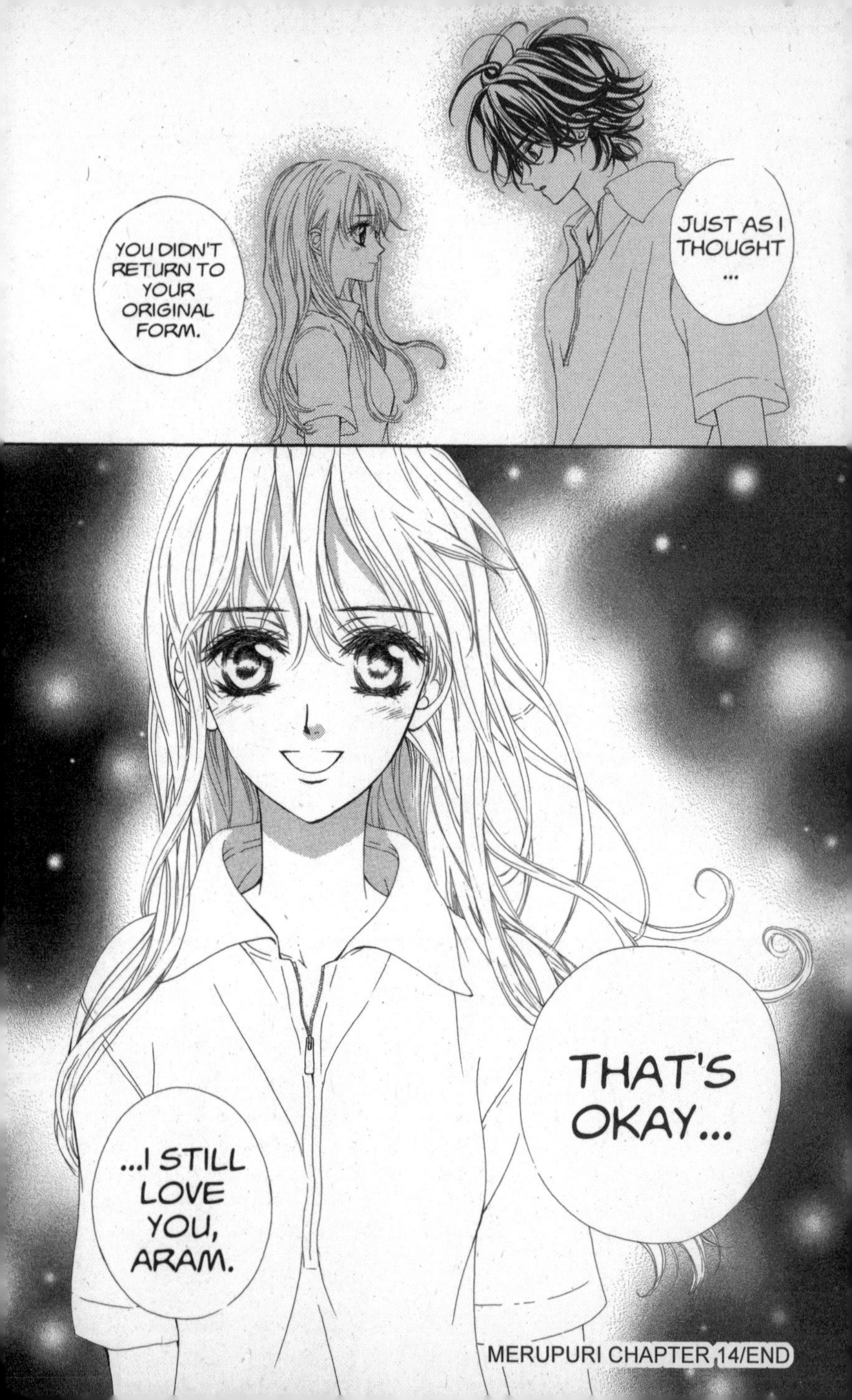
JUST AS I THOUGHT ...
YOU DIDN'T RETURN TO YOUR ORIGINAL FORM.
THAT'S OKAY...
...I STILL LOVE YOU, ARAM.
MERUPURI CHAPTER 14/END

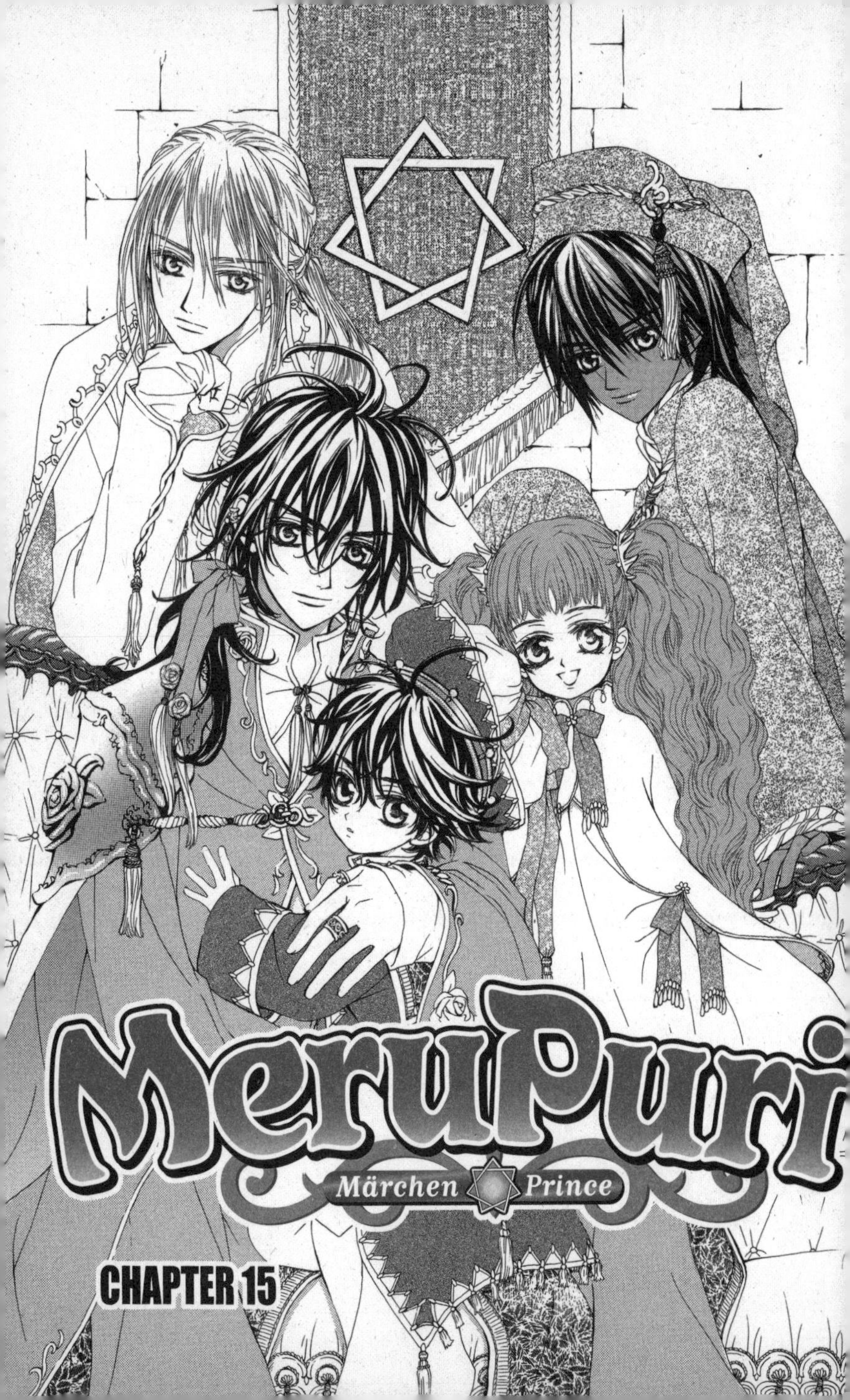
MeruPuri
Märchen Prince
CHAPTER 15

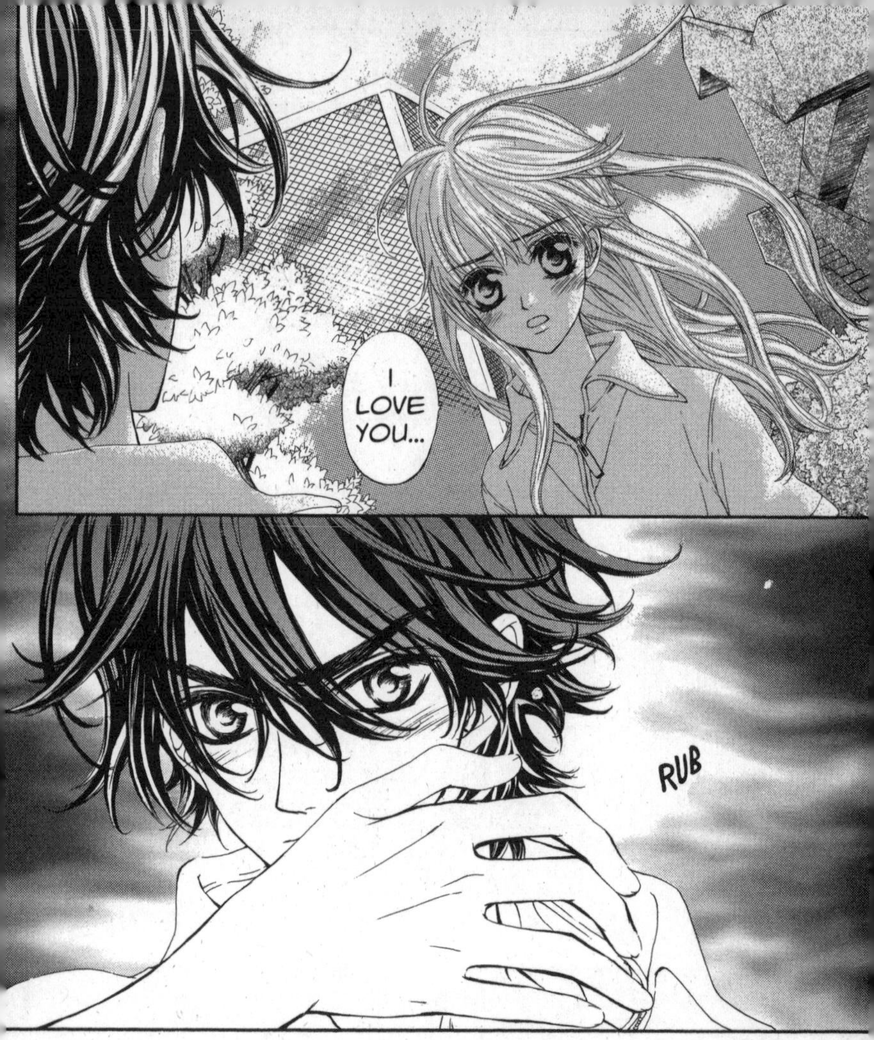
I LOVE YOU...
RUB

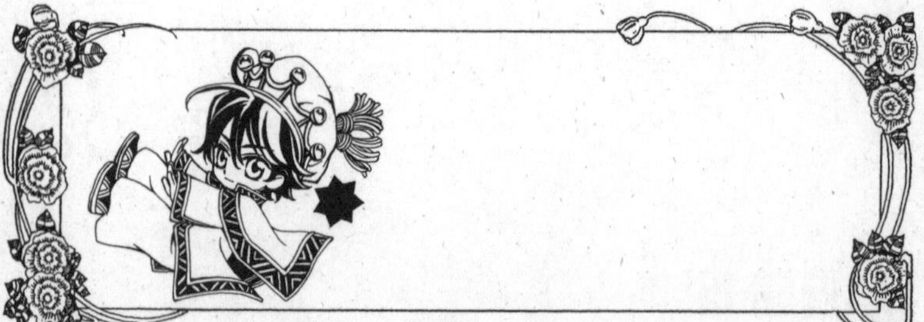

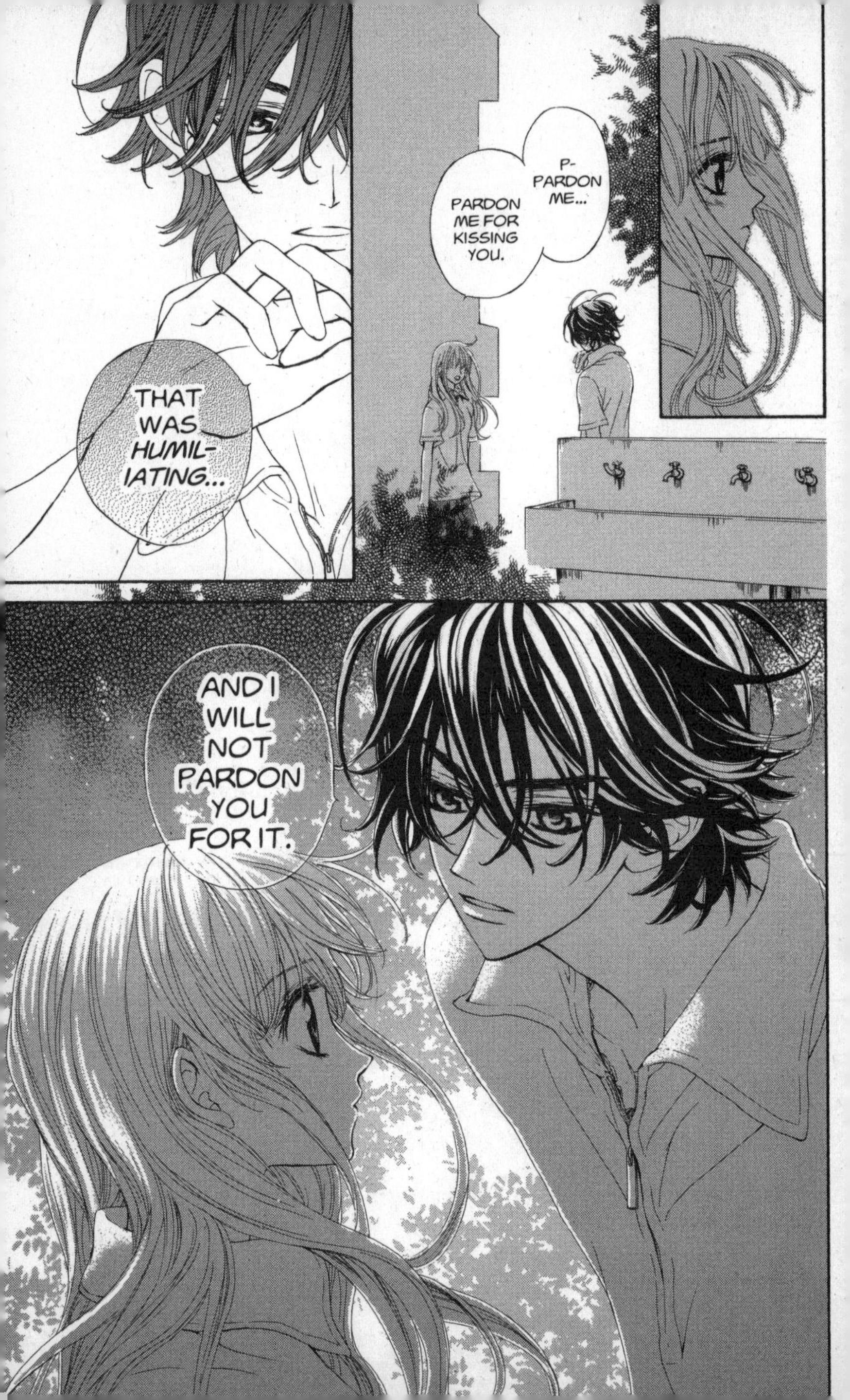
P-PARDON ME...
PARDON ME FOR KISSING YOU.
THAT WAS HUMILIATING...
AND I WILL NOT PARDON YOU FOR IT.

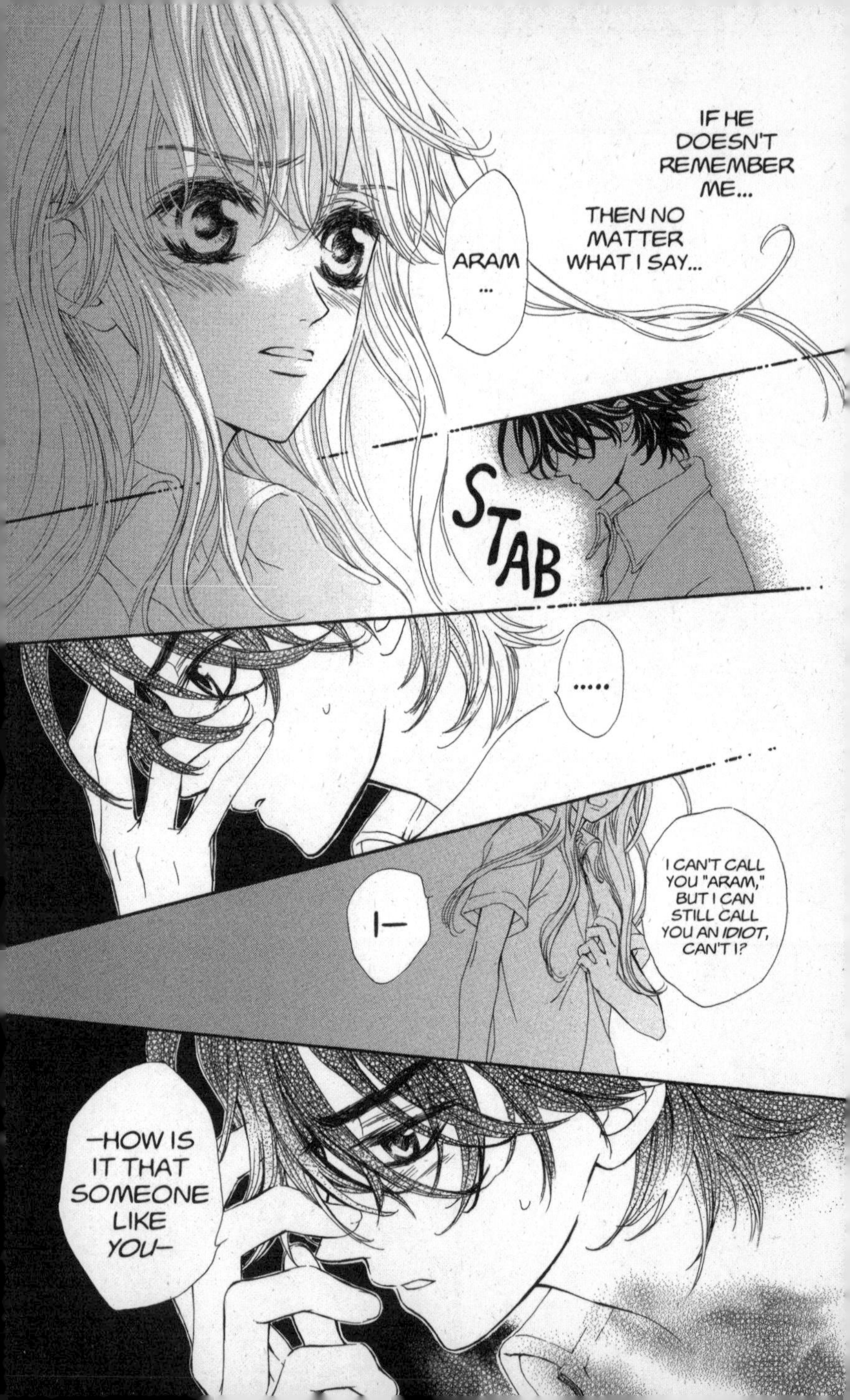

IF HE DOESN'T REMEMBER ME...
THEN NO MATTER WHAT I SAY...
ARAM ...
STAB
.....
I CAN'T CALL YOU "ARAM," BUT I CAN STILL CALL YOU AN *IDIOT*, CAN'T I?
I—
—HOW IS IT THAT SOMEONE LIKE *YOU*—

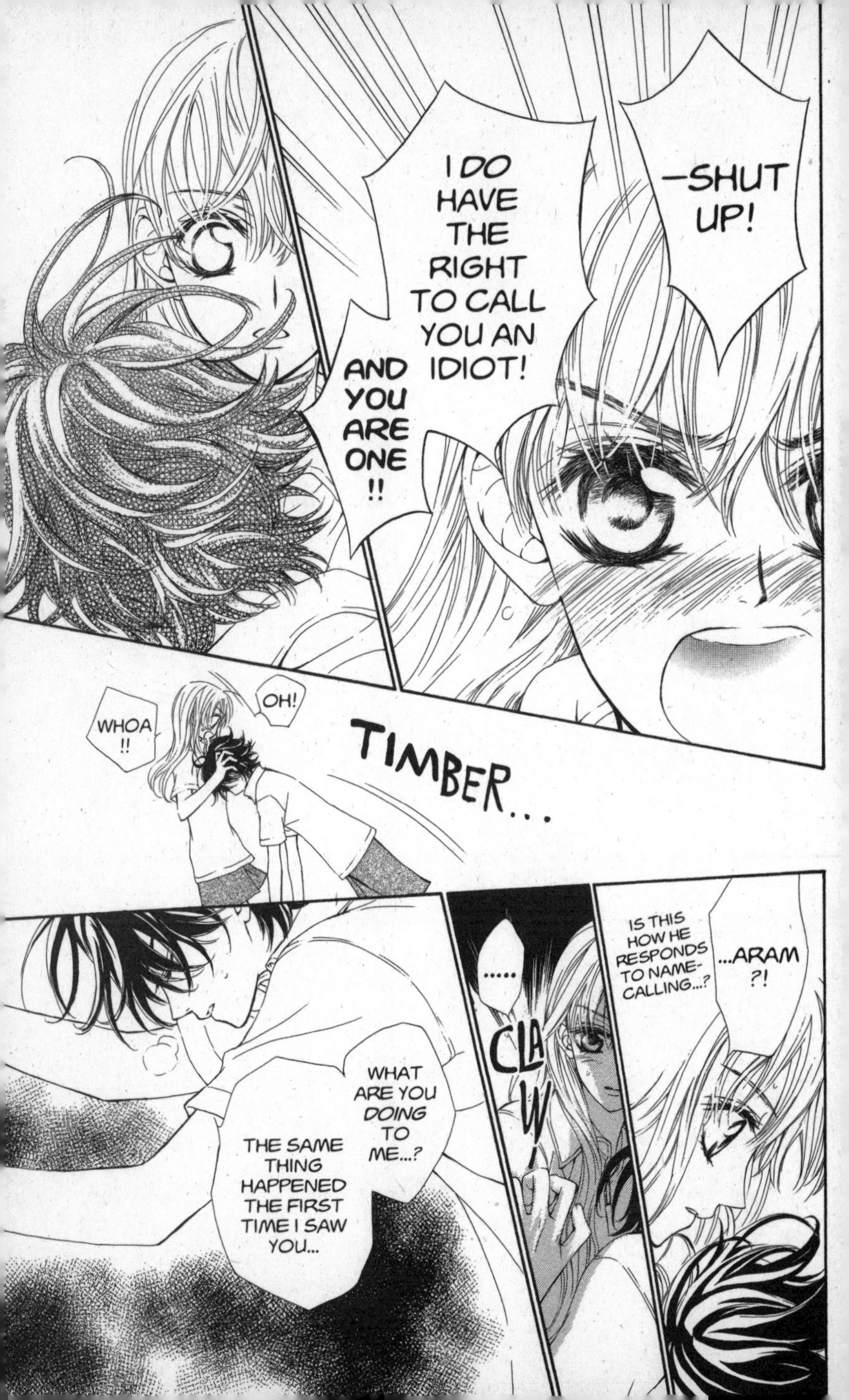

—SHUT UP!
I DO HAVE THE RIGHT TO CALL YOU AN IDIOT!
AND YOU ARE ONE !!
TIMBER...
OH!
WHOA !!
...ARAM ?!
IS THIS HOW HE RESPONDS TO NAME-CALLING...?
......
CLAW!
WHAT ARE YOU DOING TO ME...?
THE SAME THING HAPPENED THE FIRST TIME I SAW YOU...

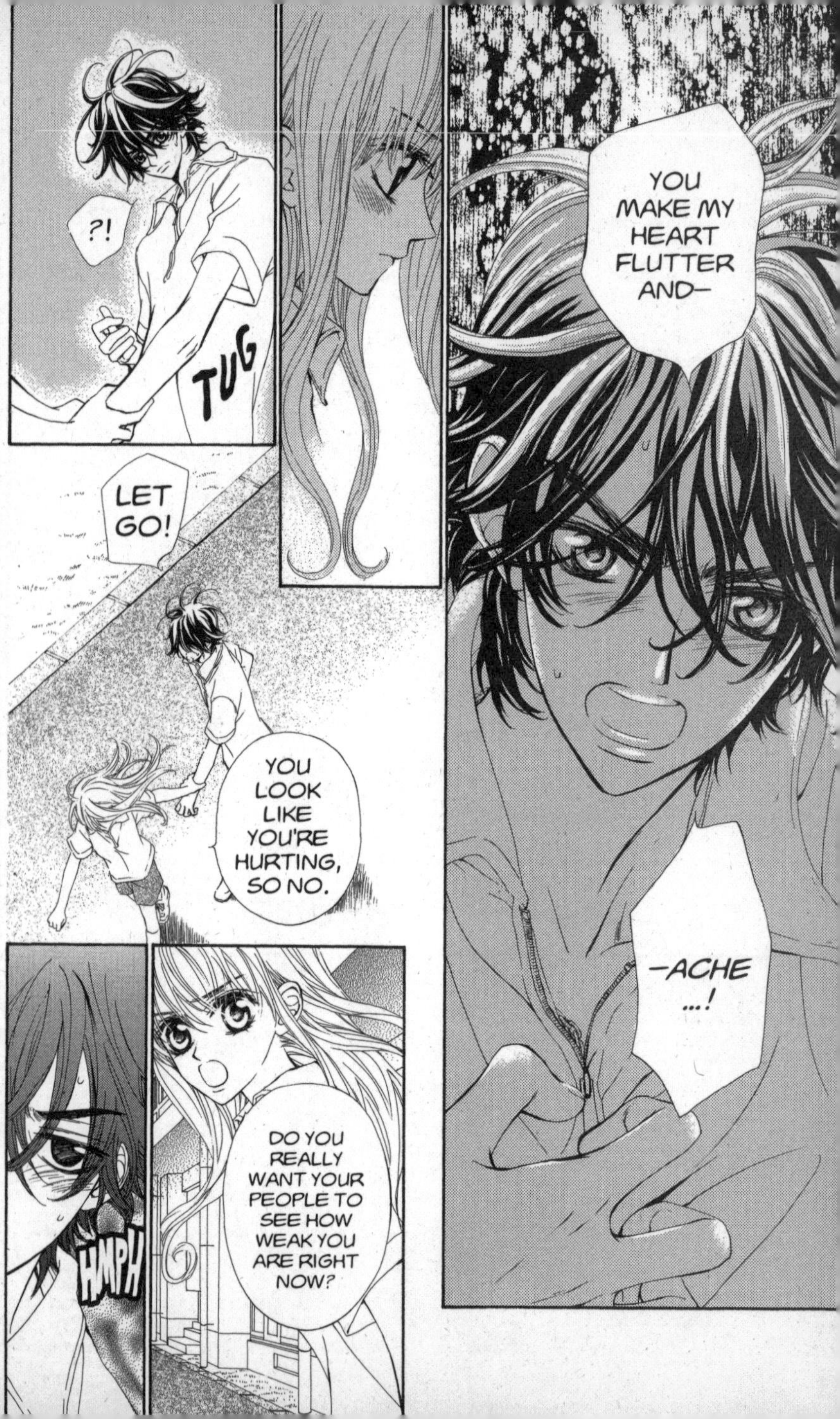
YOU MAKE MY HEART FLUTTER AND—
—ACHE ...!
?!
TUG
LET GO!
YOU LOOK LIKE YOU'RE HURTING, SO NO.
DO YOU REALLY WANT YOUR PEOPLE TO SEE HOW WEAK YOU ARE RIGHT NOW?
HMPH

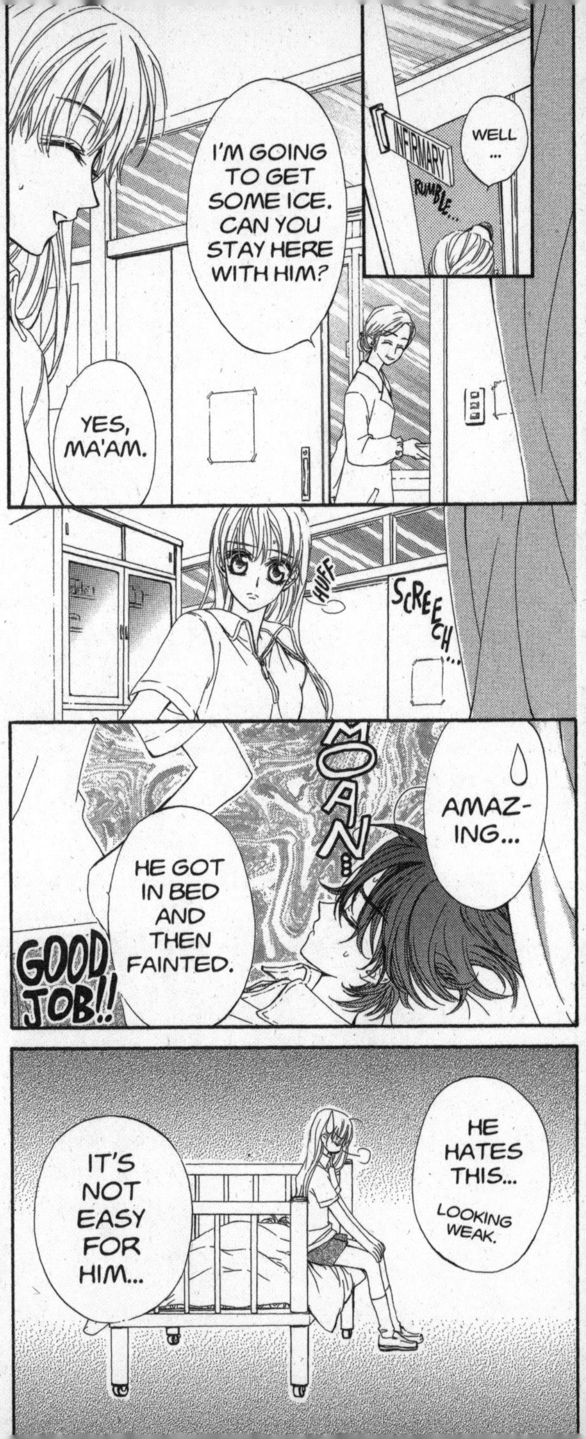
INFIRMARY
RUMBLE...
WELL ...
I'M GOING TO GET SOME ICE. CAN YOU STAY HERE WITH HIM?
YES, MA'AM.
SCREECH...
HUFF
AMAZ-ING...
MOAN...
HE GOT IN BED AND THEN FAINTED.
GOOD JOB!!
HE HATES THIS...
LOOKING WEAK.
IT'S NOT EASY FOR HIM...

IV

(Continued) More than anything, I longed to see Airi spurred into action by love...

Strangely confident that my readers would feel the same, I dropped Airi--whom I loved like my own child--into a bottomless pit of despair... (Ouch!).

In the midst of all that, drawing Jeile was pure joy! (Aah! ✿ It must be fun to be Jeile.) However, drawing Aram like he had permanent wrinkles between his eyebrows was not fun. Poor guy. If the dark didn't age him, the stress would!

Raz and Maria-bel: Airi's Enemies. Boy, do I have plans for the two of them! I know what they're doing and where they're going. I don't want to spoil Vol. 4, so I won't go into detail, but the keywords are "unfinished," "unstable," and "growth period."

...Or something like that. (Ha!)

Continued in V.

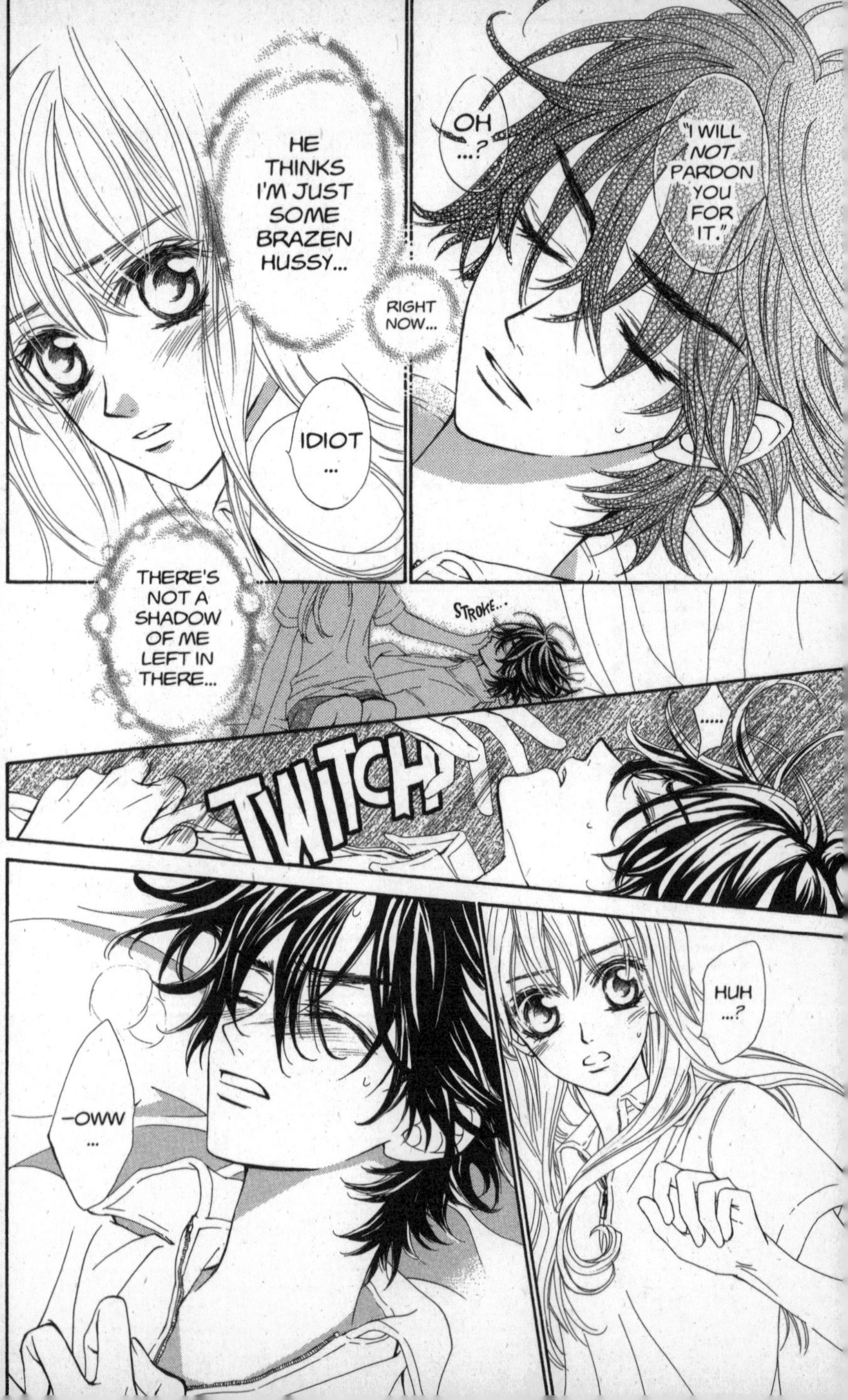
"I WILL NOT PARDON YOU FOR IT."
OH ...?
HE THINKS I'M JUST SOME BRAZEN HUSSY...
RIGHT NOW...
IDIOT ...
THERE'S NOT A SHADOW OF ME LEFT IN THERE...
STROKE...
......
TWITCH
HUH ...?
—OWW ...

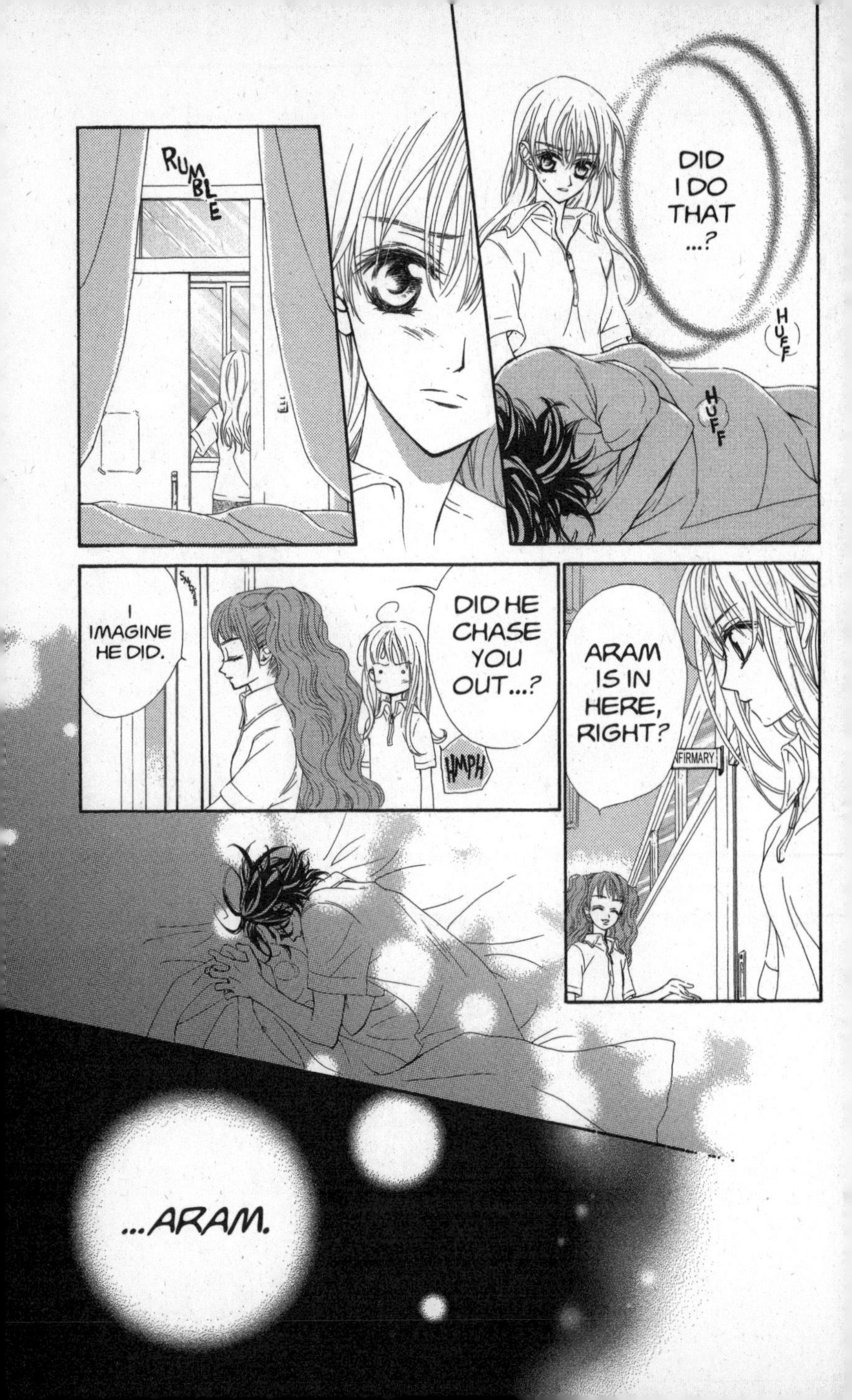
DID I DO THAT ...?
HUFF
HUFF
RUMBLE
ARAM IS IN HERE, RIGHT?
NFIRMARY
DID HE CHASE YOU OUT...?
HMPH
I IMAGINE HE DID.
...ARAM.

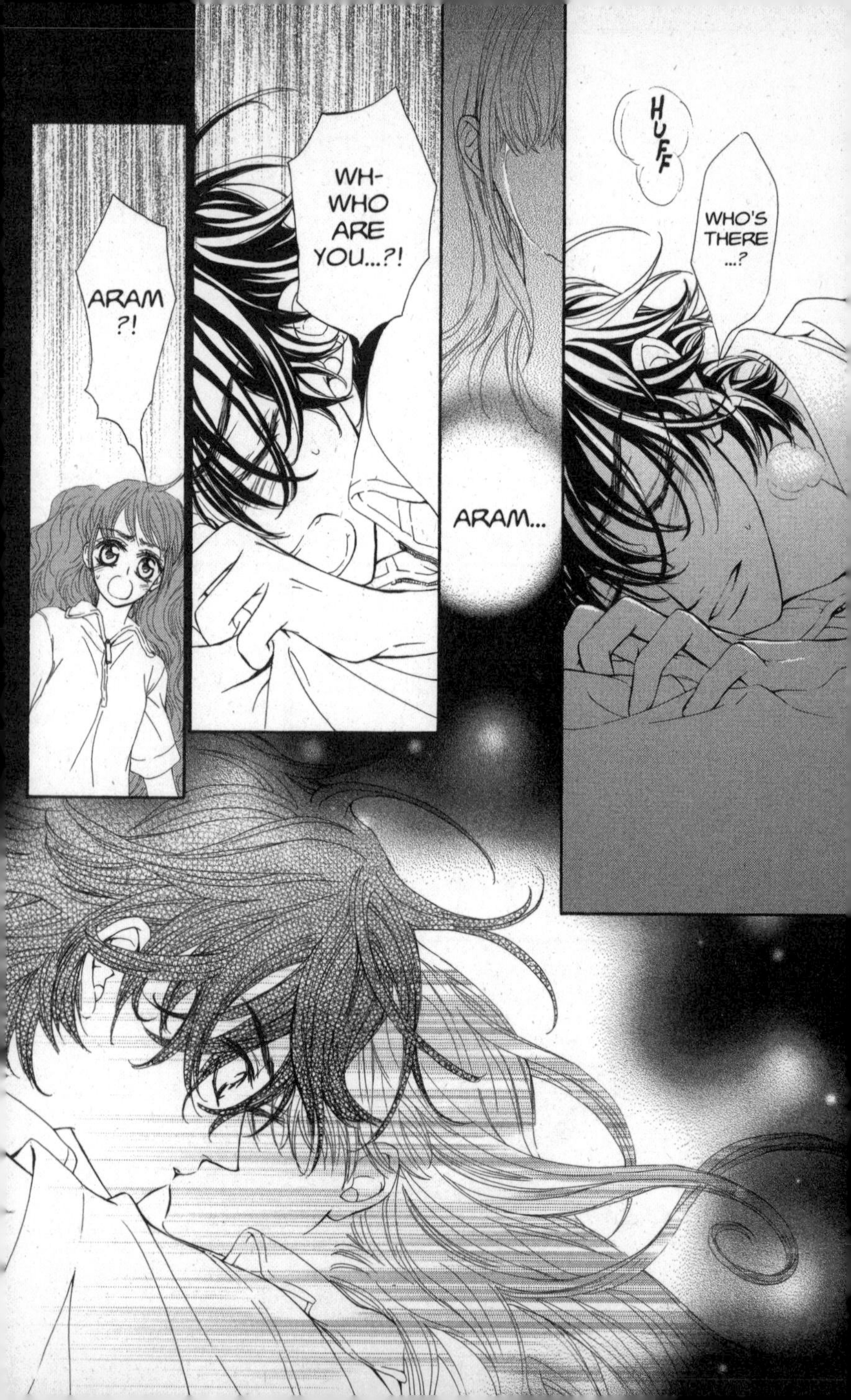
HUFF
WHO'S THERE ...?
ARAM...
WH- WHO ARE YOU...?!
ARAM ?!

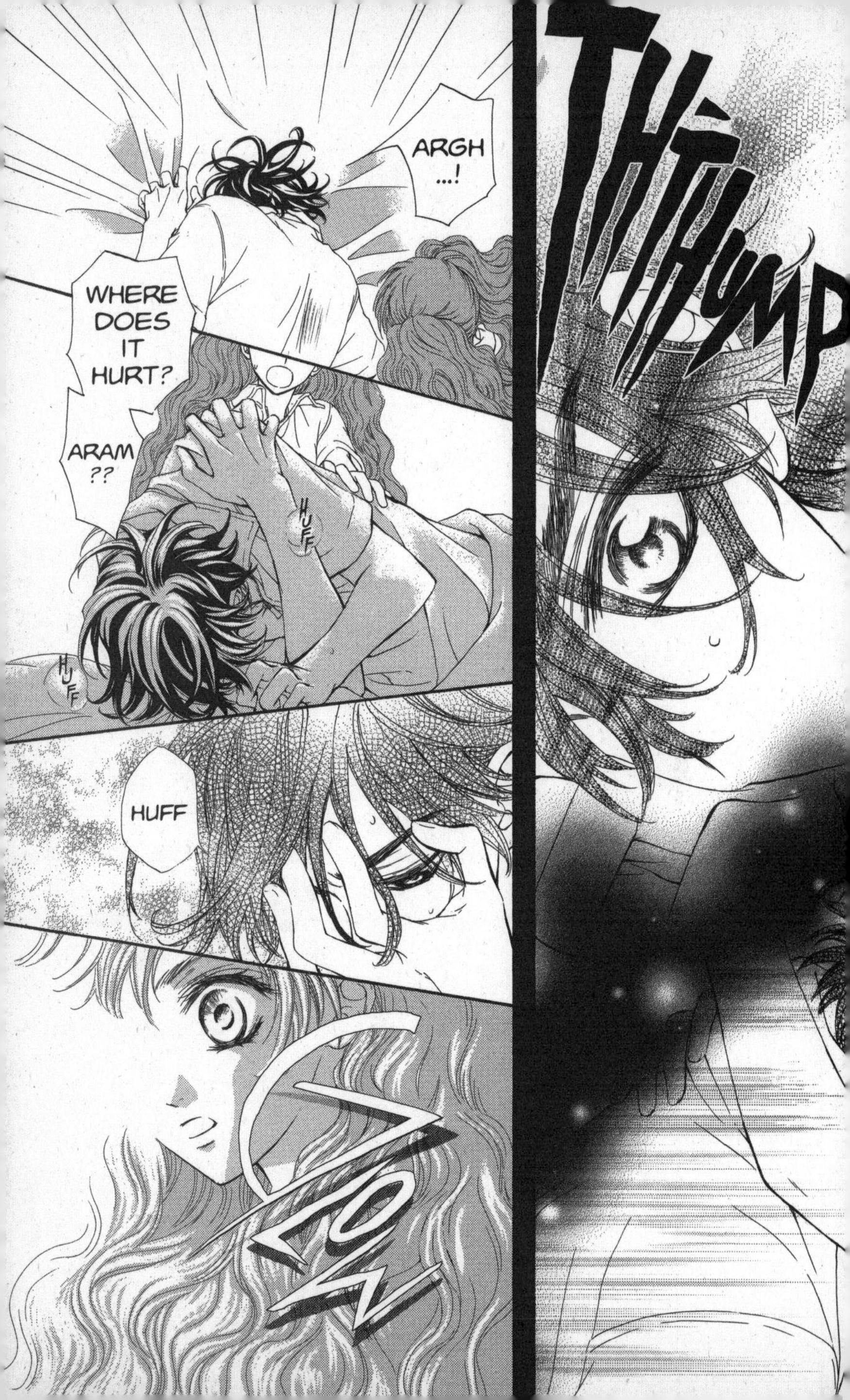
THTHUMP
ARGH ...!
WHERE DOES IT HURT?
ARAM ??
HUFF
HUFF
HUFF

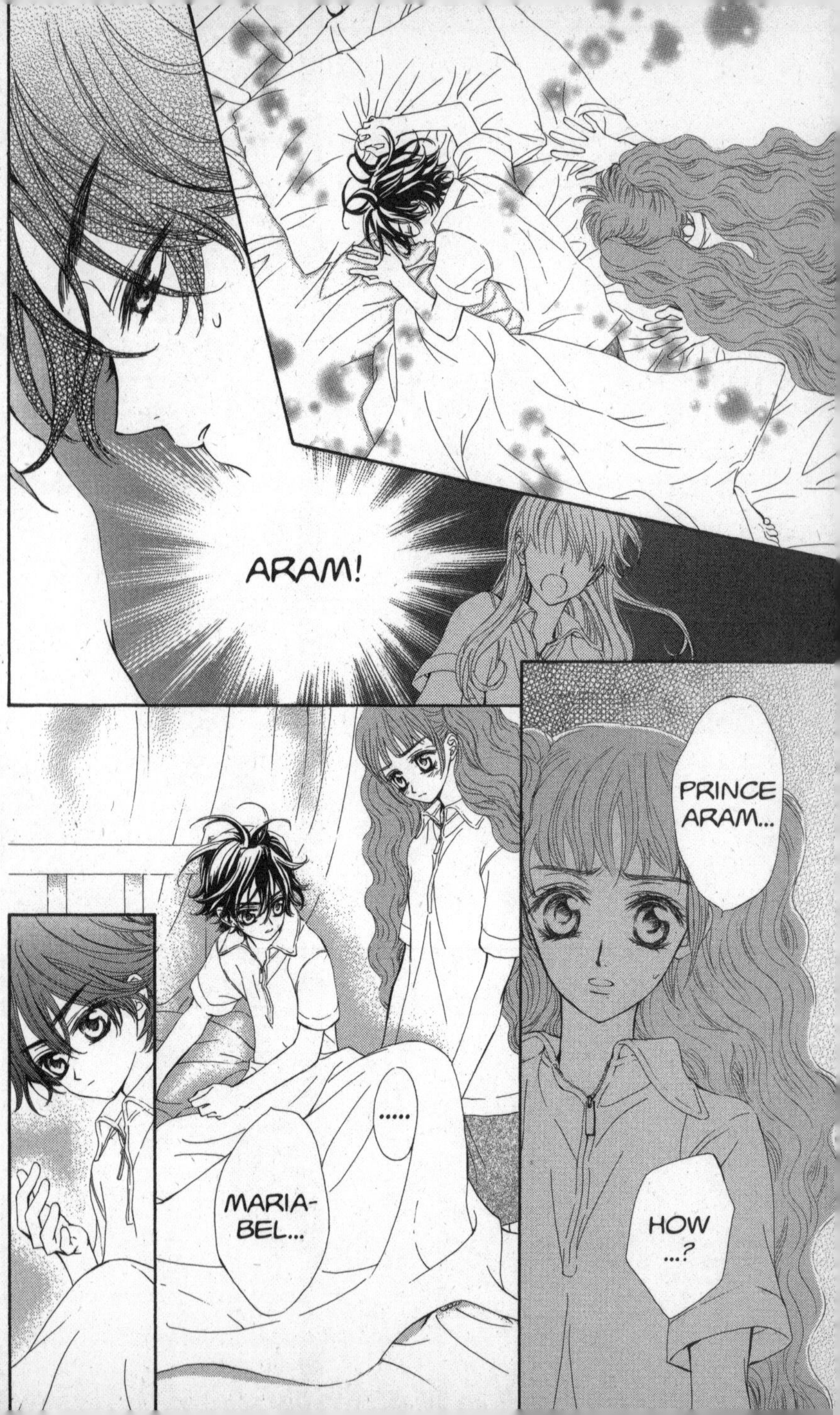
ARAM!
PRINCE ARAM...
HOW ...?
......
MARIA-BEL...

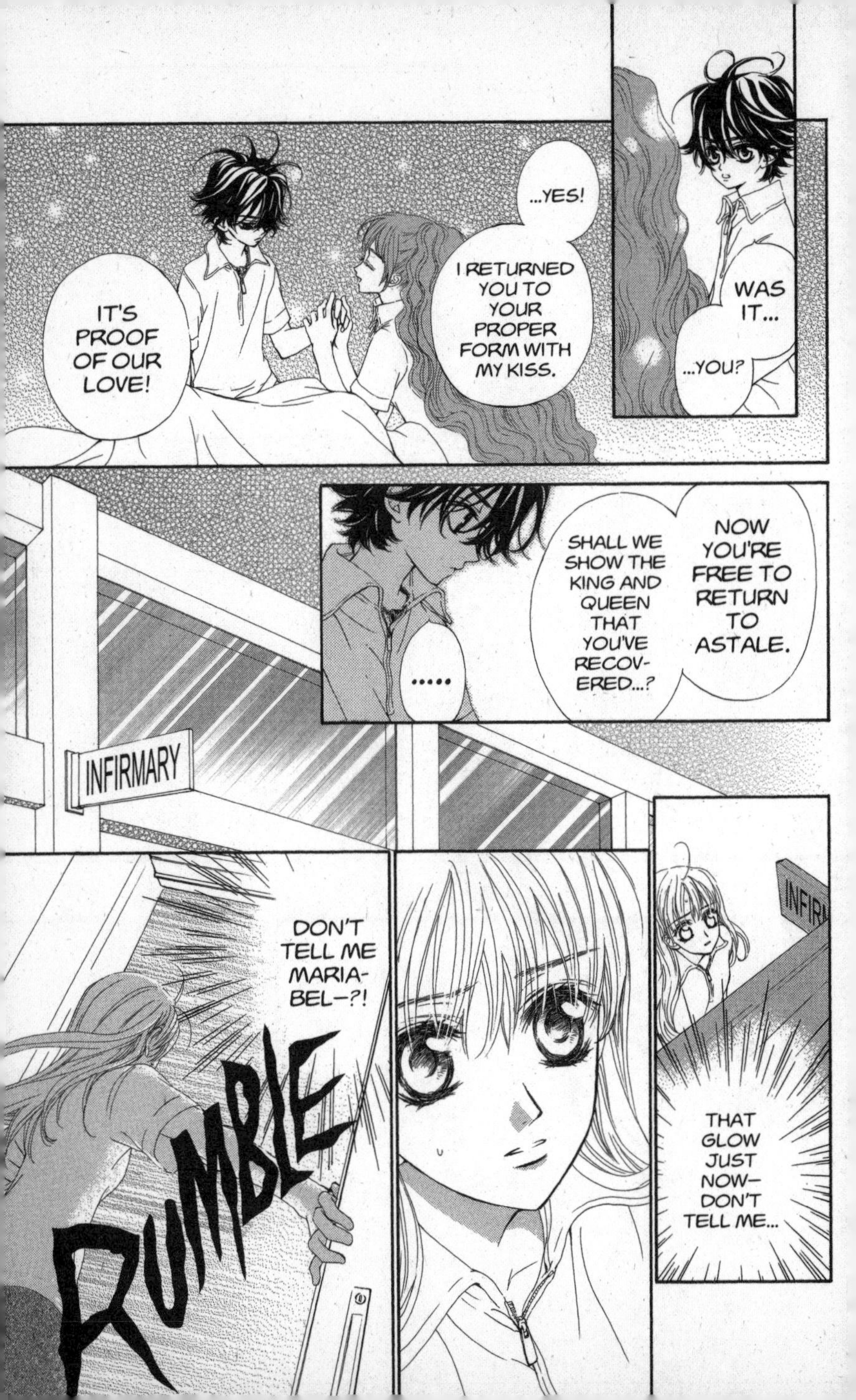
WAS IT...
...YOU?
...YES!
I RETURNED YOU TO YOUR PROPER FORM WITH MY KISS.
IT'S PROOF OF OUR LOVE!
NOW YOU'RE FREE TO RETURN TO ASTALE.
SHALL WE SHOW THE KING AND QUEEN THAT YOU'VE RECOVERED...?
......
INFIRMARY
INFIRM
THAT GLOW JUST NOW— DON'T TELL ME...
DON'T TELL ME MARIA-BEL—?!
RUMBLE

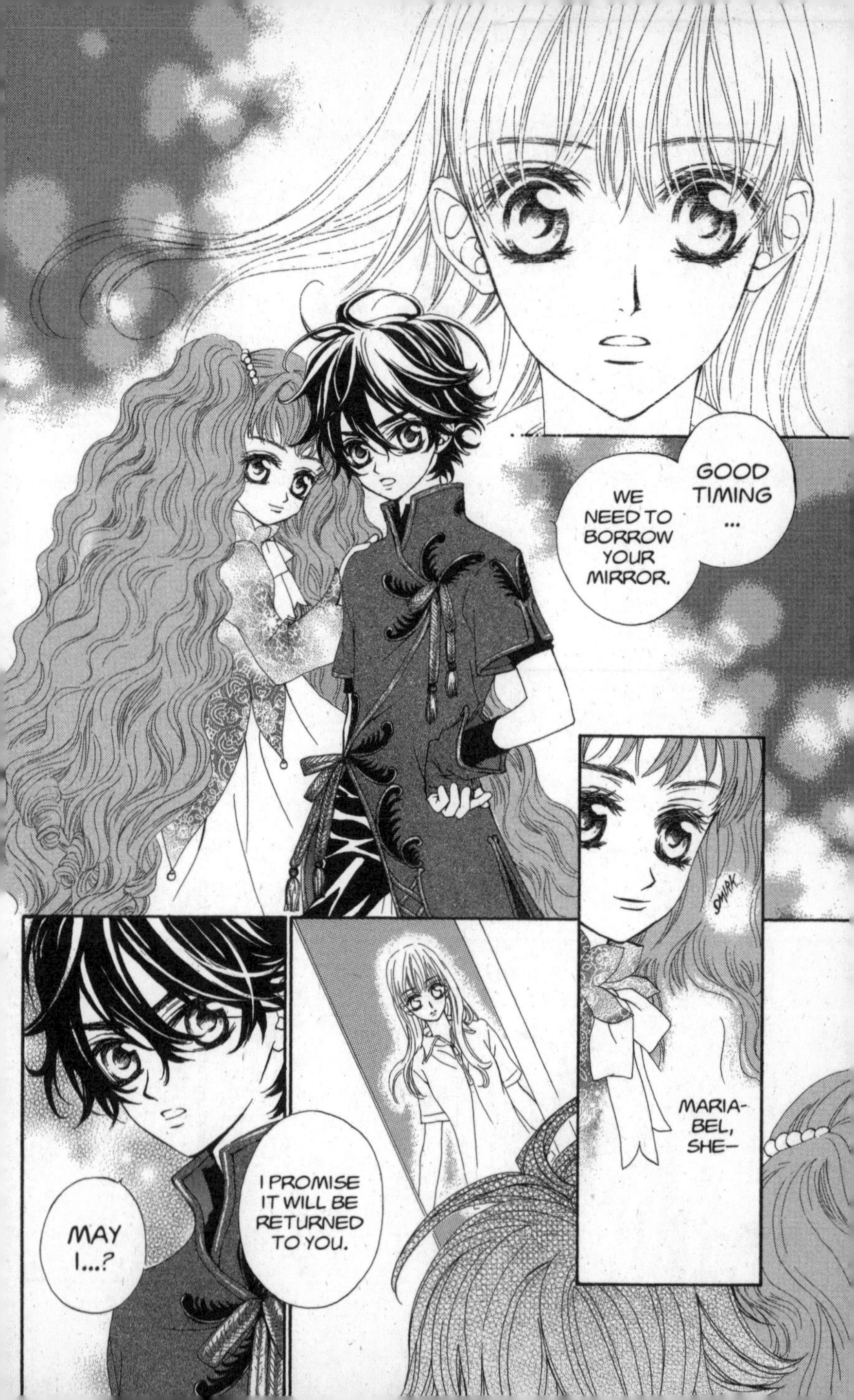
GOOD TIMING ...
WE NEED TO BORROW YOUR MIRROR.
SMIRK
MARIA-BEL, SHE–
I PROMISE IT WILL BE RETURNED TO YOU.
MAY I...?

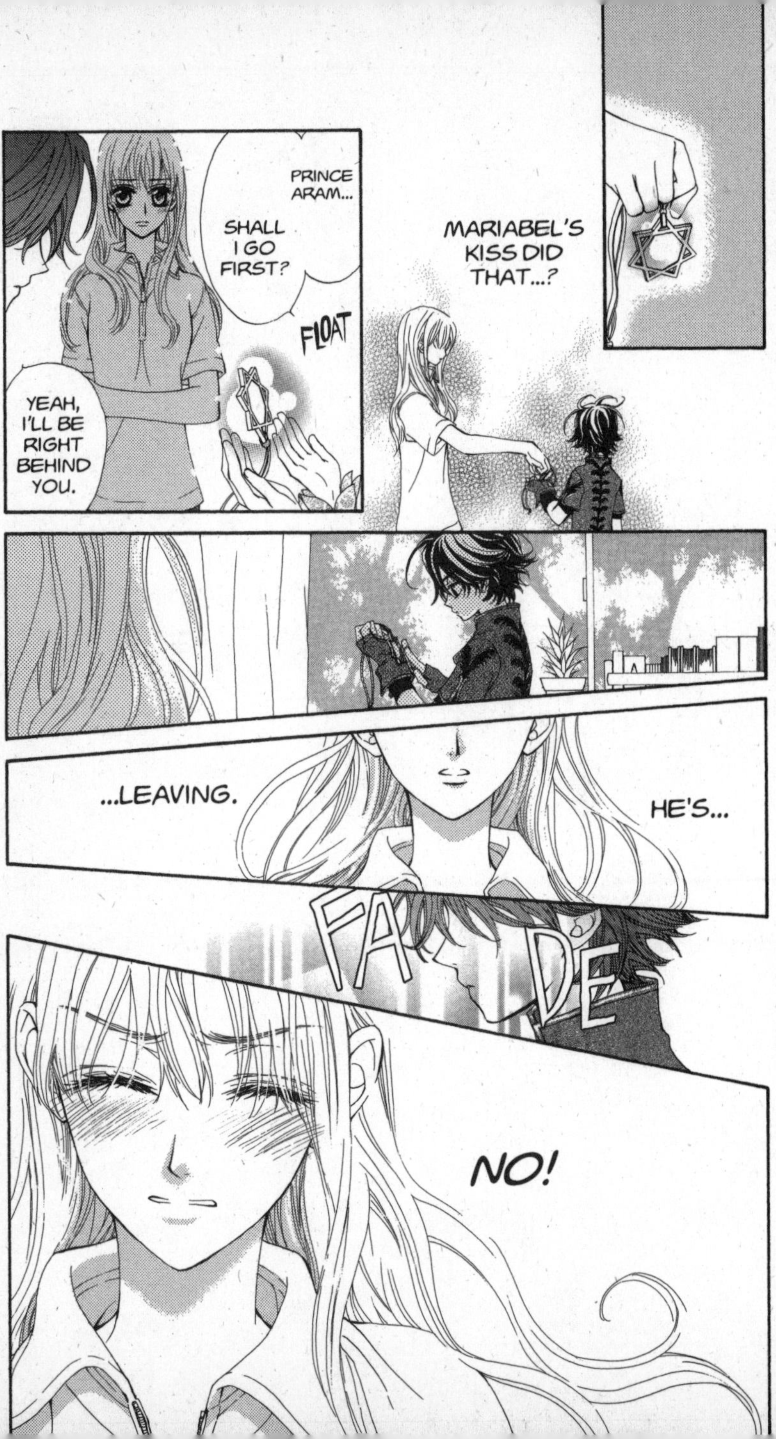
MARIABEL'S KISS DID THAT...?
PRINCE ARAM...
SHALL I GO FIRST?
FLOAT
YEAH, I'LL BE RIGHT BEHIND YOU.
HE'S...
...LEAVING.
FADE
NO!

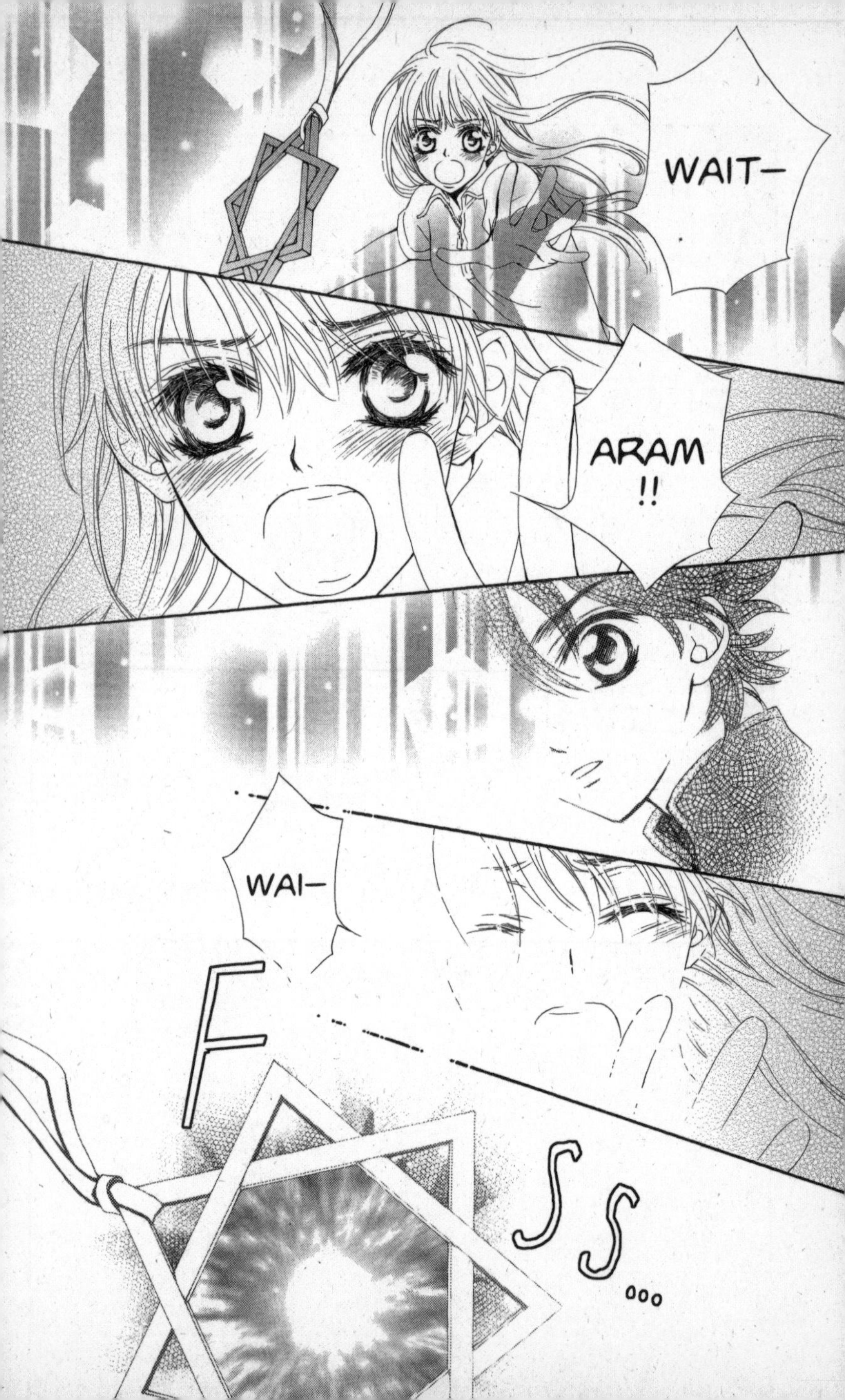
WAIT-
ARAM !!
WAI-
F
SS...

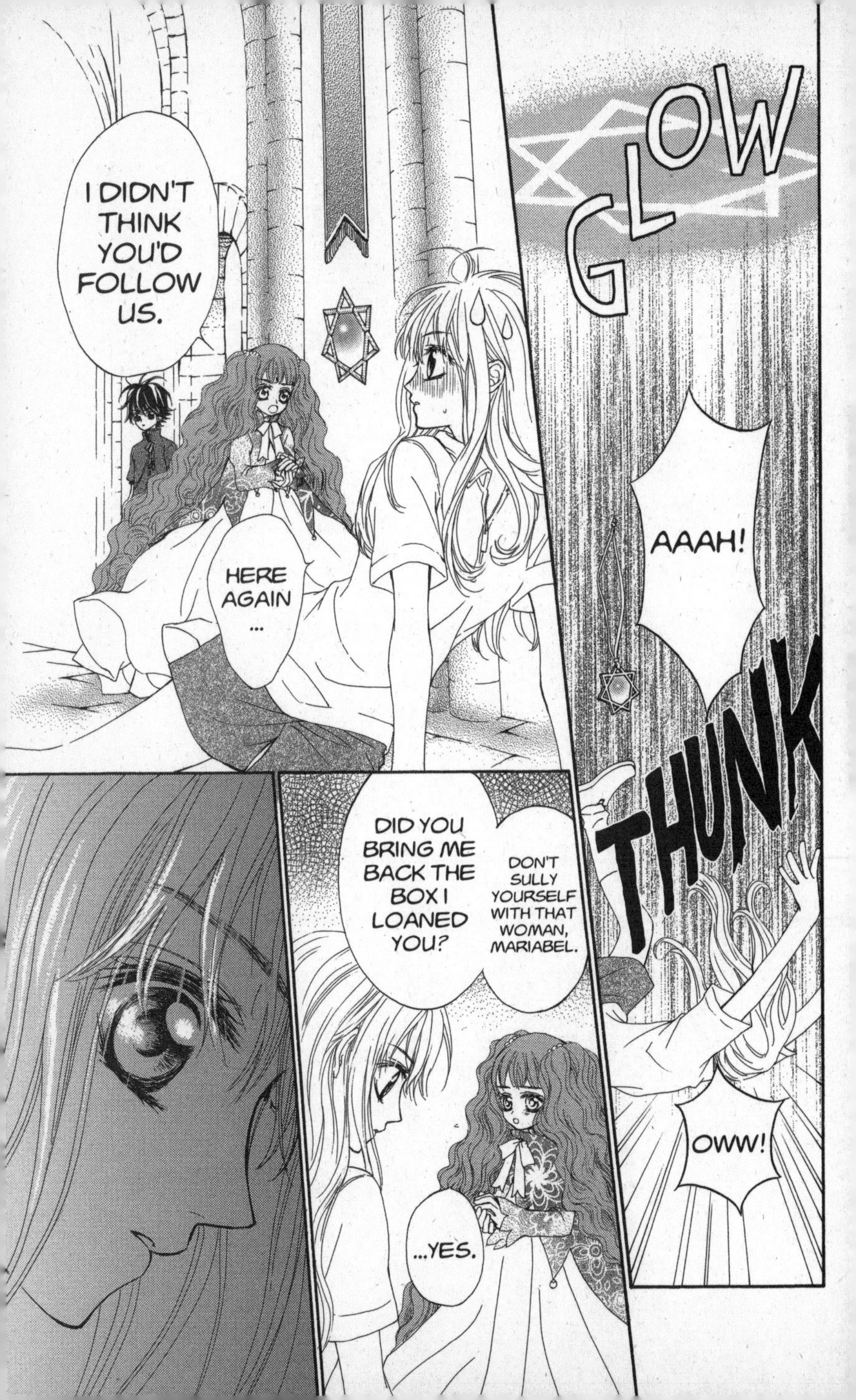
GLOW
AAAH!
THUNK
OWW!
I DIDN'T THINK YOU'D FOLLOW US.
HERE AGAIN ...
DON'T SULLY YOURSELF WITH THAT WOMAN, MARIABEL.
DID YOU BRING ME BACK THE BOX I LOANED YOU?
...YES.

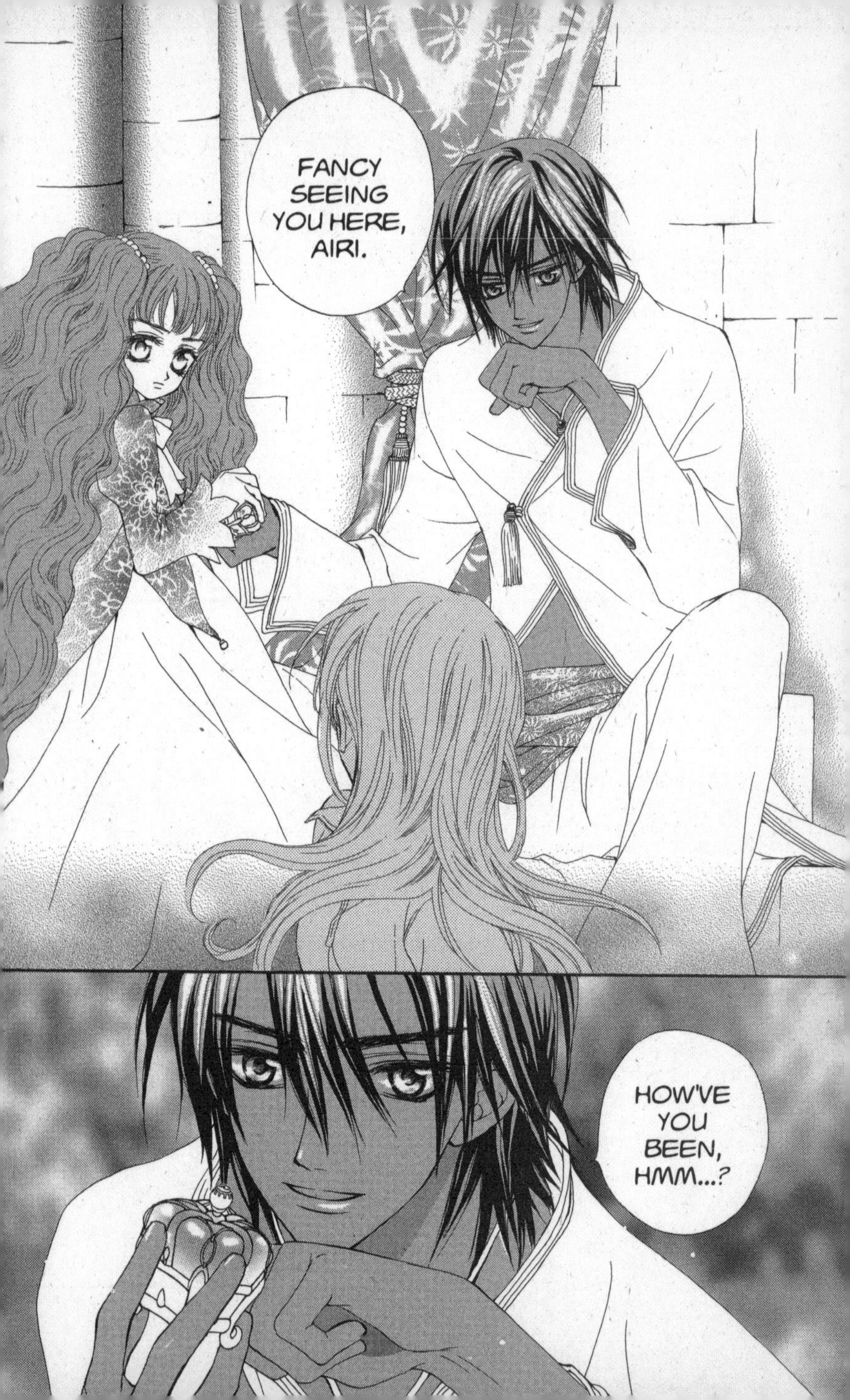
FANCY SEEING YOU HERE, AIRI.
HOW'VE YOU BEEN, HMM...?

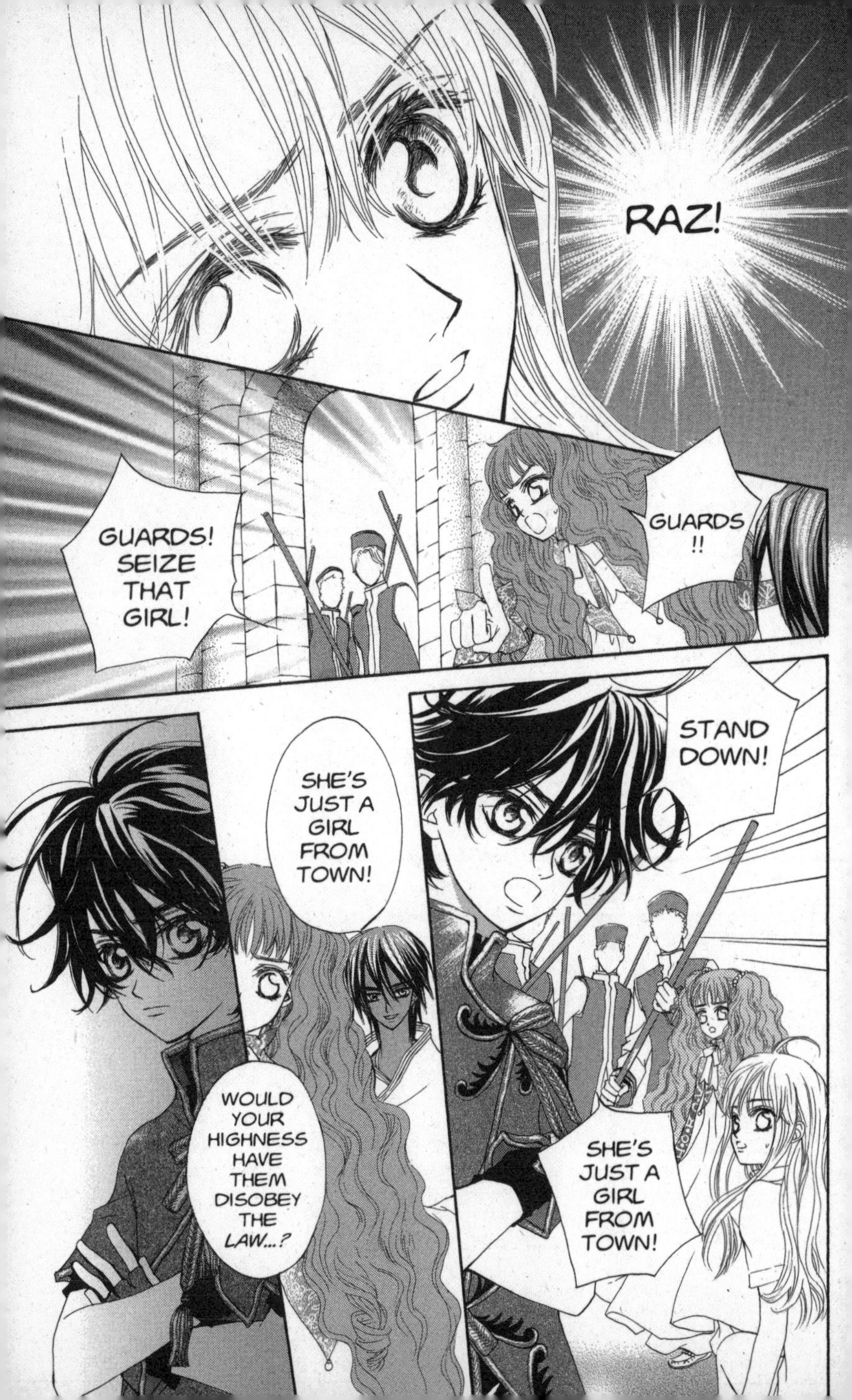
RAZ!
GUARDS !!
GUARDS! SEIZE THAT GIRL!
STAND DOWN!
SHE'S JUST A GIRL FROM TOWN!
SHE'S JUST A GIRL FROM TOWN!
WOULD YOUR HIGHNESS HAVE THEM DISOBEY THE LAW...?

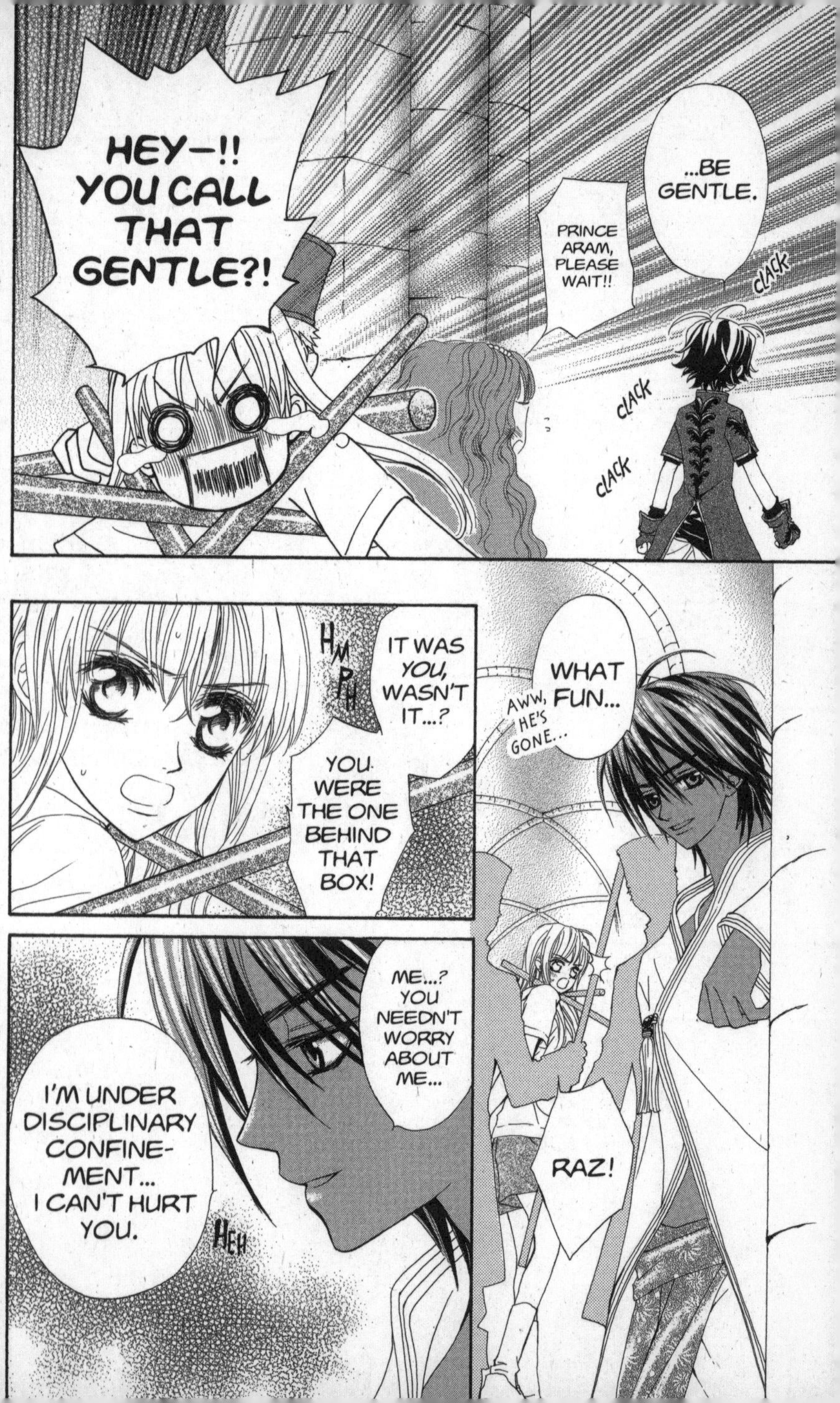
...BE GENTLE.
PRINCE ARAM, PLEASE WAIT!!
CLACK
CLACK
CLACK
HEY—!! YOU CALL THAT GENTLE?!
WHAT FUN...
AWW, HE'S GONE...
RAZ!
HMPH
IT WAS YOU, WASN'T IT...?
YOU WERE THE ONE BEHIND THAT BOX!
ME...? YOU NEEDN'T WORRY ABOUT ME...
I'M UNDER DISCIPLINARY CONFINE-MENT... I CAN'T HURT YOU.
HEH

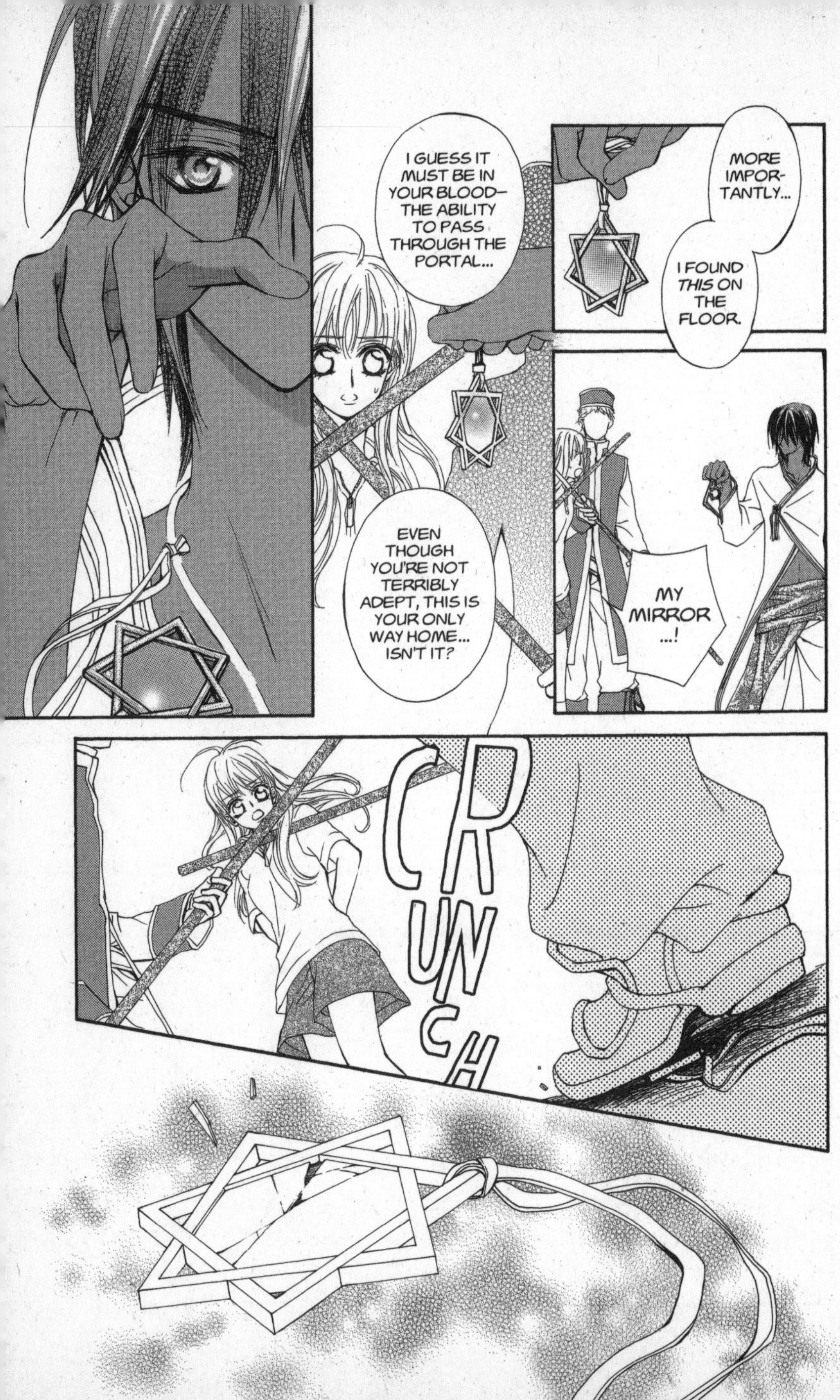

MORE IMPORTANTLY...
I FOUND *THIS* ON THE FLOOR.
MY MIRROR ...!
I GUESS IT MUST BE IN YOUR BLOOD— THE ABILITY TO PASS THROUGH THE PORTAL...
EVEN THOUGH YOU'RE NOT TERRIBLY ADEPT, THIS IS YOUR ONLY WAY HOME... ISN'T IT?
CRUNCH

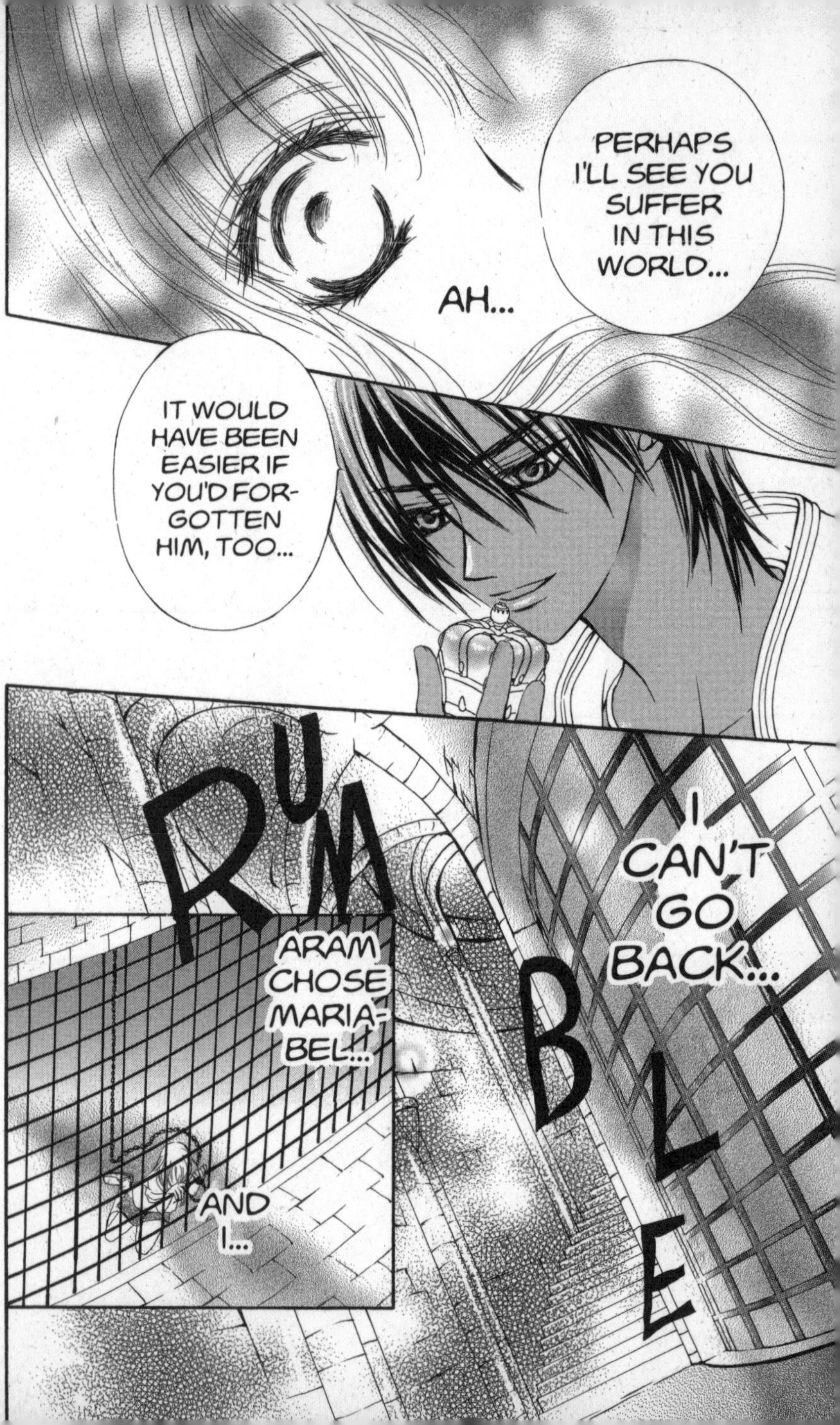
PERHAPS I'LL SEE YOU SUFFER IN THIS WORLD...
AH...
IT WOULD HAVE BEEN EASIER IF YOU'D FOR-GOTTEN HIM, TOO...
I CAN'T GO BACK...
RUMBLE
ARAM CHOSE MARIA-BEL...
AND I...

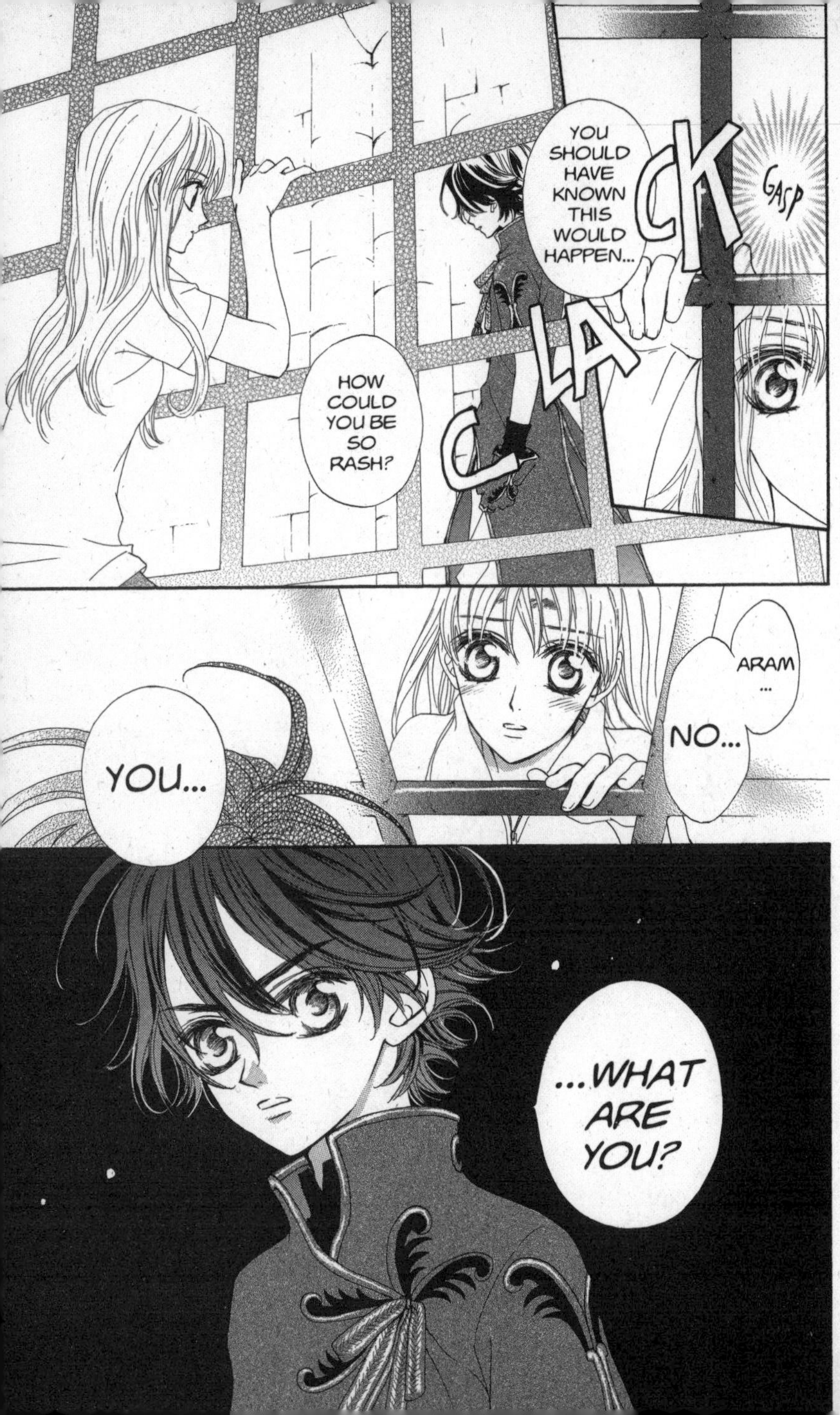
GASP
CLACK
YOU SHOULD HAVE KNOWN THIS WOULD HAPPEN...
HOW COULD YOU BE SO RASH?
ARAM ...
NO...
YOU...
...WHAT ARE YOU?

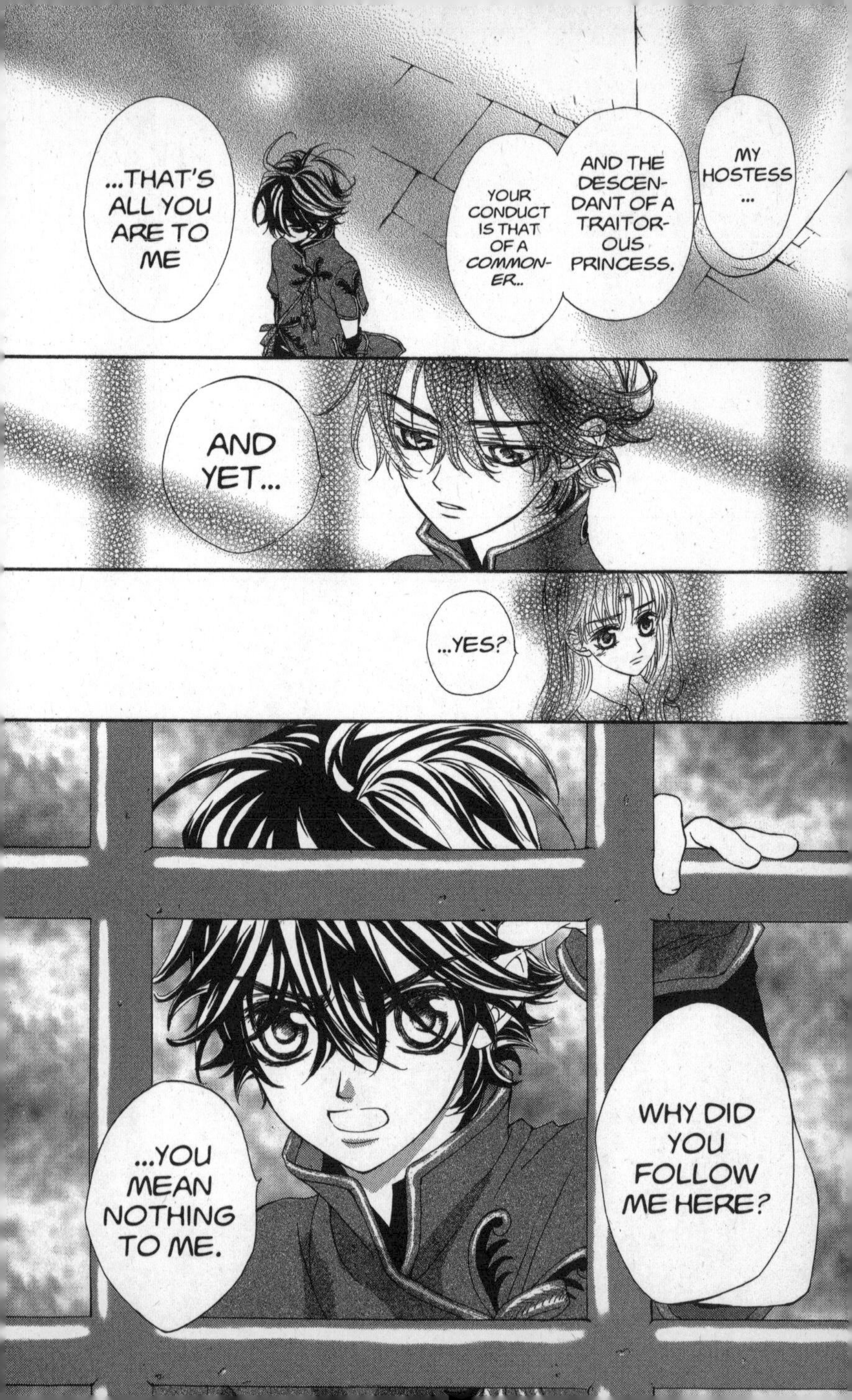
MY HOSTESS...
AND THE DESCENDANT OF A TRAITOROUS PRINCESS.
YOUR CONDUCT IS THAT OF A COMMONER...
...THAT'S ALL YOU ARE TO ME
AND YET...
...YES?
WHY DID YOU FOLLOW ME HERE?
...YOU MEAN NOTHING TO ME.

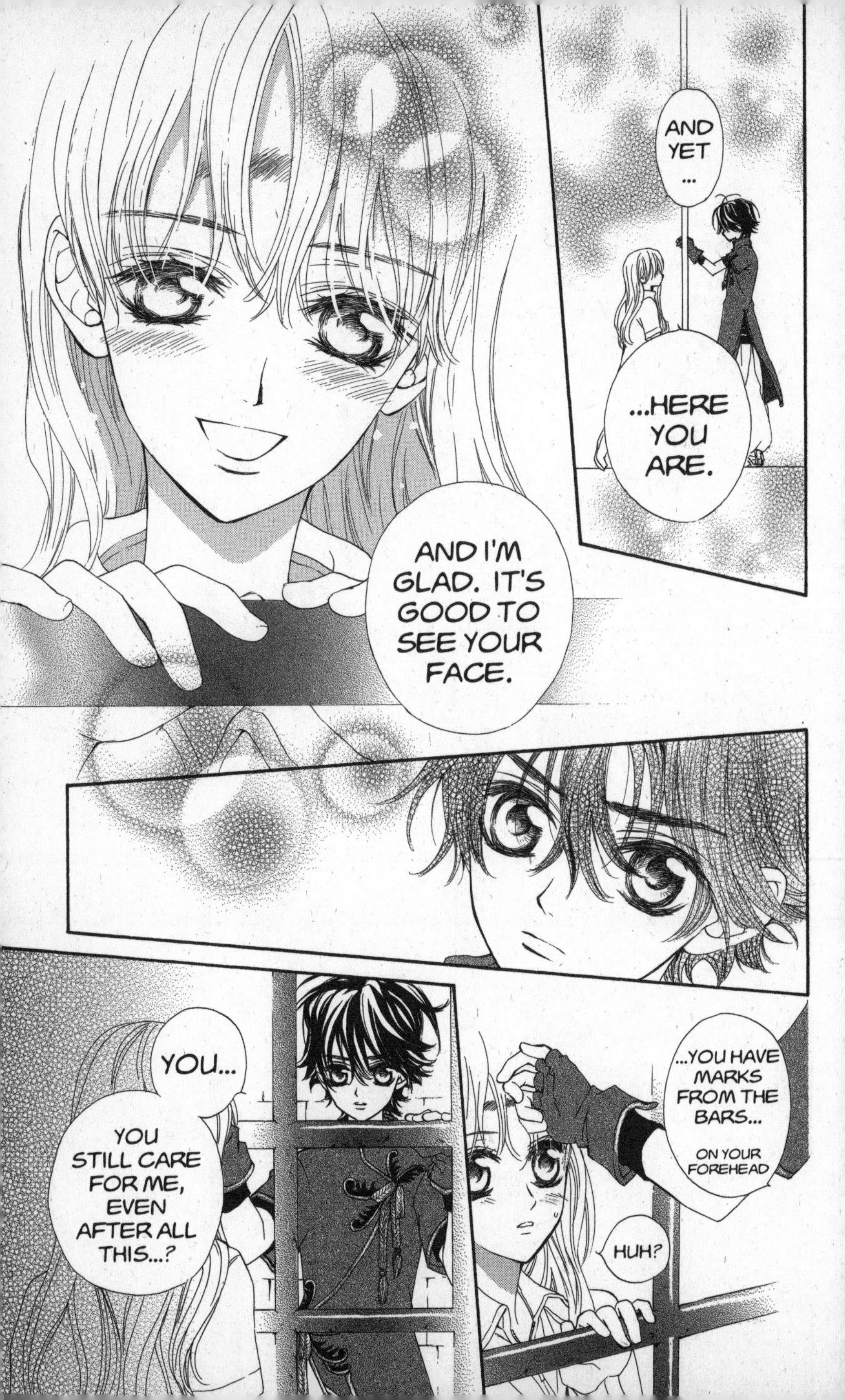
AND YET ...
...HERE YOU ARE.
AND I'M GLAD. IT'S GOOD TO SEE YOUR FACE.
...YOU HAVE MARKS FROM THE BARS...
ON YOUR FOREHEAD
HUH?
YOU...
YOU STILL CARE FOR ME, EVEN AFTER ALL THIS...?

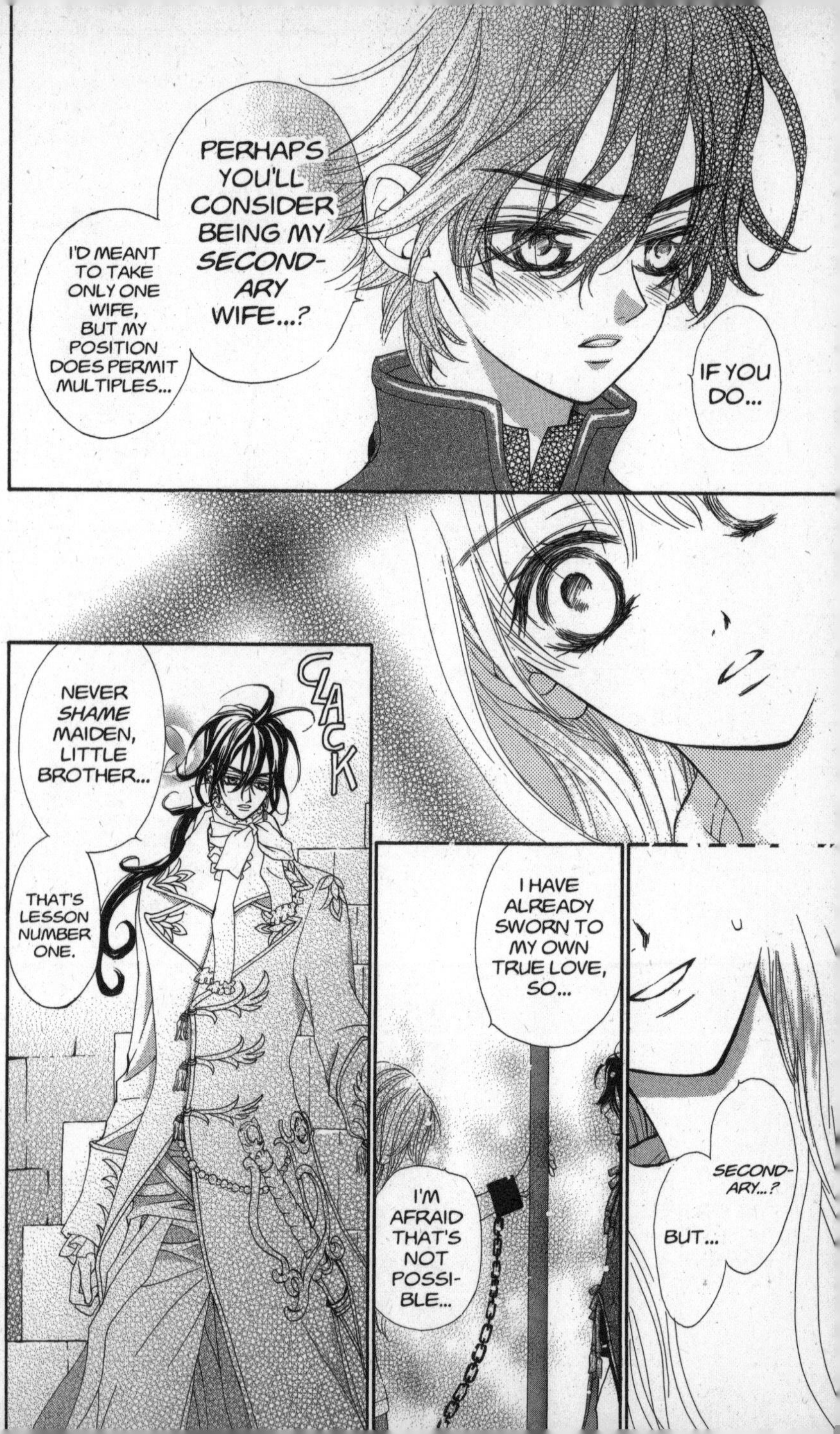
IF YOU DO...
PERHAPS YOU'LL CONSIDER BEING MY SECOND-ARY WIFE...?
I'D MEANT TO TAKE ONLY ONE WIFE, BUT MY POSITION DOES PERMIT MULTIPLES...
SECOND-ARY...?
BUT...
I HAVE ALREADY SWORN TO MY OWN TRUE LOVE, SO...
I'M AFRAID THAT'S NOT POSSI-BLE...
CLACK
NEVER *SHAME* MAIDEN, LITTLE BROTHER...
THAT'S LESSON NUMBER ONE.

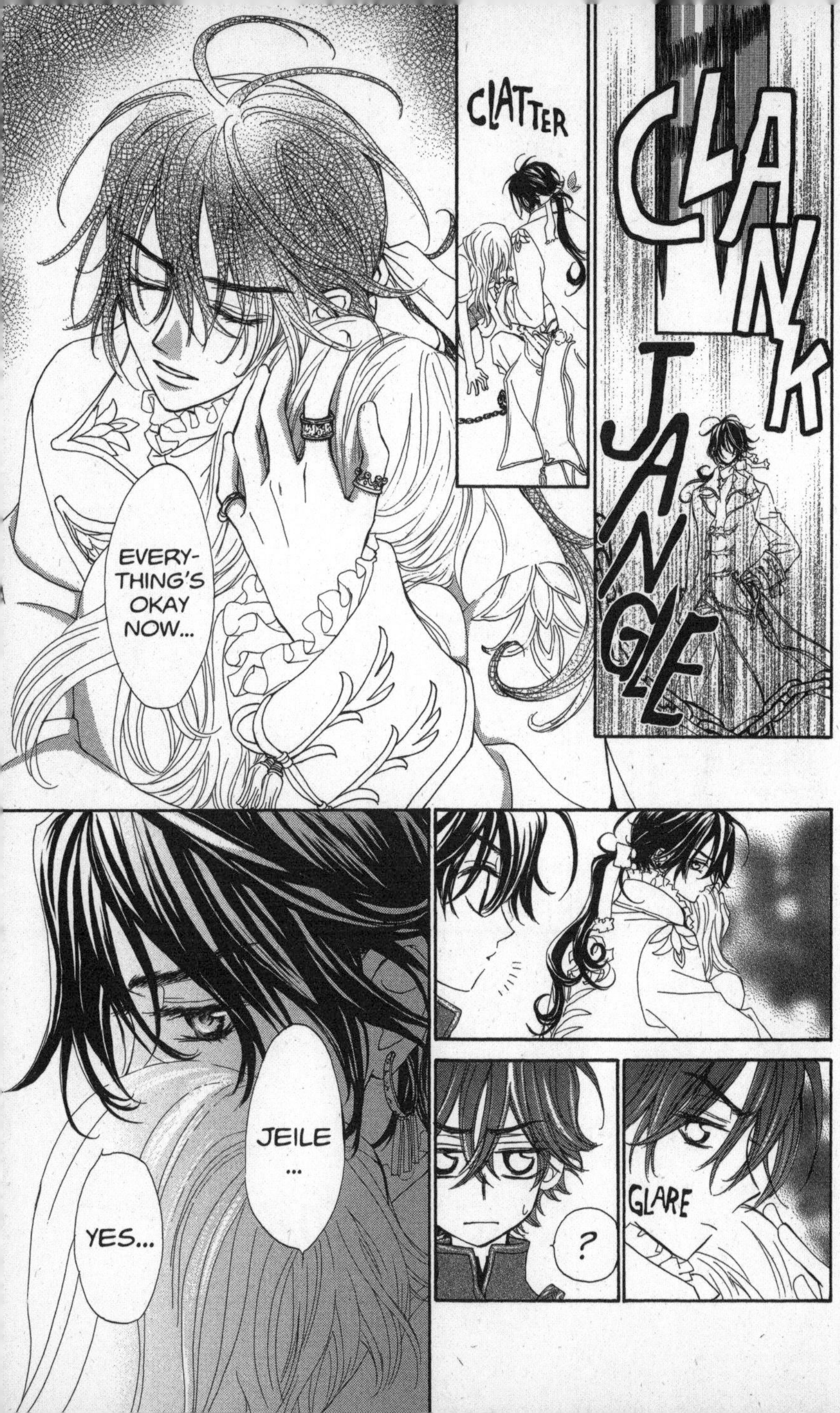
CLANK
JANGLE
CLATTER
EVERY-THING'S OKAY NOW...
GLARE
?
JEILE ...
YES...

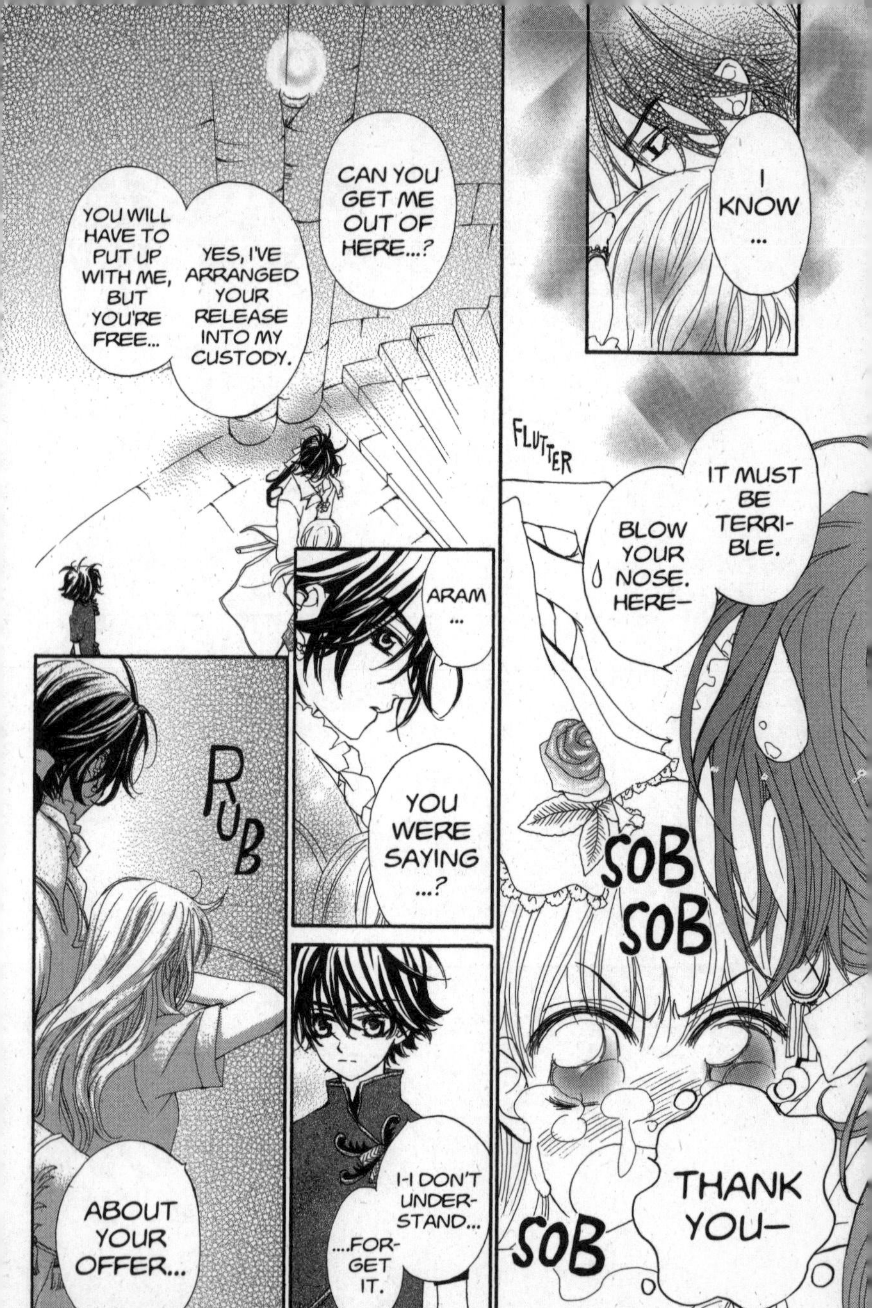
I KNOW ...
FLUTTER
IT MUST BE TERRIBLE.
BLOW YOUR NOSE. HERE–
SOB SOB
THANK YOU–
SOB
CAN YOU GET ME OUT OF HERE...?
YES, I'VE ARRANGED YOUR RELEASE INTO MY CUSTODY.
YOU WILL HAVE TO PUT UP WITH ME, BUT YOU'RE FREE...
ARAM ...
YOU WERE SAYING ...?
RUB
ABOUT YOUR OFFER...
I-I DON'T UNDERSTAND...
....FOR-GET IT.

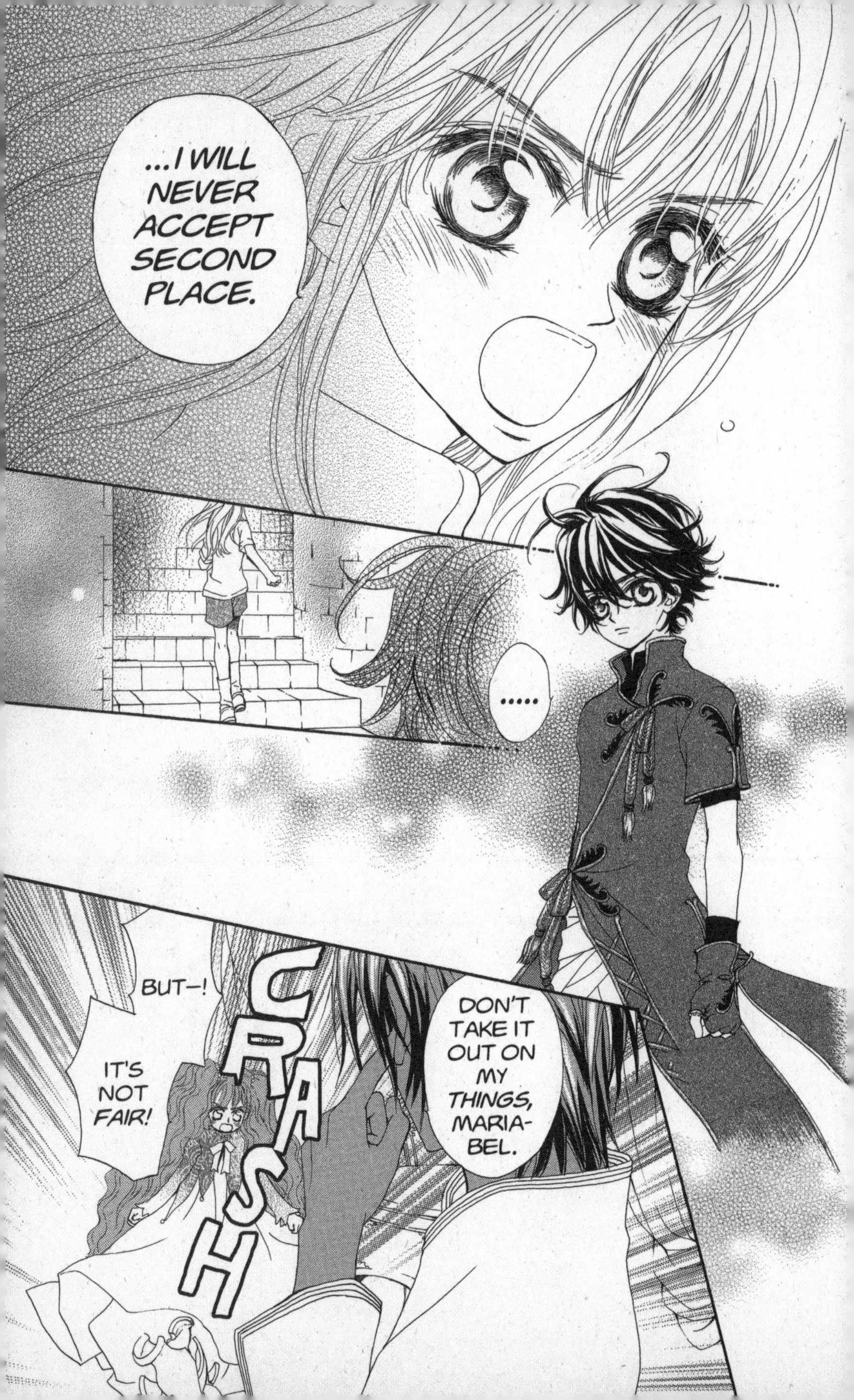
...I WILL NEVER ACCEPT SECOND PLACE.
.....
DON'T TAKE IT OUT ON MY THINGS, MARIA-BEL.
CRASH
BUT--!
IT'S NOT FAIR!

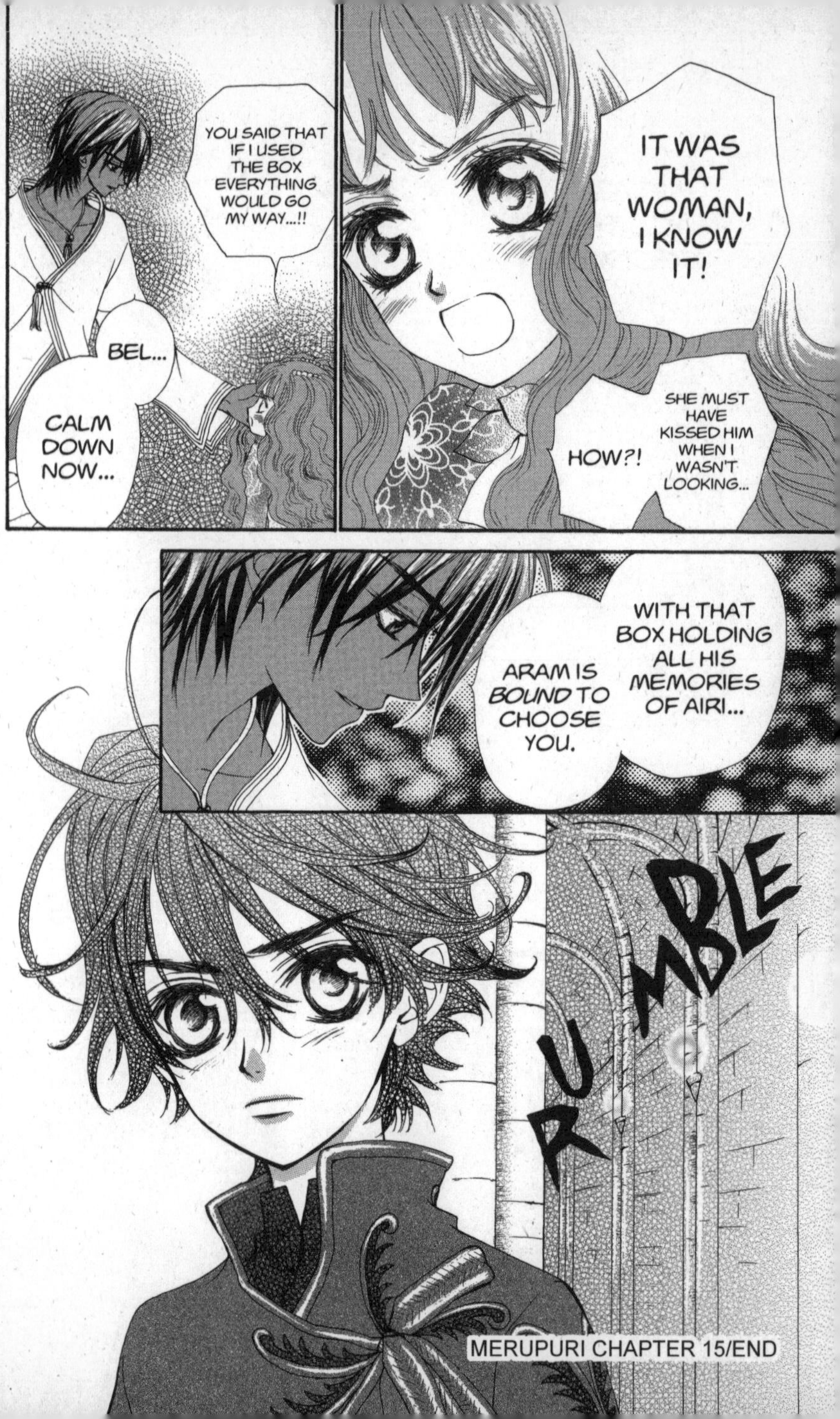
IT WAS THAT WOMAN, I KNOW IT!
SHE MUST HAVE KISSED HIM WHEN I WASN'T LOOKING...
HOW?!
YOU SAID THAT IF I USED THE BOX EVERYTHING WOULD GO MY WAY...!!
BEL...
CALM DOWN NOW...
WITH THAT BOX HOLDING ALL HIS MEMORIES OF AIRI...
ARAM IS *BOUND* TO CHOOSE YOU.
RUMBLE
MERUPURI CHAPTER 15/END

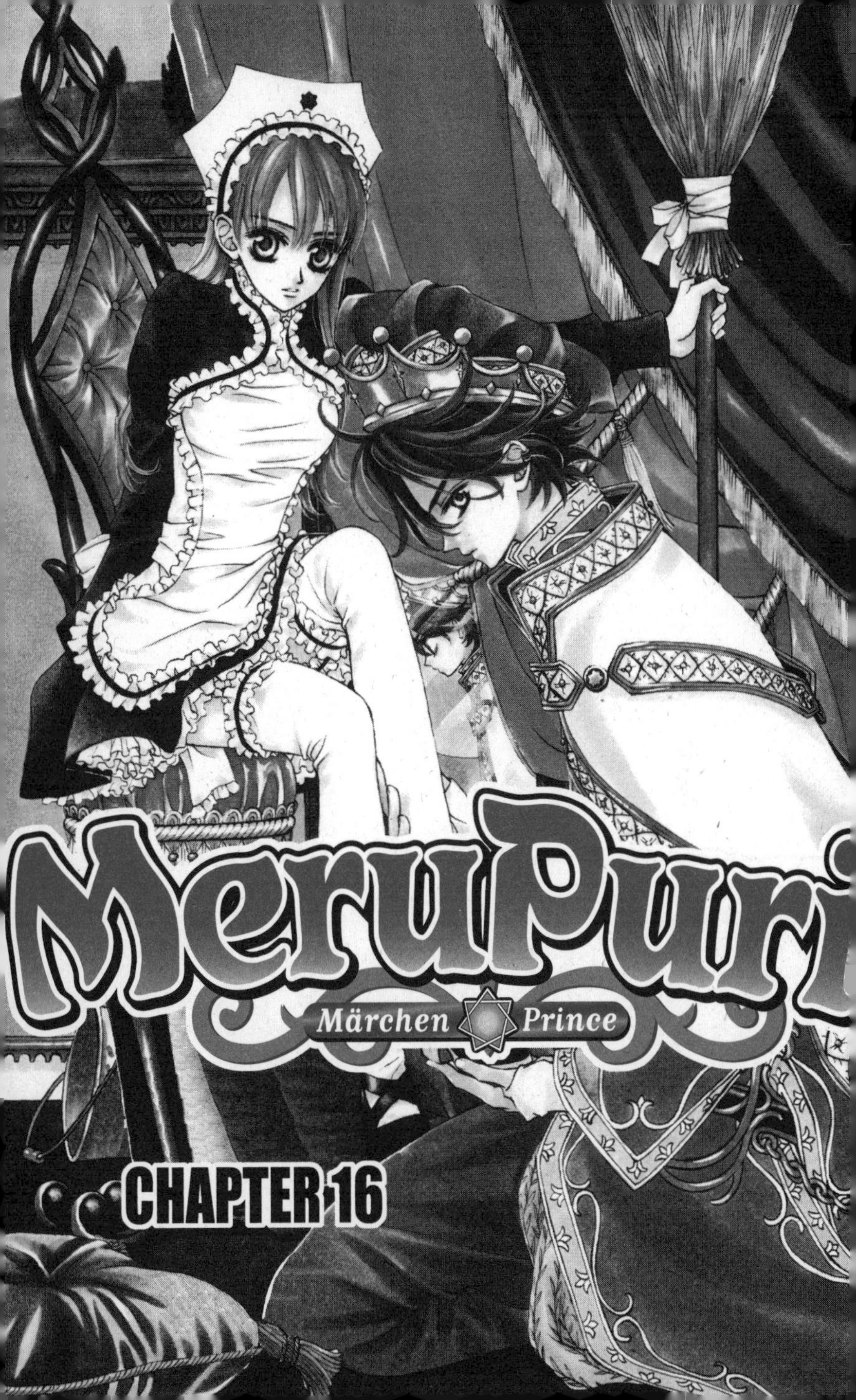
MeruPuri
Märchen Prince
CHAPTER 16

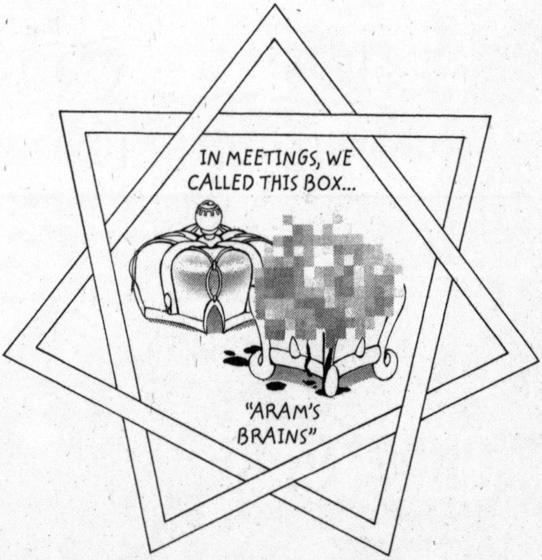
IN MEETINGS, WE CALLED THIS BOX...
"ARAM'S BRAINS"

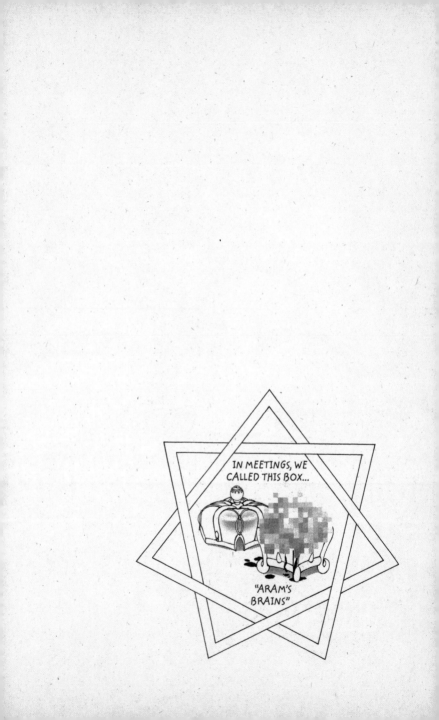

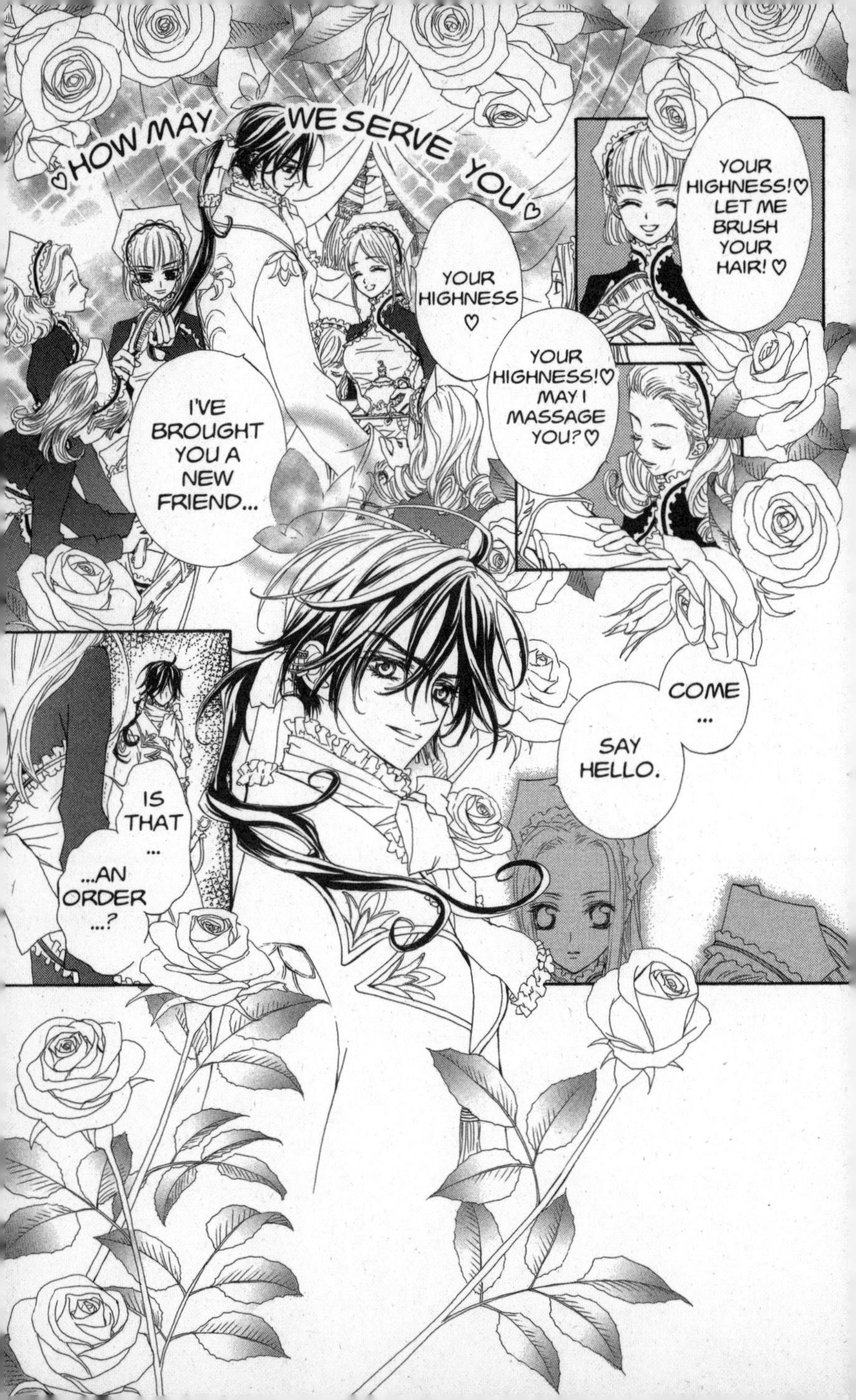
YOUR HIGHNESS!♡ LET ME BRUSH YOUR HAIR!♡
YOUR HIGHNESS!♡ MAY I MASSAGE YOU?♡
♡HOW MAY WE SERVE YOU♡
YOUR HIGHNESS ♡
I'VE BROUGHT YOU A NEW FRIEND...
COME ...
SAY HELLO.
IS THAT ...
...AN ORDER ...?

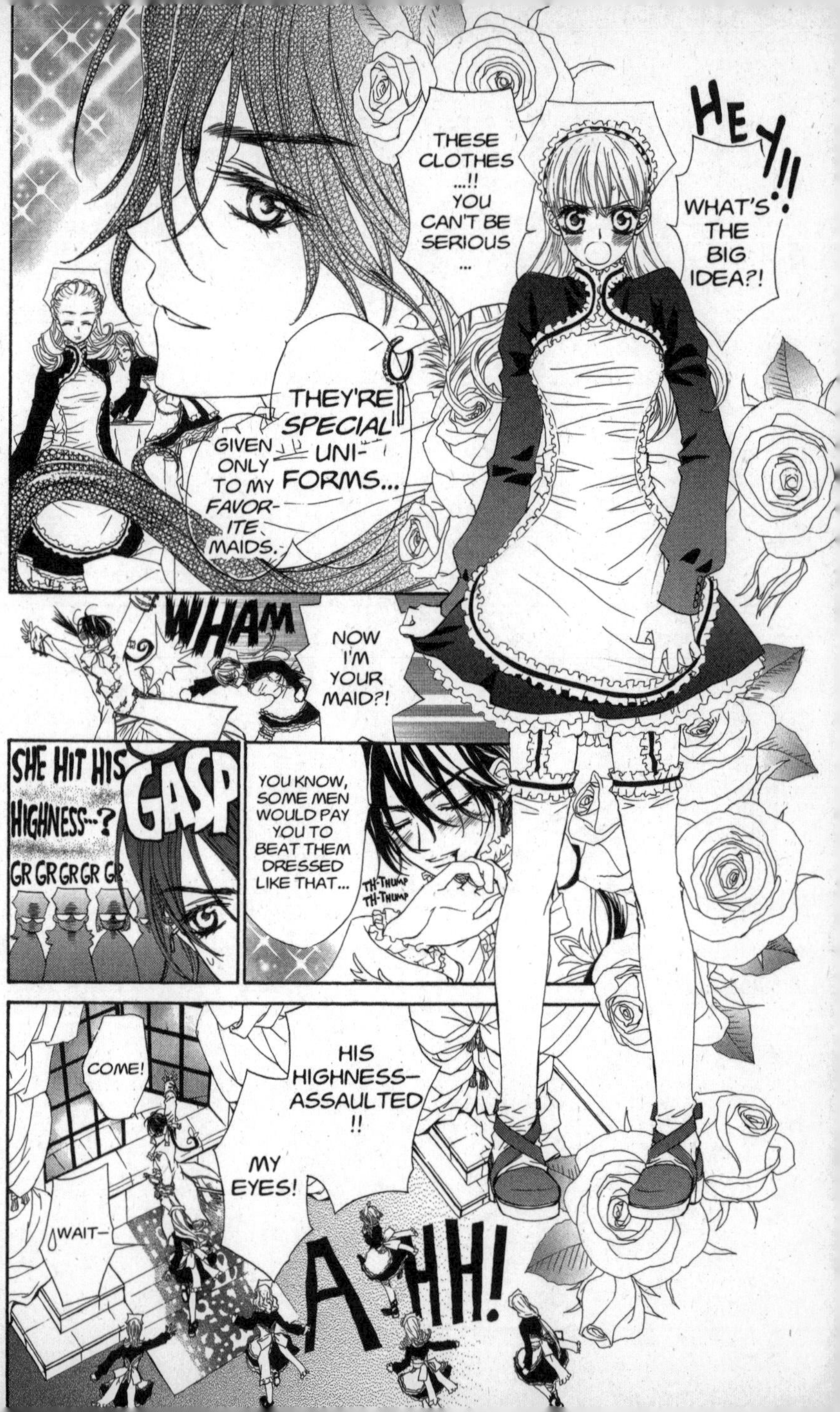

HEY!!!
WHAT'S THE BIG IDEA?!
THESE CLOTHES ...!! YOU CAN'T BE SERIOUS ...
THEY'RE SPECIAL UNI-FORMS...
GIVEN ONLY TO MY FAVOR-ITE MAIDS.
NOW I'M YOUR MAID?!
WHAM
YOU KNOW, SOME MEN WOULD PAY YOU TO BEAT THEM DRESSED LIKE THAT...
TH-THUMP TH-THUMP
GASP
SHE HIT HIS HIGHNESS--?
GR GR GR GR GR
HIS HIGHNESS-ASSAULTED !!
MY EYES!
AHH!
COME!
WAIT-

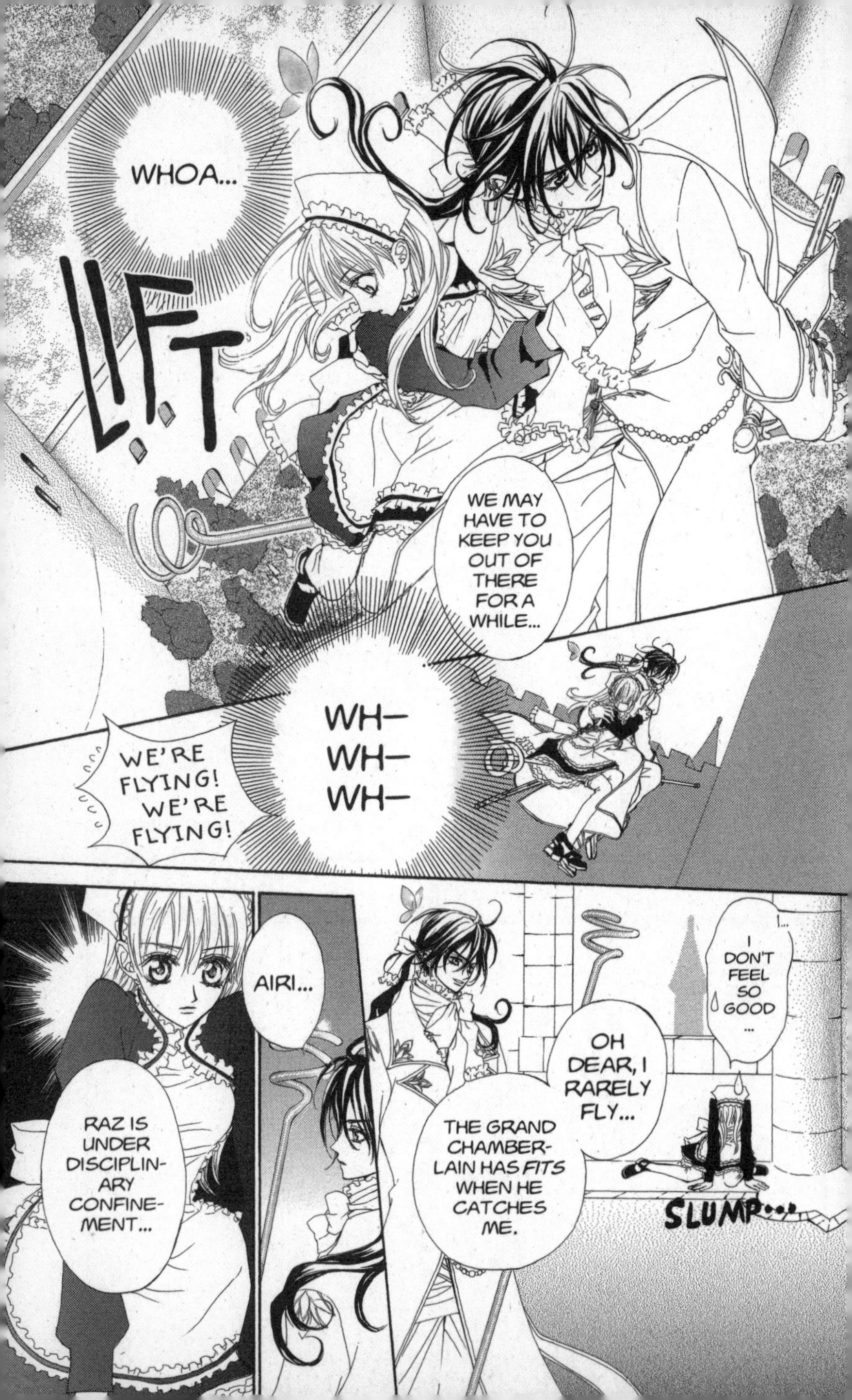
WHOA...
LIFT
WE MAY HAVE TO KEEP YOU OUT OF THERE FOR A WHILE...
WH- WH- WH-
WE'RE FLYING! WE'RE FLYING!
I... I DON'T FEEL SO GOOD...
OH DEAR, I RARELY FLY...
THE GRAND CHAMBER-LAIN HAS *FITS* WHEN HE CATCHES ME.
SLUMP...
AIRI...
RAZ IS UNDER DISCIPLIN-ARY CONFINE-MENT...

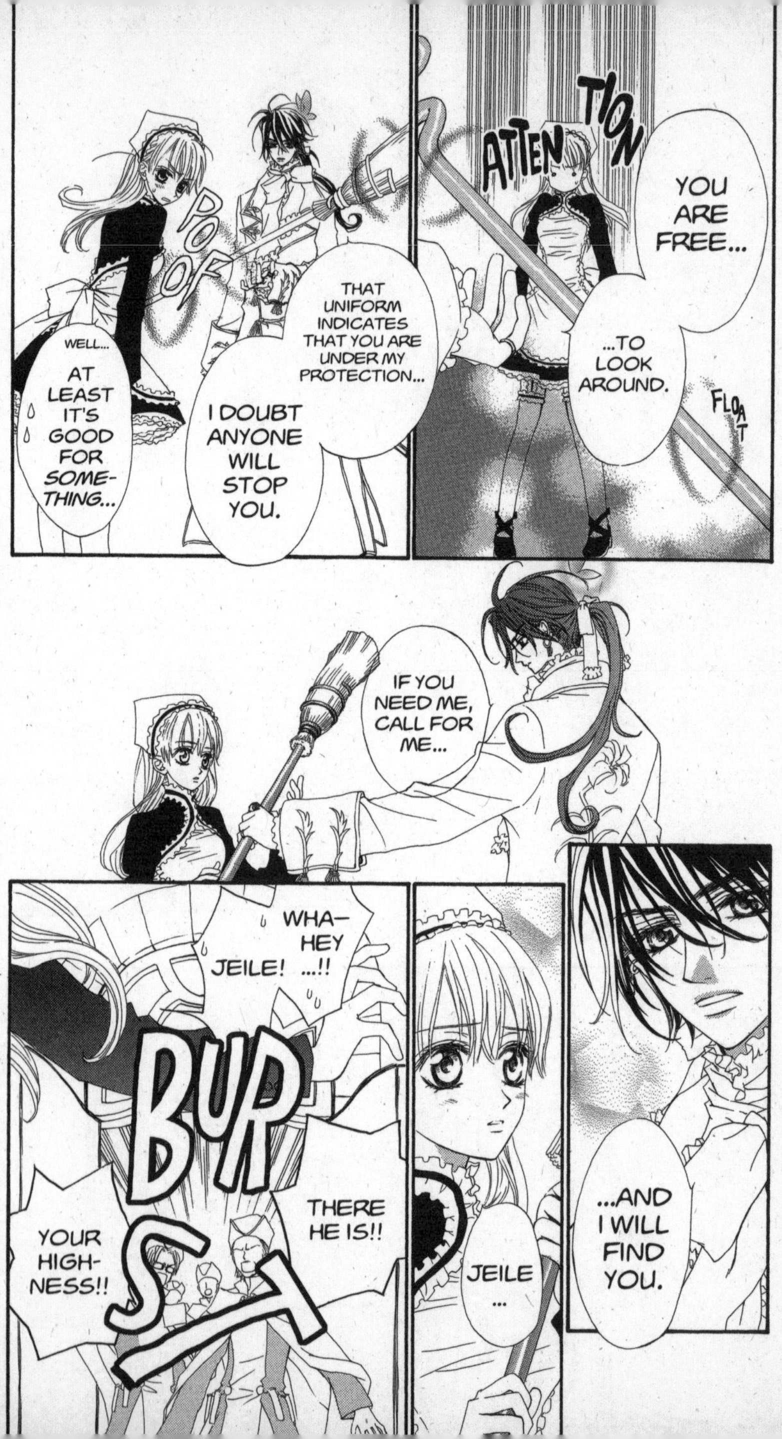
ATTEN TION
YOU ARE FREE...
...TO LOOK AROUND.
FLOAT
POOF
THAT UNIFORM INDICATES THAT YOU ARE UNDER MY PROTECTION...
I DOUBT ANYONE WILL STOP YOU.
WELL... AT LEAST IT'S GOOD FOR SOME-THING...
IF YOU NEED ME, CALL FOR ME...
...AND I WILL FIND YOU.
JEILE ...
WHA— HEY ...!!
JEILE!
BUPST
THERE HE IS!!
YOUR HIGH-NESS!!

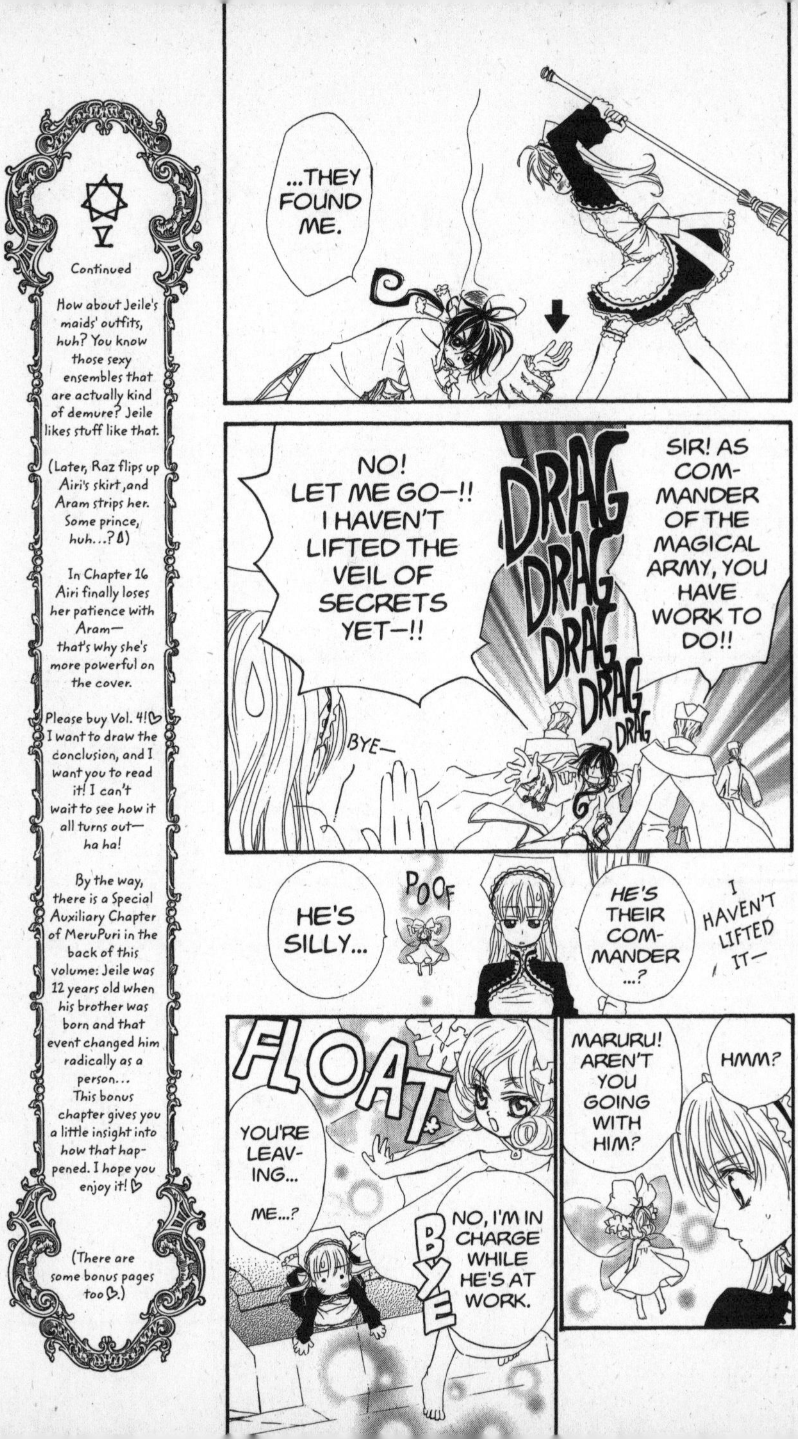
...THEY FOUND ME.
SIR! AS COMMANDER OF THE MAGICAL ARMY, YOU HAVE WORK TO DO!!
DRAG DRAG DRAG DRAG DRAG
NO! LET ME GO—!! I HAVEN'T LIFTED THE VEIL OF SECRETS YET—!!
BYE—
I HAVEN'T LIFTED IT—
HE'S THEIR COMMANDER...?
POOF
HE'S SILLY...
HMM?
MARURU! AREN'T YOU GOING WITH HIM?
FLOAT
YOU'RE LEAVING...
NO, I'M IN CHARGE WHILE HE'S AT WORK.
BYE
ME...?

Continued

How about Jeile's maids' outfits, huh? You know those sexy ensembles that are actually kind of demure? Jeile likes stuff like that.

(Later, Raz flips up Airi's skirt, and Aram strips her. Some prince, huh...?)

In Chapter 16 Airi finally loses her patience with Aram— that's why she's more powerful on the cover.

Please buy Vol. 4! ♡ I want to draw the conclusion, and I want you to read it! I can't wait to see how it all turns out— ha ha!

By the way, there is a Special Auxiliary Chapter of MeruPuri in the back of this volume: Jeile was 12 years old when his brother was born and that event changed him radically as a person... This bonus chapter gives you a little insight into how that happened. I hope you enjoy it! ♡

(There are some bonus pages too ♡.)

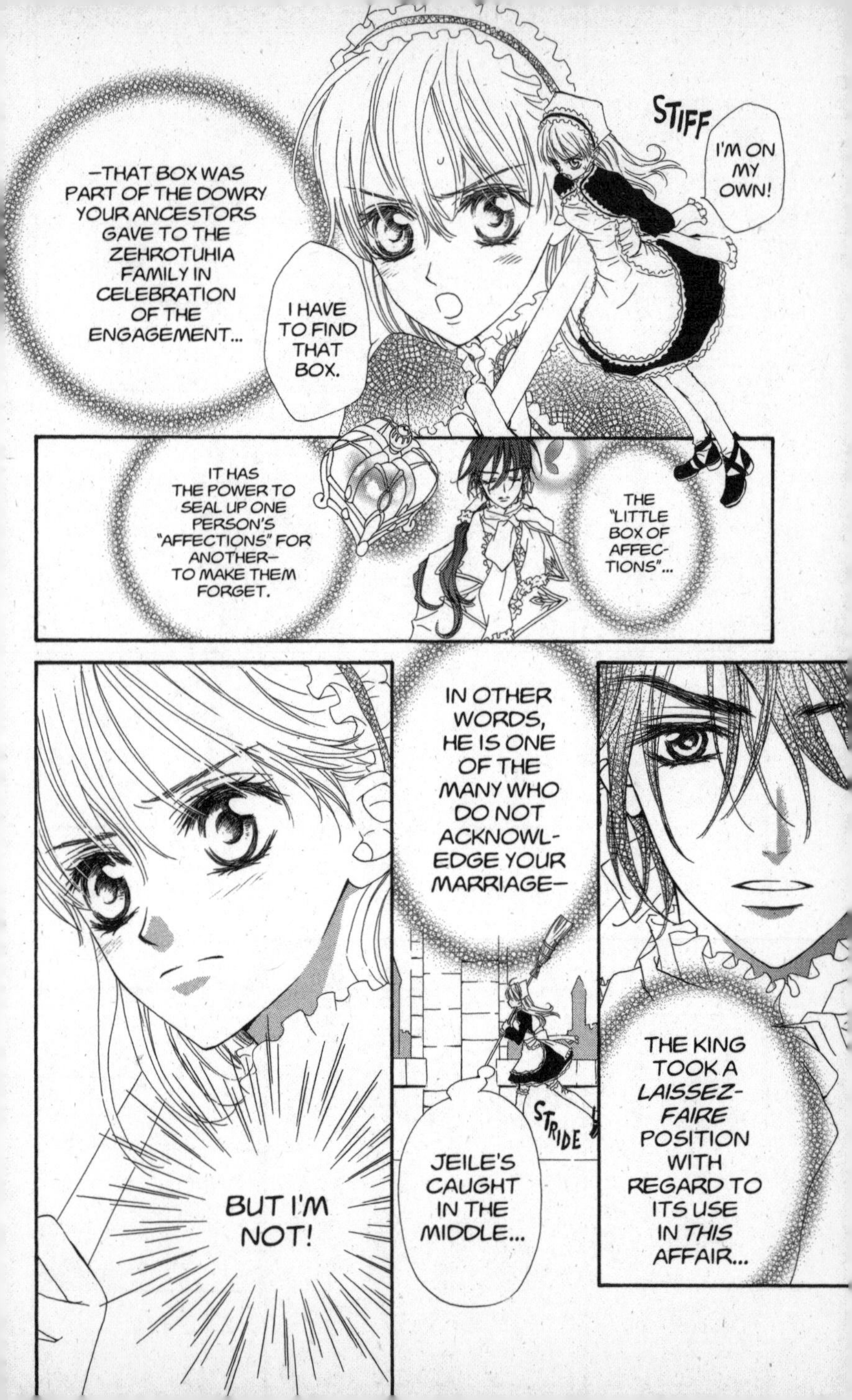
STIFF
I'M ON MY OWN!
I HAVE TO FIND THAT BOX.
—THAT BOX WAS PART OF THE DOWRY YOUR ANCESTORS GAVE TO THE ZEHROTUHIA FAMILY IN CELEBRATION OF THE ENGAGEMENT...
THE "LITTLE BOX OF AFFECTIONS"...
IT HAS THE POWER TO SEAL UP ONE PERSON'S "AFFECTIONS" FOR ANOTHER— TO MAKE THEM FORGET.
THE KING TOOK A *LAISSEZ-FAIRE* POSITION WITH REGARD TO ITS USE IN *THIS* AFFAIR...
IN OTHER WORDS, HE IS ONE OF THE MANY WHO DO NOT ACKNOWLEDGE YOUR MARRIAGE—
STRIDE
JEILE'S CAUGHT IN THE MIDDLE...
BUT I'M NOT!

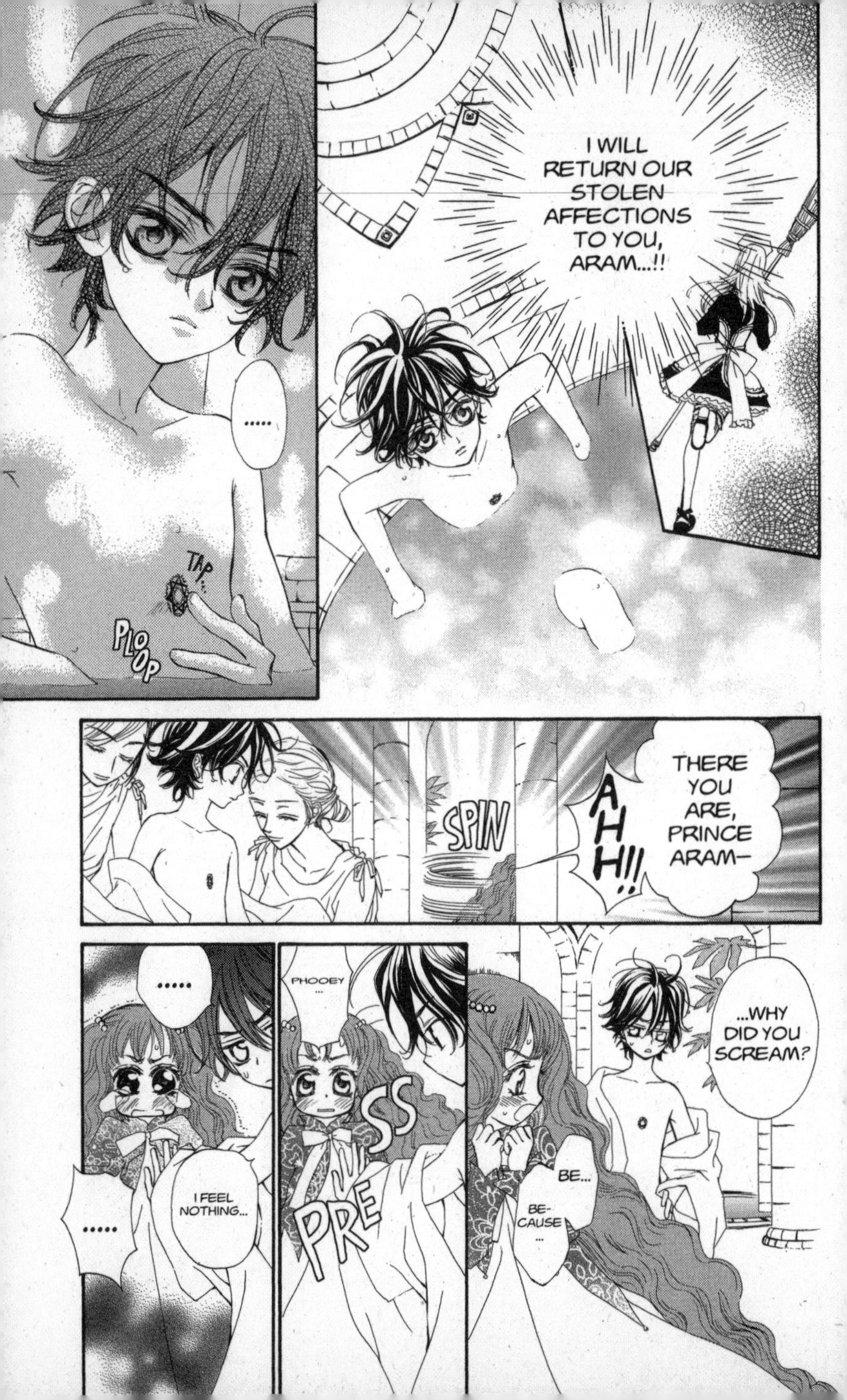
I WILL RETURN OUR STOLEN AFFECTIONS TO YOU, ARAM...!!
......
TAP...
PLOOP
THERE YOU ARE, PRINCE ARAM–
AHH!!
SPIN
...WHY DID YOU SCREAM?
BE...
BE-CAUSE...
PHOOEY...
PRESS
......
I FEEL NOTHING...
......

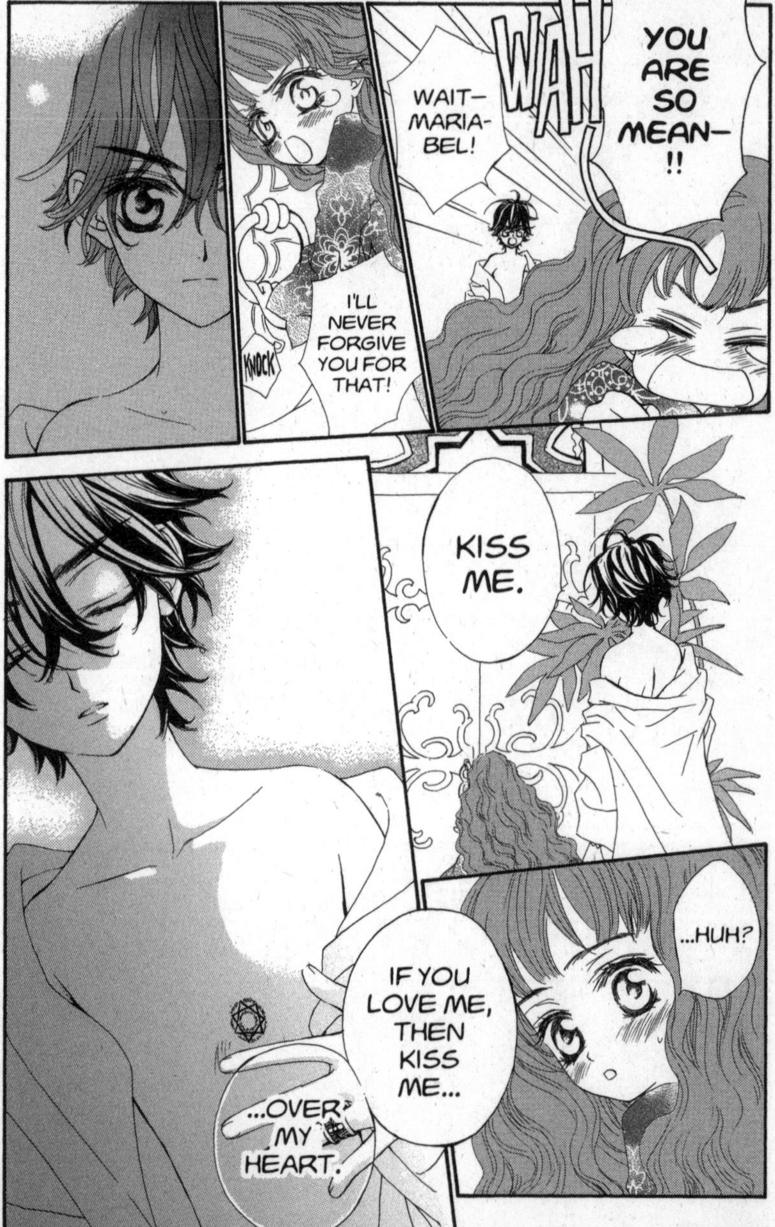
YOU ARE SO MEAN—!!
WAH
WAIT—MARIA-BEL!
I'LL NEVER FORGIVE YOU FOR THAT!
KNOCK
KISS ME.
...HUH?
IF YOU LOVE ME, THEN KISS ME...
...OVER MY HEART.

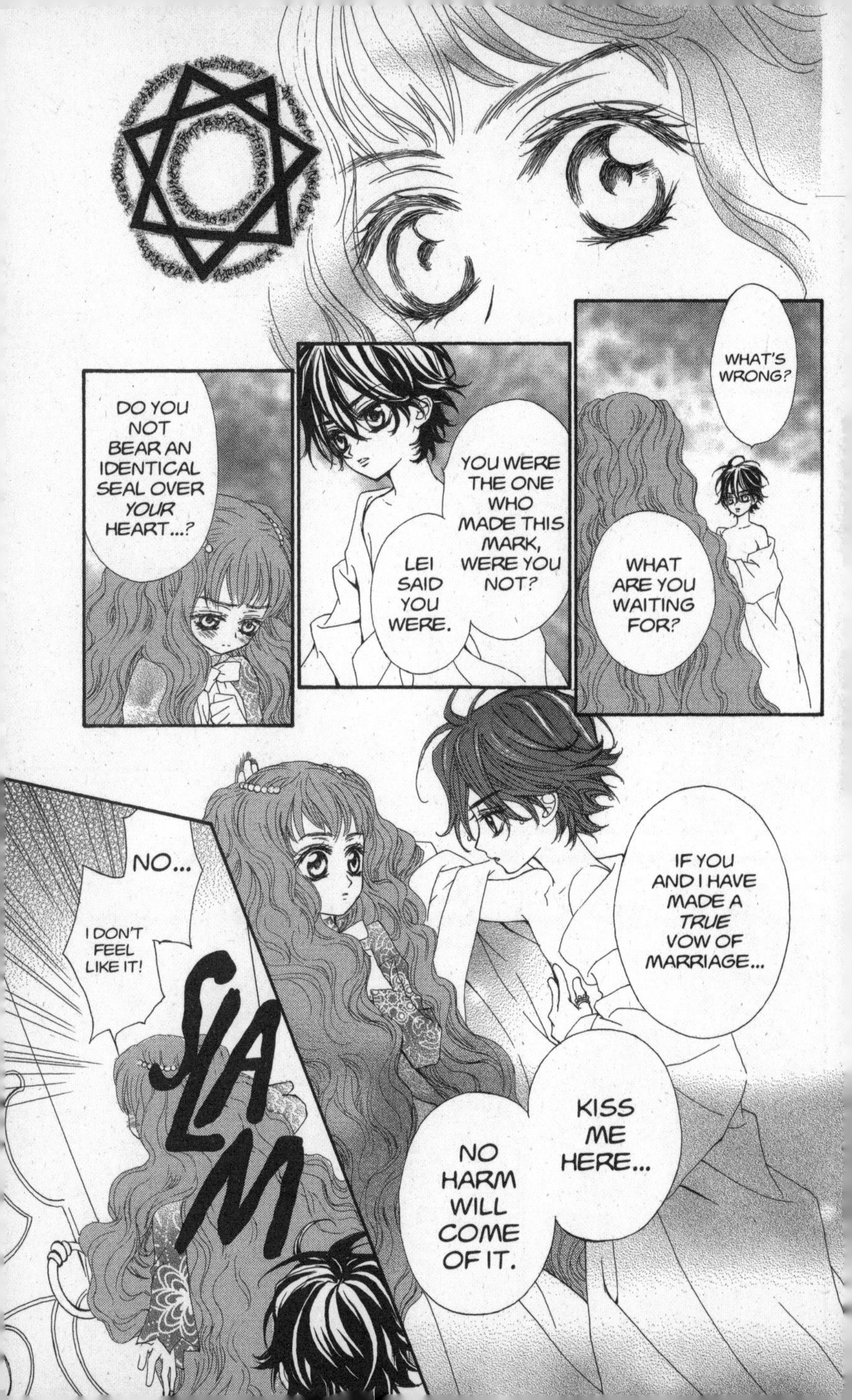
WHAT'S WRONG?
WHAT ARE YOU WAITING FOR?
YOU WERE THE ONE WHO MADE THIS MARK, WERE YOU NOT?
LEI SAID YOU WERE.
DO YOU NOT BEAR AN IDENTICAL SEAL OVER *YOUR* HEART...?
IF YOU AND I HAVE MADE A *TRUE* VOW OF MARRIAGE...
KISS ME HERE...
NO HARM WILL COME OF IT.
NO...
I DON'T FEEL LIKE IT!
SLAM

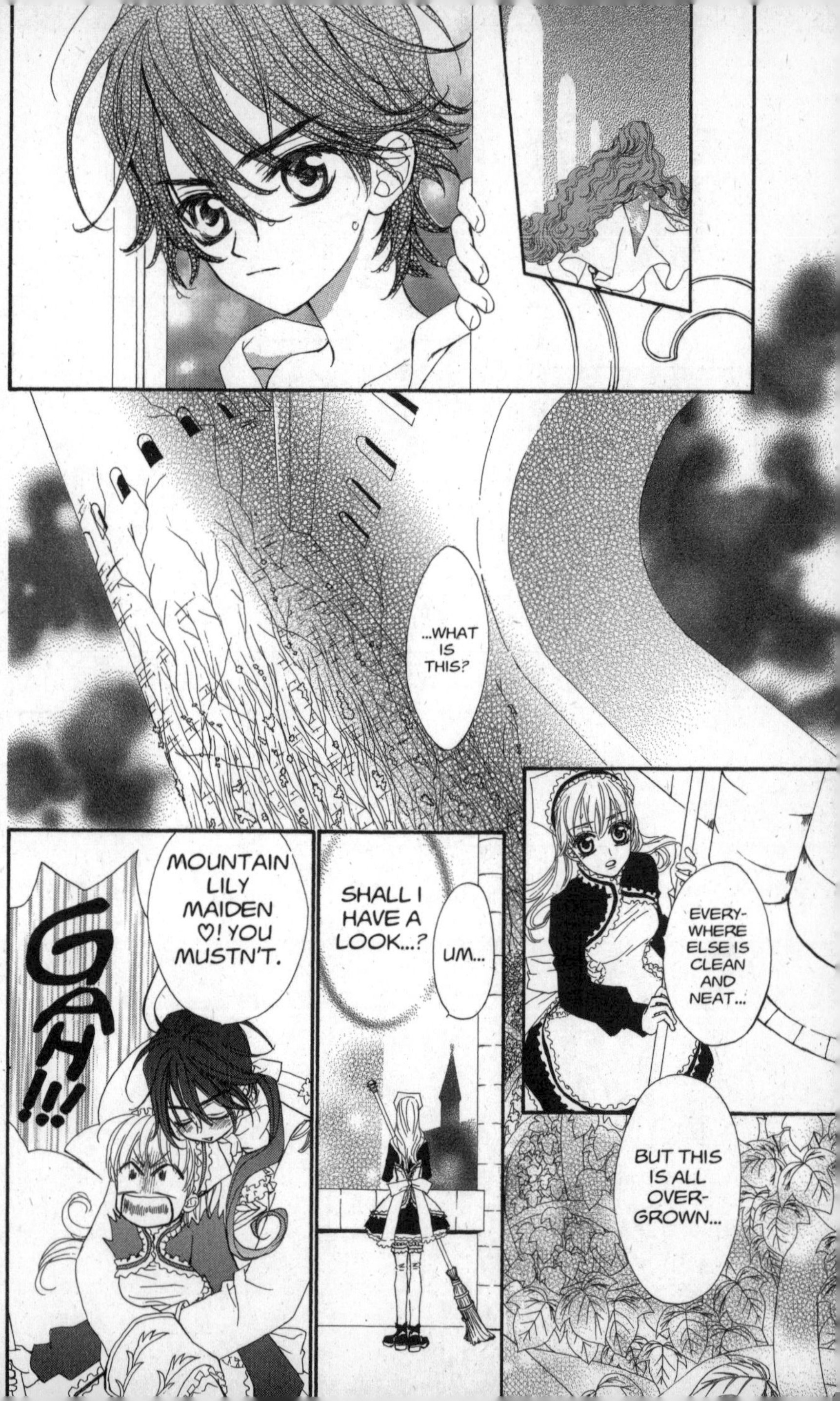
...WHAT IS THIS?
EVERY-WHERE ELSE IS CLEAN AND NEAT...
BUT THIS IS ALL OVER-GROWN...
UM...
SHALL I HAVE A LOOK...?
MOUNTAIN LILY MAIDEN ♡! YOU MUSTN'T.
GAH!!!

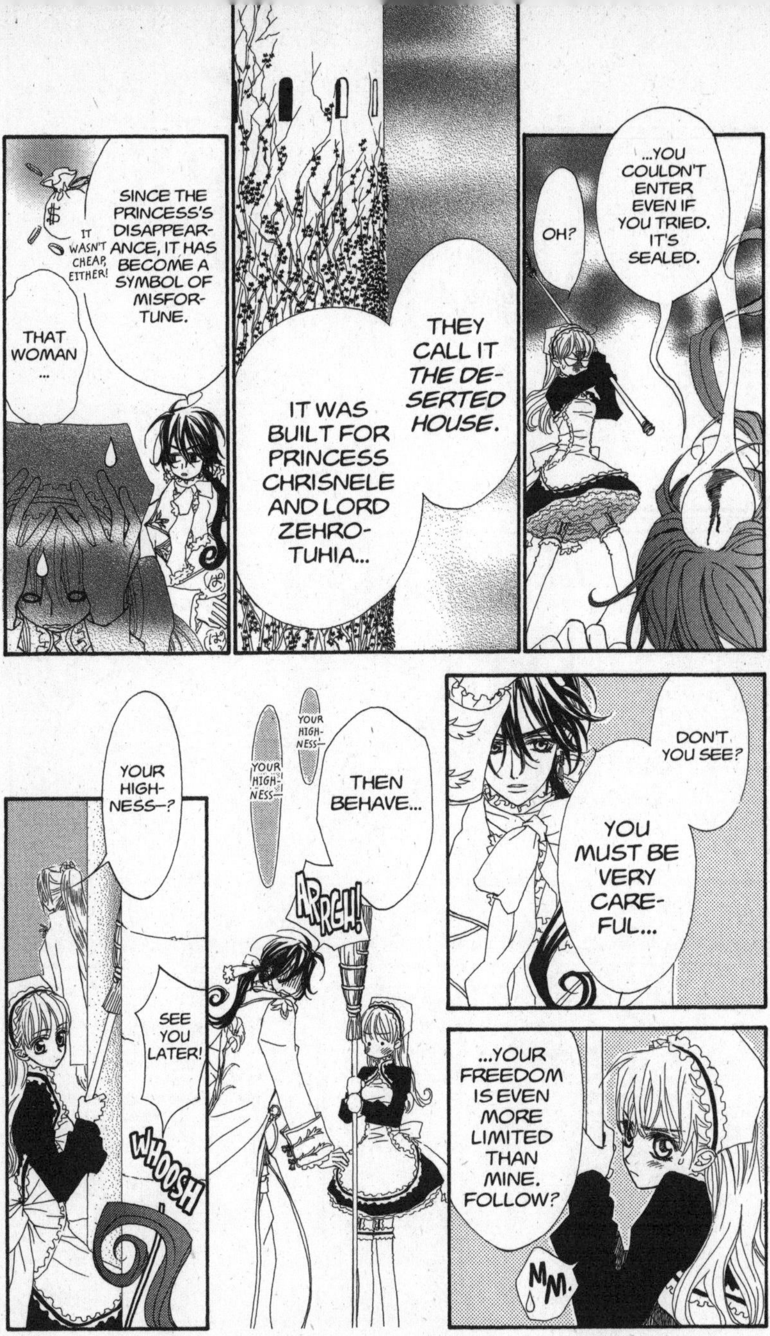
...YOU COULDN'T ENTER EVEN IF YOU TRIED. IT'S SEALED.
OH?
THEY CALL IT THE DESERTED HOUSE.
IT WAS BUILT FOR PRINCESS CHRISNELE AND LORD ZEHRO-TUHIA...
SINCE THE PRINCESS'S DISAPPEARANCE, IT HAS BECOME A SYMBOL OF MISFORTUNE.
IT WASN'T CHEAP, EITHER!
THAT WOMAN ...
DON'T YOU SEE?
YOU MUST BE VERY CAREFUL...
...YOUR FREEDOM IS EVEN MORE LIMITED THAN MINE. FOLLOW?
MM.
YOUR HIGHNESS—
THEN BEHAVE...
YOUR HIGHNESS—
ARRGH!
YOUR HIGHNESS—?
SEE YOU LATER!
WHOOSH

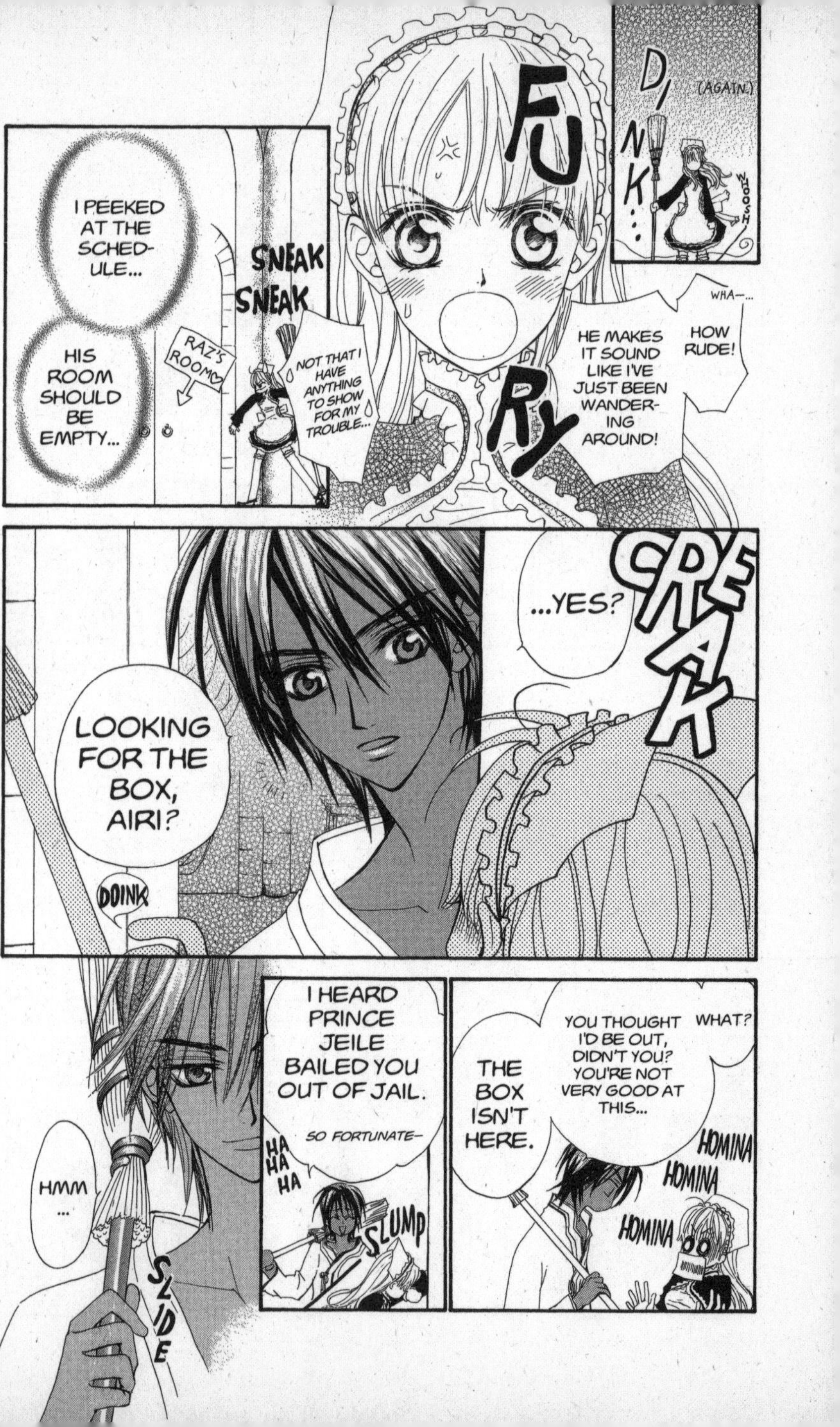
DINK...
(AGAIN.)
WHOOSH
FURY
WHA—...
HOW RUDE!
HE MAKES IT SOUND LIKE I'VE JUST BEEN WANDERING AROUND!
NOT THAT I HAVE ANYTHING TO SHOW FOR MY TROUBLE...
SNEAK SNEAK
RAZ'S ROOM♡
I PEEKED AT THE SCHEDULE...
HIS ROOM SHOULD BE EMPTY...
CREAK
...YES?
LOOKING FOR THE BOX, AIRI?
DOINK
WHAT?
YOU THOUGHT I'D BE OUT, DIDN'T YOU? YOU'RE NOT VERY GOOD AT THIS...
THE BOX ISN'T HERE.
HOMINA HOMINA HOMINA
I HEARD PRINCE JEILE BAILED YOU OUT OF JAIL.
SO FORTUNATE—
HA HA HA
SLUMP
HMM...
SLIDE

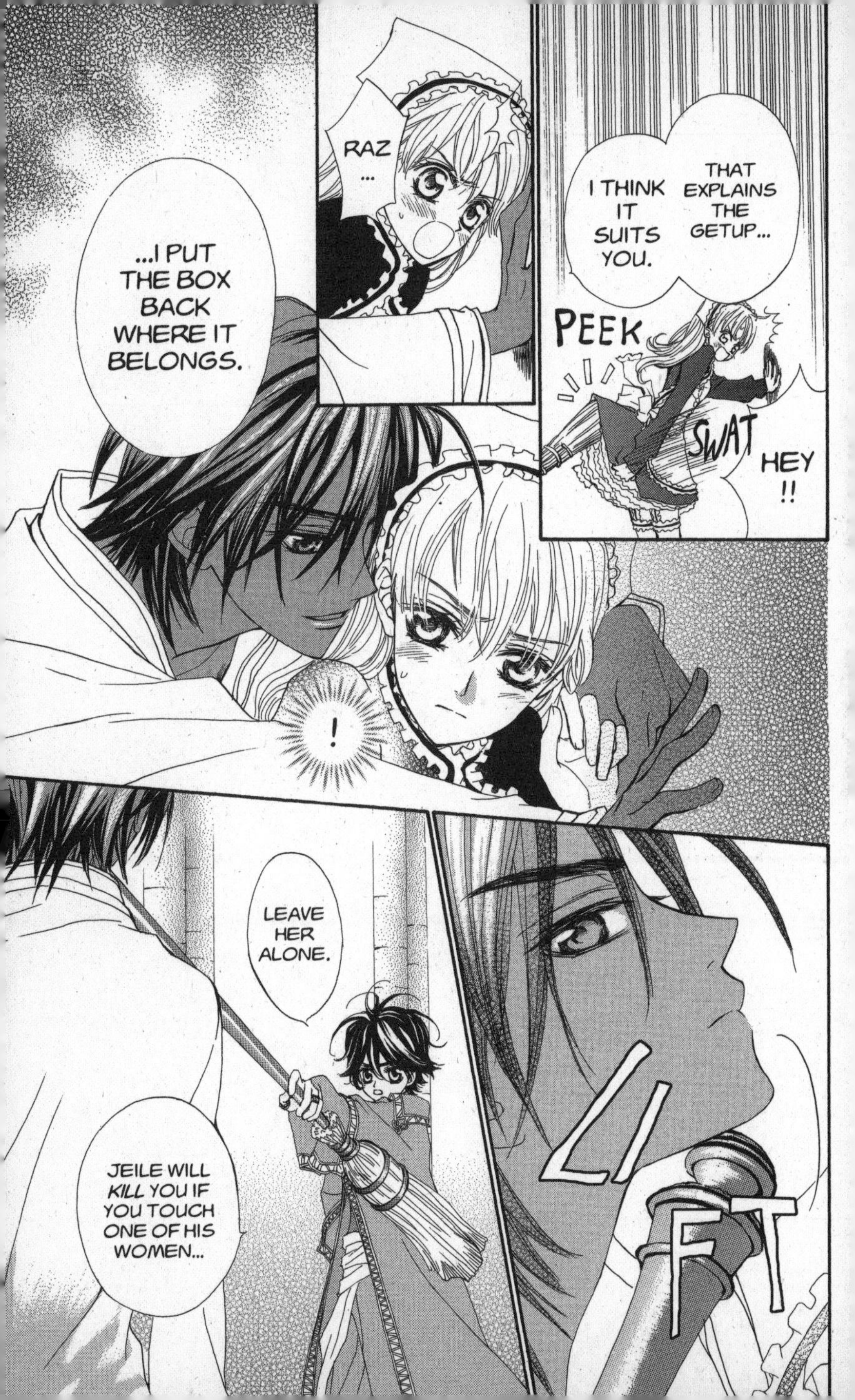
THAT EXPLAINS THE GETUP...
I THINK IT SUITS YOU.
PEEK
SWAT
HEY!!
RAZ...
...I PUT THE BOX BACK WHERE IT BELONGS.
!
LIFT
LEAVE HER ALONE.
JEILE WILL *KILL* YOU IF YOU TOUCH ONE OF HIS WOMEN...

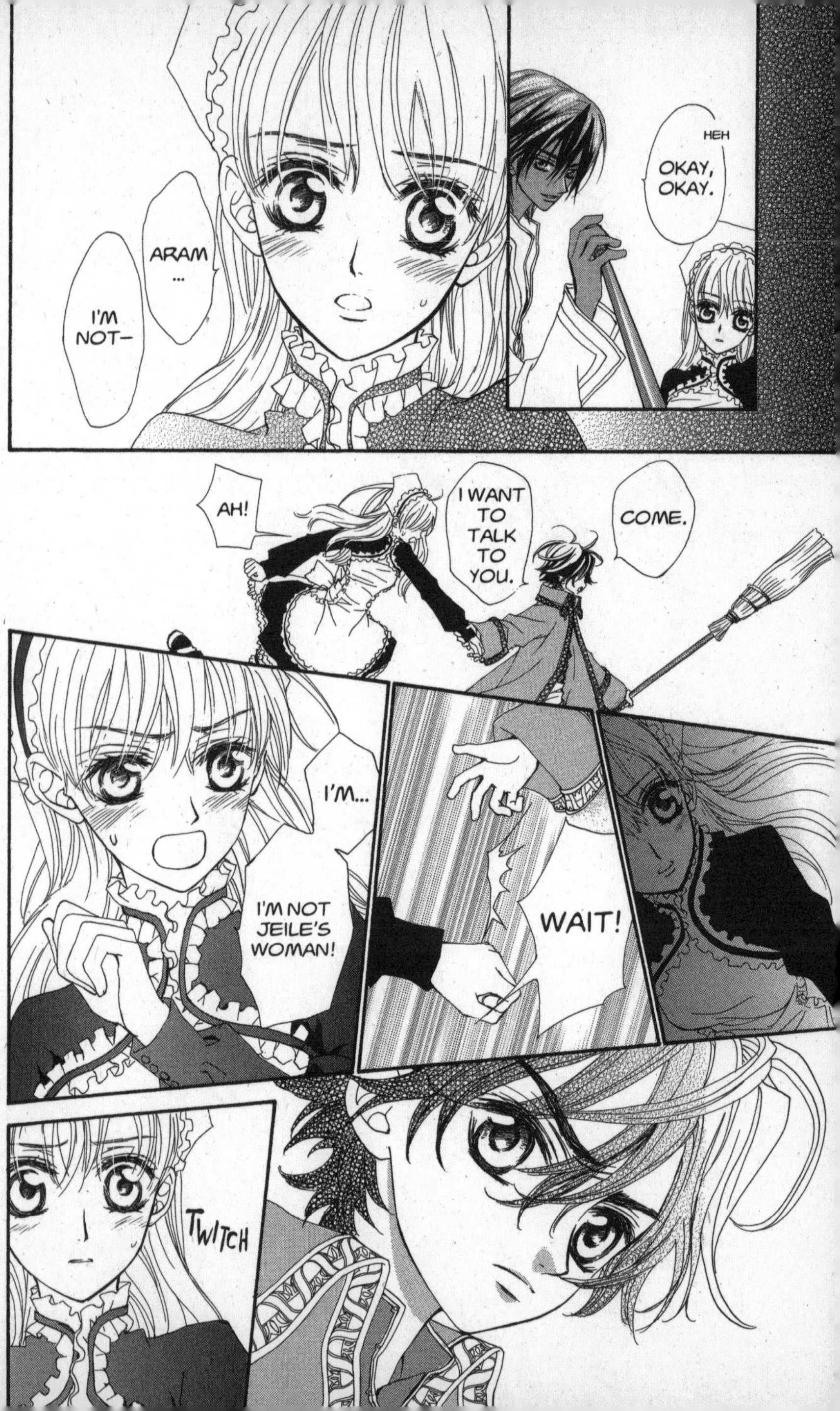
HEH
OKAY, OKAY.
ARAM ...
I'M NOT—
COME.
I WANT TO TALK TO YOU.
AH!
WAIT!
I'M...
I'M NOT JEILE'S WOMAN!
TWITCH

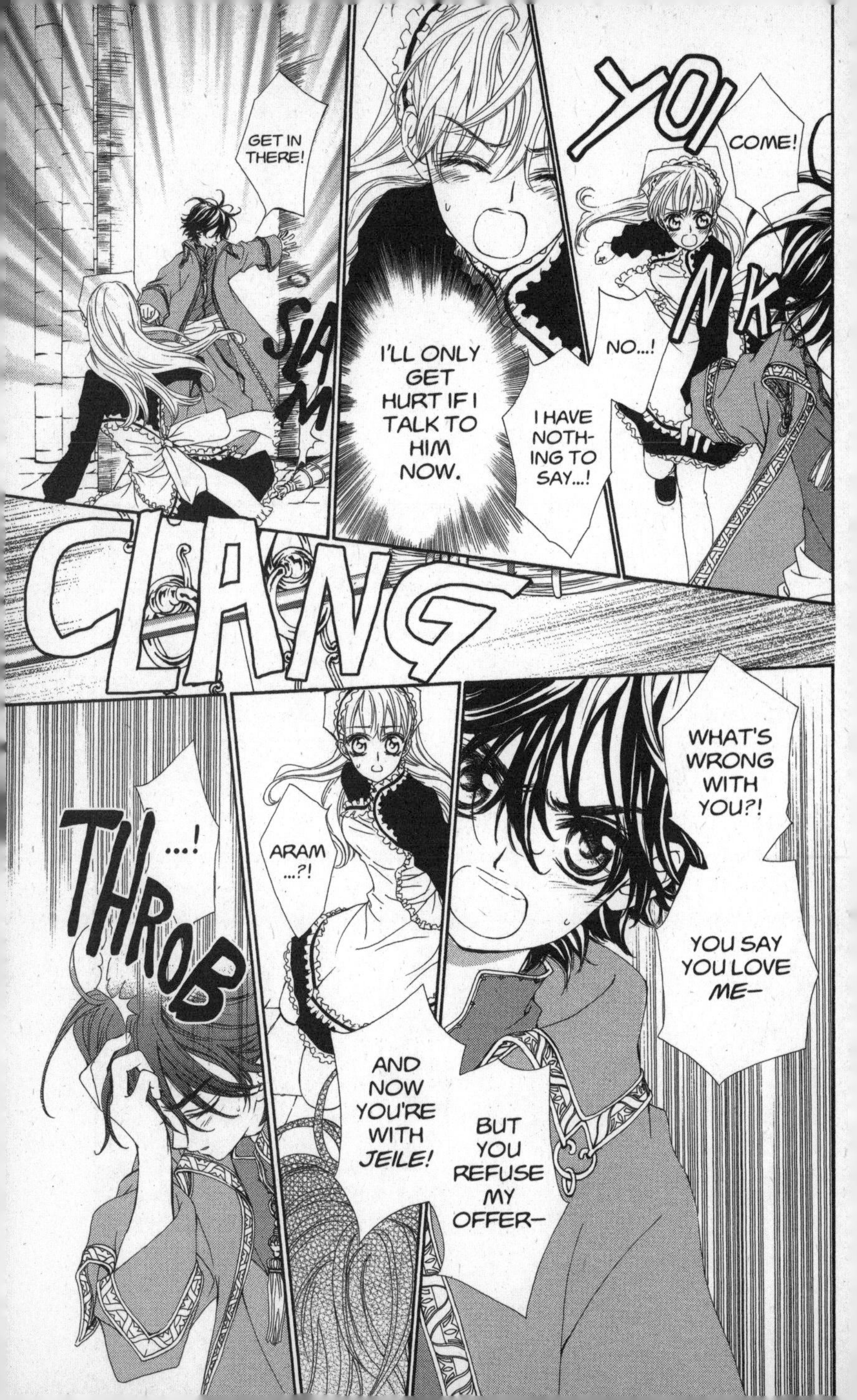
YOINK
COME!
NO...!
I HAVE NOTH-ING TO SAY...!
I'LL ONLY GET HURT IF I TALK TO HIM NOW.
GET IN THERE!
SLAM
CLANG
WHAT'S WRONG WITH YOU?!
YOU SAY YOU LOVE ME—
BUT YOU REFUSE MY OFFER—
AND NOW YOU'RE WITH JEILE!
ARAM ...?!
...!
THROB

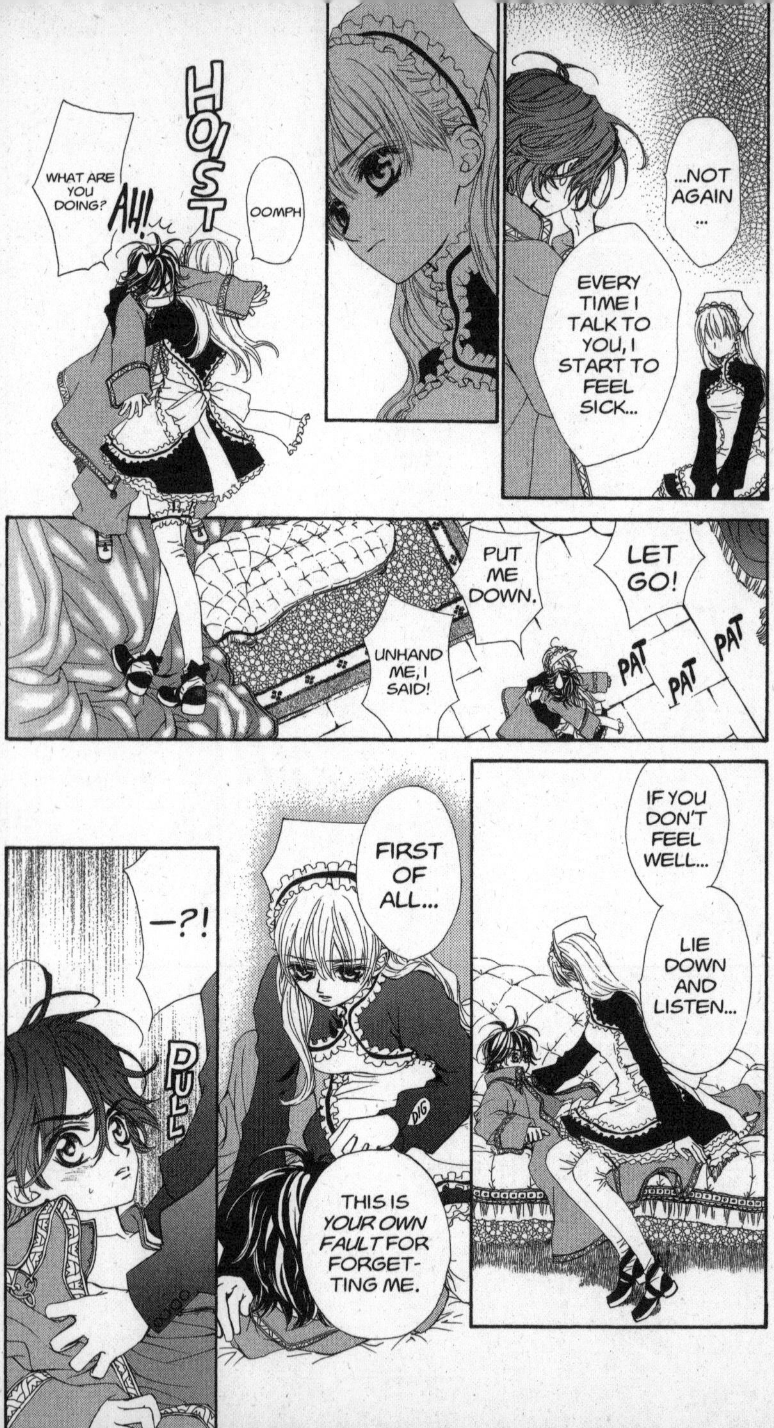
...NOT AGAIN ...
EVERY TIME I TALK TO YOU, I START TO FEEL SICK...
HOIST
OOMPH
WHAT ARE YOU DOING?
AH!
LET GO!
PUT ME DOWN.
UNHAND ME, I SAID!
PAT
PAT
PAT
IF YOU DON'T FEEL WELL...
LIE DOWN AND LISTEN...
FIRST OF ALL...
DIG
THIS IS YOUR OWN FAULT FOR FORGET-TING ME.
—?!
PULL

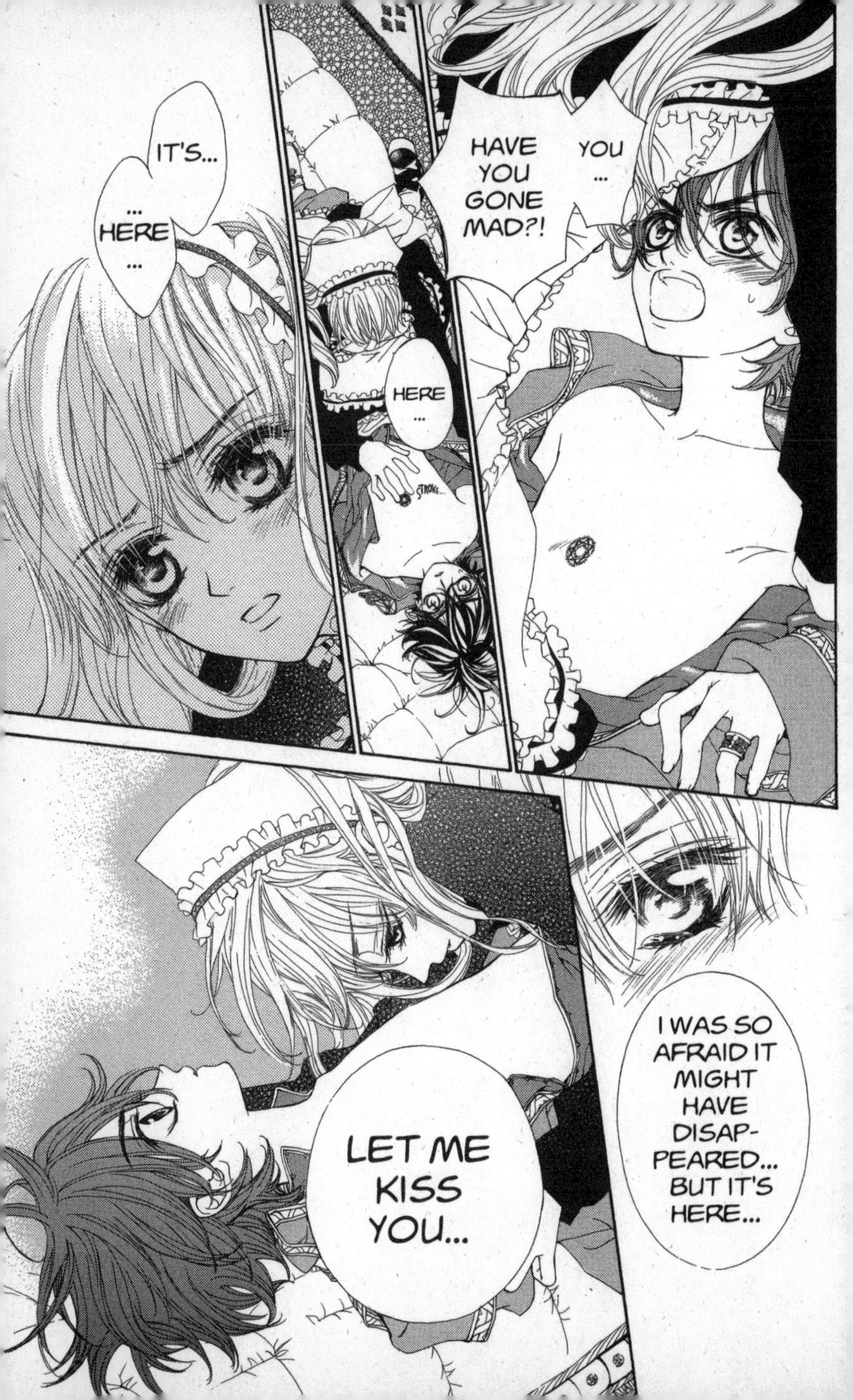
YOU ...
HAVE YOU GONE MAD?!
HERE ...
STROKE...
IT'S...
... HERE ...
I WAS SO AFRAID IT MIGHT HAVE DISAP-PEARED... BUT IT'S HERE...
LET ME KISS YOU...

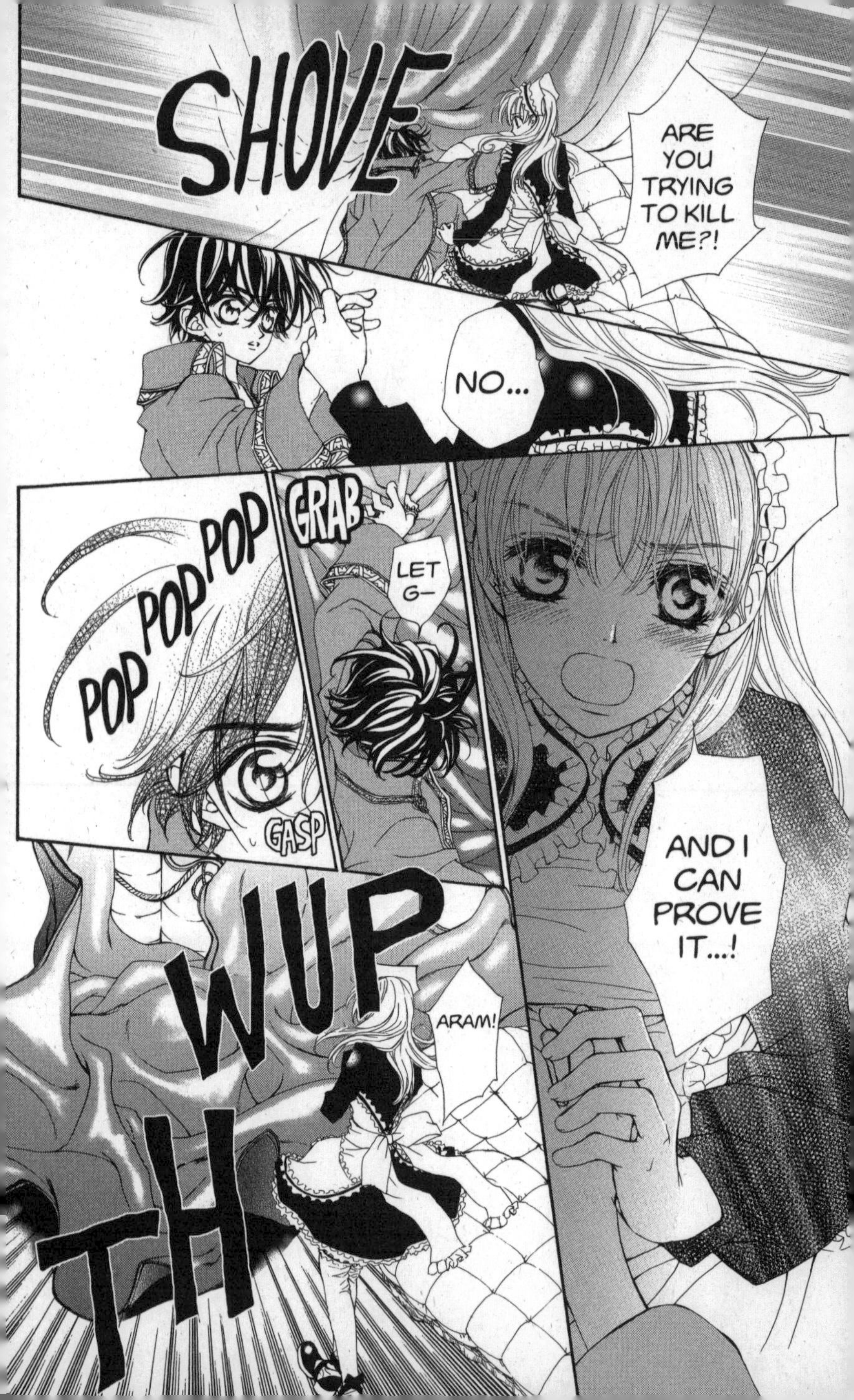
ARE YOU TRYING TO KILL ME?!
SHOVE
NO...
AND I CAN PROVE IT...!
GRAB
LET G—
POP POP POP POP
GASP
ARAM!
THWUP

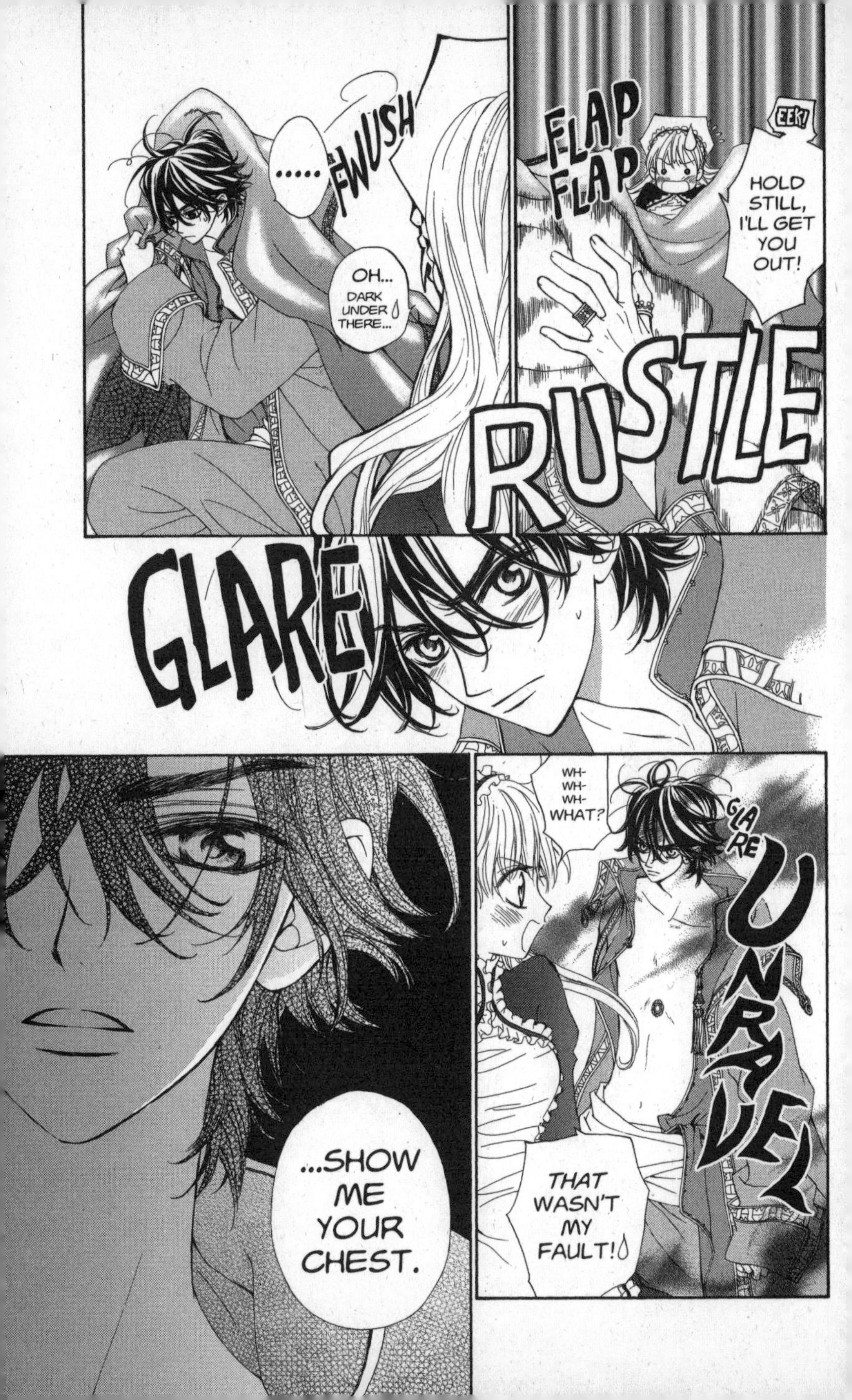
EEK!
FLAP FLAP
HOLD STILL, I'LL GET YOU OUT!
RUSTLE
......
FWUSH
OH... DARK UNDER THERE...
GLARE
WH-WH-WH-WHAT?
GLARE
UNRAVEL
THAT WASN'T MY FAULT!
...SHOW ME YOUR CHEST.

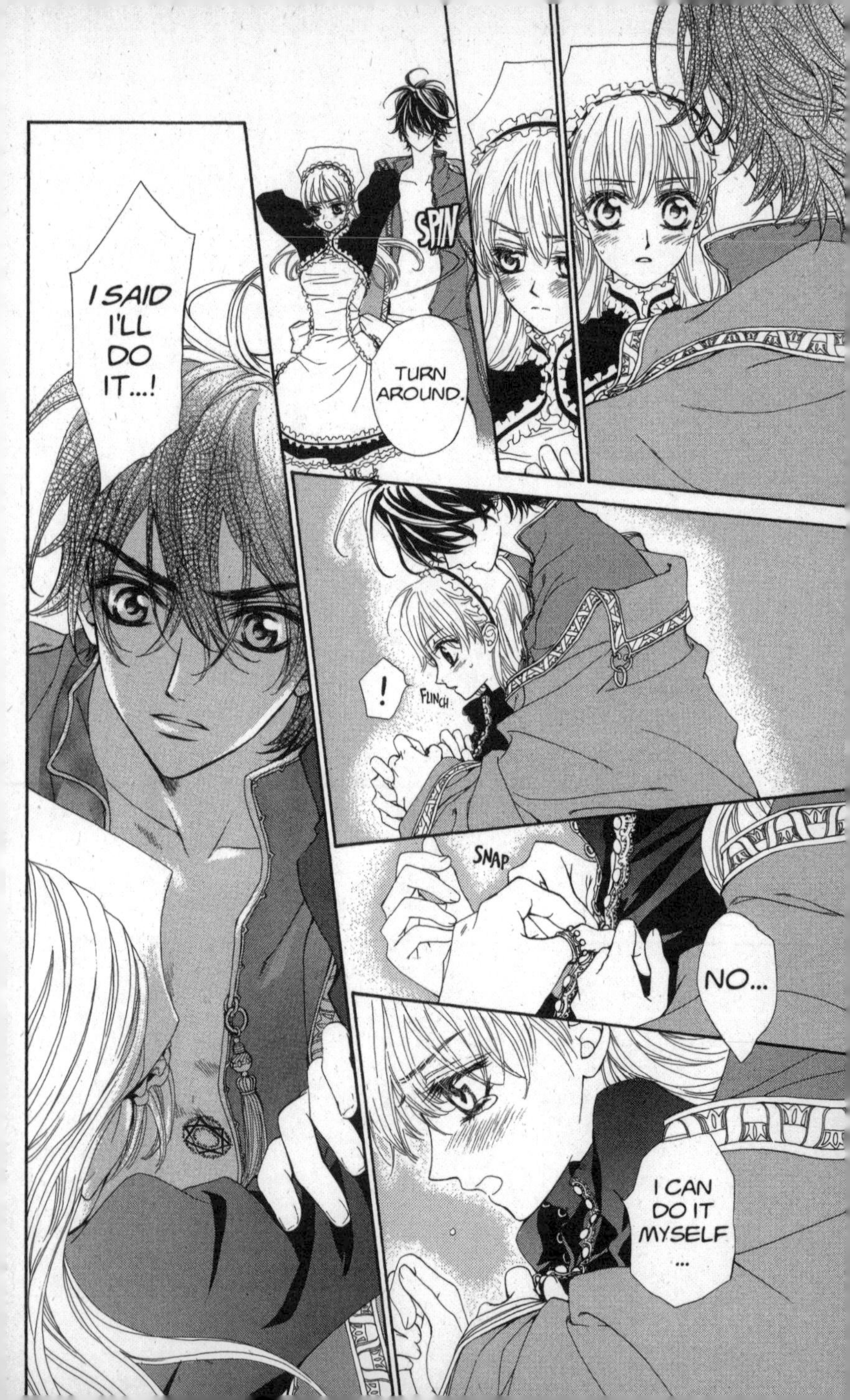
SPIN
TURN AROUND.
!
FLINCH
SNAP
NO...
I CAN DO IT MYSELF ...
I SAID I'LL DO IT...!

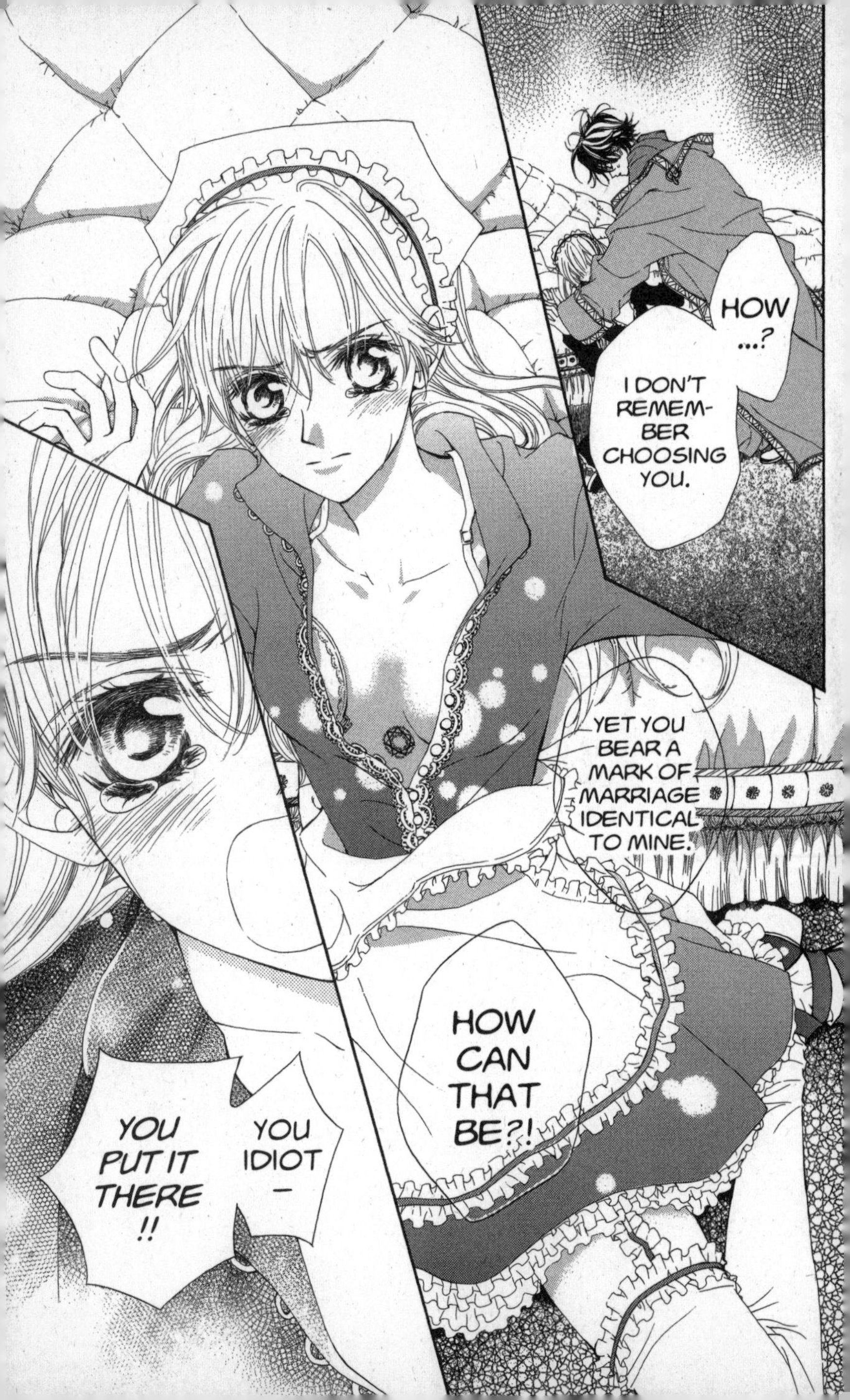
HOW ...?
I DON'T REMEMBER CHOOSING YOU.
YET YOU BEAR A MARK OF MARRIAGE IDENTICAL TO MINE.
HOW CAN THAT BE?!
YOU IDIOT —
YOU PUT IT THERE!!

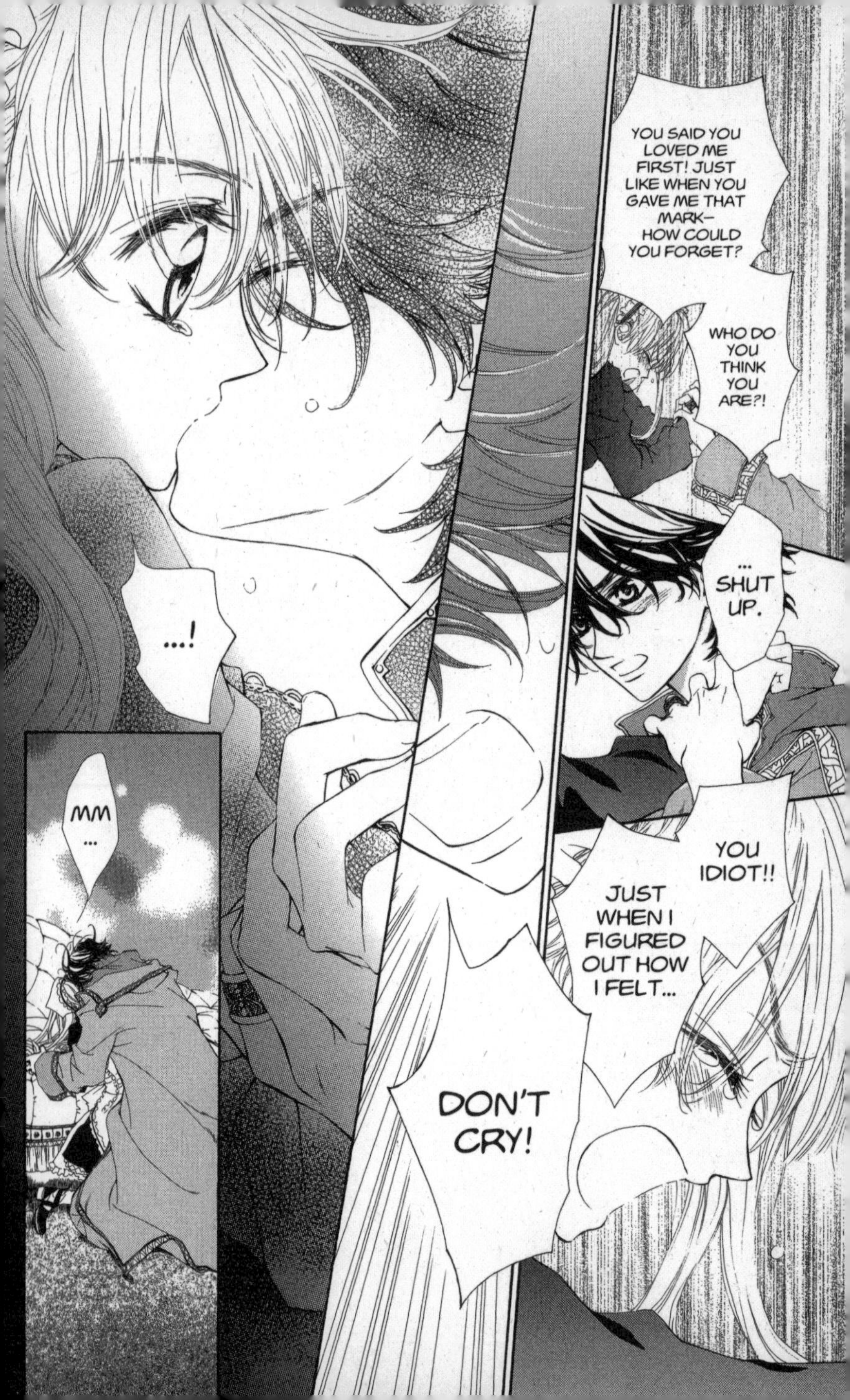
YOU SAID YOU LOVED ME FIRST! JUST LIKE WHEN YOU GAVE ME THAT MARK— HOW COULD YOU FORGET?
WHO DO YOU THINK YOU ARE?!
... SHUT UP.
YOU IDIOT!!
JUST WHEN I FIGURED OUT HOW I FELT...
DON'T CRY!
...!
MM ...

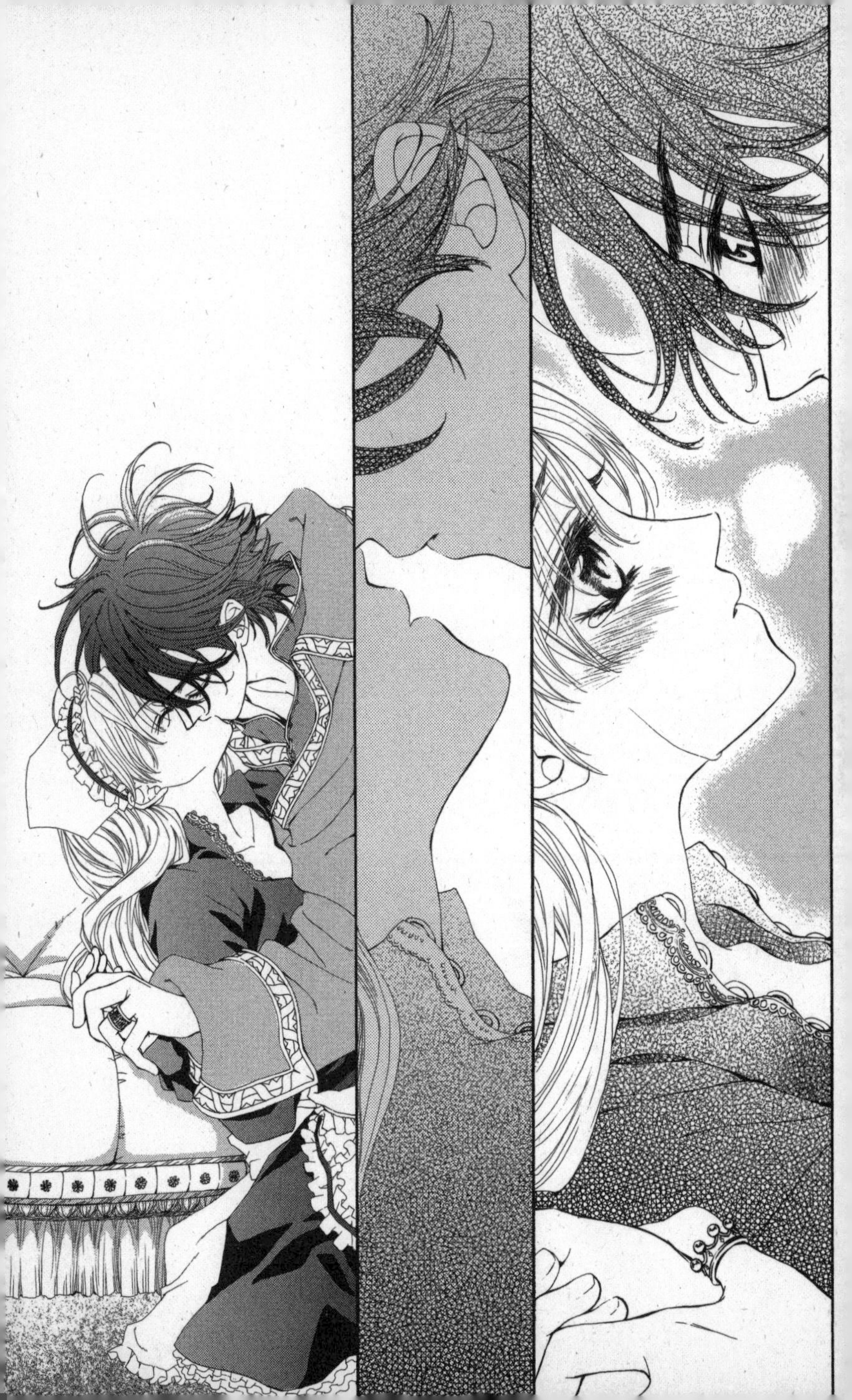

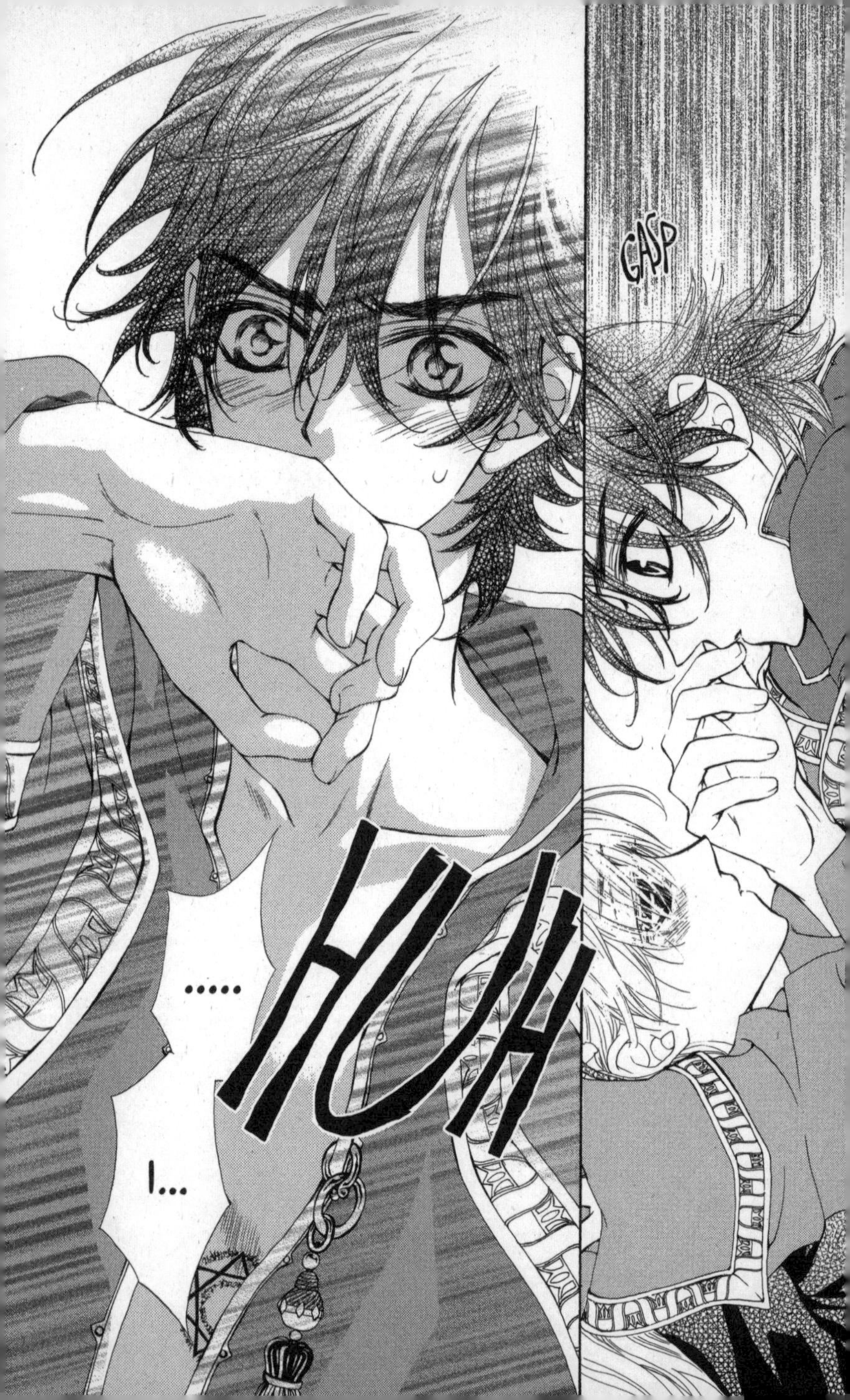
GASP
HUH
.....
I...

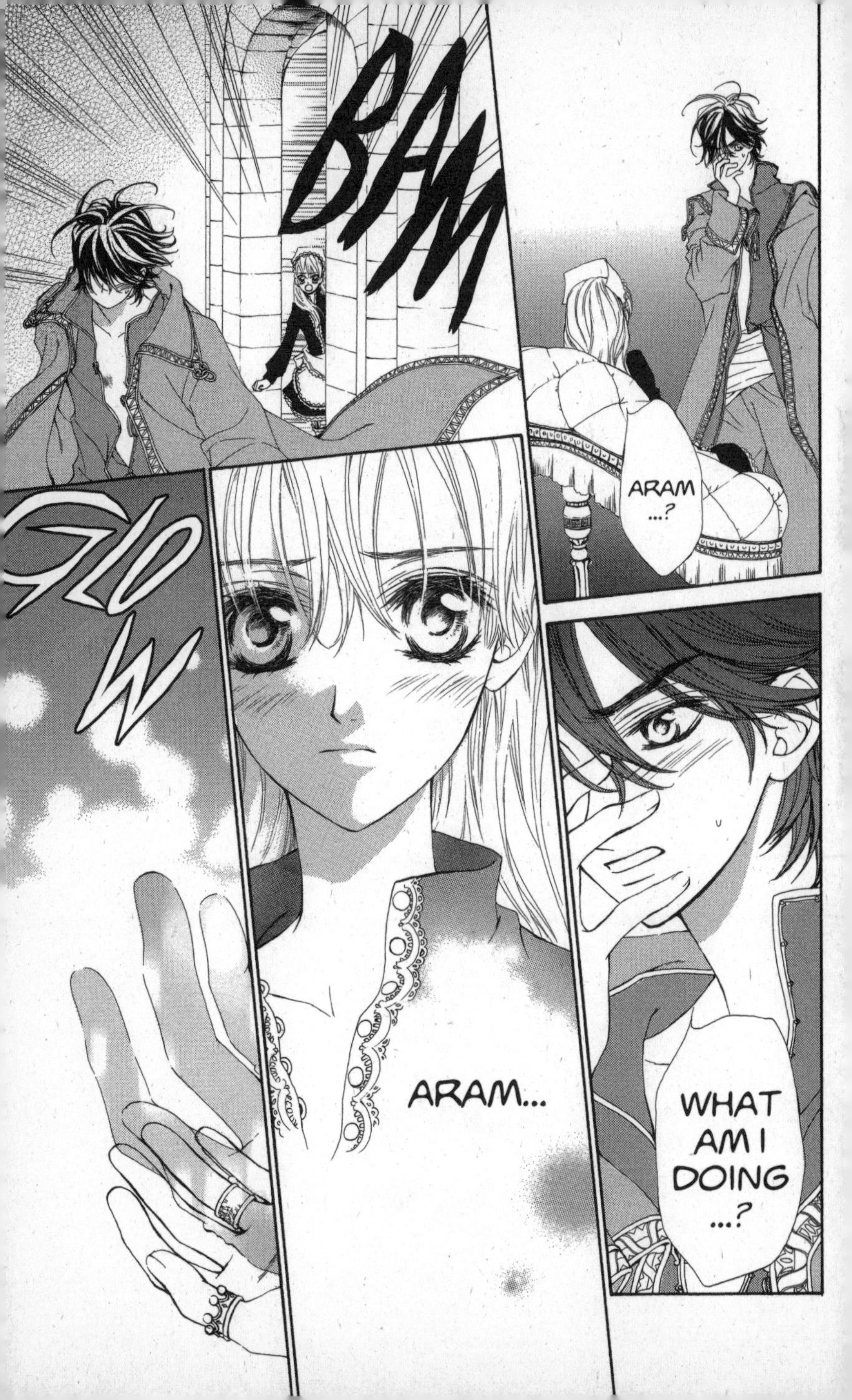
ARAM ...?
BAM
WHAT AM I DOING ...?
ARAM...
GLOW

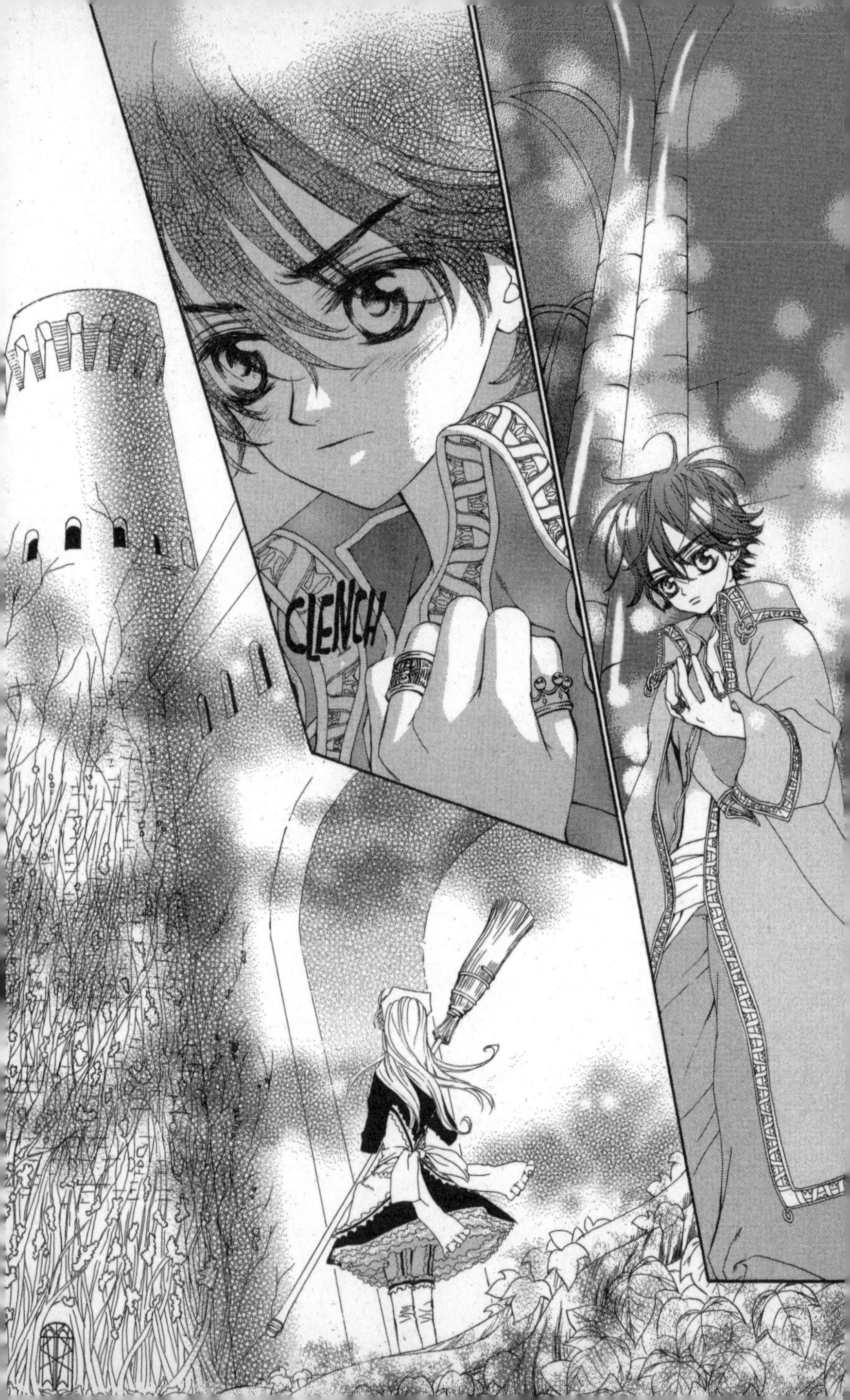
CLENCH

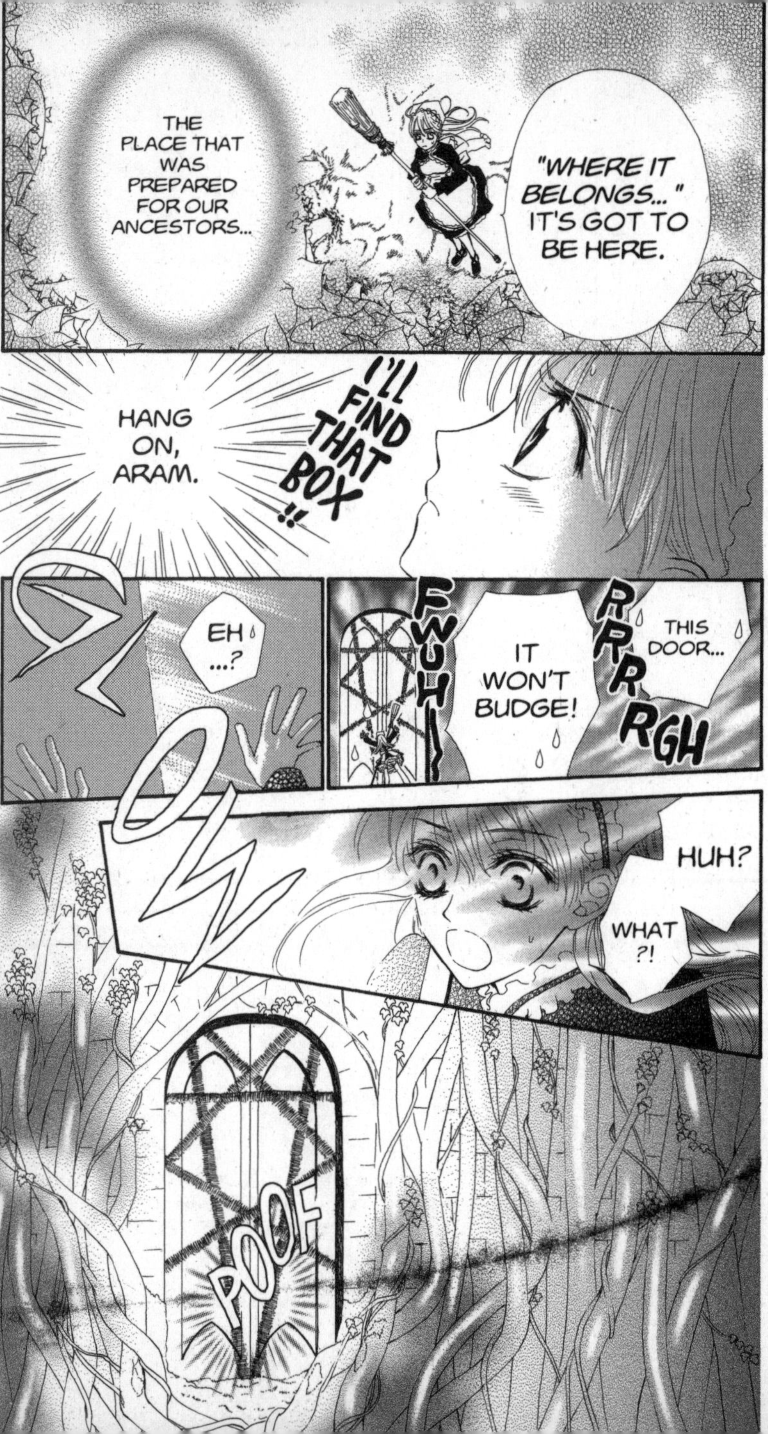
"WHERE IT BELONGS..." IT'S GOT TO BE HERE.
THE PLACE THAT WAS PREPARED FOR OUR ANCESTORS...
I'LL FIND THAT BOX!!
HANG ON, ARAM.
THIS DOOR...
RRRRGH
IT WON'T BUDGE!
FWUH
EH ...?
HUH?
WHAT ?!
POOF

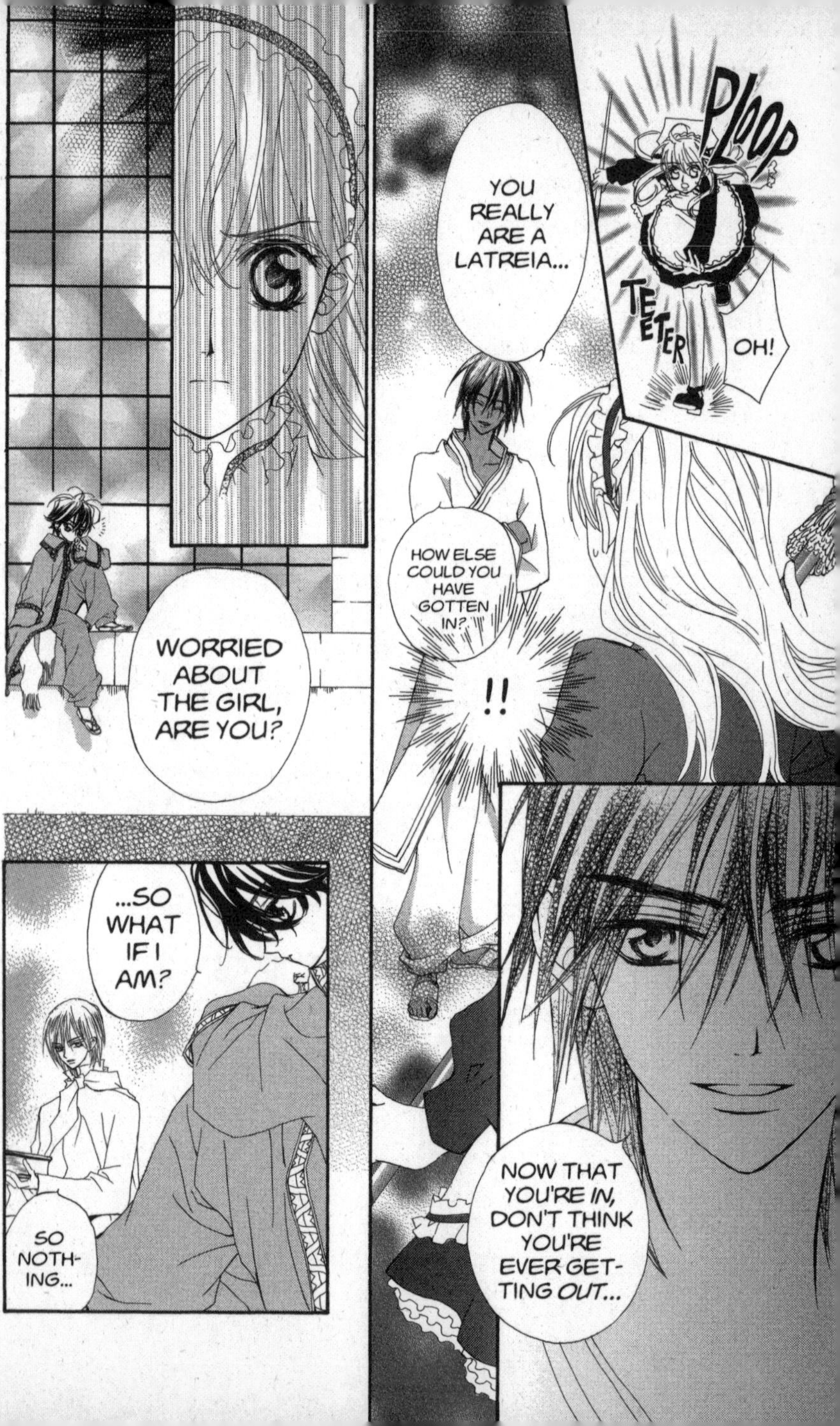
PLOOP
TETER
OH!
YOU REALLY ARE A LATREIA...
HOW ELSE COULD YOU HAVE GOTTEN IN?
!!
NOW THAT YOU'RE IN, DON'T THINK YOU'RE EVER GETTING OUT...
WORRIED ABOUT THE GIRL, ARE YOU?
...SO WHAT IF I AM?
SO NOTHING...

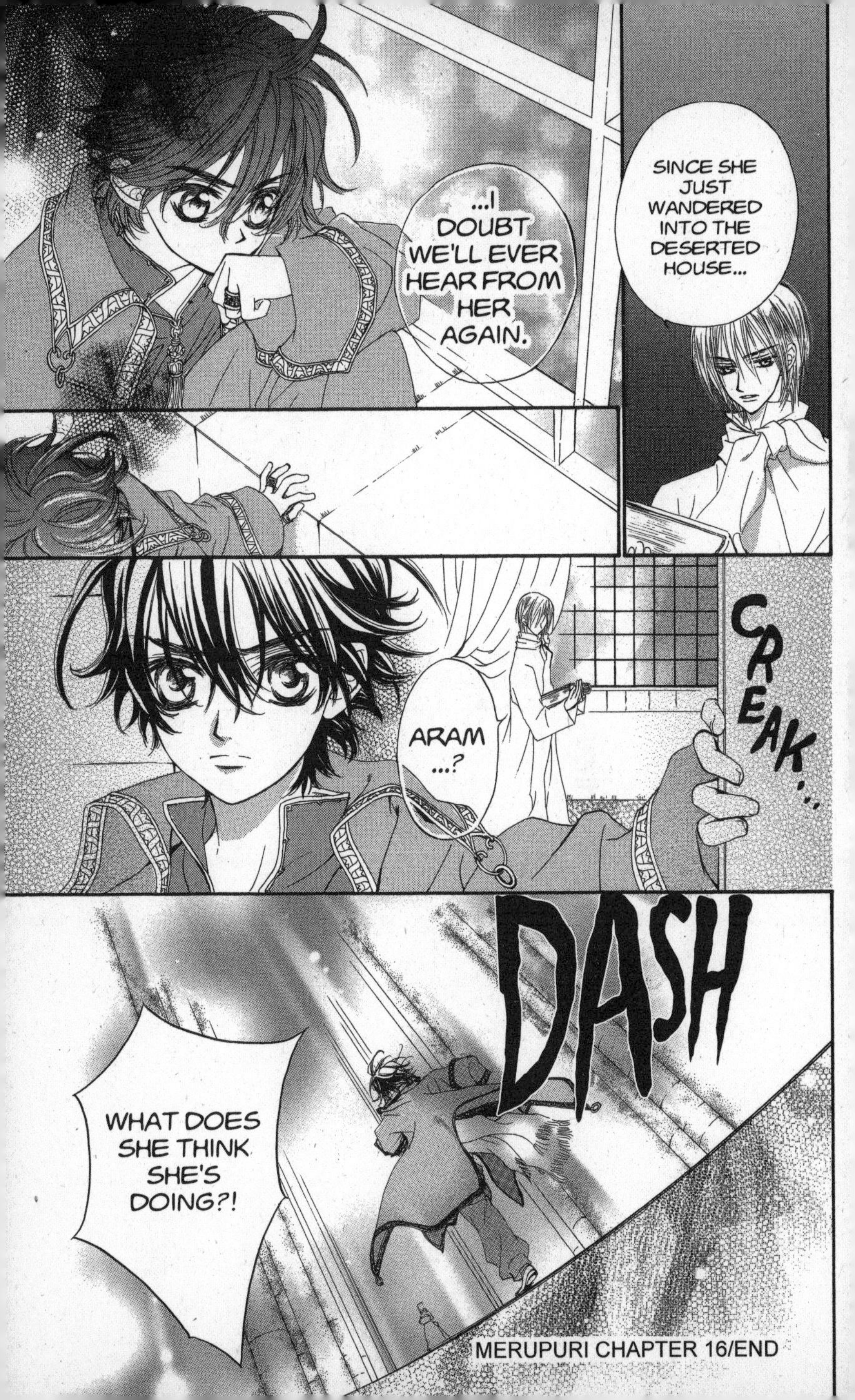
SINCE SHE JUST WANDERED INTO THE DESERTED HOUSE...
...I DOUBT WE'LL EVER HEAR FROM HER AGAIN.
CREAK...
ARAM ...?
DASH
WHAT DOES SHE THINK SHE'S DOING?!
MERUPURI CHAPTER 16/END

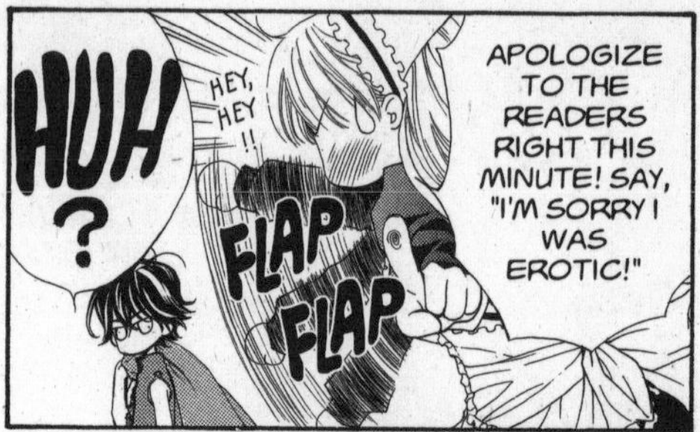
APOLOGIZE TO THE READERS RIGHT THIS MINUTE! SAY, "I'M SORRY I WAS EROTIC!"
HEY, HEY !!
HUH ?
FLAP FLAP
DON'T POINT, AIRI.

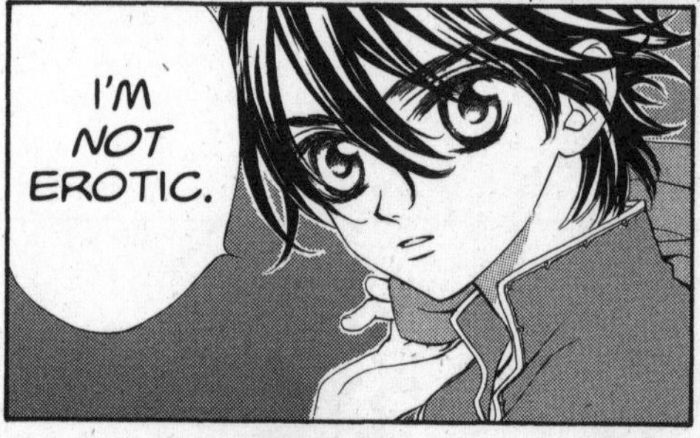
I'M NOT EROTIC.

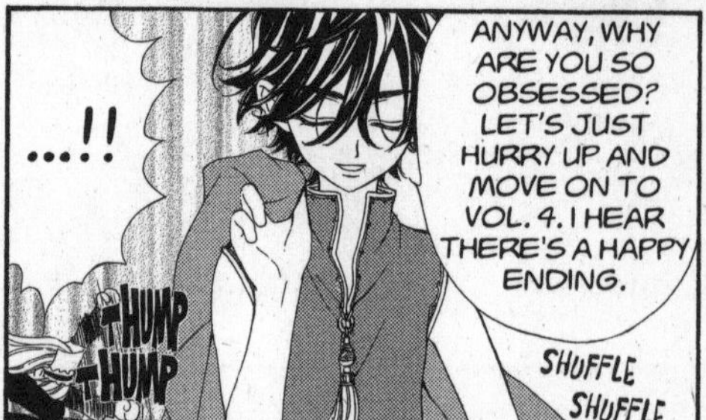
ANYWAY, WHY ARE YOU SO OBSESSED? LET'S JUST HURRY UP AND MOVE ON TO VOL. 4. I HEAR THERE'S A HAPPY ENDING.
...!!
THUMP THUMP
SHUFFLE SHUFFLE
HANG IN THERE, AIRI!

CONTINUED IN VOL. 4 ♡

AUXILIARY STORY STARTS HERE ♥

MeruPuri™
Märchen Prince

SPECIAL AUXILIARY CHAPTER

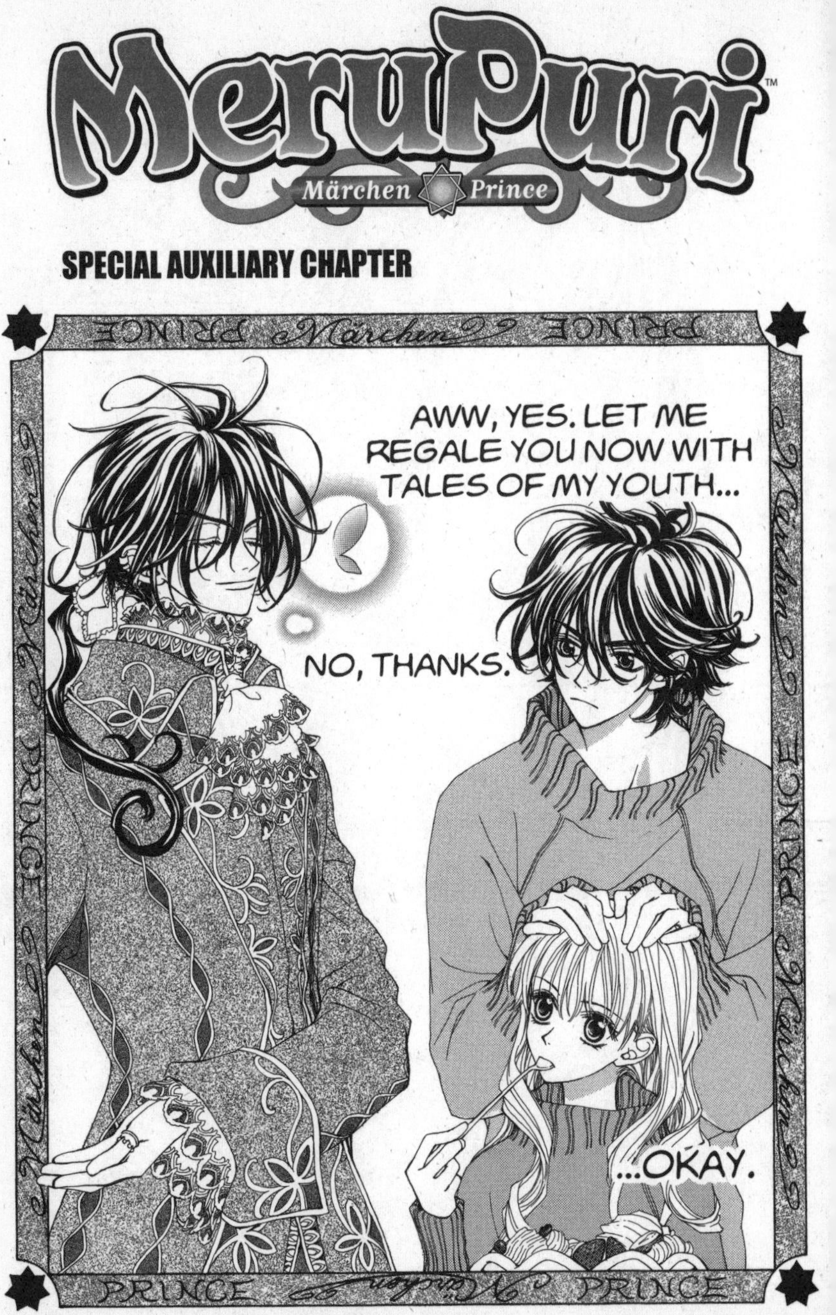
AWW, YES. LET ME REGALE YOU NOW WITH TALES OF MY YOUTH...
NO, THANKS.
...OKAY.

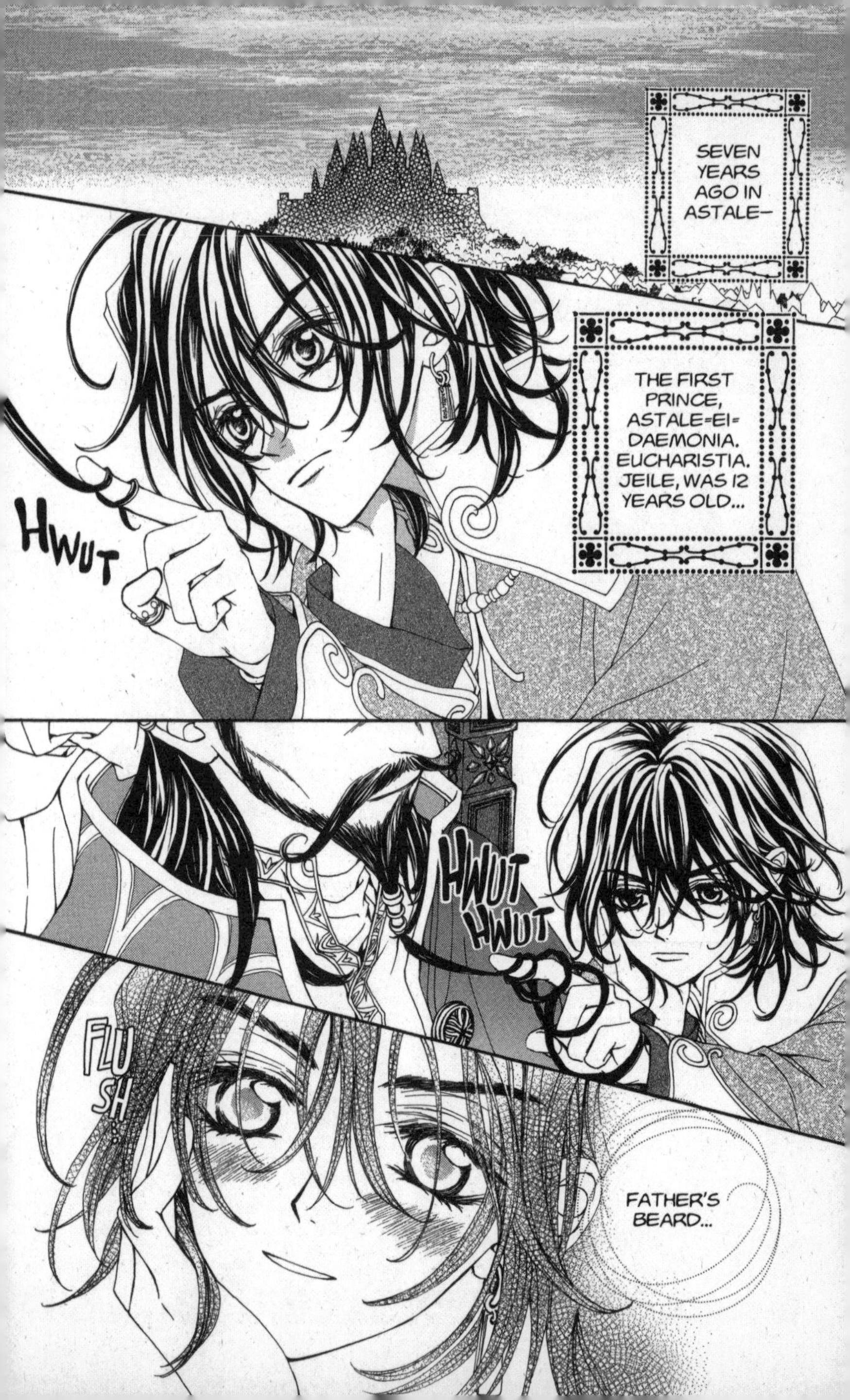
SEVEN YEARS AGO IN ASTALE–
THE FIRST PRINCE, ASTALE=EI=DAEMONIA. EUCHARISTIA. JEILE, WAS 12 YEARS OLD...
HWUT
HWUT HWUT
FLUSH
FATHER'S BEARD...

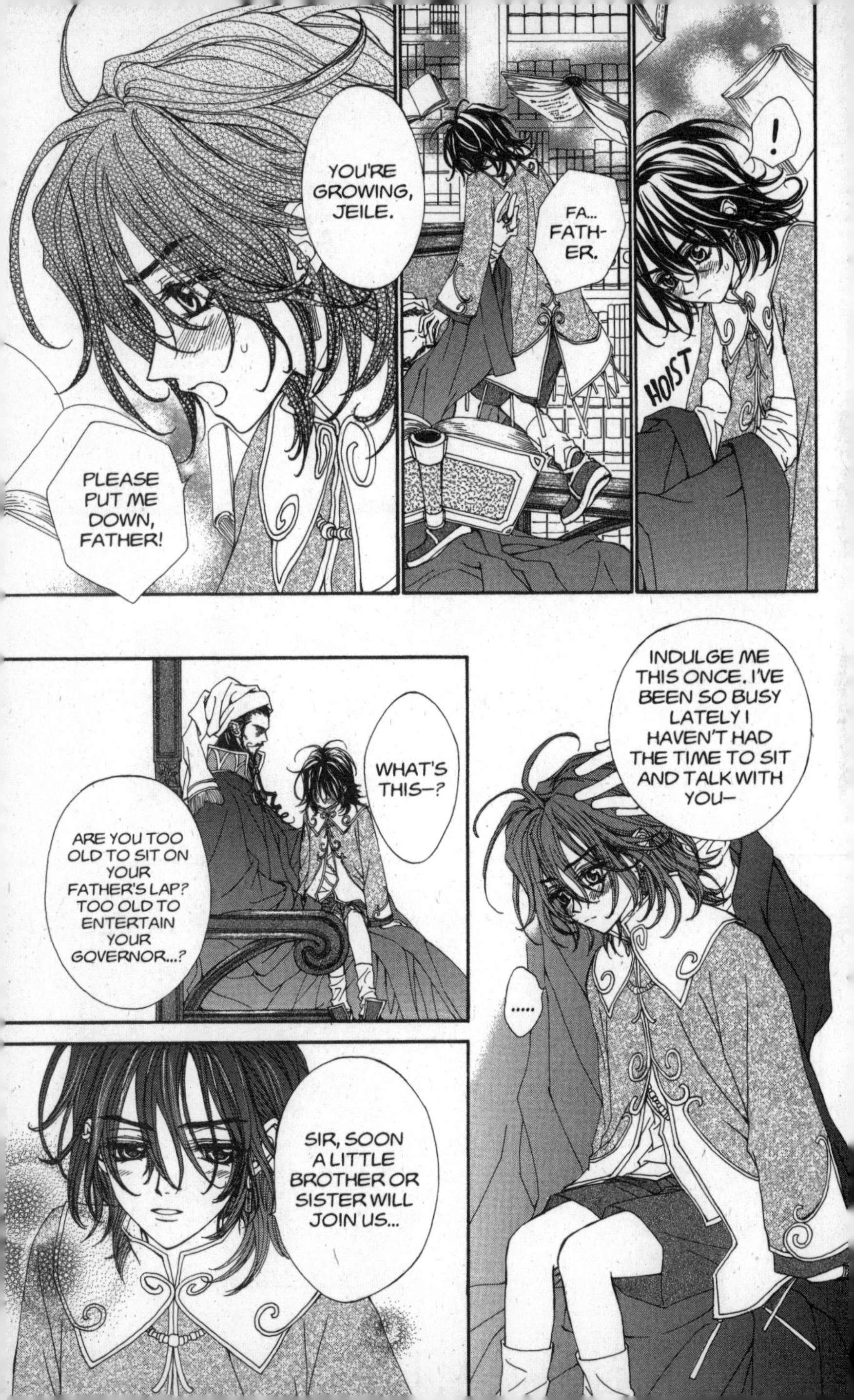
!
HOIST
FA... FATHER-ER.
YOU'RE GROWING, JEILE.
PLEASE PUT ME DOWN, FATHER!
INDULGE ME THIS ONCE. I'VE BEEN SO BUSY LATELY I HAVEN'T HAD THE TIME TO SIT AND TALK WITH YOU—
......
WHAT'S THIS—?
ARE YOU TOO OLD TO SIT ON YOUR FATHER'S LAP? TOO OLD TO ENTERTAIN YOUR GOVERNOR...?
SIR, SOON A LITTLE BROTHER OR SISTER WILL JOIN US...

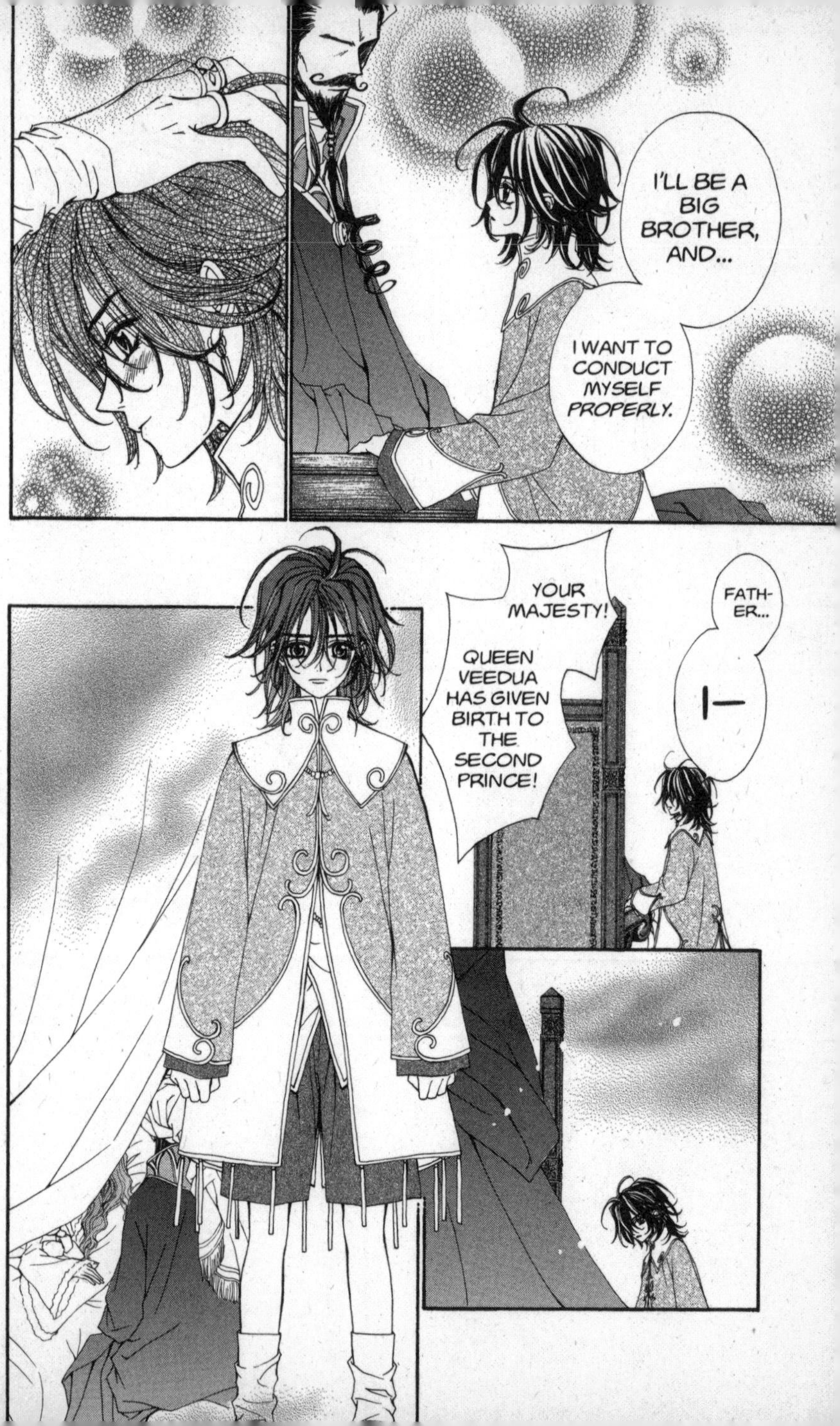
I'LL BE A BIG BROTHER, AND...
I WANT TO CONDUCT MYSELF PROPERLY.
FATH-ER...
I—
YOUR MAJESTY!
QUEEN VEEDUA HAS GIVEN BIRTH TO THE SECOND PRINCE!

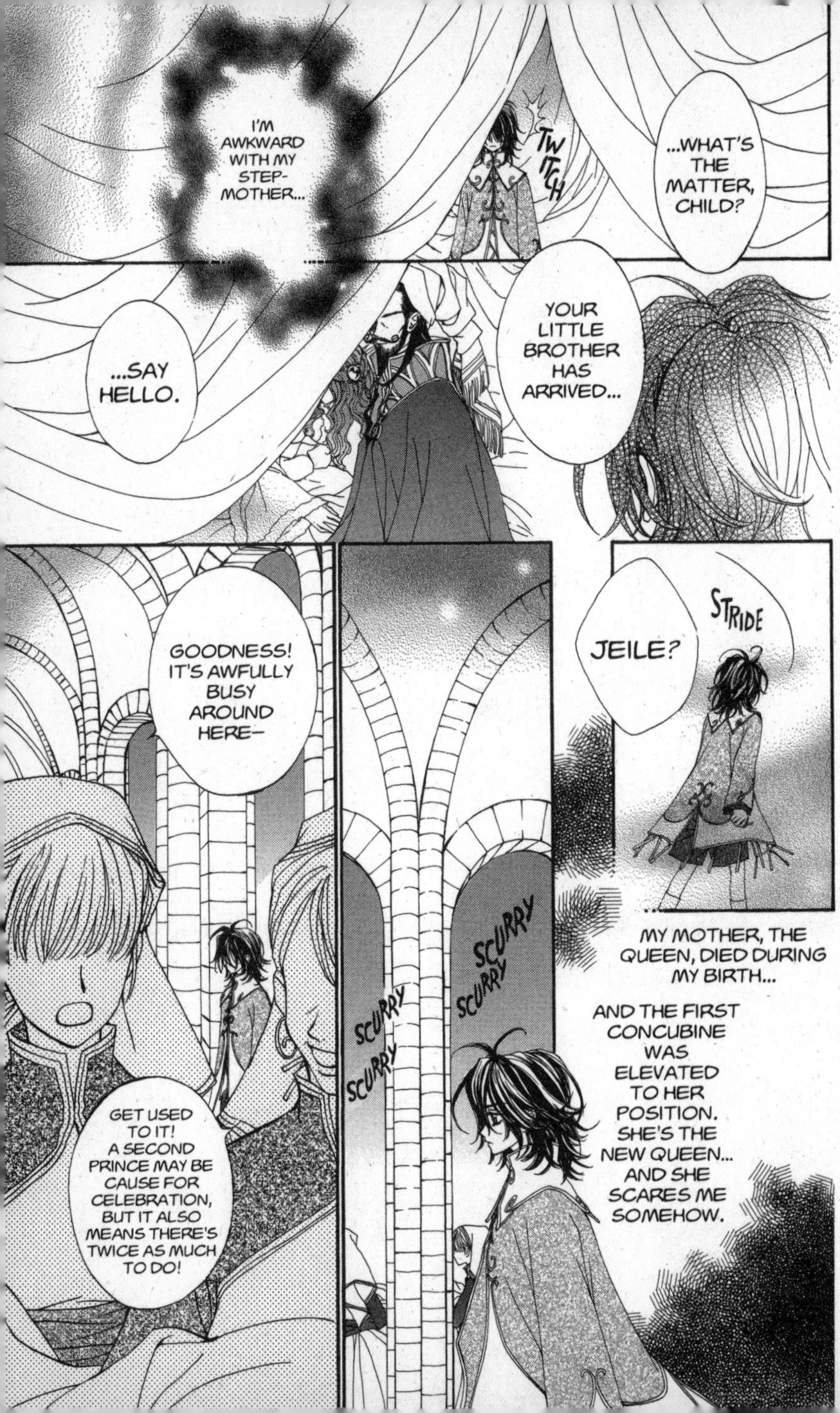

...WHAT'S THE MATTER, CHILD?
TWITCH
I'M AWKWARD WITH MY STEP-MOTHER...
YOUR LITTLE BROTHER HAS ARRIVED...
...SAY HELLO.
STRIDE
JEILE?
MY MOTHER, THE QUEEN, DIED DURING MY BIRTH...
AND THE FIRST CONCUBINE WAS ELEVATED TO HER POSITION. SHE'S THE NEW QUEEN... AND SHE SCARES ME SOMEHOW.
SCURRY SCURRY
SCURRY SCURRY
GOODNESS! IT'S AWFULLY BUSY AROUND HERE–
GET USED TO IT! A SECOND PRINCE MAY BE CAUSE FOR CELEBRATION, BUT IT ALSO MEANS THERE'S TWICE AS MUCH TO DO!

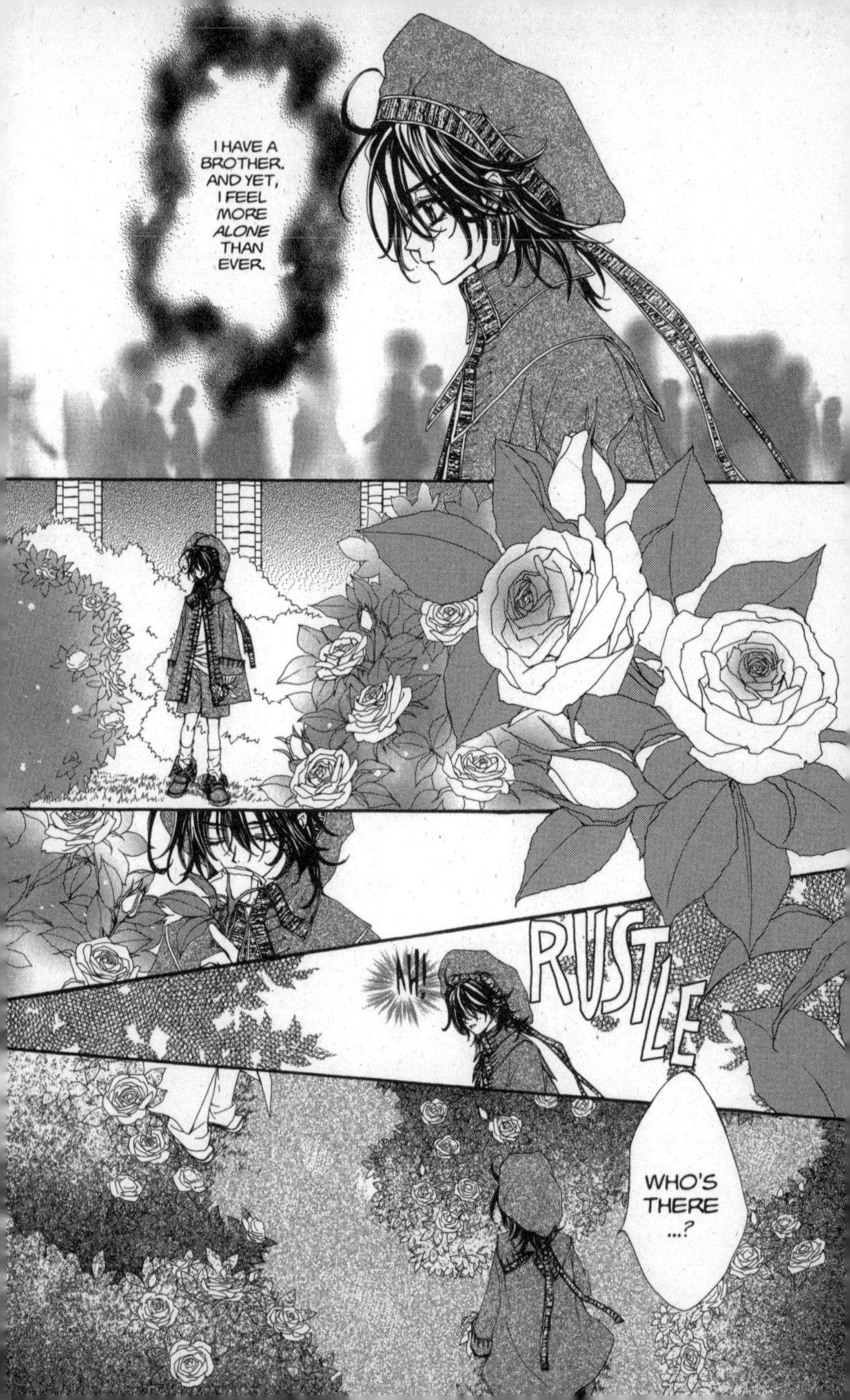
I HAVE A BROTHER. AND YET, I FEEL MORE ALONE THAN EVER.
RUSTLE
AH!
WHO'S THERE ...?

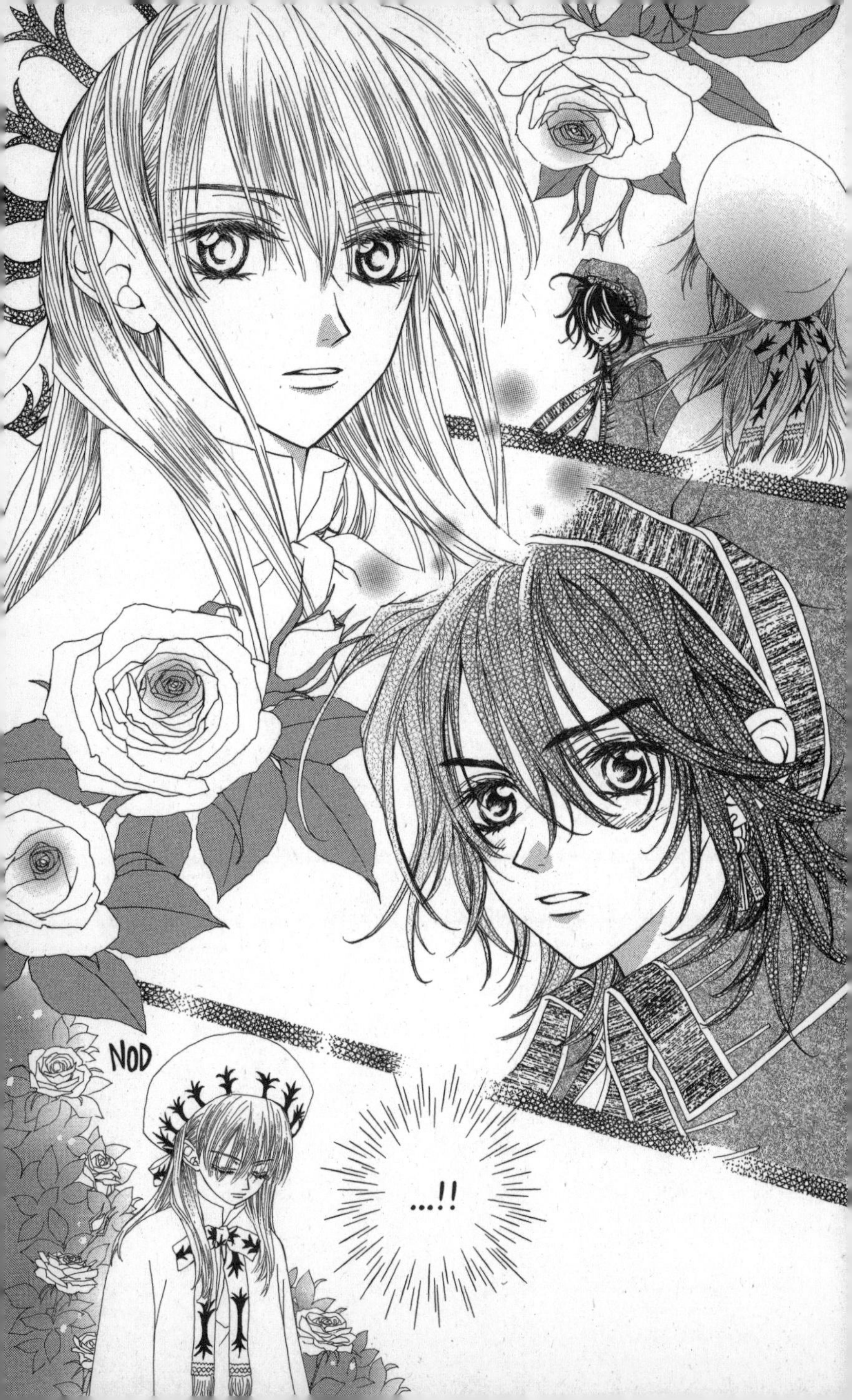
NOD
...!!

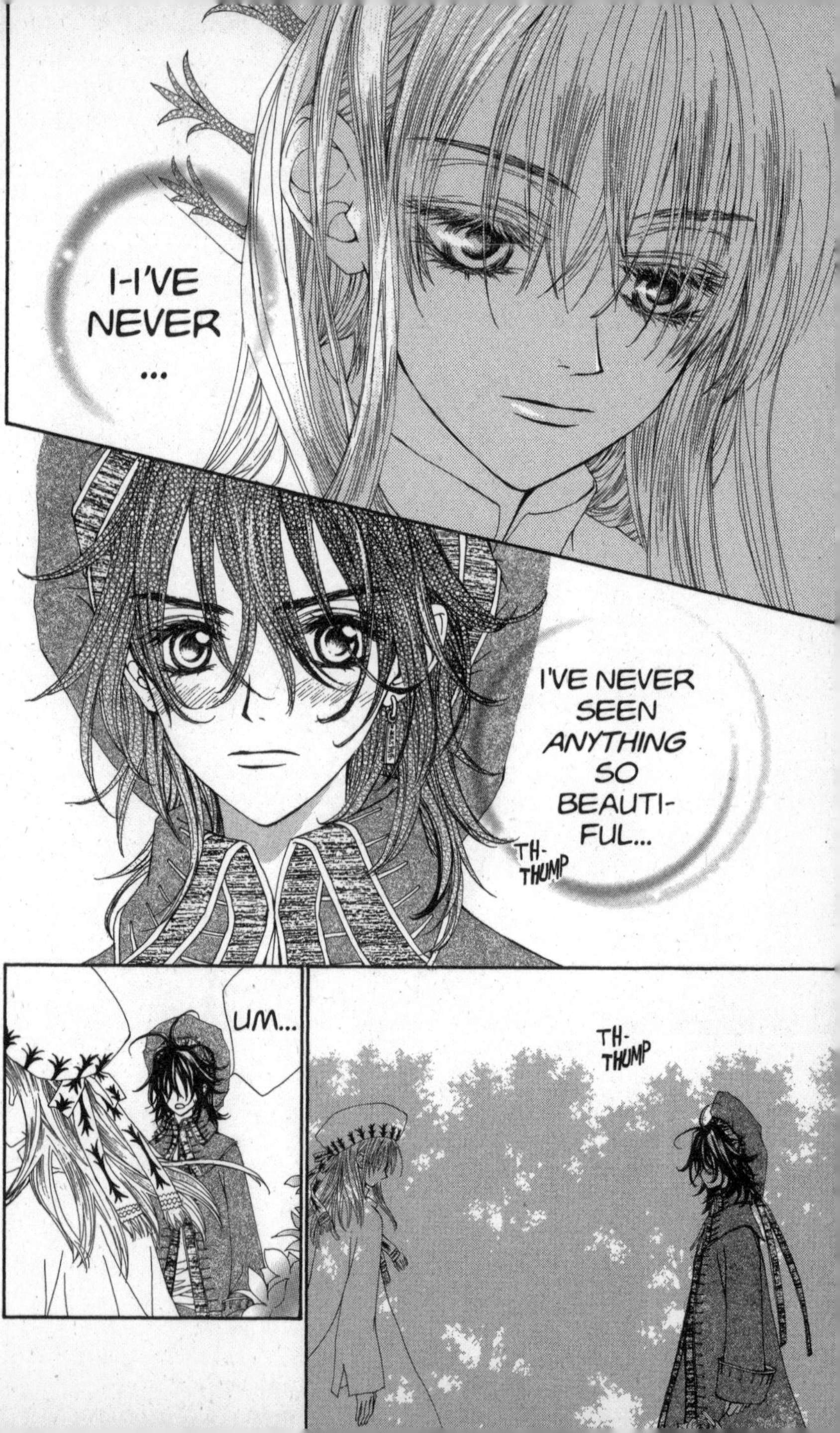
I-I'VE NEVER ...
I'VE NEVER SEEN ANYTHING SO BEAUTI-FUL...
TH-THUMP
TH-THUMP
UM...

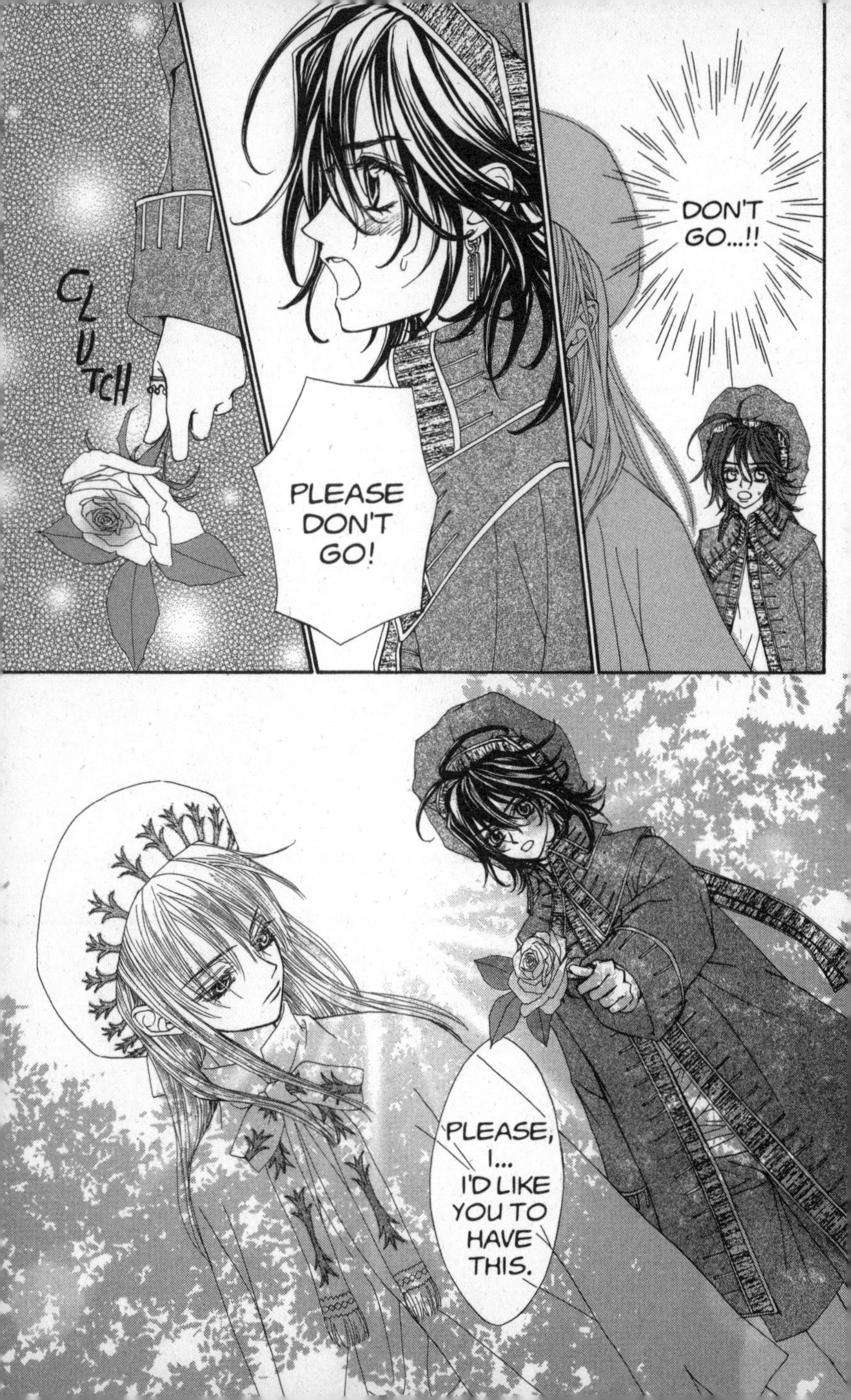
DON'T GO...!!
PLEASE DON'T GO!
CLUTCH
PLEASE, I... I'D LIKE YOU TO HAVE THIS.

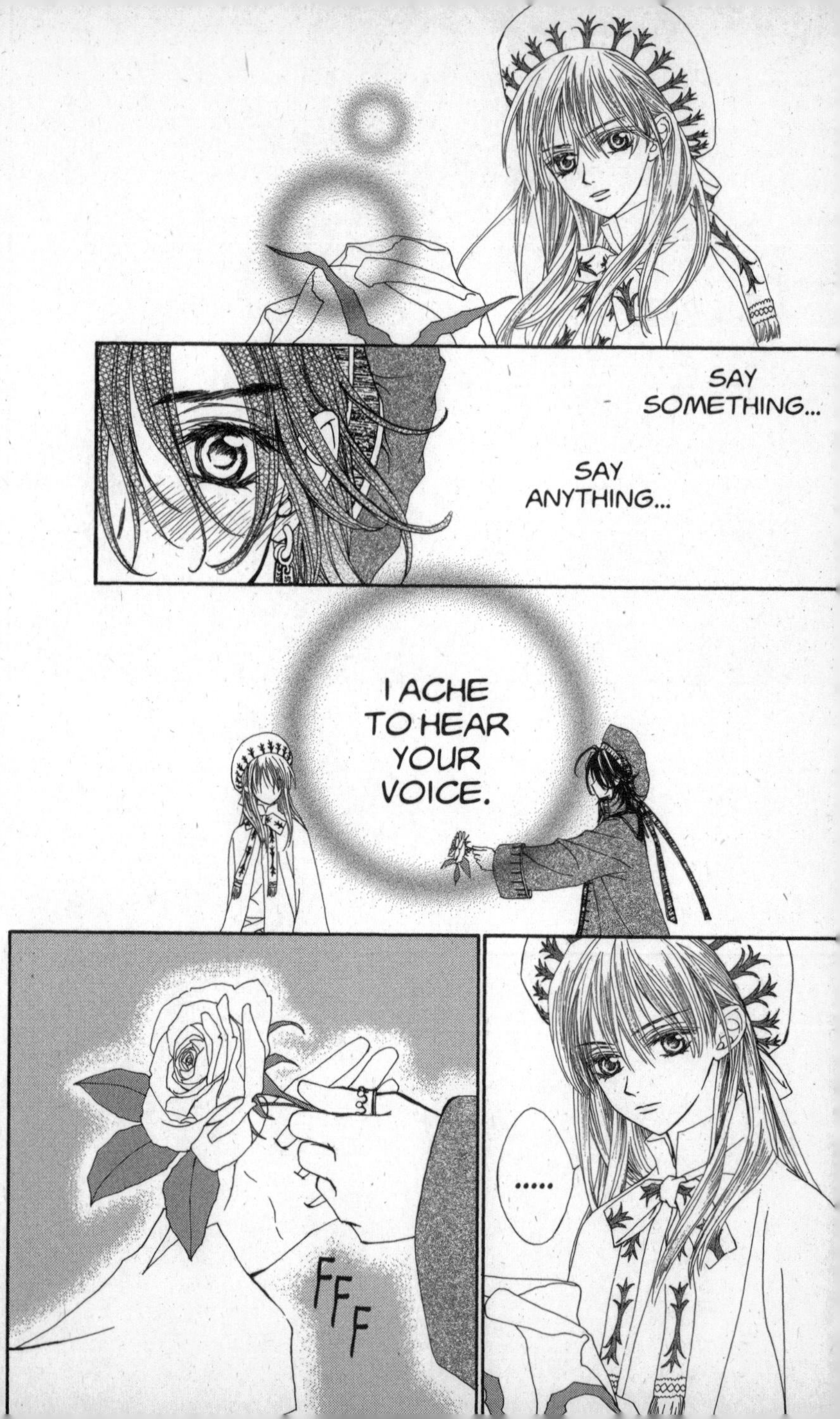
SAY SOMETHING...
SAY ANYTHING...
I ACHE TO HEAR YOUR VOICE.
.....
FFF

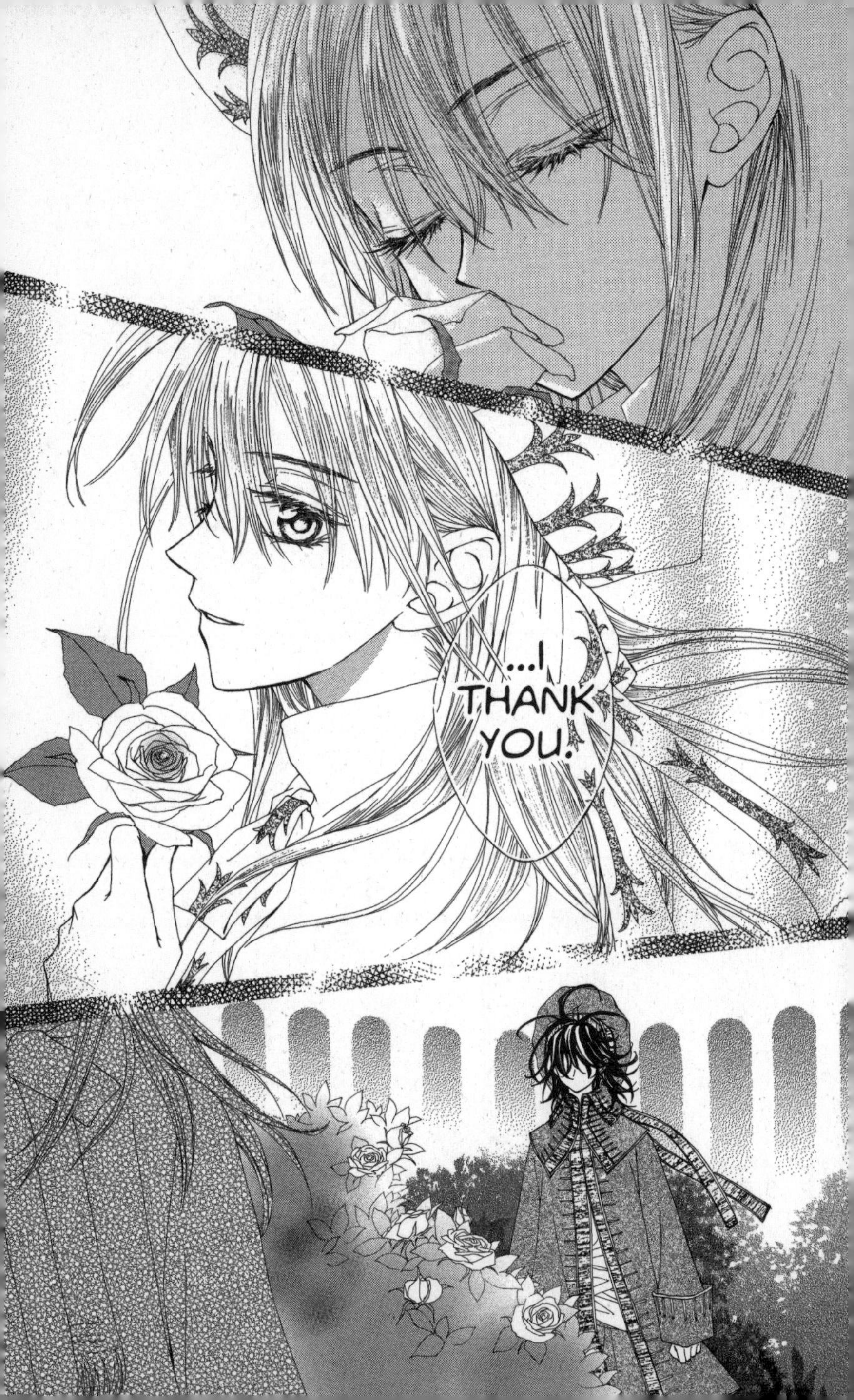
...I THANK YOU.

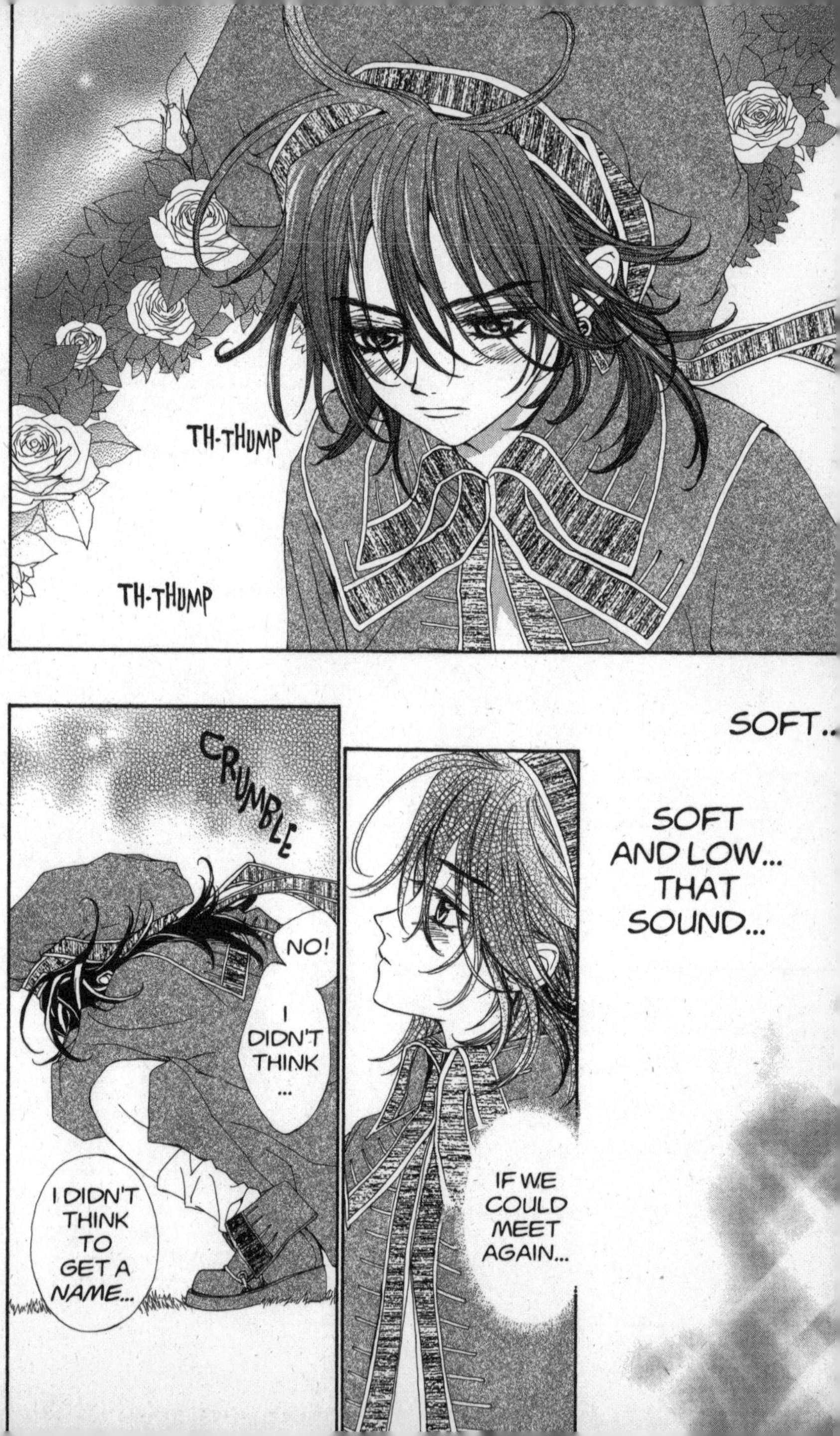
TH-THUMP
TH-THUMP
SOFT...
SOFT AND LOW... THAT SOUND...
IF WE COULD MEET AGAIN...
CRUMBLE
NO!
I DIDN'T THINK ...
I DIDN'T THINK TO GET A NAME...

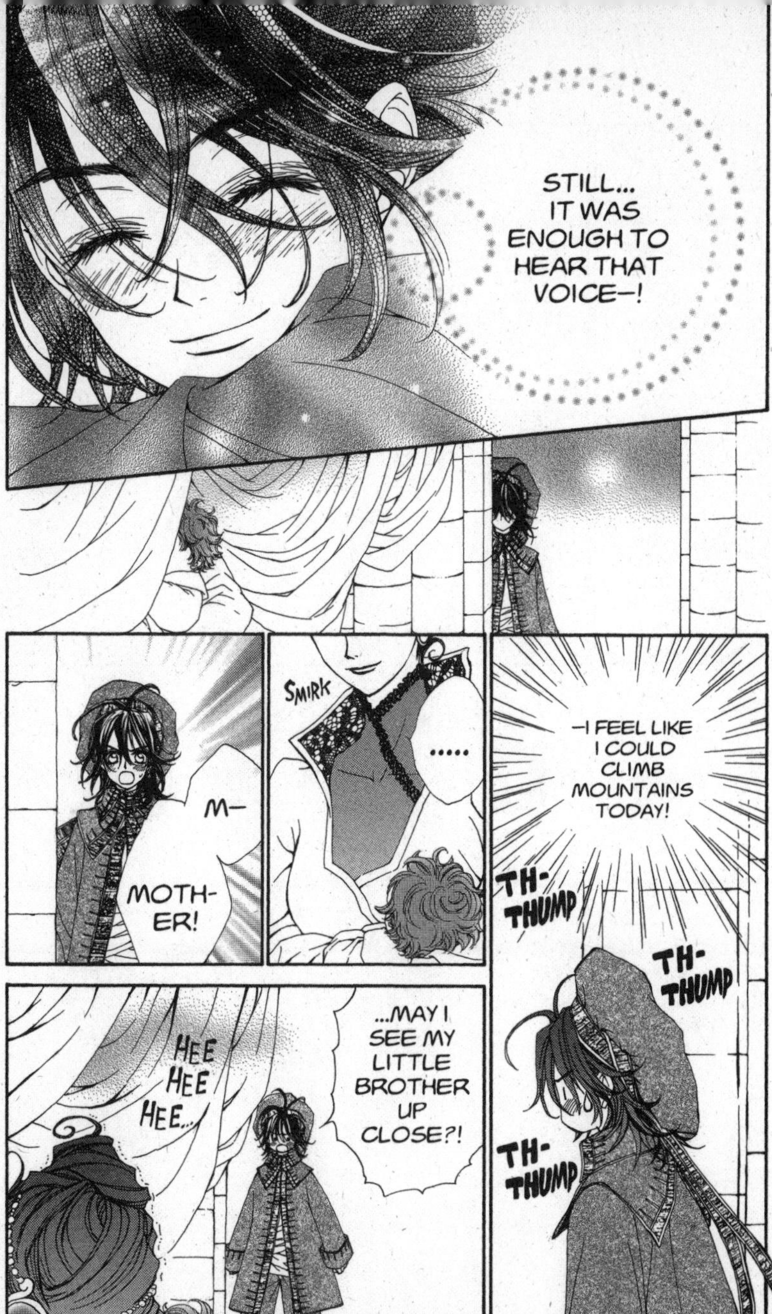
STILL... IT WAS ENOUGH TO HEAR THAT VOICE—!
—I FEEL LIKE I COULD CLIMB MOUNTAINS TODAY!
TH-THUMP
TH-THUMP
TH-THUMP
SMIRK
.....
M-
MOTH-ER!
...MAY I SEE MY LITTLE BROTHER UP CLOSE?!
HEE HEE HEE...

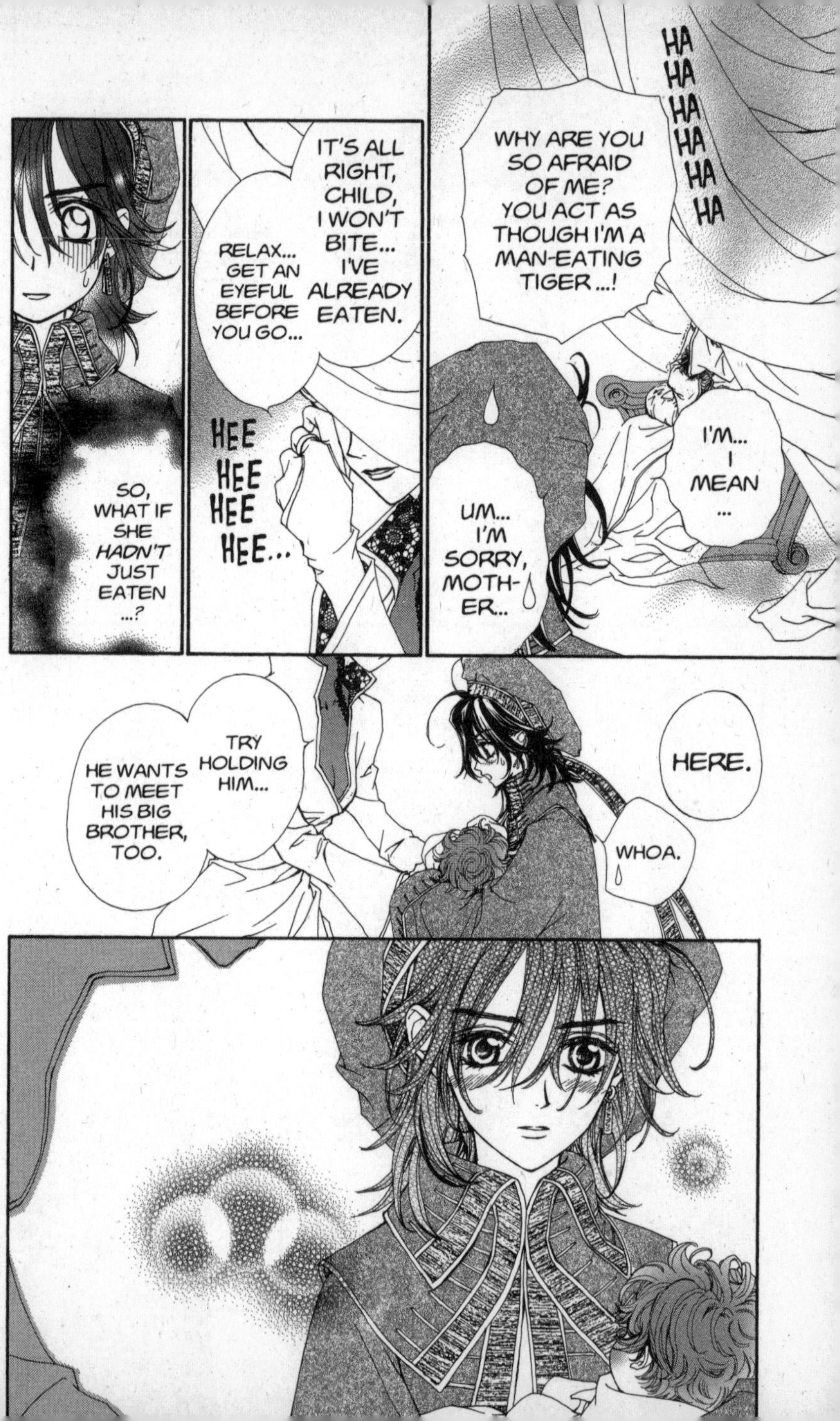
HA HA HA HA HA HA
WHY ARE YOU SO AFRAID OF ME? YOU ACT AS THOUGH I'M A MAN-EATING TIGER...!
I'M... I MEAN...
UM... I'M SORRY, MOTHER...
IT'S ALL RIGHT, CHILD, I WON'T BITE... I'VE ALREADY EATEN.
RELAX... GET AN EYEFUL BEFORE YOU GO...
HEE HEE HEE HEE...
SO, WHAT IF SHE HADN'T JUST EATEN...?
HERE.
WHOA.
TRY HOLDING HIM...
HE WANTS TO MEET HIS BIG BROTHER, TOO.

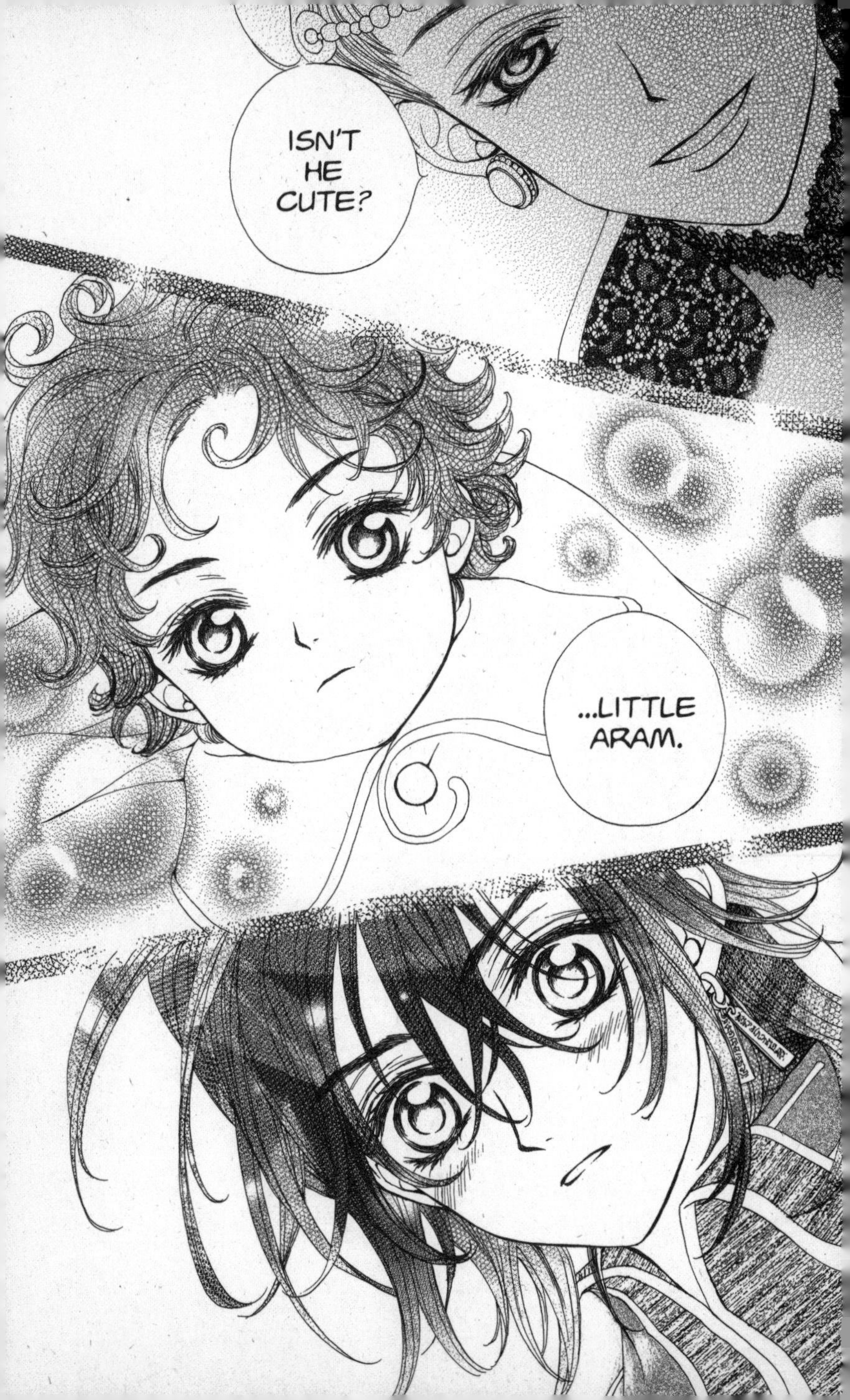
ISN'T HE CUTE?
...LITTLE ARAM.

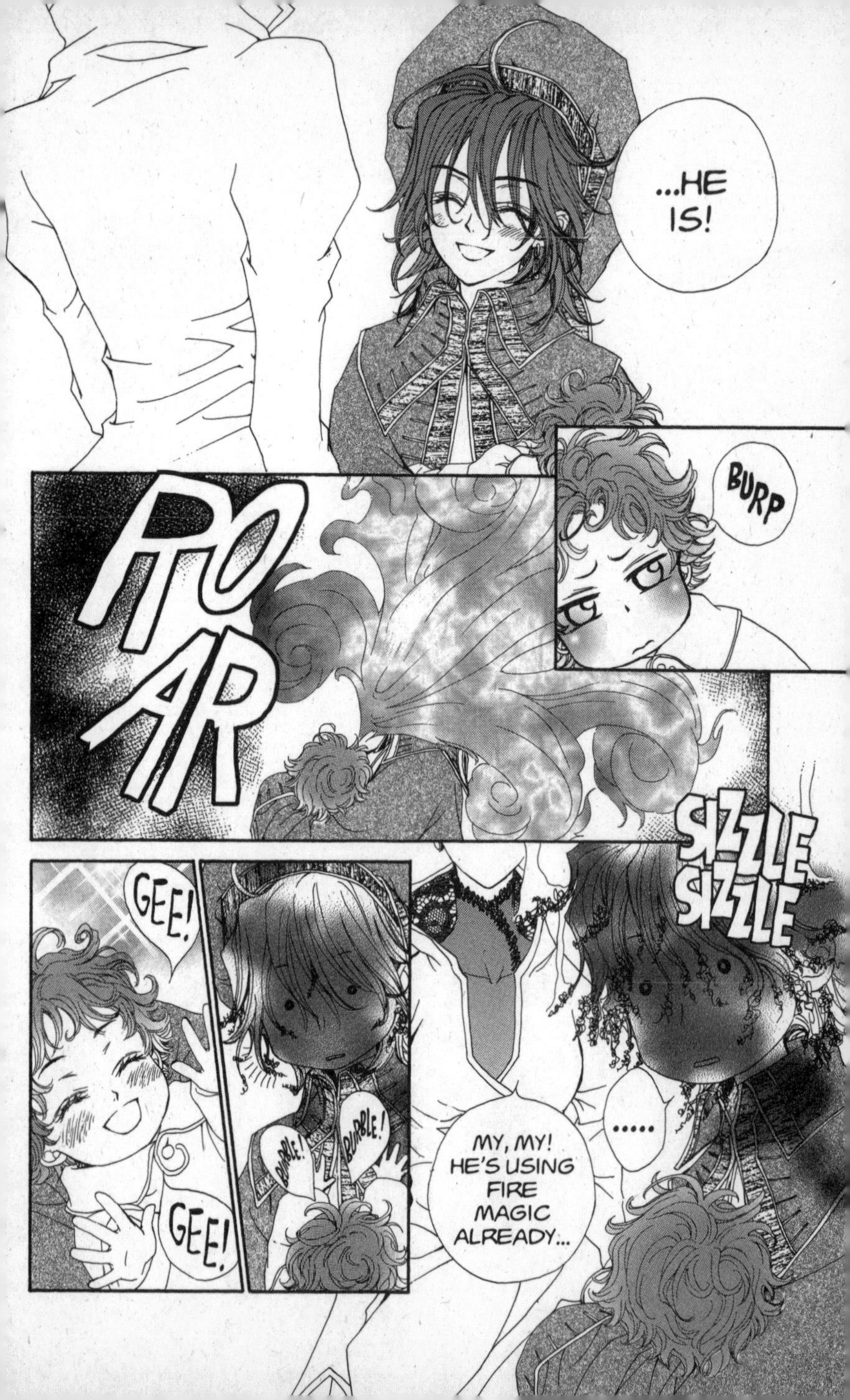
...HE IS!
BURP
POAR
SIZZLE SIZZLE
.....
MY, MY! HE'S USING FIRE MAGIC ALREADY...
BURBLE!
BURBLE!
GEE!
GEE!

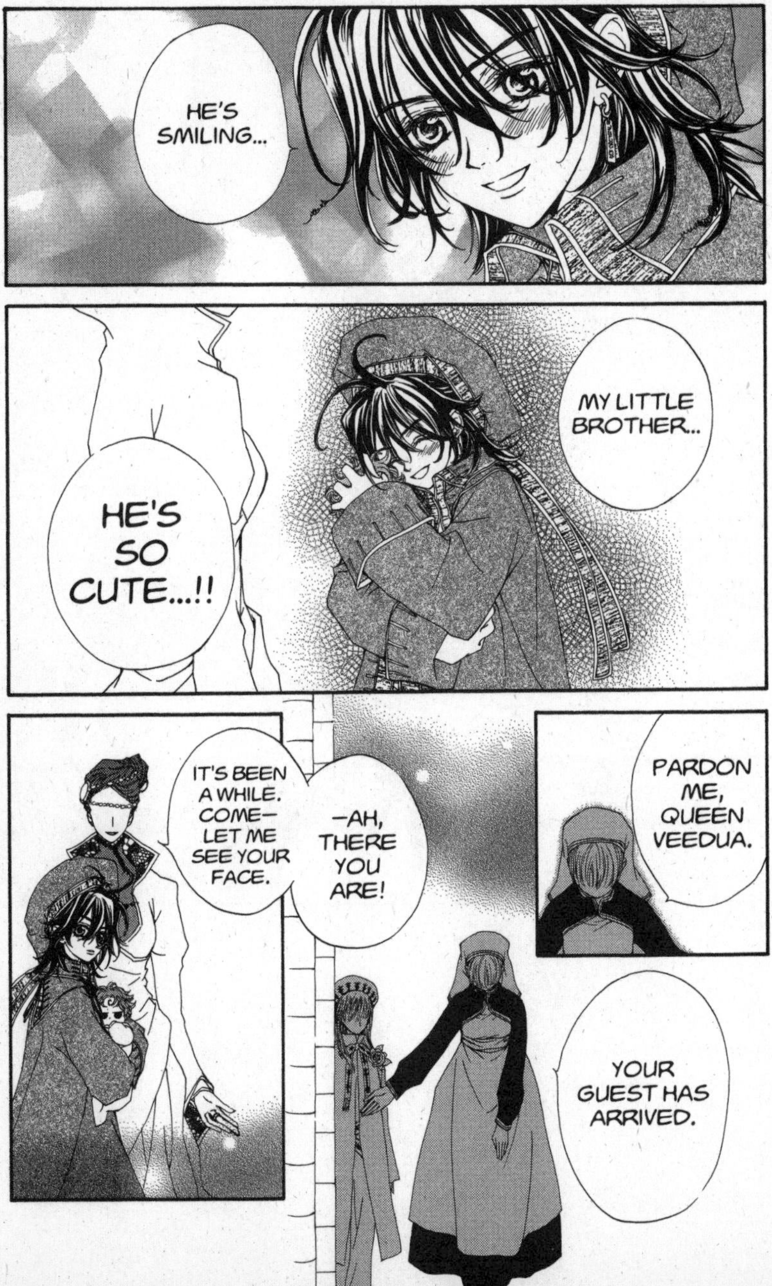
HE'S SMILING...
MY LITTLE BROTHER...
HE'S SO CUTE...!!
PARDON ME, QUEEN VEEDUA.
YOUR GUEST HAS ARRIVED.
—AH, THERE YOU ARE!
IT'S BEEN A WHILE. COME— LET ME SEE YOUR FACE.

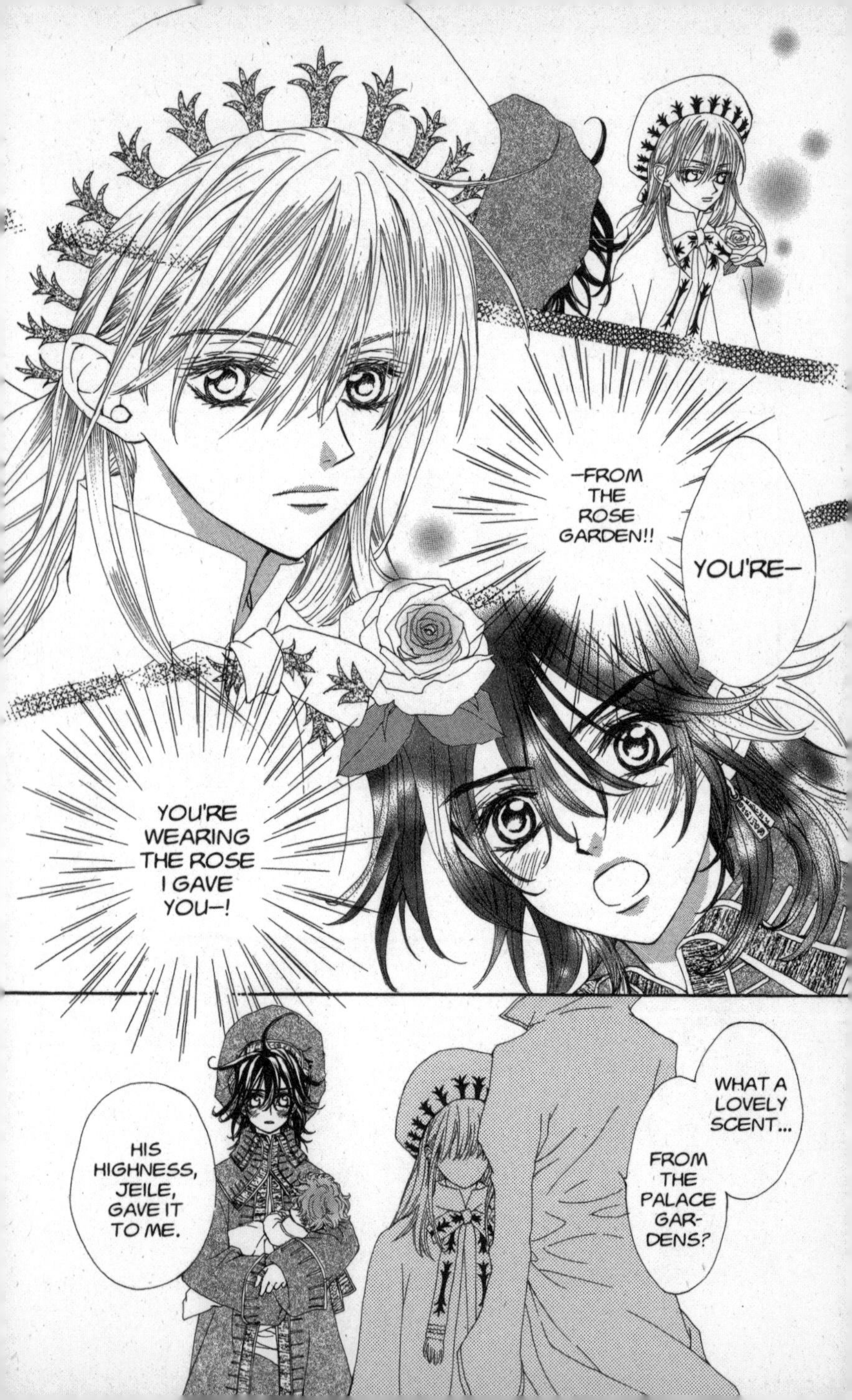
YOU'RE—
—FROM THE ROSE GARDEN!!
YOU'RE WEARING THE ROSE I GAVE YOU—!
WHAT A LOVELY SCENT...
FROM THE PALACE GAR-DENS?
HIS HIGHNESS, JEILE, GAVE IT TO ME.

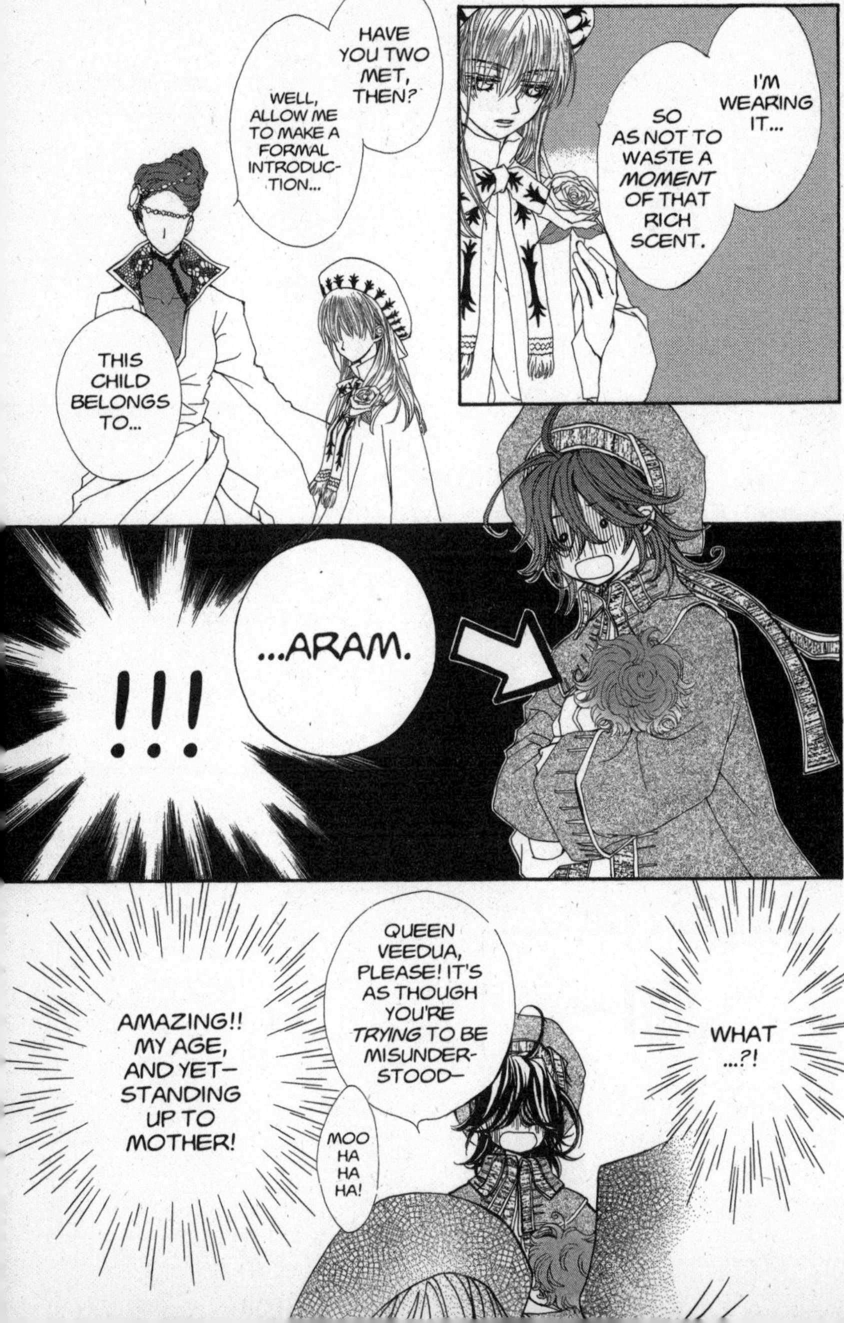
I'M WEARING IT...
SO AS NOT TO WASTE A *MOMENT* OF THAT RICH SCENT.
HAVE YOU TWO MET, THEN?
WELL, ALLOW ME TO MAKE A FORMAL INTRODUC-TION...
THIS CHILD BELONGS TO...
...ARAM.
!!!
WHAT ...?!
QUEEN VEEDUA, PLEASE! IT'S AS THOUGH YOU'RE *TRYING* TO BE MISUNDER-STOOD—
MOO HA HA HA!
AMAZING!! MY AGE, AND YET— STANDING UP TO MOTHER!

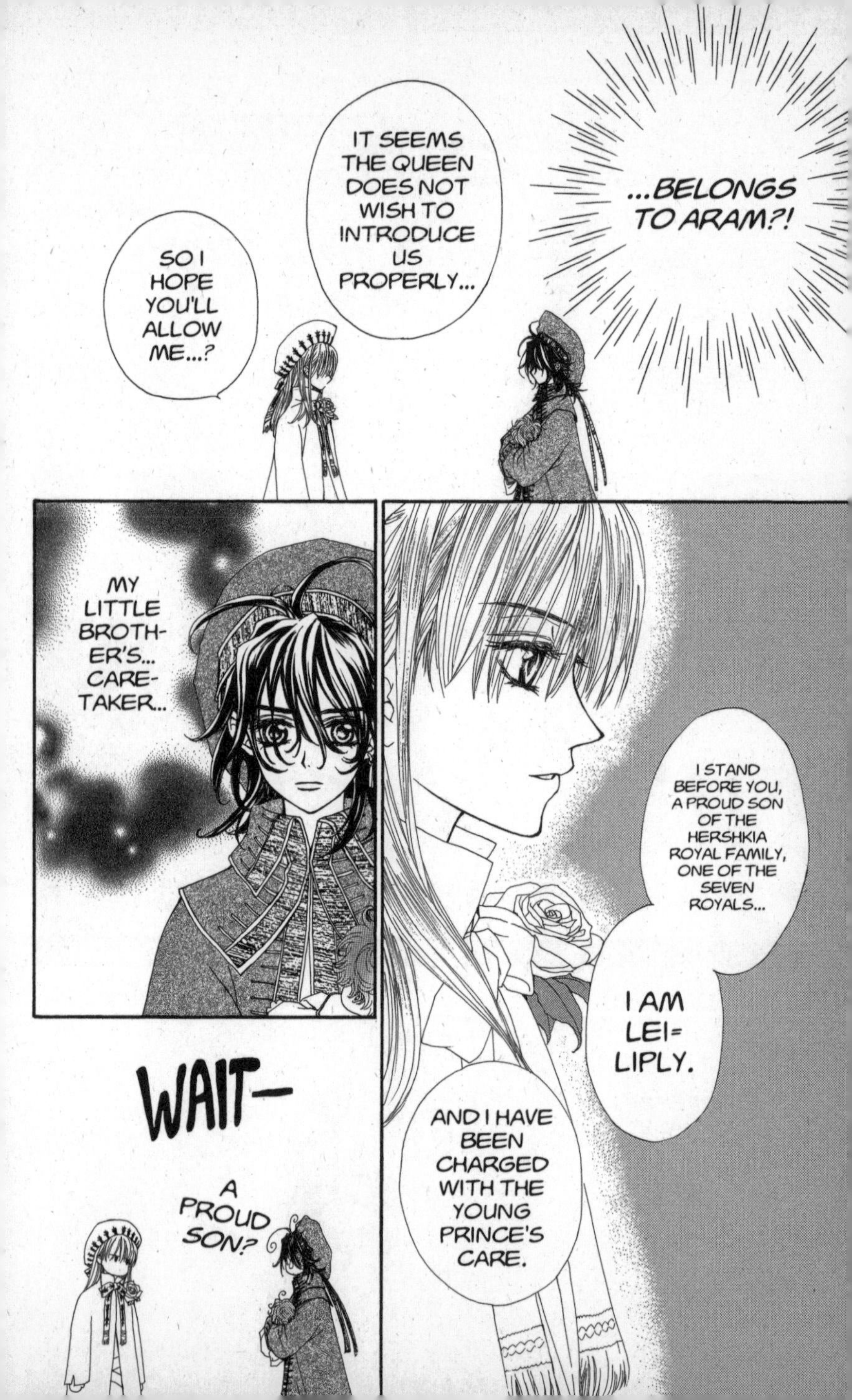
...BELONGS TO ARAM?!
IT SEEMS THE QUEEN DOES NOT WISH TO INTRODUCE US PROPERLY...
SO I HOPE YOU'LL ALLOW ME...?
I STAND BEFORE YOU, A PROUD SON OF THE HERSHKIA ROYAL FAMILY, ONE OF THE SEVEN ROYALS...
I AM LEI=LIPLY.
AND I HAVE BEEN CHARGED WITH THE YOUNG PRINCE'S CARE.
MY LITTLE BROTHER'S... CARETAKER...
WAIT-
A PROUD SON?

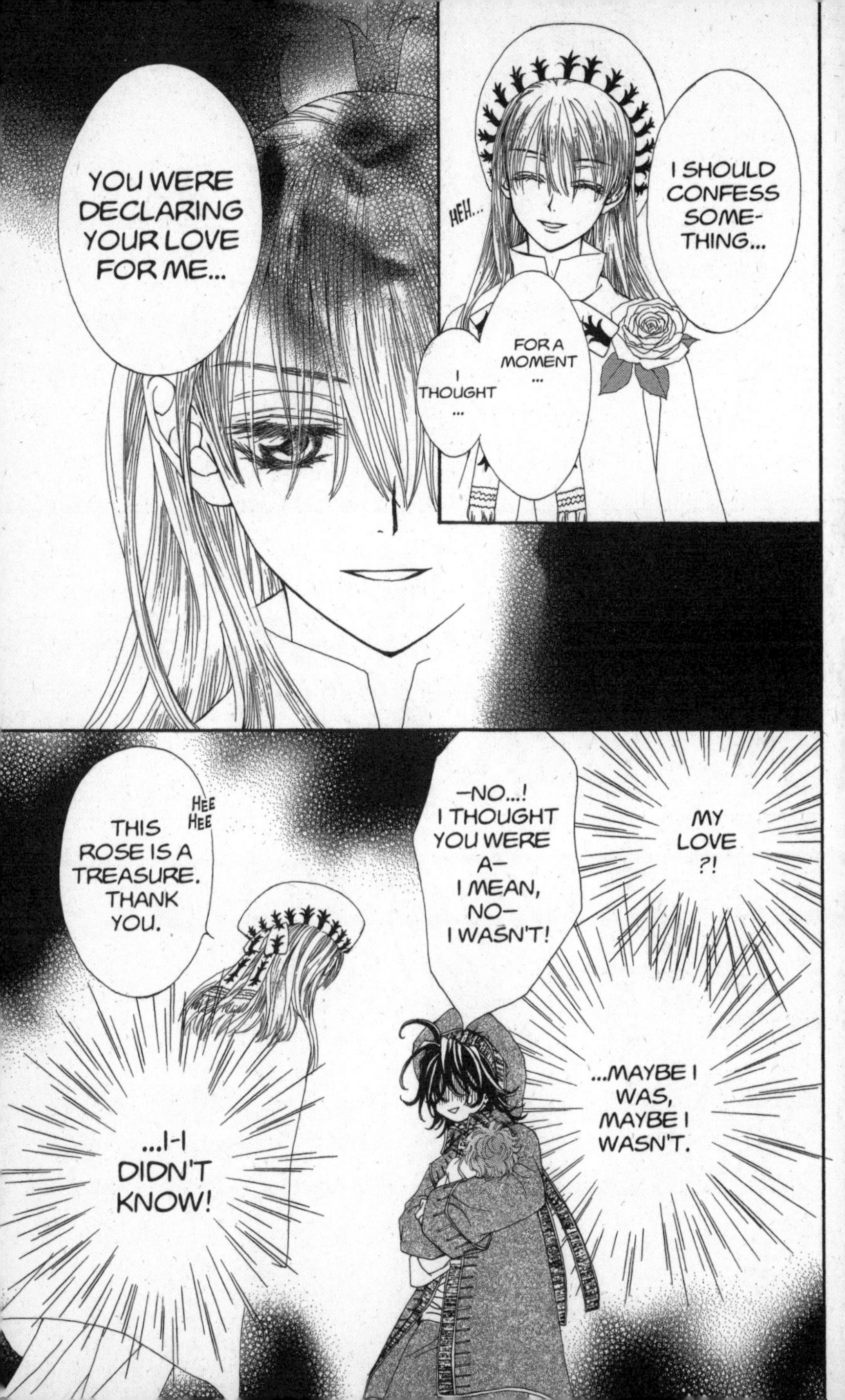
I SHOULD CONFESS SOME-THING...
HEH...
FOR A MOMENT ...
I THOUGHT ...
YOU WERE DECLARING YOUR LOVE FOR ME...
MY LOVE ?!
—NO...! I THOUGHT YOU WERE A— I MEAN, NO— I WASN'T!
HEE HEE
THIS ROSE IS A TREASURE. THANK YOU.
...MAYBE I WAS, MAYBE I WASN'T.
...I-I DIDN'T KNOW!

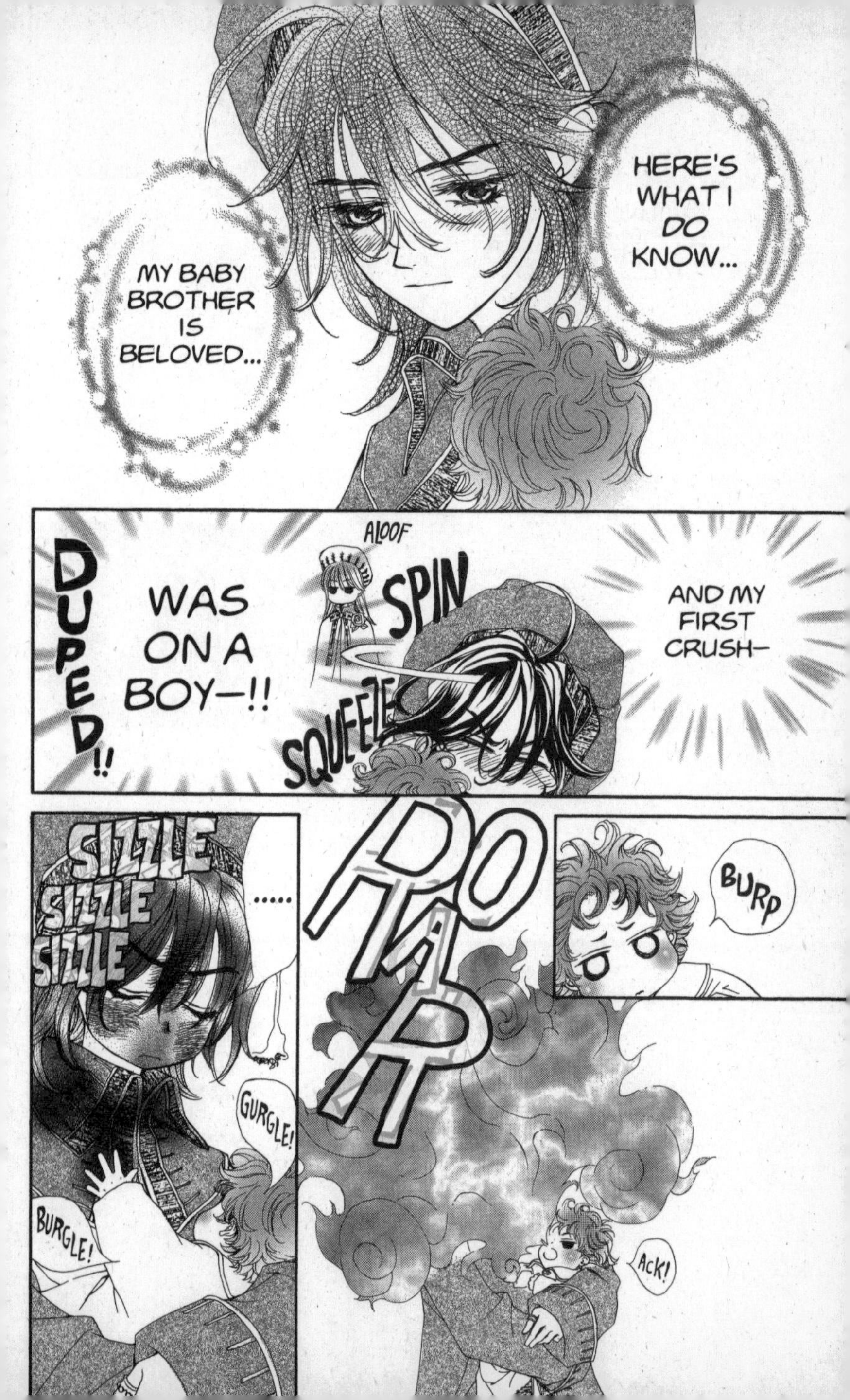
HERE'S WHAT I DO KNOW...
MY BABY BROTHER IS BELOVED...
AND MY FIRST CRUSH-
ALOOF
SPIN
SQUEEZE
WAS ON A BOY-!!
DUPED!!
BURP
ACK!
SIZZLE
SIZZLE
SIZZLE
.....
GURGLE!
BURGLE!

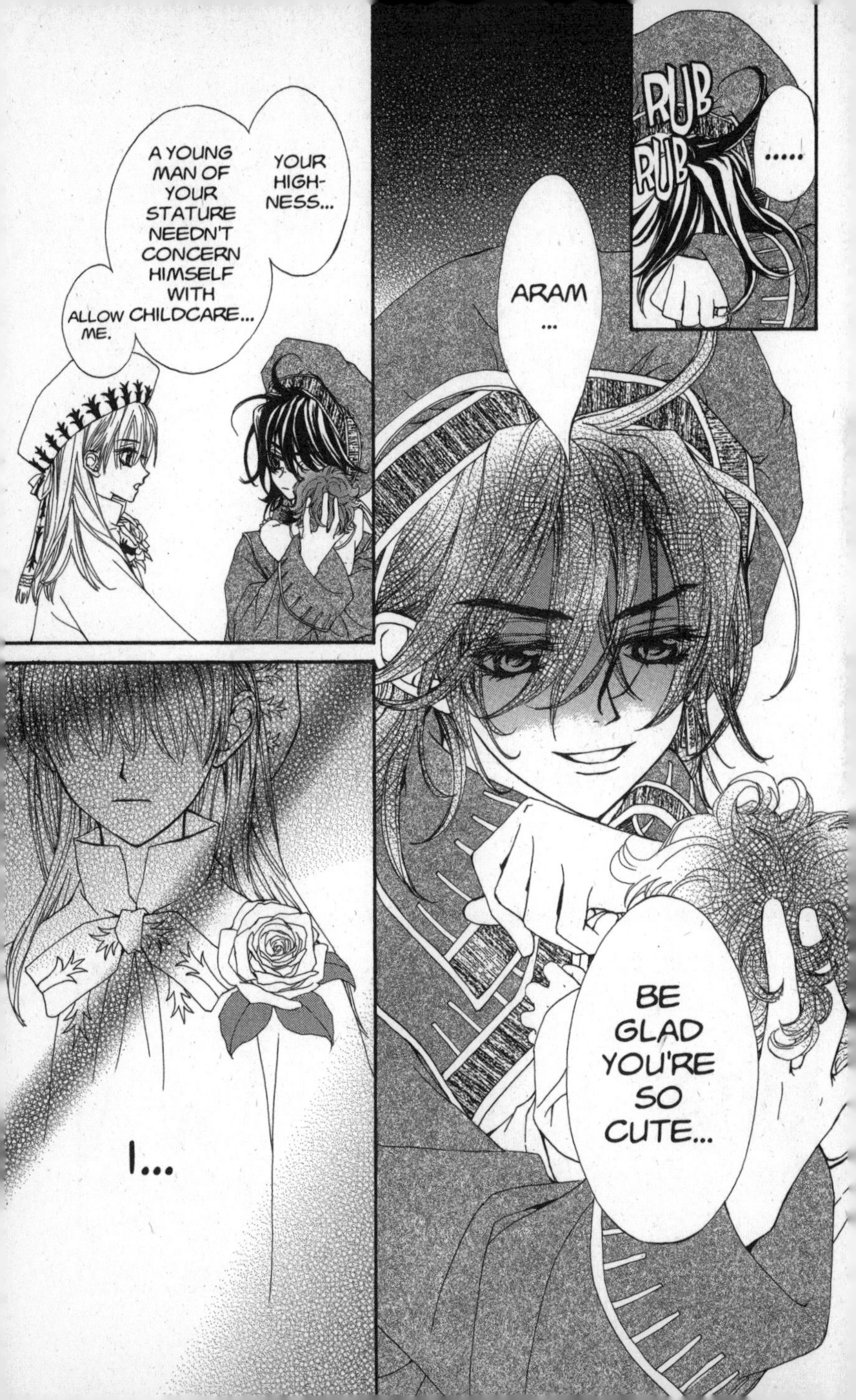
RUB RUB
.....
ARAM ...
BE GLAD YOU'RE SO CUTE...
YOUR HIGHNESS...
A YOUNG MAN OF YOUR STATURE NEEDN'T CONCERN HIMSELF WITH CHILDCARE...
ALLOW ME.
I...

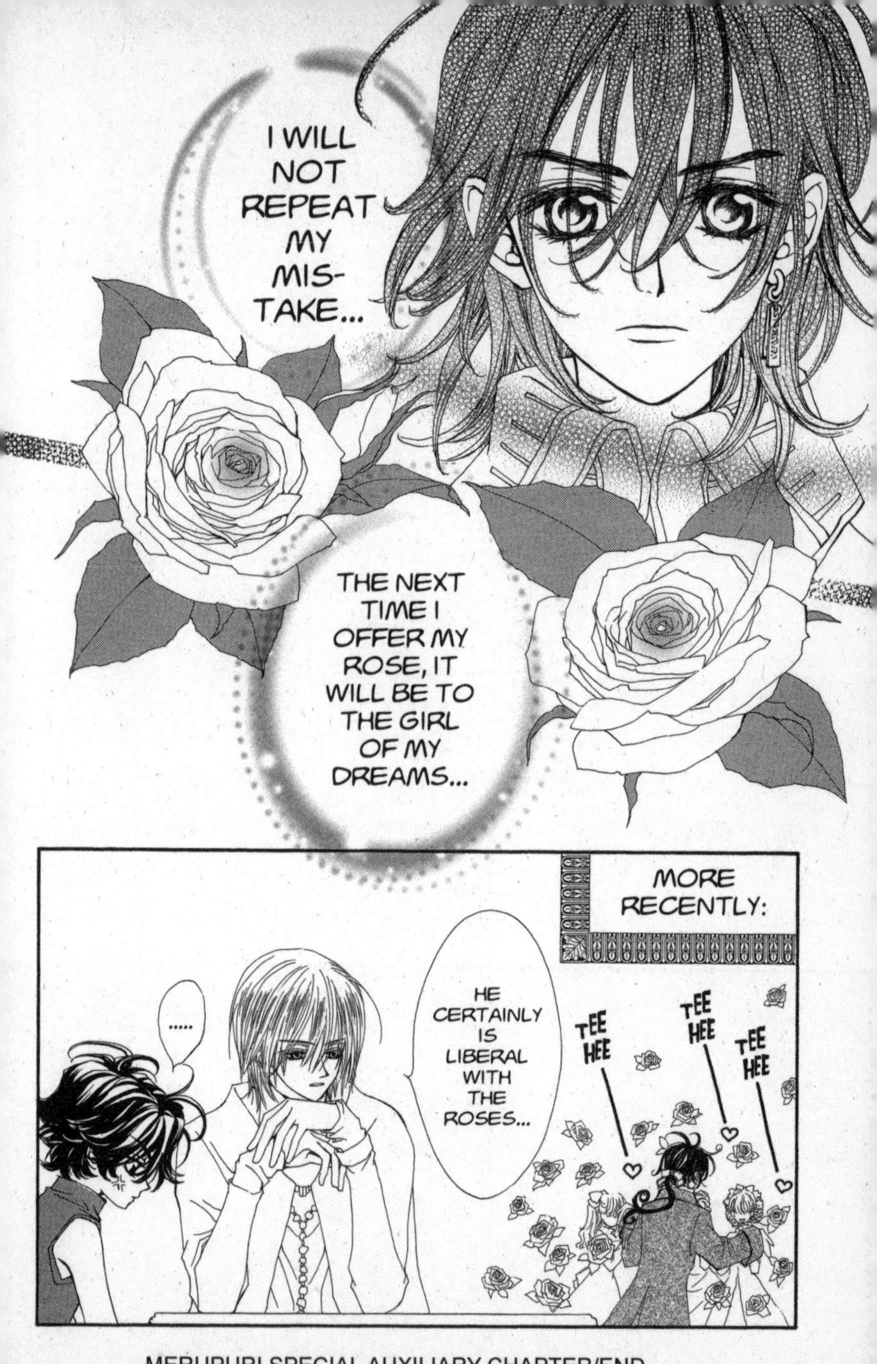
I WILL NOT REPEAT MY MIS-TAKE...
THE NEXT TIME I OFFER MY ROSE, IT WILL BE TO THE GIRL OF MY DREAMS...
MORE RECENTLY:
TEE HEE
TEE HEE
TEE HEE
HE CERTAINLY IS LIBERAL WITH THE ROSES...
......

MERUPURI SPECIAL AUXILIARY CHAPTER/END

MARURU STANDS GUARD WHILE JEILE IS WORKING.

BONUS PAGES START HERE 🖤

THINKING.

HWUT
HWUT

OUCH—!
JEILE—!

HWUT

HWUT

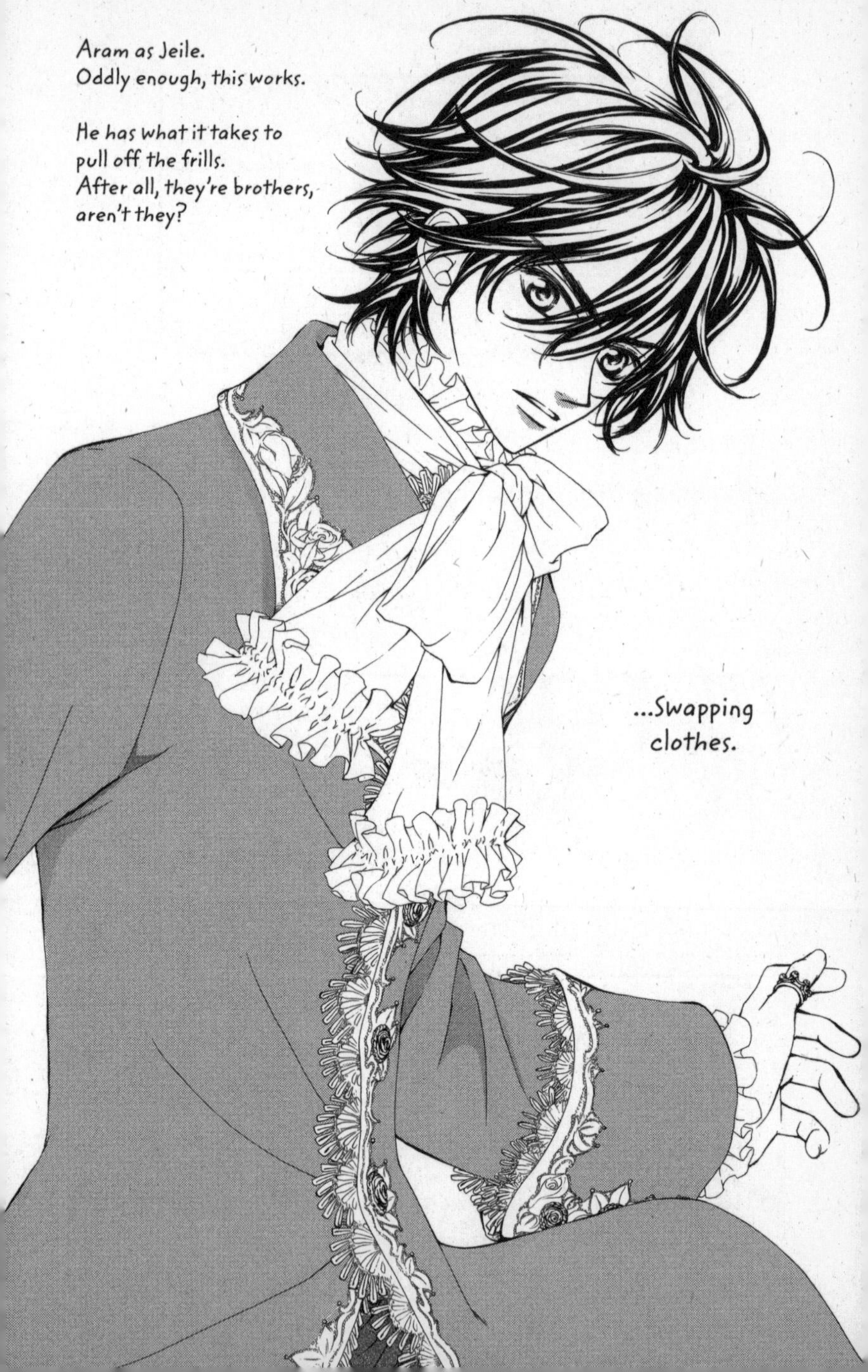
Aram as Jeile.
Oddly enough, this works.
He has what it takes to pull off the frills.
After all, they're brothers, aren't they?
...Swapping clothes.

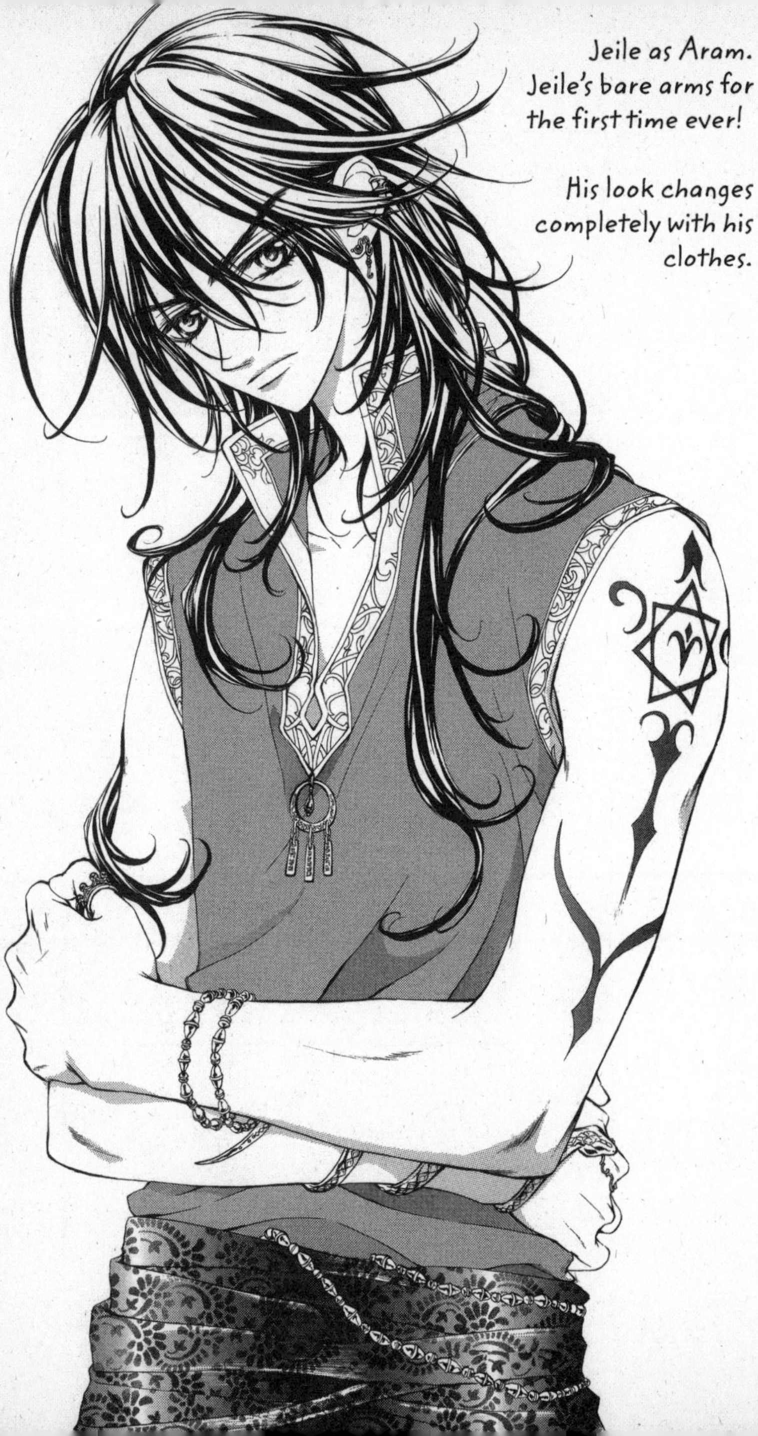

Jeile as Aram.
Jeile's bare arms for the first time ever!

His look changes completely with his clothes.

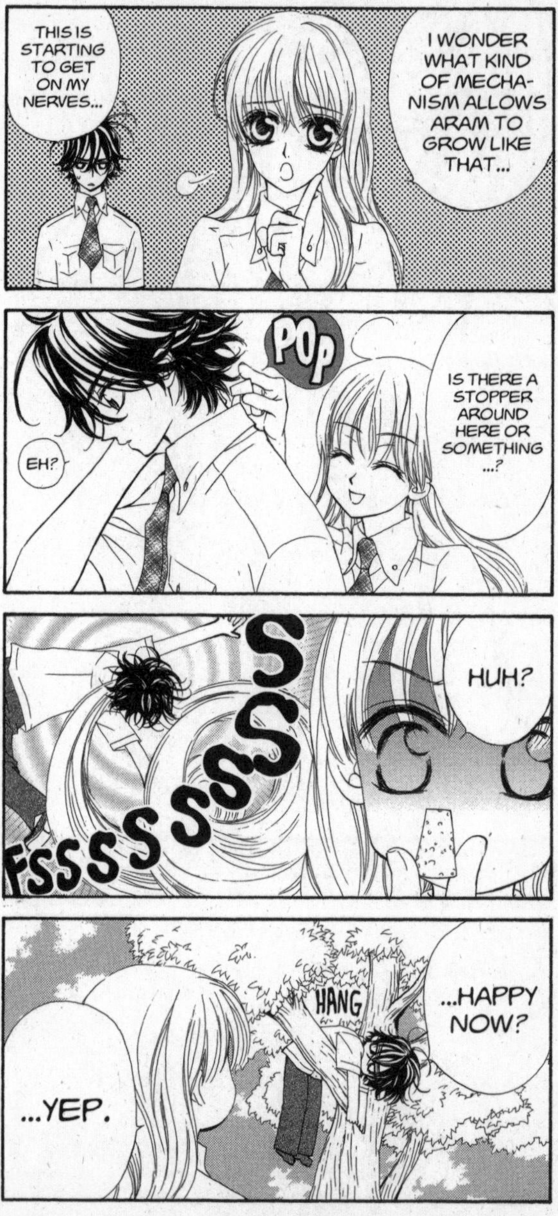
I WONDER WHAT KIND OF MECHA-NISM ALLOWS ARAM TO GROW LIKE THAT...
THIS IS STARTING TO GET ON MY NERVES...
IS THERE A STOPPER AROUND HERE OR SOMETHING ...?
POP
EH?
HUH?
FSSSSSSSSS
...HAPPY NOW?
HANG
...YEP.

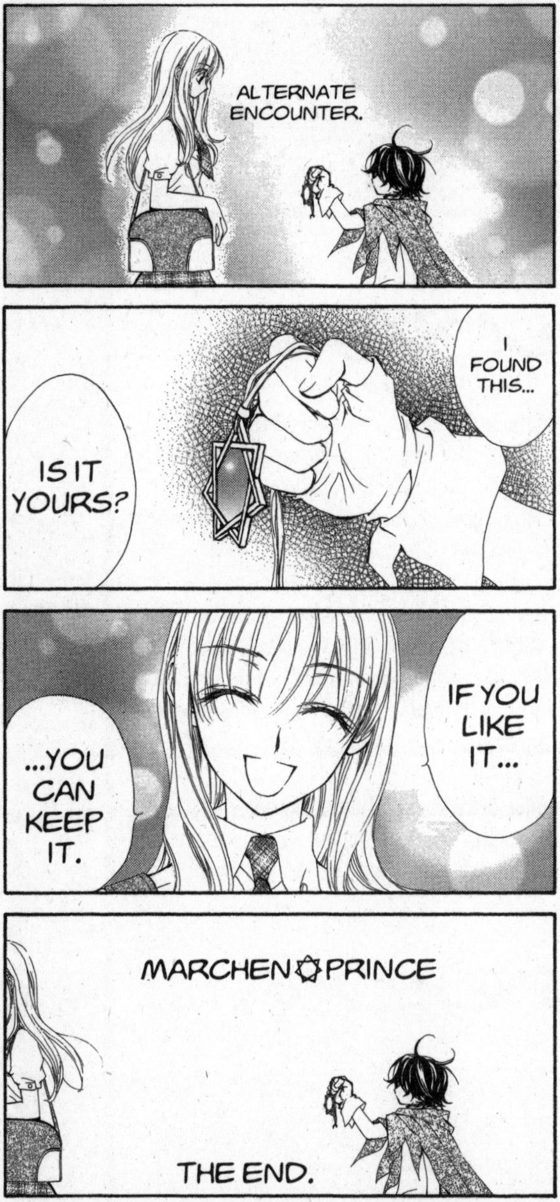
ALTERNATE ENCOUNTER.
I FOUND THIS...
IS IT YOURS?
IF YOU LIKE IT...
...YOU CAN KEEP IT.
MARCHEN PRINCE
THE END.

A former bookstore shopkeeper, **Matsuri Hino** burst onto the manga scene with her title *Kono Yume ga Sametara* (When This Dream Is Over), which was published in *LaLa DX* magazine. Hino was a manga artist a mere nine months after she decided to become one.

With the success of her popular series *Toraware no Minoue* (Captive Circumstance), and *MeruPuri*, Hino has established herself as a major player in the world of shojo manga. Her new title, *Vampire Knight*, currently runs in *Monthly LaLa* magazine.

Hino enjoys creative activities and has commented that she would have been either an architect or an apprentice to traditional Japanese craft masters if she did not become a manga artist.

MERUPURI: MÄRCHEN PRINCE, VOLUME 3
The Shojo Beat Manga Edition

STORY AND ART BY
MATSURI HINO

English Adaptation/Kelly Sue DeConnick
Translation/Priscilla Yim
Touch-up Art & Lettering/Andy Ristaino
Design/Courtney Utt
Editor/Michelle Pangilinan

Printed in Canada

Published by VIZ Media, LLC
P.O. Box 77010
San Francisco, CA 94107

Shojo Beat Manga Edition
10 9 8 7 6 5
First printing, December 2005
Fifth printing, May 2010

www.viz.com

store.viz.com